Steinbeck and the Environment

Edited by
Susan F. Beegel
Susan Shillinglaw
Wesley N. Tiffney, Jr.

Steinbeck and the Environment

Interdisciplinary Approaches

With a Foreword by
Elaine Steinbeck

The University of Alabama Press

Tuscaloosa and London

Library of Congress Cataloging-in-Publication Data

Steinbeck and the environment : interdisciplinary approaches / edited
    by Susan F. Beegel, Susan Shillinglaw, and Wesley N. Tiffney, Jr.,
    with a foreword by Elaine Steinbeck.
        p.   cm.
    Essays originally presented at a conference held in Nantucket,
Mass., in May 1992.
    Includes bibliographical references (p.   ) and index.
    ISBN 0-8173-0846-6 (alk. paper)
    1. Steinbeck, John, 1902–1968—Knowledge—Nature—Congresses.
2. Steinbeck, John, 1902–1968—Knowledge—Science—Congresses.
3. Environmental protection in literature—Congresses.   4. Human
ecology in literature—Congresses.   I. Beegel, Susan F., 1954–   .
II. Shillinglaw, Susan.   III. Tiffney, Wesley N.
PS3537.T3234Z8669   1997
813'.52—dc20   96-36276

British Library Cataloguing-in-Publication Data available

In Memoriam

Professor Stanley Brodwin,

1930–1995

The untold want by life and land ne'er granted,
Now voyager sail thou forth to seek and find.
                              —*Walt Whitman*

Contents

Part Five: Overviews

Foreword
Elaine Steinbeck

Since my husband John Steinbeck died in 1968, I have, I am thankful to say, led a very busy life. I have an apartment in New York to manage and a little house near the sea in Sag Harbor, Long Island. I am the matriarch of a large and scattered family, and I have a happy social life with many dear friends.

Most important of all, I am concerned with the work of John Steinbeck. That's the part of my life I like best. I enjoy working with his literary agents, his publishers at home and abroad; I love talking about his books on television and in all kinds of interviews. In fact, for years I kept myself so busy with this aspect of his literary career that I had never been able to attend any of the Steinbeck seminars and festivals held in various parts of the country.

Then, in 1992, there came a special invitation from Susan Beegel, Wes Tiffney of the UMASS Nantucket Field Station, and my friend Susan Shillinglaw of the Steinbeck Research Center, San Jose State University. A three-day meeting was to be held to discuss Steinbeck and the environment—and it would take place on Nantucket, one of John's very favorite spots in the world.

We spent the first summer of our marriage on the island in 1951, in a little house on a bluff high above the Atlantic Ocean, next to the Sankaty Lighthouse. John wrote a great part of *East of Eden* there, and he spent as much time as possible on the sea, in the sea, and studying that particular bit of sea. He became involved with the Marine Biology Station in Woods Hole, Massachusetts, marine biology being the second love of his life, just after writing.

So I accepted with enthusiasm the invitation to go to Nantucket.

It was a delightful affair, attended by many interesting Steinbeckians of all ages, scholars and students. The meetings were long, and the speeches were often intense and absorbing. I had a wonderful time, and I am happy to invite you to share some of the experience of the seminar as expressed in this book.

Acknowledgments

Many people helped implement the conference "Steinbeck and the Environment," which was held on Nantucket Island, Massachusetts, in May 1992 and was the original source of the papers presented in this anthology. The conference was cosponsored by the Steinbeck Research Center of San Jose State University, San Jose, California, and the University of Massachusetts Nantucket Field Station. Our thanks to Dean John K. Crane of the College of Humanities and Arts and former library head Ruth Hafter, San Jose State University, for financial support. Craig Kochersberger of SJSU designed the program. Douglas F. Beattie of the UMASS Field Station staff provided essential logistical support.

A number of people helped make the conference a special occasion. Particular thanks are due to Elaine Steinbeck, a real trouper about fog and lost luggage. She generously attended every session of the conference and enriched the experience of all with her delightful contributions to our discussions. Mr. and Mrs. Edwin Thrower kindly hosted a reception for conference participants at their home, "Footlight," the Nantucket cottage where John Steinbeck wrote much of *East of Eden*. John and Elaine Steinbeck's friend, Mrs. Nathaniel Benchley, together with Mr. Livingston D. Watrous, helped us to reconstruct that summer of 1951, while marine biologist Dr. James T. Carlton, director of the Williams College/Mystic Seaport Program in Maritime Studies, connected us with Dr. Joel Hedgpeth and Virginia Scardigli, who knew John Steinbeck and Ed Ricketts during their Cannery Row days.

The Nantucket community welcomed visiting scholars. Albert F. Egan, Jr., and the Egan Foundation made available the historic Admiral Coffin School as a meeting place. Mary K. Beman of Mitchell's Book Corner provided publicity and a topical book exhibit.

Philip Read and the staff of the Jared Coffin House hotel extended exemplary hospitality to conference participants. Dr. Joseph P.

Grochowski of the Nantucket Research and Education Foundation opened the doors of the Town of Nantucket Marine Laboratory. Nathaniel and Melissa Philbrick led a walking tour of historic Nantucket. Mary Ellen Mack provided hospitality and essential services at an end-of-conference picnic held on the UMASS Field Station grounds.

Folksinger Geoff Kaufman, director of Music Programs at Connecticut's Mystic Seaport Museum, gave an outstanding concert of environmental ballads and authentic 1930s songs from his days aboard the *Clearwater*. Once Steinbeck scholars begin singing it's hard to stop them, and Geoff gave us memorable music long after the concert had officially ended, and into the small hours of the morning.

Finally, our sincere thanks to all the Steinbeck conference participants who contributed in so many ways to discussion, collegiality, and fellowship both during the academic program and after hours. We feel the result of everyone's contributions was a conference and a collection of papers that John Steinbeck himself would have enjoyed.

Susan F. Beegel
Susan Shillinglaw
Wesley N. Tiffney, Jr.

Permissions

We thank those who kindly gave permission to reproduce the following materials:

David N. Cassuto's "Turning Wine into Water: Water as Privileged Signifier in *The Grapes of Wrath*" appeared originally in *Papers on Language and Literature*, V. 29, No. 1, Winter 1993. Copyright © 1993 By the Board of Trustees, Southern Illinois University. Reprinted by permission.

Brian Railsback's "Searching for 'What Is': Charles Darwin and John Steinbeck" appeared originally in Brian Railsback, *Parallel Expeditions: Charles Darwin and the Art of John Steinbeck* (Moscow: University of Idaho Press, 1995).

Robert DeMott's "Working at the Impossible: *Moby-Dick*'s Presence in *East of Eden*" appeared originally in *Steinbeck's Typewriter: A Collection of Essays* (Troy, New York: Whitson Publishing, 1996).

Abbreviations

AAA = *America and Americans*
BB = *Burning Bright*
COG = *Cup of Gold*
CR = *Cannery Row*
EOE = *East of Eden*
IDB = *In Dubious Battle*
JN = *Journal of a Novel: The East of Eden Letters*
LSC = *The Log from the Sea of Cortez*
LV = *The Long Valley*
OMM = *Of Mice and Men*
PH = *The Pastures of Heaven*
SLL = *Steinbeck: A Life in Letters*
SOC = *Sea of Cortez: A Leisurely Journal of Travel and Research*
SQ = *Steinbeck Quarterly*
ST = *Sweet Thursday*
TAKA = *The Acts of King Arthur*
TF = *Tortilla Flat*
TGOW = *The Grapes of Wrath*
TGU = *To a God Unknown*
THG = *The Harvest Gypsies*
TMID = *The Moon Is Down*
TP = *The Pearl*
TWB = *The Wayward Bus*
TWC = *Travels with Charley in Search of America*
WD = *Working Days: The Journals of The Grapes of Wrath*
WOD = *Winter of Our Discontent*

Steinbeck and the Environment

Introduction

The problem of how three editors might write an introduction to Steinbeck and the Environment *together seemed insurmountable until we decided to adopt the useful evolutionary principle of niche partitioning. Here each of us has contributed his or her own introductory perspective, approaching this volume's title subject from the respective points of view of biologist, Steinbeck specialist, and generalist in American literature. We are hopeful that the reader will find the interdisciplinary approach helpful from the start, using our points of convergence to locate the universals in the scientific and humanistic experience of Steinbeck's writing and our points of departure to gauge what our different disciplines can contribute to one another.*

A SCIENTIST'S PERSPECTIVE
Wesley N. Tiffney, Jr.

This volume presents papers by researchers of two basic types. The first group consists of people whose primary interest is in American literature and literary criticism. The second group comprises practicing scientists. This characterization of contributors does not mean that the literary cadre is not interested in science or that the scientists are not interested in literature—quite the opposite, as all the authors represented here have enthusiastically contributed to this interdisciplinary anthology.

My background is essentially scientific, so I will seek to introduce this volume from a generally scientific standpoint. First I will attempt to provide some definitions and common ground for terms and concepts often used in the following essays. Then I will attempt to explain why I feel many of Steinbeck's works appeal strongly to scientists.

Ecology, Environment, Environmentalists, and Environmental Science
Ecology in the sense of man's awareness of interrelationships among organisms themselves and between organisms and their environ-

ment is not new. One does not need formal training to recognize that without herbivores there would be no lions and that palm trees cannot grow at the North Pole. Ecology did not emerge as an intellectual concept and academic discipline, however, until the nineteenth century.

Darwin's 1859 presentation of the evolutionary idea, with his and others' subsequent elaboration of it, is fundamental to the development of ecological thinking. Although there were glimmerings before 1859, it would be very difficult to form concepts of interrelationships among organisms and with the environment without the concept of change and adaptation that is the driving force in developing these relationships. The leading German proponent of Charles Darwin's organic evolution concept, Ernst Haeckel, proposed the term *Oekologie* in 1866 and defined it as the comprehensive science of the relationship of the organism to the environment. Even before this codification, people such as the German Alexander von Humboldt (1769–1859), and British investigators William MacGillivray (1796–1852) and John G. Baker (1834–1920), had accomplished serious research into plant distribution relative to physical environmental factors (Sheail 1987, 3).

By 1900, a number of people were practicing the new "science" of ecology, although the results were often criticized for sloppiness and lack of standards. In England, Arthur G. Tansley (1871–1955) set out to improve this situation; he was abetted by Frederic E. Clements (1874–1945) in the United States. Tansley established a journal, the *New Phytologist* (literally "plant student"), in 1901 and then assisted in forming the British Ecological Society in 1913. Its carefully refereed journals continue to present the finest of ecological research today. Beginning in 1897, Clements published significant works on American plant ecology, establishing high standards for such work in the United States. The American Ecological Society formed in 1915 and began publishing its journal in 1920 (Sheail 1987, 16–42). By the late 1930s, the emphasis of ecological thought and research was on the relationship between organisms and the physical environment, following the early motto of the American Ecological Society: "All forms of life in relation to environment."

By the time Ed Ricketts studied with Warder C. Allee (1885–1955) at the University of Chicago and Steinbeck attended Stanford classes and worked at the Hopkins Marine Laboratory, ecology was a well-established and well-respected discipline. Allee was a pioneer of modern "population biology," an approach more concerned with interactions among organisms than simply with their environmental relations. From about 1920 until the 1950s, Allee published a series of papers on animal sociobiology and a book, *Animal Aggregations: A Study in General Sociology* (1931), that Ricketts and Steinbeck took with them on their trip to the Gulf of California (Astro 1973, 15). Allee noted that aggregations of animals could often withstand stresses, either from environmental factors or from other organisms, that individuals could not survive. For example, if organisms ranging in complexity from bacteria and protozoa to goldfish are not present in sufficient numbers, they cannot aggregate for mutual support and cannot survive in many marginal habitats (Scott 1958). Allee's concept of cooperation among organisms made him the harbinger of a new wave in ecology, and he exposed Ricketts to this very advanced thinking.

Astro (1973, 44–45) points out that Steinbeck came under the influence of teachers espousing the "superorganism" idea when he studied at the Hopkins Marine Station in 1923. This school believed that survival of cells, organs, individuals, or higher organizations depended on the orderly cooperation of all the component parts. Thus conditioned by education and predilection, Steinbeck and Ricketts embarked on some mutual advanced thinking of their own.

Neither Ricketts nor Steinbeck would recognize the terms "environment," "environmentalist," or "environmental scientist" as they are used today—although if given definitions and examples they would understand quickly. The terms have either changed their meanings or did not exist in the days when Ricketts and Steinbeck were active.

To the two friends in Monterey, "the environment" meant the physical surroundings of living plants and animals—air, water, weather, salinity, and temperature. Today, "environment" has come to mean man's surroundings—flora, fauna, and physical habitat—with particular emphasis on how man has damaged that environment and how he must now set about putting it right. I suggest that

Ricketts and Steinbeck were progenitors of the present definition of "environment," but I feel it would be a mistake to believe they held that concept in its current form.

"Environmentalists," as presently defined, were rare in Ricketts's and Steinbeck's day. Now an environmentalist is that admirable person who belongs to Greenpeace and seeks to destroy whaling vessels, or who at least belongs to the Sierra Club, is probably a liberal, and commendably votes for the interests of redwoods and spotted owls— as I do. An environmentalist is a politically active organism. Steinbeck was certainly "politically active" when he wrote *The Grapes of Wrath*; he recognized the Dust Bowl as a politically created environmental disaster, and I am confident that both he and Ricketts would have considered themselves friends of the natural world. Nevertheless, I still think we should not evaluate the two men by current "environmentalist" standards.

"Environmental science" was not a recognized specialty in the 1930s. Today's environmental scientists are people doing the useful work of monitoring air and water quality, seeking out point or nonpoint discharge sources of pollution, and keeping track of fluctuating plant and animal populations. Others are administrators working in government agencies to devise, test, and enforce environmental regulations. Some are highly educated theoretical scientists. Neither Ricketts nor Steinbeck would be regarded as an environmental scientist today, because neither was doing these things. Rather both men were advanced early ecologists, not only evaluating organisms in relation to the physical environment, but also considering living populations, including man, in relation to each other.

When we discuss Ricketts or Steinbeck as ecologists, or speak of them as early environmentalists, it will be important to keep the above history and distinctions in mind. Although the precepts of good ecology have not changed, the terminology surrounding our concept of "environment" and the word's connotations certainly have. And if some of their ideas and philosophy seem a little naive and self-evident, or their marine collecting practices seem "environmentally incorrect" to us today, remember that fifty-five years have passed since *Sea of Cortez* saw print, and our ideas and approaches have changed. Ricketts and Steinbeck were pioneer ecological thinkers and we should not chastise them for lacking the benefit of our "modern" and "enlightened" ideas.

Why Steinbeck Speaks to Scientists

I am pleased to be the token biologist associated with this project because several of John Steinbeck's works speak strongly to biologists and particularly to that strange subset of characters I belong to, the "field biologist." *Cannery Row, Sweet Thursday, Travels with Charley,* and particularly *The Log from the Sea of Cortez* are my personal favorites, and many colleagues share my tastes. To me, Steinbeck's *Log* provides a fine description of ecological field biology.

Ed Ricketts and John Steinbeck set out on a serious scientific expedition to the Gulf of California, although the description of the trip was anything but serious at times. Their objective "was to observe the distribution of invertebrates, to see and record their kinds and numbers, how they lived together, what they ate, and how they reproduced (*LSC* 2). They prepared with great care, stocking the *Western Flyer* with preserving chemicals of all descriptions and seemingly endless quantities of specimen containers, but still ran short during the six-week voyage.

Steinbeck, Ricketts, and the *Western Flyer*'s crew worked hard during the trip and returned with an impressive catch. Some of the collections Ricketts sold on the commercial market (he made his living this way), but the bulk of the material was distributed to scientific specialists for identification. In 1940 the Gulf of California was virtually unknown territory for marine biologists, and half of the collections Ricketts and Steinbeck made there represented entirely new species or significant range extensions for known species. Today, some fifty lots of preserved echinoderms and starfish relatives (plus the human embryo so admired by Ed Ricketts's father) are preserved at the California Academy of Science in San Francisco. These came to the Academy from W. K. Fisher, echinoderm specialist, director of the Hopkins Marine Laboratory, and an associate of Ricketts.

Although the pranks, parties, drinking, and sex stick in the memory, *Cannery Row* and *Sweet Thursday* also reflect a scientist doing serious work. Benson comments that the Doc of these novels is characterized as a man "who spends much of his time going for beer, counseling misfits and prostitutes, chasing girls, and partying." He notes that Ed Ricketts did all of these things but concludes that, "in actuality, Ed was a serious, energetic man who spent most of his time working" (Benson 1984, 194).

Then there is Ed Ricketts's and Jack Calvin's serious and delightful *Between Pacific Tides* (1939). It continues to be an innovative sourcebook, not simply a list of organisms and collecting sites, but organized by habitat (protected coast, open coast, bays and estuaries) and emphasizing the natural history and aesthetics of the animals it covers. As such, *Between Pacific Tides* was a great departure from the "dry ball" lists published before its first appearance and, periodically updated, remains current, if not still ahead of its time, today.

Both Ricketts and Steinbeck liked to have fun, but both took their work seriously. Practicing scientists do science because they think it is important, and they are serious about doing their work well. An earnest approach to work bonds the two men to other scientists and to practitioners of other disciplines as well. Scientists appreciate Steinbeck, the famous literary figure and Nobel Prize winner, for understanding their work and taking it seriously.

But this is definitely not to say that scientists in general and field ecologists in particular don't manage to have various sorts of fun (very few field biologists are "dry balls"). Again, the accounts of high jinks in Steinbeck's books ring true to many scientist readers: "We sat on a crate of oranges and thought what good men most biologists are, the tenors of the scientific world-temperamental, moody, lecherous, loud-laughing, and healthy." They tend to "proliferate in all directions " (*LSC* 33). Later in the gulf, the expedition crosses the trail of an earlier field biologist, John Xántus, who truly proliferated in all directions—leaving in his wake "a whole tribe of Xantuses" (*LSC* 72). I won't shock present readers or embarrass my colleagues by citing similar examples from personal or vicarious experiences.

Then there is Murphy's Law. Few field biologists are religious in a conventional sense, but most, like Ed Ricketts, are notably superstitious. Also, most possess a sense of humor. Offhand I cannot think of a field biologist who does not believe in Murphy's Law (Sod's Law in Britain). According to this law, "Anything that can go wrong will go wrong," and one of its many corollaries is that "machines work perfectly until you really need them." Practicing scientists, in field or laboratory, frequently experience the immutable truth of this most basic principle. The Hansen Sea Cow, the outboard motor portrayed in *The Log from the Sea of Cortez*, is a classic example:

It completely refused to run: (a) when the waves were high, (b) when the wind blew, (c) at night, early morning, and evening, (d) in rain, dew, or fog, (e) when the distance to be covered was more than two hundred yards. But on warm, sunny days when the weather was calm and the white beach close by—in a word, on days when it would have been a pleasure to row—the Sea-Cow started at a touch and would not stop. (LSC 25)

Very few scientists and certainly no field biologist can read this passage without remembering the essential piece of gear, functioning perfectly ashore or in the laboratory, that just plain died afloat or in the field.

Finally, scientists empathize with Steinbeck because they share his need to know how it all works. The very basis of scientific curiosity is to seek to understand, in as unbiased a way as possible, how the natural world—from the tide pool to the stars—really works. Ricketts and Steinbeck strive to achieve "is" thinking and quest for a "unified field theory" of ecology. They may not have succeeded, but striving toward these or similar goals is the essence of science.

Steinbeck and Ricketts's outstanding idea is that microcosm and macrocosm are interacting entities and part of a grand, interlaced continuum embracing human society. Within this continuum, no part can do without the whole. As the essays in this volume demonstrate, literature and literary critics are not isolated from the ideas and products of science, and scientists do not live apart from the concepts and reality of literature. Here, both are parts of the intellectual whole.

Note

I am indebted to Alan Baldridge, librarian of the Hopkins Marine Station, and Dustin Chivers, senior curator, Department of Invertebrate Zoology, California Academy of Science, for information on the importance and fate of the Ricketts/Steinbeck collections.

A STEINBECK SCHOLAR'S PERSPECTIVE
Susan Shillinglaw

> Most of the feeling we call religious, most of the mystical out-
> crying which is one of the most prized and used and desired
> reactions of our species, is really the understanding and the
> attempt to say that man is related to the whole thing, related
> inextricably to all known and unknowable.
> —*Log from the Sea of Cortez*

John Steinbeck and marine biologist Edward F. Ricketts met in 1930, when Steinbeck moved to his parents' summer home in Pacific Grove, California. There he matured as a writer. There he and Ricketts stimulated, challenged, and refined one another's thinking. To appreciate their shared ecological perspective, which received its fullest statement in *Sea of Cortez* (1941), it may be well first to recognize their common romanticism: Steinbeck grew up reenacting the stories of King Arthur, and Ricketts had a lifelong fondness for the poetry of Whitman. Neither was narrow-minded, linear, or materialistic. Meaning resided, for both, in the juncture of the physical and the intangible. Their ecological holism had not only biological but also metaphysical dimensions.

Long before Steinbeck met Ricketts he was struggling to articulate holistic concepts, to conceive of a human's place in a living whole. His earliest published fiction focuses on a character drawn to nature. In "Fingers of Cloud," which ran in a 1924 Stanford *Spectator*, the restless heroine Gertie flees her home and finds temporary solace and consoling visions on a mountaintop. This romantic escape is her single moment of bliss, for she descends the mountain into a bad marriage. But this story highlights Steinbeck's inclination to identify or measure a character against nature, both as physical place and as metaphysical symbol. He would repeatedly acknowledge humanity's intimate and essential ties with its environment. As he was writing *To a God Unknown* in 1930, he kept a journal intended for his college roommate, Carlton Sheffield, and in that journal he records an idea that adumbrates Gertie's quest and his own ecological bent: "Each figure is a population and the stones—the trees, the muscled mountains are the world—but not the world apart from man—the world and man—the one inseparable unit man and his environment.

Why they should ever have been understood as being separate I do not know. Man is said to come out of his environment. He doesn't know when" (Stanford University Library).

Steinbeck's 1930 statement goes a long way toward explaining his ecological holism. In the novel he wrote "for" Sheffield (he often imagined an audience for his works in progress), *To a God Unknown*, the hero's tragic flaw is that he wrestles to forge a unit—Joseph Wayne and his burgeoning ranch, Joseph Wayne and the mysterious rocks—rather than accepting the natural rhythm of nature that the Indians around him so instinctively acknowledge—years of drought followed by years of rain. Joseph, in contrast, stands defiant. Most of Steinbeck's memorable characters must learn not to do so. His most sympathetic figures are sculpted in their environments, often first glimpsed as intimately linked to a place both sustaining and threatening, as is the whole of nature. Fog hangs over Elisa Allen's valley, suggesting her isolation. Lennie and George seek refuge (from economic and social predators) by a stream that evokes fragile safety; the Joads are Oklahomans, their identity forged in contact with the land they must abandon; and the hard drinking paisanos (defiantly antiestablishment) reside on a hill both physically and spiritually above mercantile Monterey. In its dominant metaphor, *Cannery Row* (1945) sees the enclave of bums and whores, of Doc and Lee Chong, as a human tide pool. In each work Steinbeck rejects the notion of a man-centered universe and describes commensal relationships in an interconnected whole. In short, to *see* any situation fully, whether it be a migrant exodus or a strike in the central valley or Monterey's Cannery Row, is to acknowledge the interaction between humans and their environment.

Typically in his novels, one character does recognize connections. These wise counselors are men who stand apart or occasionally the women who articulate an alternative vision that implicitly denies male linearity. Jackson Benson has called these farsighted characters Merlin figures, more or less magical characters who recognize the living whole, both physical and metaphysical. They interpret: Slim, Casy, Pilon, and Doc in *Cannery Row* and the Chinese Lee in *East of Eden*. Juanito in *To a God Unknown* is a wise counselor, as is the problematic Margie Young-Hunt in *The Winter of Our Discontent*. As visionary, the Merlin figure is the artist, the creator, and he has a little of both Steinbeck and Ricketts in him. In life these two friends, like the farsighted characters, sought connections.

The essays in this collection examine this interconnectedness that Steinbeck and Ricketts long sought to articulate and define in conversation, in letters, in essays, and, for Steinbeck of course, in fiction. Their magnum opus was *Sea of Cortez,* published in 1941, the collaborative work that is the focus of several of these analyses. At the time of publication, Lewis Gannet commented that this book held "more of the whole man, John Steinbeck, than any of his novels." And more of Ed Ricketts. The work represents a decade of thought, and it may be well to step back from Steinbeck's novels to see the context that shaped the thinking of both men. Long a subject of critical debate, their symbiotic relationship is difficult to unravel. Richard Astro, for one, in his pioneering study *John Steinbeck and Edward F. Ricketts: The Shaping of a Novelist,* champions the marine biologist as the wellspring of Steinbeck's biological naturalism. By self-admission a "shameless magpie," Steinbeck, others concur, absorbed Ricketts's philosophical ideas: nonteleological, or "is," thinking; the group man concept; and biological holism.

A better model to characterize the relationship between Steinbeck and Ricketts, however, may be borrowed from their own investigations, the ecological one of interconnection. Key psychological and philosophical issues worked out between the two men were debated, refined, and recorded separately, as each strove to articulate a model of the universe that integrated physical and spiritual realms, reality and symbolic context. They sought to articulate "larger relationships," in Ricketts's words, "between human society and the given individual, between man and the land, and between man and his feeling of supra-personal participation from within" (Stanford University Library, "Thesis and Materials for a Script on Mexico" 1). Steinbeck's holistic "solution," if you will, focused on connections between nature, man, and group; Ricketts's, perhaps the more abstract of the two, concentrated on man's potential for "breaking through" to some reality beyond the physical. Ricketts's cosmology embraced the scientist's grasp of matter and the metaphysician's awareness of "the inward things."

The year 1932 was, I believe, the generative time, perhaps the annus mirabilis for Ricketts's lab circle. That year Joseph Campbell lived briefly in Pacific Grove. That year Steinbeck was working on *To a God Unknown,* arguably his most mystical work. Steinbeck "used to talk about putting unconscious symbols in his work," reported Richard Albee about Steinbeck's writing during that time; "he explicitly talked about working with symbols." Joseph Campbell sheds further insight into Steinbeck's state of mind when he first knew the writer: "Nature power was the generator of myth as far as Steinbeck was concerned," he told Steinbeck's biographer, admitting that he learned more from Steinbeck about myth than vice versa (Benson 1984, 223). During that remarkable year, Campbell, Ricketts, and Steinbeck—all reading the poetry of Robinson Jeffers, the writings of Carl Jung, and the works of Spengler—were similarly struggling to find a universal commonalty, a source, a way of tying together human experience, nature, myth, symbol, and mysticism—each in his own way. Each recognized, in Ricketts's words, "the trait that has enabled the works of Plato, Lao Tzu, Christ, Jung, etc. to live. . . . I think it's one of the deepest and most significant quests in human life." Ricketts later wrote to Henry Miller: "The people are few who speak from 'the other side' " (2 July 1941).[1] In 1932, Steinbeck, Ricketts, and Campbell—"following the Jeffers lead," said Campbell (14 September 1939)—sought words for the connections they felt.

The correspondence between Ricketts and Steinbeck was burned—by the writer himself—when the marine biologist died in 1948. Campbell and Steinbeck had a falling out. And the reclusive Jeffers certainly never made it over the hill from Carmel to join the group that gathered at Ricketts's lab. But one can tentatively—and here rather briefly—reconstruct what was under discussion at the lab during what Campbell called "our year of crazy beginnings" (14 September 1939) through the correspondence between Ricketts and Campbell. Not having seen the marine biologist for seven years, Joseph Campbell wrote to him in 1939, mentioning that "the project" he was working on last time he saw Ed was a "synthesis of Spengler and Jung. I have been diligently at work on the project these seven silent years, Joyce's new work, 'Finnegans Wake,' is the closest thing I have found to a complete resolution of the problem" (22 August 1939).

Ricketts responded immediately: "In continuation of the things we discussed I have worked up three essays that pretty well sum up the world outlook, or rather the inlook, that I have found developing in myself more and more during the years" (25 August 1939). For Ricketts, "the problem" of unity was resolved by the "extra humanists, the breaking thru gang: Whitman, Nietzsche, Jeffers, Jung, Krishnamurti. Stevenson in Will-o the will, a lodging for night. Emerson's oversoul. James Stevens knew it. Conrad Youth and Heart of Darkness. Steinbeck To a God Unknown and In Dubious Battle" (Ricketts's notes). All were willing, in Ricketts's mind, to grasp a sense of the whole, to "break through" tangible reality to a spiritual awareness. In 1939, he sent Campbell the essays that outline the core of his thought: "Non-Teleological Thinking" (the Easter Sunday sermon in *Log*), "Philosophy of Breaking Through," and "A Spiritual Morphology of Poetry," each of which Campbell critiques and endorses. Both men resolved "the problem" by unifying fields of thought: in poetry, in biology, and in myth each found both vivid reality and a reaching beyond.

During those same seven years, of course, Steinbeck published his best fiction. "I have been especially interested in John Steinbeck's notions because they develop widely the holistic concepts being felt specifically in modern biology," Ricketts wrote late in the 1930s. For Steinbeck, "the problem" of unity found focus in stories about group man and the potential of the whole, in the higher calling of Tom and Ma Joad, and of course in the biological holism articulated in *Sea of Cortez*. Composing the "Log" section using Ed's daily journals of the trip and undoubtedly recalling years of conversation, Steinbeck "carefully builds" a text—to paraphrase Ricketts (31 December 1941)—that conveys immediacy, connection, and a sharp awareness of a cosmic whole. Joseph Campbell acknowledges as much in a letter to Ricketts after he read the book:

And I think that the book form discovered by you and John is perhaps as close to the life form itself as [a] book could possibly be to life. The on-and-on carelessness of the first two hundred pages, with the cans of beer and the vague chewing the fat; and then, emerging out of all this, the great solid realization of 'non-teleological thinking': and then again, that moment just before the entering of Gueyamas, when a realization of two realistic worlds, in the most moving way presenting itself; gradually, meanwhile, the dominant theme of the work is emerging, and from this remark

and from that, we understand that society itself is an organism that these
little intertidal societies and the great human societies are manifestations
of common principles; more than that: we understand that the little and
the great societies are themselves units in a sublime, all inclusive organ-
ism, which breathes and goes on, in dream-like half consciousness of its
own life-processes, oxidizing its own substance yet sustaining its wonder-
ful form. Suddenly, then the life goes out of the trip and we are on our
way back to the laboratory to follow this great thing through in a more
exact set of terms. (26 December 1941)

Ricketts responds that no critic to date has gotten his "sense of the whole."

Certainly the essays here fill gaps in our appreciation of Stein-beck's approach to "the problem," a holistic appreciation of life. For too long, the voice of Edmund Wilson has echoed through Steinbeck studies: the author's biological holism is simply his tendency to see a character in its lowest common denominator as a kind of instinc-tive animal. These essays offer a healthy corrective to that view, en-gaging the reader in the full context of Steinbeck's holistic imagina-tion.

Note

1. The letters to and from Edward F. Ricketts, as well as other materials by Ricketts cited in this essay, are located in the Ricketts Archive of Stanford Uni-versity Library.

A GENERALIST'S PERSPECTIVE
Susan F. Beegel

Alas for the generalist in American literature who must follow the director of a *Cannery Row*–style, "rubber boot" biology lab and the director of the Steinbeck Research Center in introductory discussion of "Steinbeck and the Environment." Pondering what might remain for me to contribute, I am forced to conclude that my only strength lies in my comparative ignorance—an ignorance perhaps more typi-cal than Wes Tiffney's or Susan Shillinglaw's knowledgeability, an ignorance that challenges Steinbeck's place in the canon of Ameri-can literature, an ignorance blind to what Steinbeck and other West-ern writers have to offer a nation in deepening environmental crisis and an ignorance urgently requiring the antidote this volume pre-scribes.

A New Englander born and bred, I had my own earliest experience with Steinbeck in a devastating encounter with a selection from "The Red Pony" in an anthology of "best-loved horse stories" for girls. Like most children, I did *not* love stories where the pony dies and could not fathom Steinbeck's inclusion with *truly* beloved writers of horse stories: Marguerite Henry, Walter Farley, Enid Bagnold, Anna Sewall. I was too young to recognize that the feeling evoked by "The Red Pony" was the feeling of reading a good book, the feeling that it had all happened to me.

On then to junior high and high school, where those taut novellas and excellent teaching tools—*The Pearl* and *Of Mice and Men*—were dutifully and dully presented. Remembering the buzzard dipping its beak in the dead pony's eye, I approached Steinbeck cautiously, but public education in this country is well designed to prevent books from "happening" to students, as they learn the black-and-white, compare-and-contrast, *Monarch Notes* approach to literature that passes for "criticism" in high school.

That was the end of the road for Steinbeck in my formal education. I did my undergraduate and doctoral work at traditional, ivy-covered Eastern schools. Steinbeck was not on the syllabi of the American literature surveys at Wellesley, nor was he included in the list of twentieth-century American writers one could read for Ph.D. orals at Yale. At some point, thinking of teaching a course on American literature of the 1930s, I read *The Grapes of Wrath* and was both profoundly moved and terribly bewildered by its exclusion from the canon presented to me. But if Steinbeck was mentioned at all at Yale in the era of deconstruction, it was with an urbane sneer, and the sneer of the Eastern literary establishment is an intimidating sneer indeed.

I encountered a corrective sneer in Wes Tiffney's lab. Somehow, upon my wandering in to pass the time of day with the various scientists at work there, Wes forced me to confess aloud that I had never read *Log from the Sea of Cortez* or *Cannery Row,* and well do I remember the shattering silence that greeted this announcement. Microbe hunter Sam Telford paused in drawing blood from a mouse, and marine biologist Dave Carlin abandoned his observations of hermit crab shell selection to stare at a strange phenomenon of nature—an illiterate with a doctorate in English.

It seems that in passing through the doors of the laboratory I had entered an alternate world with an alternate canon. The biologists ranked *Log from the Sea of Cortez* and *Cannery Row* among their great books, the works from which they draw spiritual sustenance and a sense of vocation, right up there with Darwin's *Voyage of the "Beagle."* Not to have read them was inconceivable. Indeed, marine biologist Jane Wulff tells me that if she were going to be stranded on a desert island and could take just one book, it would be *Log from the Sea of Cortez.* Because Wulff does much of her teaching from vessels under sail, being marooned is not an entirely far-fetched possibility, and she does carry a copy of *Log* with her just in case. This is canonicity with a vengeance, a passion for Steinbeck utterly removed from the tepid response of the Eastern literary establishment's "dry ball" humanists, "worried about titles and preferment and the gossip of the Faculty Club" (*LSC* 71–72).

The astonished disapproval of the biologists launched me on my first *real* reading of Steinbeck, a tentative dipping into *Cannery Row* that turned into a Steinbeck binge, one of those first readings with the vividness of entering new country, of a first dive on a coral reef, of a first walk in old-growth forest. That reading in turn sent me West, to an American Literature Association meeting in California, where I sought out a Steinbeck session chaired by Susan Shillinglaw and experienced my first serious discussion of Steinbeck unaccompanied by the gurgle of aquarium pumps and the rustle of laboratory mice. Once again, I seemed to have stumbled into an alternate world with an alternate canon, as the enthusiasm for Steinbeck of Western scholars of American literature is more nearly equivalent to that of marine biologists than that of Eastern humanists.

I've ventured to mention my carefully cultivated and expensively educated Eastern ignorance of Steinbeck here, as well as my "conversion" by field biologists and Californians, because no less a Steinbeck scholar than Jackson Benson has told me my experience is "typical." "The East," said Jack, Steinbeck's preeminent biographer and a native Californian, "believes the West has no culture." And biologists, he assured me, especially those whose work involves unraveling the intricate mysteries of ecological relationships, have always known about Steinbeck what Eastern humanists have yet to learn. If the marginalization of Steinbeck I've encountered is indeed "typical," then the canon of American literature is deficient both in ecological and in Western thinking, a deficiency that may prove as hazardous to America and Americans as the "reckless dumping of sewage and toxic industrial wastes" or "the belching of uncontrolled products from combustion of coal, coke, oil, and gasoline" (*AAA* 127).

Because of his scientific training, Steinbeck's understanding of the environment and human dependence on it is perhaps unique among the canonical American writers of his generation. For F. Scott Fitzgerald, progenitor of our Tom Wolfes and Jay McInernys, the "fresh green breast of the New World" was a source of nostalgia only, replaced by the ash heaps and glittering towers of the city, run down and destroyed by a newly mobile society whose pleasure is "breaking things," as Myrtle Wilson is run down and destroyed by the "death car" that mingles her "thick dark blood" with the dust and leaves her "left breast . . . swinging loose like a flap" (Fitzgerald 138, 182).

For Sinclair Lewis, progenitor of our Cheevers and Updikes, poet laureate of suburban banality, the concept of wilderness as escape is absurd. His George F. Babbitt yearns "like a trapper in a North Canada movie" to "plunge through the forest, make camp in the Rockies, [and be] a grim and wordless caveman" (Lewis 238). During his trip to Maine, Babbitt manages to spit from a hotel dock into a "delicate and shivering" lake while "the pines rustled" and "the mountain glowed," but ten days after his return to Zenith, it is as though the trip had never been (238, 247).

Even Ernest Hemingway, who all his life actively sought "the last good country" (a concept now embraced by the Nature Conservancy's "Last Great Places on Earth" campaign) and who could write such hymns of oneness with the natural world as "Big Two-Hearted River" and *The Old Man and the Sea,* fled before environmental degradation rather than confront it, endlessly exchanging despoiled country for more virgin soil, leaving one son to be a Kenyan game warden, leaving another to be a fish and game commissioner, and leaving his widow to donate land to the Nature Conservancy. Hemingway's consideration of human responsibility to the land does not extend beyond observing the rules of ethical hunting and fishing. The land does offer his characters refuge and refreshment, but when it ceases to do so, they move on.

Contrast this scenario with that in a Steinbeck novel, where setting becomes habitat. More than a backdrop, habitat is an integral part of his fictive ecology. The destiny of the land is intimately related to the destiny of the people, and vice versa. *The Grapes of Wrath* is rich with examples. Consider, for example, this passage on human exploitation of the land, the destruction of prairie sod by mechanized plowing: "Behind the tractor rolled the shining disks, cutting the earth with blades—not plowing but surgery, pushing the cut earth to the right where the second row of disks cut it and pushed it to the left; slicing blades shining, polished by the cut earth. And pulled behind the disks, the harrows combing with iron teeth so that the little clods broke up and the earth lay smooth" (*TGOW* 37–38). The rape of the land leads to this Dust Bowl portrait of a species displaced by habitat destruction—

The people came out of their houses and smelled the hot stinging air and covered their noses from it. And the children came out of the houses, but they did not run or shout as they would have done after a rain. Men stood by their fences and looked at the ruined corn, drying fast now, only a little green showing through the film of dust. The men were silent and they did not move often. And the women came out of the houses to stand beside their men—to feel whether this time the men would break. (TGOW 3–4)

The farming practices of agribusiness, the big tractors sent in by the banks, destroy the fertility of Oklahoma—and when the surviving Joads finally reach California's promised land, land that should be an Eden of abundance, they find it also in the grip of agribusiness, of corporations that plow crops back into the earth to drive up prices while people starve to death. The dependence of people on the land they destroy is underscored when Rose of Sharon—malnourished, ill from exposure, and weakened by her labors picking cotton, that most soil-destructive and water-profligate of crops—gives birth to a stillborn baby. The "blue shriveled little mummy" is a reminder that the ability to reproduce is "all" in evolutionary terms and that by destroying the fecundity of the earth the agribusinessmen have destroyed the fecundity of their own species (*TGOW* 489). "Go down an' tell 'em," Uncle John adjures the infant corpse as he sets it adrift on a flooding stream (493).

Steinbeck too was one of the first to understand the fragility of the sea, a habitat that many people of his day assumed was inexhaustible. The impoverished community of *Sweet Thursday*, where the women have nothing to sell but their sexuality and the men have no work, is the by-product of overfishing, of human greed that has destroyed what ought to have been a self-sustaining industry—and that greed is marching on:

The canneries themselves fought the war by getting the limit taken off fish and catching them all. It was done for patriotic reasons, but that didn't bring the fish back. As with the oysters in Alice, *"They'd eaten every one." It was the same noble impulse that stripped the forests of the West and right now is pumping water out of California's earth faster than it can rain back in. When the desert comes, people will be sad; just as Cannery Row was sad when all the pilchards were caught and canned and eaten.* (ST 3)

Not for nothing is the postwar madam of the Bear Flag Restaurant called Fauna. The human characters of Cannery Row are as dependent on the health of their habitat as other creatures.

The characters in Steinbeck's fiction are also intimately related to one another in the ecological web of interrelationships we call economy. This point is tragically demonstrated in *The Grapes of Wrath*, as the collapse of the banks drives families like the Joads off their land, and comically in *Cannery Row*. In a hilarious parody of the Crash of 1929, those Skid Row capitalists, Mack and the boys, who understand the principle of leverage perfectly, work out an agreement with Lee Chong, the grocer, to obtain material goods (tobacco, whiskey, Coca-Cola, steak, peaches, bacon and eggs) for frogs (worth five cents a piece to Doc). Lee Chong, recognizing that he has a "stranglehold on the consumers," charges a "five-frog margin" in addition to his usual "grocery mark-up," and "the poison of greed . . . creep[s] into the innocent and laudable merchandising agreement" (CR 227–29).

The ostensibly altruistic motive for the great frog caper is a party for Doc. But as Mack himself confesses, in a contemplative moment by the campfire: "We worked it out that we wanted to give Doc a party. So we come out here and have a hell of a lot of fun. Then we'll go back and get the dough from Doc. There's five of us, so we'll drink five times as much liquor as he will. And I ain't sure we're doin' it for Doc. I ain't sure we ain't doin' it for ourselves" (CR 190–91). Mack and the boys are for the moment motivated most strongly by their thirst for alcohol and lust for a good time. After plundering the available supply of frogs, the Cannery Row bums launch in Doc's absence a truly pathological party, a destructive carnival that involves every member of the community (passers-by, clients of a rival whorehouse, a wandering drunk) in a kind of ecological chain reaction and finally results in the escape of the frog capital, the collapse of Lee Chong's investment, and the smashing of that sacred space, Doc's lab. The event causes the normally gentle Doc to punch Mack in "a cold calculated punishing way" and poisons the atmosphere for weeks until a second party, one with an ecology based on cooperation and generosity (Doc's birthday presents include a quilt made of whores' lingerie and a 1916 Chalmers piston), restores Cannery Row's sense of community.

In Steinbeck's work the most redemptive sense that humans have is a kind of consciousness of the ecological web, a sense of their interdependence on one another, as when Rose of Sharon gives her breast to a starving man (TGOW 501–2) and a sense of the evolutionary, even revolutionary strength to be found in cooperation, rather than competition: "Here is the node, you who hate change and fear revolution. . . . two men are not as lonely and perplexed as one. And from this first 'we' there grows a still more dangerous thing: 'I have a little food' plus 'I have none.' If from this problem the sum is 'We have a little food,' the thing is on its way, the movement has direction. . . . This is the beginning—from 'I' to 'we' " (TGOW 165).

Novel as ecology, setting as habitat, characters as fauna, cooperation as redemption—the understanding of the environment that pervades Steinbeck's work results from a profoundly interdisciplinary habit of mind and a uniquely interdisciplinary friendship. If Steinbeck was a novelist who thought as an ecologist, his influential friend Ed Ricketts, the original "Doc," was a marine biologist who thought as a philosopher. Science and the humanities are not compartmentalized in their minds. The "diamond-true child voices of the Sistine Choir" and Sanskrit poetry are as much a part of Doc's laboratory as aquariums and pickled specimens (*CR* 210, 297). The apparent confusion about his roles (to the boys, the "Doc" honorific makes him an expert on Darling's canine distemper; in *Sweet Thursday* he is given a telescope instead of a microscope) is unwarranted, all forms of knowledge are his purview. He is expected to understand such subjects as the prayer of stinkbugs and the rage of octopi. The boys treat him very much as Hamlet treats Horatio when the ghost appears—"Thou art a scholar, speak to it."

Of course an interdisciplinary habit of mind is to be expected from an ecologist, one who takes the interconnectedness of all things as a first principle. No potential relationship is too inappropriate for exploration. A comic manifestation of that spirit is Doc's experimental willingness to put beer in a milkshake and drink it. But this spirit operates in other, more profound ways, as well. The marine biologist's understanding of ecology is as mystical, as religious, as it is "data-based" or scientific. *Log from the Sea of Cortez* contains Steinbeck's most complete expression of ecology as *the* humanistic doctrine, binding both Judaeo-Christian and scientific thought:

Man is related to the whole thing, related inextricably to all reality, known as unknowable. This is a simple thing to say, but the profound feeling of it made a Jesus, a St. Augustine, a St. Francis, a Roger Bacon, a Charles Darwin, and an Einstein. Each of them in his own tempo and with his own voice discovered and reaffirmed with astonishment that all things are one thing and that one thing is all things—plankton, a shimmering phosphorescence on the sea and the spinning planets and an expanding universe, all bound together by the elastic string of time. (LSC 257)

Was Steinbeck different because he studied biology, evolution, and ecology? Certainly. But he was also different in part because he was from the West, a native Californian. Wallace Stegner reminds us that "the West is short-grass plains, alpine mountains, geyser basins, plateaus and mesas and canyons and cliffs, salinas and sinks, sagebrush and Joshua tree and saguaro deserts," that "there is nothing in the East like the granite horns of Grand Teton or Teewinot, nothing like the volcanic neck of Devil's Tower, nothing like the travertine terraces of Mammoth Hot Springs, nothing like the flat crestline and repetitive profile of the Vermilion Cliffs" (1992, 45). Inhuman in scale, such country, unlike the domesticated landscapes of the East, teaches humility even as it invites exploitation in the form of irrigated agriculture, mining, grazing, and lumbering.

Perhaps Steinbeck's Western origins more than anything else give him his "transcendent sense of place" (Stegner 1992, 149). But he also understood the West as a place that would continue to test our attitudes toward the land. The American frontier ends on the beaches of the Pacific, as Steinbeck well knew (recall the old men in *The Red Pony,* hating the sea because it stopped them). And if early twentieth-century California was no longer a frontier, as "frontier" might have been understood by the pioneers of the Oregon Trail, nevertheless it remained throughout the 1930s the goal of a new westward migration. California's agricultural lands, to a nation willfully ignoring the fact that irrigation and desertification go hand in hand, held out the hope of abundance during the worst depression of our history.

When a frontier ends, we must begin to consider confronting not a wilderness of virgin land but the still more frightening wilderness of man's exploitative, even rapacious character. Toward the end of his life, writing in *America and Americans*, Steinbeck was optimistic enough to hope that, although "it was full late when we began to realize the continent did not stretch out to infinity," we might extend to the land as well as to one another the transcendent consciousness of interdependence that suffuses *The Grapes of Wrath:* "We are no longer content to destroy our beloved country. We are slow to learn; but we learn. . . . And we no longer believe that a man, by owning a piece of America, is free to outrage it" (*AAA* 129–30).

Nevertheless, we still live in a world where a New York publishing house can reject a classic book such as Norman Maclean's *A River Runs Through It* because "these stories turned out to be Western stories. . . . these stories have trees in them" (Maclean ix). The masses of our nation's population continue to be crowded into the great cities and sprawling suburbs of our Eastern Seaboard, and the majority of our colleges and universities are crowded there as well. Steinbeck's position in the urban academy remains marginal because his stories are Western stories, and not only do they have trees in them, they have "the living moving flowers of the sea, nudibranchs and tetribranchs, the spiked and nobbed and needly urchins, the crabs and demi-crabs" and even "little unborn humans, some whole and others sliced thin and mounted on slides" (*CR* 135). "Western Biological"—the very name of Doc's lab, a place where "you can order anything living . . . and sooner or later you will get it"—summarizes the intellectual threat Steinbeck poses to many Eastern ecophobes (*CR* 135–36).

For a long time now, deconstruction and its theoretical progeny have held sway in American literary criticism. Jonathan Culler celebrates, in all seriousness, such poststructuralist critical thinking with a telling metaphor:

Deconstruction's procedure is called "sawing off the branch on which one is sitting". . . . If "sawing off the branch on which one is sitting," seems foolhardy to men of common sense, it is not so for Nietzsche, Freud, Heidegger, and Derrida; for they suspect that if they fall there is no "ground" to hit and that the most clear sighted act may be a certain reckless sawing, a calculated dismemberment or deconstruction of the great cathedral-like trees in which Man has taken shelter for millennia. (in Lehman 61–62)

Contrast this statement with a passage from *America and Americans*:

Quite a few years ago when I was living in my little town on the coast of California a stranger came in and bought a small valley where the Sempervirens redwoods grew, some of them three hundred feet high. We used to walk among these trees, and the light colored as though the great glass of the Cathedral at Chartres had strained and sanctified the sunlight. The emotion we felt in this grove was one of awe and humility and joy; and then one day it was gone, slaughtered, and the sad wreckage of boughs and broken saplings left like nonsensical spoilage of the battle-ruined countryside. And I remember that after our rage there was sadness, and when we passed the man who had done this we looked away, because we were ashamed for him. (AAA 130)

Can such a critic and such a writer coexist? Steinbeck, of course, is writing about trees, not literary theory, but it is perhaps little wonder that some elements of the clear-cut groves of academe are uncomfortable with a writer of his earnestness and sense of moral responsibility. Like Charley the poodle refusing to pay his "devoirs" to the redwood tree, poststructuralist critics can be, in Steinbeckian terms, "non-appreciators" (*TWC* 188, 191), and one goal of this volume might be to drag them to the trunk and rub their noses against the realities of constructed nature and constructed language.

Fortunately, the wheels of literary fashion turn. No more a "dry ball" writer than a "dry ball" biologist, Steinbeck is an important patriarch for a younger generation of Western writers (Edward Abbey, Ivan Doig, Rick Bass, Gretel Ehrlich, William Least Heat Moon, Leslie Marmon Silko, Terry Tempest Williams), whose books, unabashedly, have trees in them and who are changing the face of American literature as they address our intensifying environmental crisis. Like the great Sea of Cortez biologist John Xántus, Steinbeck as a writer had "the warmth and the breadth . . . [to] proliferate in all directions" and to leave a "whole tribe" of Steinbecks (*LSC* 71–72).

For those of us who believe, with Steinbeck, that "great writing" should be "a staff to lean on, a mother to consult, a wisdom to pick up stumbling folly, a strength in weakness, and a courage to support sick cowardice" (*JN* 115–16), there is much to learn from his work. Particularly, there is much to learn about how we can combat our "tendency toward irresponsibility," our tendency to "conduct ourselves as our ancestors did, stealing from the future for our own clear and present profit" (*AAA* 127).

Here, in the pages of *Steinbeck and the Environment*, in the spirit of Doc's lab, we have gathered marine biologists and literary critics, a philosopher, an environmental policy maker, and even the senior investigator of a Mars mission, to consult great writing on the most interesting of all subjects—how to stop our reckless sawing and attain the state of cooperation and the transcendent recognition of ecological interdependence that will alone ensure the survival of our species and its brethren.

Part One: Origins

ONE

John Steinbeck
and Ed Ricketts:
Understanding Life in
the Great Tide Pool

James C. Kelley

James Kelley draws on a wide range of philosophies to show how Steinbeck and Ricketts almost literally anticipated the New Age school of "deep ecology." To the superorganism concept Steinbeck was exposed to at the Hopkins Marine Station and the idea of group cooperation among organisms Ricketts received from W. C. or Warder Clyde Allee at the University of Chicago, Kelley adds the concepts of transcendent and visceral thinking that contributed to Ricketts's goal of "breaking through" to a holistic concept of the world ecosystem. The essay also contrasts Ricketts's idea of the "deep smile" of primitive peoples living close to nature with the ethic of nature subjugation practiced by "advanced" European cultures. Kelley concludes that Steinbeck and Ricketts viewed science based on ecological principles as a "noble human undertaking" and a rational means of achieving global understanding. The philosophy of Sea of Cortez *is increasingly relevant to our preparation for today's "green revolution."*

One of the most important social changes in these last decades of the twentieth century is, surely, the "greening" of the world population. The widespread concern for the environment and the effect of this concern on the political process and on the amount of money we are devoting to understanding human environmental impacts and reversing their effects are unprecedented in human history. This concern may be a natural response by an organism to environmental change. The Gaia Hypothesis (Lovelock 1972, 215) predicts this sort of response as organisms work to regulate their environment to make it more habitable (such a regulatory effort presumably occurs even if the uninhabitable features are of their own making). To some degree, our environmental awareness must be due to the Apollo space program, which allowed us, for the first time, to see our little water planet from the outside. To some less obvious but no less profound degree, the awareness may have been conditioned by John Steinbeck, who gave expression to Ed Ricketts's philosophical thoughts. These thoughts contain all of the primary elements of what "New Age" writers, thinking they have found something new and revolutionary, call "deep ecology." In fact, the thinking by Steinbeck and Ricketts on the subject is considerably more sophisticated than much of the recent work. This chapter will explore some of these ideas and how they may condition environmental concern.

Ecological Thinking, Rational Understanding

Ricketts's mentor, W. C. Allee, traces the origins of ecology to Empedocles, Aristotle, and Theophrastus but recognizes the development of the field in its modern form as beginning with the use of the name (*Oekologie,* or oecology) by Haeckel in 1869 (Allee et al. 34). The field experienced a rapid expansion and sophistication in the first three decades of this century, during which both Allee himself and William Emerson Ritter were major contributors. The Gaia concept is, of course, more recent. The term was introduced by Lovelock in 1972 (579), but in 1989 (215) he traced its origins to the work of the remarkable Scottish geologist James Hutton in 1788 (Hutton 209–304).

John Steinbeck was certainly interested in the subject we now call ecology at least from his Stanford years; in 1923, he and his sister Mary took summer session courses in marine biology at the Hopkins Marine Station in Pacific Grove. It was a short walk down from the Eleventh Street house to the tide pools between Lover's Point and Cabrillo Point (China Point), which they visited often as children. The instructor in his summer biology course, Charles Vincent Taylor, was a doctoral candidate at Berkeley, a student of Charles Kofoid, and heavily influenced by the work of William Emerson Ritter, former chairman of the Zoology Department and, in 1911, founding director of Scripps Institution of Oceanography (Benson 1984, 240). As chair, Ritter had taught the University of California's summer marine biology course on the Hopkins property in 1892 (Ritter 1912, 148). Ritter used the "superorganism" model for what we would today call an ecosystem. This model worked well for Steinbeck in the form of the "phalanx" concept for "group man," prominent in *In Dubious Battle*, "The Leader of the People," and *The Grapes of Wrath* (Astro 1973, 61).

When John met Ed Ricketts in 1930, Ed was fresh from the powerful influence of Warder Clyde Allee at the University of Chicago. Allee wrote extensively on group behavior among animals and was interested in the ways in which the group modifies, for example, the feeding or reproductive behaviors of its individual members. Allee developed some of the fundamental principles of the discipline of ecology and certainly was one of the most important contributors to the rapid development of the field in the early decades of this century. He was a powerful personal figure, and the University of Chicago, at the time, was a major force in both ecology and marine biology through his efforts and those of the pioneering and prolific invertebrate zoologist Libbie Hyman.

A third perspective, although not strictly ecological and still in its formative stage, was provided by the young Joseph Campbell, Ed's neighbor on Fourth Street in Pacific Grove and a regular visitor to Ed's lab in 1932. Joe Campbell was, at the time, exploring both the common denominators of the mythologies of the world's peoples and also, after his time in Germany with Carl Jung, the needs of our "collective unconscious" and how and why we develop our mythologies. Joe was infatuated with Carol Henning Steinbeck, and it was Carol who introduced Joe, John, and Ed to the often allegorical poetry of Robinson Jeffers. Jeffers, by then living in Carmel, greatly influenced all three (Larsen and Larsen 179).

The mix of ecological and mythological concepts provides a philosophical basis that pervades much of Steinbeck's work from at least *Tortilla Flat* (1935) to *The Log from the Sea of Cortez* (1951). The ecological treatment of intertidal communities was the significant innovation of *Between Pacific Tides,* by Ricketts and Jack Calvin, and the principle of the interconnectedness of everything is an essential part of Joseph Campbell's later work. He was fascinated by the notion that all humans share a set of primitive ideas, the *Elementargedanken* of German anthropologist Adolf Bastian. In Campbell's analysis these primitive ideas may be born of Jung's collective unconscious (*Masks*

of God 45). In this formulation the mythological work yields a basically ecological explanation (i.e., one of the ways in which our species adapts to its environment is by explaining the wonders of the
world through our mythology—or through our science).

Transcendent Understanding, "Breaking Through"

John was fascinated with Ed's scientific temperament. In a radio
script interview on his advocacy on behalf of the Okies in *The Grapes
of Wrath*, the novelist said that "the only heroes left are the scientists
and the poor" (Benson 1984, 402). He admired Ed's objectivity and
his ability to think nonteleologically, to observe natural phenomena
for excruciatingly long periods without drawing conclusions as to
the causes of the observed behaviors. The story of Hazel and the
stinkbugs in *Cannery Row* provides the ultimate display of nonteleological irony to illustrate this point:

> *[When Hazel, observing typical stinkbug behavior, asks] "Well, what
> they got their asses up in the air for?" . . .*
> *"I think they're praying," said Doc.*
> *"What!" Hazel was shocked.*
> *"The remarkable thing," said Doc, "isn't that they put their tails up in
> the air—the really remarkable thing is that we find it remarkable. We can
> only use ourselves as yardsticks. If we did something as inexplicable and
> strange we'd probably be praying—so maybe they're praying."*
> *"Let's get the hell out of here," said Hazel. (CR 147–48)*

Ed Ricketts's ability to study the phenomenon under investigation
as it is, without leaping to causal conclusions, is certainly an element
of good science, but it led Ed to seek another kind of transcendence.
Ed was fond of advocating what he called getting the "*toto* picture,"
the kind of holistic, synthetic thinking that is essential in ecology
(Hedgpeth 1978, pt. 2, 26). It was the pursuit of this kind of systemic
understanding that led Ed to develop the philosophy of "breaking
through." The idea of breaking through implies the existence of a
kind of understanding that goes beyond anything possible by
scientific observation and deductive reasoning alone. I will refer to
this kind of understanding as *transcendent understanding.*

Ed attributes the terminology to Robinson Jeffers in "Roan Stallion":

> Humanity is the mould to break away from, the crust to
>   break through, the coal to break into fire,
> The atom to be split.
>   Tragedy that breaks man's face and a white
>   fire flies out of it; vision that fools him
> Out of his limits, desire that fools him out of his
>   limits, unnatural crime, inhuman science,
> Slit eyes in the mask; wild loves that leap over the
>   walls of nature, the wild fence-vaulter science,
> Useless intelligence of far stars, dim knowledge of the
>   spinning demons that make an atom,
> These break, these pierce, these deify, praising their
>   God shrilly with fierce voices: not in a man's
>   shape
> He approves the praise, he that walks lightning-naked
>   on the Pacific, that laces the suns with planets
> The heart of the atom with electrons: what is humanity
>   in this cosmos? For him, the last
> Least taint of a trace in the dregs of the solution;
>   for itself, the mould to break away from, the coal
> To break into fire, the atom to be split.
>   (Jeffers 140 [emphasis added])

It should be clear from the emphasized phrase, in this part of the poem, that Jeffers expects science itself to break through. In his 1938 poem, "The Purse-Seine," in a mode very much like Ricketts's own, Jeffers breaks through from the description of sardine fishing to see the sardines in a seine net as symbolic of humans pressed together in cities, dependent on one another and the artificial life support systems that keep them trapped in the urban environment (Jeffers 588).

In another use of the phrase, Ed's professor W. C. Allee, in chapter 11 of *Cooperation Among Animals* entitled "The Peck Order and International Relations," says that the biologist must "break through" the confines of his discipline and try to understand how his knowledge may be applied to international relations. He writes:

It may have come as a surprise to some that there is evidence from modern experimental studies in group biology that bears on international problems. The biological information at hand is incomplete and must be used with caution, but the urgency of the situation [the world political disarray after World War I] has seemed to me to necessitate breaking through the reticence of the research biologist to set forth, and even to summarize briefly, some of the human implications growing out of recent work with animal aggregations. (202)

If Ed did not take the phrase from Allee, certainly he and John followed the advice with some enthusiasm. Interestingly, Joseph Campbell uses the same phrase in *The Mask of God* (4).

The notion of breaking through, especially when it follows a long period of rational contemplation, is a remarkably Zen idea. The achievement of "satori" was discussed in Zen texts owned by Steinbeck and Ricketts (DeMott 1984, 69 and 108), particularly D. T. Suzuki's *Essays in Zen Buddhism,* which we know was in Ed's library at the lab, as were Lao Tze's *Tao teh Ching* and the Taoist poetry of Li Po in S. Obata's *The Works of Li-Po* (Hedgpeth 1978, pt. 2, 23). These works reverberate with various versions of the phrase "the Tao which can be Tao-ed is not the real Tao." In Lionel Giles's 1905 translation, Lao Tze says, "The Tao which can be expressed in words is not the eternal Tao" (5). In Ed's essay "The Philosophy of Breaking Through," he uses the first translation, which is that of Dwight Goddard. Hedgpeth says that Ed had the 1919 edition in his library and further that "John Steinbeck often looked through Ed's books; and if John read Lao Tse, it was probably Ed's copy. My first sight of John Steinbeck was as he was standing beside a bookshelf in Ed's place with a book in his hand" (Hedgpeth 1978, pt. 2, 23). In the essay Ed focuses on the enlightenment achieved after a long struggle, a theme that spans the cultural range from the *Tao teh Ching* to the Grail Romance (*Masks of God* 197) and that is central to the Judaeo-Christian tradition from the Exodus to the Passion and Resurrection of Jesus Christ.

In "About Ed Ricketts," Steinbeck says of Ed, "He was walled off a little, so that he worked at his philosophy of 'breaking through,' of coming out through the back of the mirror into some kind of reality which would make the world seen dreamlike. This thought obsessed him" (*LSC* lxii).

Visceral Understanding

We have seen an awareness of at least two levels of understanding that were of interest to Steinbeck and Ricketts: the empirical scientific understanding that comes from studying the natural world and a transcendent understanding achieved by breaking through. The second is clearly more than an inductive synthesis from observational results. The full realization of the idea requires transcendence in the mystical sense used in Zen Buddhism. In addition to these two forms, there is a third that I will call visceral understanding. This is an intuitive and innate understanding of the world. Steinbeck used the term "racial memory," and it is clear from the pantheistic exploration of the oneness of man and nature in *To a God Unknown* that John came to this notion independently of Ed, although by the time the novel was published in 1933 it showed Ed's influence (Astro 1973, 81–88). Beginning with Webster Street's unfinished play *The Green Lady,* which already took this pantheistic view, John built on the idea with such passages as "There was a curious femaleness about the interlacing boughs and twigs, about the long green cavern cut by the river through the trees." To take another example, in Joseph Wayne's orgasmic experience on the land: "He stamped his feet into the soft earth. Then the exultance grew to be a sharp pain of desire that ran through his body in a hot river. He flung himself face downward on the grass and pressed his cheek against the wet stems. His fingers gripped the wet grass and tore it out, and gripped again. His thighs beat heavily on the earth" (*TGU* 11). The catharsis appears in Joseph's dying words "I am the land, and I am the rain. The grass will grow out of me in a little while" (*TGU* 261).

Ed Ricketts came to a different but sympathetic idea from his marine work. In his essay "The Tide," he says: "We have to envision the concept of the collective pattern associationally involved in instinct, to get an inkling of the force behind the lunar rhythm so deeply rooted, and so obviously and often present in marine animals and even in higher animals and man" (Hedgpeth 1978, pt. 2, 64). Consider Ed's statement, in the same essay, discussing the notion proposed by George Darwin (son of Charles Darwin) that earlier in earth history the tides were much stronger:

It is nevertheless far-fetched to attribute the lunar rhythm status actually observable in breeding animals of the tide controlled breeding habits of the California grunion, of the Polynesian palolo worm, of Nereis, of Amphineura, etc., wherein whole collections of animals act as one individual responding to a natural phenomenon, to the present fairly weak tidal forces only, or to coincidence. There is tied up to the most primitive and powerful social (collective) instinct, a rhythm "memory" which effects everything and which in the past was probably far more potent than it is now. (Hedgpeth 1978, pt. 2, 64)

John's rewritten version in *Sea of Cortez* reads:

It would seem far-fetched to attribute the strong lunar effects actually observable in breeding animals to the present fairly weak tidal forces only, or to coincidence. There is tied up to the most primitive and powerful racial or collective instinct a rhythm sense or "memory" which affects everything and which in the past was probably more potent than it is now..It would at least be more plausible to attribute these profound effects to devastating and instinct-searing tidal influences active during the formative times of the early race history of organisms; and whether or not any mechanism has been discovered or is discoverable to carry on this imprint through the germ plasms, the fact remains that the imprint is there. The imprint is in us and in Sparky and in the ship's master, in the palolo worm, in mussel worms, in chitons, and in the menstrual cycle of women. (SOC 34)

The notion that humans and all living things share some sort of common animus, that we are all interconnected spiritually, is a central theme of the "new" deep ecology. The notions of visceral understanding pervade modern environmentalist, animal welfare, and feminist writing. An interesting example was provided in 1990 when Adrienne Zihlman of the University of California at Santa Cruz and Mary Ellen Morbeck of the University of Arizona organized a meeting on female primatology. They closed the meeting to men on the grounds that "women scientists think differently about those topics than men do—possibly even understanding them better because they are women" (Dusheck 1494). The argument is commonly heard that one cannot really understand what it is like to be black, or gay, or female, for example, unless one is black, or gay, or female. This sort of alleged special knowledge could be gained through experiential learning, but clearly in the female primatology case it is said to be an example of visceral understanding.

One of the tenets of the "New Age" sense of visceral understanding is that it is a shared understanding of the interconnectedness of everything, especially humans, with everything else in the universe. Fritjof Capra, in 1991, writes:

a very useful distinction has emerged during the past two decades, the distinction between deep ecology and shallow ecology. In shallow ecology, human beings are put above nature or outside nature, and, of course, this perspective goes with the domination of nature. Value is seen as residing in human beings; nature is given merely use value, or instrumental value. Deep ecologists see human beings as an intrinsic part of nature, as merely a special strand in the fabric of life. (Capra and Steindl-Rast 85)

But half a century earlier John and Ed wrote:

"Let's go wide open. Let's see what we see, record what we find, and not fool ourselves with conventional scientific strictures. We could not observe a completely objective Sea of Cortez anyway, for in that lonely and uninhabited Gulf our boat and ourselves would change it the moment we entered. . . . Let us go," we said, "into the Sea of Cortez, realizing that we become forever a part of it, that our rubber boots slogging through a flat of eelgrass, that the rocks we turn over in a tide pool, make us truly and permanently a factor in the ecology of the region. We shall take something away from it, but we shall leave something too." (SOC 3)

Steinbeck and Ricketts explore other manifestations of this sort of visceral understanding. In the second chapter of Sea of Cortez, there is a long discussion about boats and how people, especially men, rapped three times on the hulls of boats on display at Macy's in New York. This is almost certainly John's observation, but of this almost instinctive behavior they write:

Can this have been an unconscious testing of hulls? . . . How deep this thing must be, the giver and the receiver again; the boat designed through millenniums of trial and error by human consciousness, the boat which

has no counterpart in nature unless it be a dry leaf fallen by accident in a
stream. And Man receiving back from Boat a warping of his psyche so
that the sight of a boat riding in the water clenches a fist of emotion in his
chest. . . . This is not mysticism, but identification; man, building his
greatest and most personal of all tools, has in turn received a boat-shaped
mind, and a boat, a man-shaped soul. His spirit and the tendrils of his
feeling are so deep in a boat that the identification is complete. (SOC 15)

In another form, visceral understanding may be manifested in group behavior of animals and humans, when, as Ed says in the above lines from "The Tide," "whole collections of animals act as one individual responding to a natural phenomenon." This idea of course pervades Steinbeck's novels and has been explored at length by Richard Astro (1973, 61), where John's formulation is the phalanx concept.

A theme central to the phalanx concept is the notion that the collection of individuals in an ecosystem, a group, or as a superorganism, exhibits a purpose, a personality, and an energy transcending that of the individuals who make up the superorganism. The superorganism, like a person drinking alcohol, may even exhibit behaviors that are inimical to the survival of individual components (e.g., brain cells) of the system. In *In Dubious Battle* Doc Burton says, "The pleasure we get in scratching an itch causes death to a great number of cells. Maybe group-man gets pleasure when individual men are wiped out in a war" (132). When Joy and Jim die, Mac turns the events into energy for the superorganism. "I want to see if it'd be a good idea for the guys to look at him tomorrow. We got to shoot some juice into 'er some way. . . . If Joy can do some work after he's dead, then he's got to do it. There's no such things as personal feelings in this crowd" (185).

The phalanx concept was one that had interested John for some time, but it certainly took shape and developed substance from his conversations with Ed Ricketts. As John wrote to George Albee in 1933,

I can't give you the whole thing [the phalanx concept] completely in a
letter, George. I am going to write a whole novel with it as a theme, so
how can I get it in a letter? Ed Ricketts has dug up all the scientific mate-
rial and more than I need to establish the physical integrity of the thing. I

have written the theme over and over and did not know what I was writing, I found at least four statements of it in the God. . . . When your phalanx needs you it will use you, if you are the material to be used. You will know when the time comes, and when it does come, nothing you can do will let you escape. (SLL 81)

Are Visceral and Transcendent Understanding the Same Thing?

In the Tibetan Buddhist and Hindu sense, transcendence is pretty clearly a monotonic increase in spirituality from one plane of being to a more enlightened one. The sense in which Ed Ricketts uses the concept of breaking through, however, is closer to the Zen Buddhist concept (Suzuki 229–66). In describing the human progression in his "Philosophy of Breaking Through" essay, Ed says:

Children and probably peasants, maybe old-fashioned farmers and laborers also, are unawakened, unconscious, live unknowingly in the flow of life; naive. The much larger conscious group includes a huge sophisticated majority either seeking, puzzled, bitter, or resigned; and a small mellow minority who, usually later in life, are luminously adjusted to their lot, whatever it may be. . . . In occasional naturally wise people (these are rare), the mellow may proceed directly from the naive. . . . [Usually] There is the original naive, child-like or savage belief in a personal deity. This is ordinarily followed, soon after the function of intellectual cognition develops and is honestly put to work on the problem, by a period of loss, bitterness, and atheistic insistence: the sophisticated stage. Then by breaking through as a result of acceptance of struggle with its challenge of work in attempting a deeper understanding, some feeling for the symbolism of religion, knowledge of the "deep thing beyond the name," of "magic" and if the "dog within," ultimately may illuminate the whole scene. The attempt toward conscious understanding of what formerly was accepted naively as a matter of traditional course, apparently imposes a struggle from which only the breakers-through emerge into the mellow group. (Hedgpeth 1978, pt. 2, 78)

Of particular interest is the sense that Ed portrays of the "deep thing" in, for example, the Indians of Baja California, who are extremely generous—

But some of the things offered, the spiritual and friendship things, I have a feeling are offered out of the "deep thing" which underlies both spiritual and physical; in other words they are given for what they are themselves, without either physical or spiritual expediency. You can't easily tell, because the words and actions are identical for the superficial or expedient thing, and for the deep thing. The only discriminating quality I've heard of is what the Upanishads call "the high and fine intuition of the wise." (Hedgpeth 1978, pt. 2, 134)

Ed raises the same point in his "antiscript" to John's *The Forgotten Village,* in which he talks of the "deep smile" of Mexican peasants as "evidence of internal adjustment and happiness" before they are influenced by modern living (Hedgpeth 1978, pt. 2, 172–82). The perception of native peoples living in ecological balance with the natural world has led to speculation that there is a deep harmony between these people and the environment that is lost when people start driving cars, living in air conditioned buildings, and surviving twice as long through the advances of modern medicine. This is certainly part of Ed's idea of the "deep smile," but whether this sort of instinctive harmony is the same state as is achieved by breaking through is a bit unclear. Ed and John talk of the Baja California Indians as living in a sort of dream state. "They actually seem to be dreaming. . . . They seemed to live on remembered things, to be so related to the seashore and the rocky hills and the loneliness that they are these things" (*SOC* 75). As we have seen earlier, John uses the same term in describing Ed's idea of transcendence: "he worked at his philosophy of 'breaking through,' of coming out through the back of the mirror into some kind of reality which would make the world seem dreamlike. This thought obsessed him." If the two states are the same, then consciousness "wraps around," and transcendent understanding merges into visceral understanding. If the states are different, and are instead end points on a continuum with rational or scientific understanding separating them, the model is obviously a very different one.

Implications for Environmental Understanding

Two common themes in contemporary environmental thinking are (1) that we, as members of the world population, must develop an appreciation of the large-scale, synthetic interconnectedness of everything that happens on the planet ("Think globally") and (2) that we, as individuals, must reestablish local ecological balance by environmentally responsible behavior ("Act locally"). It would seem that the first of these themes is best accomplished by a kind of breaking through, a kind of at least synthetic, if not transcendent, thinking. Certainly Allee would have been comfortable with this extension of his scientific ecological understanding, and neither Ed nor John was particularly shy about these sorts of conceptual leaps. The second of these themes may require rediscovering the "deep smile" of native peoples, reestablishing our connections to the natural world. No one doubts that Ed, through his mystical approach to science, nor John, in his literary celebrations of the natural world, had, to a significant degree in their own lives, accomplished just that.

As we have seen, we can view our understanding of our world as progressing from a sort of instinctive understanding, to an understanding refined by our scientific study of the world, and finally breaking through to an understanding of the global ecosystem as whole. Alternatively, we can view ourselves as coming, shortly after birth, out of a state of harmony with our world, passing through a period of searching in which we struggle to develop a rational understanding of our world, to, finally—if we allow ourselves to do so—achieving an enlightenment that reestablishes our sense of harmony with the universe.

A highly romanticized version of the second view is popular today, in which we hear that primitive peoples are in possession of both the instinctive harmony and the transcendent harmony but that victims of Western civilization, especially those perceived to be responsible for advancing that culture, are trapped in a sort of purgatory of rational disharmony (e.g., the popular films *The Emerald Forest* and *Dances with Wolves*). Some feminist literature suggests that it is not the rational step itself that is at fault but rather the current form of science that is the problem. Harding, for example, suggests changing the rational part of the process:

Women need sciences and technologies that are for women and that are for women in every class, race, and culture. Feminists (male and female) want to close the gender gap in scientific and technological literacy, to invent modes of thought and learn the existing techniques and skills that will enable women to get more control over the conditions of their lives. Such sciences can and must benefit men, too—especially those marginalized by racism, imperialism, and class exploitation; the new sciences are not to be only for women. But it is time to ask what sciences would look like that were for "female men," all of them, and not primarily for the white, Western and economically advantaged "male men" toward whom benefit from the science has disproportionately tended to flow. (Harding 5)

Capra argues that the current form of the rational step, of science, is simply offtrack and calls for a course correction:

Many of us in the new-paradigm movement believe that this association of man dominating nature, which is a patriarchal attitude, has to be divorced from science. We would like to see emerge again a science in which scientists cooperate with nature and pursue knowledge in order to learn about natural phenomena and be able to "follow the natural order and current of the Tao," as the Chinese sages put it. That is how I understand the traditional medieval notion of pursuing science "for the glory of God." (Capra and Steindl-Rast 12)

Capra blames Francis Bacon for getting science off course in the first place. "Ever since Francis Bacon, the aim of most scientists has been the domination of nature and the exploitation of nature" (Capra and Steindl-Rast 30). The accusation is interesting because Bacon, rather than arguing for a utilitarian science, clearly advocated full appreciation of nature by a combination of empiricism and rational thought. In "De Augmentis Scientiarum," he writes: "Now the first kind [of natural history] which aims either to please by the agreeableness of the narrative or to help by the use of experiments, and is pursued for the sake of such pleasure or profit, I account as far inferior in importance to that which is the stuff and material of a solid and lawful induction, and may be called the nursing mother of philosophy" (Bacon 430). In "Novum Organum," in a delightfully biological admonition, one that Ed and John would surely have appreciated, Bacon wrote: "Those who have handled sciences have been either men of experiment or men of dogmas. The men of experiment are like the ant; they only collect and use; the reasoners resemble spiders, who make cobwebs out of their own substance. But the bee takes the middle course; it gathers its matter from the flowers of the garden and of the field, but transforms it and digests it by a power of its own" (Bacon 288).

The contemporary environmentalist movement seems somewhat schizophrenic about science as an enterprise. For example, while celebrating the sophisticated biochemistry that provides the understanding of, say, heavy metals in the biosphere, the movement condemns the geochemistry that freed these same metals from the lithosphere. The simple resolution is that science is a tool and can be used for good or ill, but this view clearly begs the deeper philosophical question as to whether science, as one aspect of rational understanding, is an inevitable and necessary step in the human progress from instinct to enlightenment or whether it is a Western European juggernaut, blind to instinct and antithetical to enlightenment, which must be stopped before it destroys what is left of the global ecosystem.

It is clear not only that John and Ed were comfortable with science in those days just prior to World War II but that they viewed science as both a noble human undertaking and an essential step in progress of human understanding, as the requisite antecedent to breaking through to transcendent understanding. While decrying with equal vehemence the war half a world away and the ecological damage to the Sea of Cortez by Japanese bottom trawlers, they did not conclude that if only we stopped doing science, or if we limited our science to its beneficial utilitarian applications, the world would be a better place. They were comfortable accepting science as one of the ways we find our place in the universe, and they clearly saw that ecology itself is neither deep nor shallow and that the scientist determines the level of synthesis and transcendence of the science: "Perhaps it is the same narrowing we observe in relation to ourselves and the tide pool—a man looking at reality brings his own limitations to the world. If he has strength and energy of mind the tide pool stretches both ways, digs back to electrons and leaps space into the universe and fights out of the moment into non-conceptual time. Then ecology has a synonym which is ALL" (*SOC* 85).

The view that we as humans come into the world with a visceral understanding that is both mystical and instinctive, that we respond to our environment by trying to understand it, perhaps through our science, and that if we succeed in this rational understanding we can break through and see that our "racial memory" and our science are steps in a very human progression toward a global understanding is an optimistic and positive one. It contrasts with the "science as aberration" philosophies advanced by some New Age writers and may well resolve the schizophrenia of some in the environmentalist movement.

John Steinbeck and Ed Ricketts offered a philosophy more than fifty years ago that is increasingly relevant. Their work may have helped to condition us for the "green revolution." Revisiting their writing and their lives may help us understand what is going on in our own environmentally conscious lives of today.

Note

I wish to recognize and thank Graham Wilson, with whom I began teaching the course "Steinbeck and Ricketts: Literature and the Sea" nineteen years ago and who has taught me much of what I know about the literature; Joel Hedgpeth and Dora Henry (the barnacle lady in "About Ed Ricketts") who have taught me much of what I know about Ed; Mike Gregory whose stewardship of the NEXA program allowed us to teach the course; and our students who have kept us all going. NEXA is an interdisciplinary program that investigates the areas of "convergence" between the sciences and the humanities in courses in which members of the two faculties teach together on a topic of common interest. Initial funding for NEXA was provided by the National Endowment for the Humanities.

TWO

Steinbeck on Man and Nature:
A Philosophical Reflection

Richard E. Hart

The theory of literary naturalism holds that man's fate is determined by natural, social, and economic laws and that he has no free will. Hart argues for a modified, or philosophical naturalism in Steinbeck's early works, including "The Red Pony" and Of Mice and Men. *Yes, Steinbeck writes about the land, using simple people as characters, and is entranced with and interested in preserving their ecological and natural integrity. But Steinbeck is also concerned with "non-teleological thinking," expressing what "is" rather than what he might wish. Natural forces may push man into a given situation, but man, caught in that situation, may still make a choice. Such acts of free will, argues Hart, cast Steinbeck as a "soft determinist" (or "soft naturalist"), believing that man is both determined by his environment and capable of making independent decisions.*

There's a line of old men along the shore hating the ocean because it stopped them.
"The Red Pony"

Maybe the challenge was in the land; or it might be that the people made the challenge.
—"Afterword," *America and Americans*

It is true that we are weak and sick and ugly and quarrelsome but if that is all we ever were, we would millenniums ago have disappeared from the face of the earth, a few remnants of fossilized jaw bones, a few teeth in strata of limestone would be the only mark our species would have left on the earth. Now this I must say and say right here and so sharply and so memorably that it will not be forgotten in the terrible and disheartening things which are to come in this book; that although East of Eden is not Eden, it is not insuperably far away.
—*Journal of a Novel: The "East of Eden" Letters*

This essay examines the unique form of John Steinbeck's naturalism and the ambiguous, somewhat paradoxical view of the relation between man and nature found in his fictional creations, with particular reference to some of the early work. Perhaps words such as "ambiguous" and "paradoxical" are not perfectly suitable in this context and, in any case, may seem strangely out of place in a project that hopes to demonstrate convincingly the philosophically coherent and insightful ideas that Steinbeck presented regarding man and nature. Ironically, as the existentialists have made us realize, philosophical clarity often grows out of perplexity and ambiguity. It simply goes with the territory of life and experience. With sufficient patience and analysis, however, we can begin to see the unity and depth of Steinbeck's philosophy. Though I may be nearly a lone voice in this realm, I take strong exception to the fairly common charge, like that once made by Stanley Edgar Hyman in a review of the *Sea of Cortez* for the *New Republic*, that Steinbeck was simply preoccupied with "rambling philosophizing" for its own sake. His was simply too mature and serious an intellect to fall prey to idle musings or dilettantish posturing. Gloria Gaither rightly says, "Any discussion of Steinbeck the social reformer, Steinbeck the artist/writer, Steinbeck the journeyer, Steinbeck the marine biologist, remains inconclusive without a deep appreciation for and genuine understanding of Steinbeck the philosopher" (Gaither 43).

An eloquent indication of Steinbeck's treatment of the relation between man and nature was captured, I believe, by Anders Österling, a permanent secretary of the Swedish Academy, in the presentation address (1962) that he delivered when Steinbeck was awarded the Nobel Prize: "But in him we find the American temperament also in his great feeling for nature, for the tilled soil, the wasteland, the mountains, and the ocean coasts, all an inexhaustible source of inspiration to Steinbeck in the midst of, and beyond, the world of human beings" (Frenz 574). The philosophically intriguing aspect of this observation, which will be elaborated here, is the phrase "in the midst of, and beyond." A great feeling for nature in the midst of the world of humans and beyond the world of humans—just what does this mean or imply?

Steinbeck's early "California" fiction is typically described as firmly ensconced within the tradition of naturalism. His characters are seen as simple and "natural," and in terms of habits, idioms, customs, and experience, Steinbeck is obviously on intimate terms with them. Thus if they are both simple and "natural" (an alleged unity of labels that many philosophers, particularly metaphysicians, have readily embraced), so must he be. As Österling and countless others have noted, the early Steinbeck was a writer of the land and its natural inhabitants, morally disposed to the preservation of nature's integrity. He was, in his thinking and work, both a functional part of nature and a student/appreciator of nature. Yet he was no simple-minded sentimentalist (though he could be sentimental on other counts) or popularizing nature freak. His on-again, off-again university education and long collegial association with scientist and collector Ed Ricketts demonstrate that he was formally trained and experienced in the biological and marine sciences. But he superseded the inherent limits and understandings of science, complementing science with a deeply appreciative understanding of nature from aesthetic and philosophical perspectives. In other words, Steinbeck's naturalism was no simple, unidimensional matter. Nature for the scientist, the theologian, and the romantic may well be a rather clearly defined, unequivocal reality. But what becomes of nature, its conceptualization and presentation, in the hands of a passionate artist, trained scientist, spiritually inclined nonbeliever, occasional romantic and transcendentalist like Steinbeck? A closer look at naturalism is necessary, in both its literary and its philosophic formulations.

Although undoubtedly generalized, a useful standard account of "literary naturalism" is represented by the sort of received opinion found in the *Oxford Companion to American Literature*: "Naturalism, critical term applied to the method of literary composition that aims at a detached scientific objectivity in the treatment of natural man. . . . It conceives of man as controlled by his passions, or by his social and economic environment and circumstances . . . in this view, man has no free will" (cited in French *John Steinbeck* 1975, 37). "Literary naturalism," thus defined, coincides with at least one pervasive aspect of "philosophical naturalism" as it has come to be conceived in the twentieth-century American context.[1] This version suggests that all instances of natural objects—a stone, a leaf, a horse, a human being—exist within spatiotemporal and causal orders. Persons, like rocks or oceans, are but one species of natural object and are no less subject to natural laws, in terms of the processes that, in the case of people, make up mental and social life, than any other parts of nature. Just as the scientist's application of natural or scientific method to the explanation of volcanoes or the movement of planets is both appropriate and useful, so, too, does the same approach to persons explain what makes them work. Clearly, much of what we today understand in the realms of genetics, psychological conditioning, medicine, and human instinctual behavior, among other phenomena, is directly attributable to the assumptions and methods of this aspect of naturalism.

On such an account then, man and nature appear coextensive, unified, compatible, and relatively harmonious in terms of operations and explanatory principles. Regarded in a literal sense, man is a determined, fully constituted unit of nature at the mercy of nature's forces, its arbitrary and sometimes capricious doings. Man is substantially the sum product of natural factors—genetics, social conditioning, and, as the Greeks knew, even pure chance or fate (Moira). Inescapably, man is but one element among many interrelated elements within the system of nature—a discrete cog in the vast machine. Steinbeck articulated this fundamental insight when, in the *Log from the Sea of Cortez,* he summarized his cosmic worldview in these words: "All things are one thing and . . . one thing is all things—plankton, a shimmering phosphorescence on the sea, and the spinning planets and an expanding universe, all bound together by the elastic string of time. It is advisable to look from the tide pool to the stars and then back to the tide pool again" (*LSC* 257).

One might be tempted to say that nature, poetically or spiritually rendered, is man's true source, an authentic home, a kindly, albeit amoral, friend and nurturer that treats persons neutrally rather than cruelly as other people all too often seem to do when they crave money or power over values. For instance, consider such ambivalent longings for nature as George and Lennie's dream in *Of Mice and Men* of lasting solace on their never-to-be-realized couple of acres ("An' live off the fatta the lan' " [14]) or boy Jody's desire in "The Red Pony" to be absorbed into the mysterious, comforting though scary mountains, those taller, darker Santa Lucias, "Curious secret mountains . . . when the sun had gone over the edge in the evening and the mountains were a purple-like despair, then Jody was afraid of them" (*LV* 242).

But yet another, complementary dimension of "philosophical naturalism" is also, it turns out, central to Steinbeck's ideas about man and nature. Moreover, when we consider the claims of scholars such as Edwin H. Cady and Warren French ("Naturalism seems to fit only theoretical examples of a misguided theory"), this aspect of philosophical naturalism serves as a much-needed corrective to the narrow and impossible confines of literary naturalism (cited in Bloom 1987, 65). While it may well be that, from the scientist's perspective, the natural universe as a whole operates according to neutral, indifferent forces of cause and effect, nature nonetheless contains within it unique value-bearing, value-creating, value-acting sorts of entities, namely, human beings.

Humans both have and constantly pursue values through deliberation and action. Though a distinctive biological unit within the natural order, man is never wholly reducible in any way to the other parts or categories of nature. Significantly, man is *both* the same and different. To the extent that human persons, unique in status and function, engage in acts of valuing they reflect at least a measure of free will, they become "moral" beings, and thus must accept responsibility for choices and actions. Among all the elements constitutive of nature, only man can and does rise up against determinism through an exercise of will and moral consciousness (notably a fundamental insight at the core of Jean-Paul Sartre's magnum opus, *Being and Nothingness*).

As John J. Conder has pointed out, Steinbeck's insistence on the two sides of the self—the species self integrated within nature, as over against the social self that inclines toward "mechanical man"— provides the ground for his "idiosyncratic way of harmonizing determinism and freedom." Man's (individual and group man) achievement of rational consciousness entails freedom and responsibility for actions. But there is more. In reflecting on *The Grapes of Wrath*, Conder suggests:

Man's possession of instinct roots him in nature [makes him part of nature], but he is different from other things in nature, as Steinbeck makes clear by describing in Chapter 14 man's willingness to "die for a concept"

*as the "one quality [that] is the foundation of Manself . . . distinctive in
the universe." And this emphasis on man's uniqueness in nature, so inextricably related to his will, in turn limits the scope of the novel's historical
determinism. (cited in Bloom 1988, 102–3)*

Simply stated, determinism is tempered, though never completely
overcome, by freedom.

My argument, then, regarding Steinbeck's outlook, is basically a
simple one, though it reflects profound philosophical insight. It extends Conder's position full force into the realms of philosophical
naturalism and existential choice. Steinbeck's early work formulates
and dramatically re-presents the two-sided and, at times, confound-
ing version of philosophical naturalism precisely in his literary portrayal of the paradoxical nature of human existence, of man in nature. For Steinbeck, to be a human person is tantamount to being
caught in a paradox, to be engaged, sometimes unwittingly, in living
with and working through the dilemma of being at once both a
determined unit of nature and a free, value-articulating individual
forever called upon to act. In a vivid, existential sense, Steinbeck's
fiction thus articulates through art the "lived experience" of the
complexities and paradoxes of naturalism.

So man is in fact both free and not free, an apparently unassailable
truth about the human condition, a reality philosophers have labeled
"soft determinism" as a counterbalance to inflexible "hard determinism." In Steinbeck the blend is between his "scientific mechanism"
and "humanistic vitalism" and follows logically from his empiri-
cally derived theory of "nonteleological thinking," which concerns
itself with what "is" the case rather than what "could," "should," or
"might" be. As a determined product of environment, in the broadest
sense, individuals sometimes cannot help themselves, cannot be or
do otherwise.

It thus comes as no surprise that Steinbeck's characters are often
cast as though they are in an epical struggle with fickle nature or
even their own uncontrollable passions and instincts. While a truth-
ful claim about man and his condition, this *alone* could not suffice
for Steinbeck, for it would imply that the characters, and their creator, the naturalistic writer, cannot attempt any moral judgments and
must necessarily be inclined toward pessimism. Contrarily, in Stein-

beck's work we witness the intersection, the complementarity, of the determinism of nature *and* man's freedom of existence, in other words, both scientific "cause and effect" and nonteleological "is" thinking. Simplistic or reductionistic models of naturalism will not do, for they either bury man in nature or seek to separate him from it. Philosophically and aesthetically, Steinbeck can be both an environmental determinist, broadly construed, and a "humanist" whose characters illustrate strong ethical qualities of choice and action.

Over and against the at times overwhelming forces of nature and fate, many of Steinbeck's early characters embody a compensating humanistic value that affirms the significance of the individual person no matter how lowly or seemingly ill equipped for the world. Man thus reveals a subtle kind of moral grandeur in his everyday life, in relations among common people such as gamblers, ranch hands, drunks, prostitutes, migrant laborers. Difficult though it may be, man *can* help himself through an act of will, thereby affirming the primacy of human dignity. In this respect, one cannot ignore Steinbeck's affinity with the idealism of American transcendentalists such as Emerson, Thoreau, and Whitman who tend to portray man as simultaneously individualistic and selflessly altruistic.

If the preceding is at all an accurate account, it is easy to see how for Steinbeck nature could be ambiguously conceived as both friend and enemy and, in turn, man himself variously celebrated for his courage and moral conquests (e.g., *In Dubious Battle*) and berated for his crass self-interest and sought-after superiority over nature (consider, e.g., the commercialization and abuse of the land and its people in *The Grapes of Wrath*). Man at times displays his *freedom* through moral grandeur and, at other times, through wanton hubris against the forces of nature that frustrate his ambitions. For a telling illustration, simply recall (in "The Red Pony") boy Jody's grandfather describing that "line of old men along the shore hating the ocean because it stopped them" from their onward push to the west, from the "westering" that was their very modus operandi.

How is this hypothesis regarding Steinbeck's vision of naturalism manifest in one of his early works? A brief summary of some key aspects of one early novel, *Of Mice and Men* (the work Peter Lisca has called "a symbolic construct of man's psychological and spiritual as well as his social condition" [294]), provides further evidence for the argument here advanced. On the side of environmental determinism, consider the character Lennie. Obviously, his inherited mental defects and developmental experiences have cast him as something of a pawn of nature, a victim of forces he can never seem to control. Consequently, he lovingly squeezes the life out of every living creature that comes into his hands and paws at women's clothing without fully realizing the meaning or consequences of his acts. By contrast his partner, George, is cast as the thinker, the decision maker, the caretaker of Lennie, and, I would argue, the ultimately free, moral agent who vividly illustrates the two aspects of Steinbeck's naturalism. George is free to choose—indeed, in a sense, condemned to freedom—but he is, also, determined by powerful forces within himself and the world—his lusts, his original promise to Lennie's aunt to look after him, his penchant for dreaming and fantasizing, his acquiescence to gambling and drink, and even, in the end, his overpowering love for Lennie.

In this vein, one of the earliest Steinbeck scholars, Harry Thornton Moore, was correct in pointing out that, regarding many of the characters in *Of Mice and Men*, "George and Lennie and Candy and Crooks and some of the others are caught in this situation, they are lonely and homeless and yearning." But he was wrong in concluding that George is simply a shattered protagonist who goes down in spiritual defeat, a character "no more than pathetic" who "attracts sympathy because he has to lose his friend Lennie" (51). Surely, George's dream is shattered, but he survives and goes on. Likewise, I disagree with Warren French's assertion that, in the end, George "is helpless in the hands of an indifferent and imperfect nature" (cited in Bloom 1987, 76). Both miss the second, enhancing dimension of naturalism (and the second aspect of the self, in Conder's terms), conceived philosophically. George chose; he acted in one way rather than another. He could simply have walked away and left Lennie to the mob, but he didn't. Both interpreters ignore the intense moral dilemma and its courageous and sad, even heroic, resolution that distinguishes the ending of this powerful story. The conclusion Steinbeck presents is as fine an example as one can find in literature of the anguished, yet imperative, nature of moral choice. Choice is tough, and often all will not go well, but it must be done. Any self-reflective human being knows this before all else.

At the end of the tale, Lennie knows, as do we the readers, that he has again done wrong but that he can't really help himself, can't help what he is or will be in the future. George has, even through denial, always known this bitter truth. Lennie thinks George may finally abandon him, as well he should (rationally speaking) in order to save his own skin. Along the quiet bank of the Salinas River, a refuge of comforting nature, the drama reaches fever pitch. There seems no way out. The lynchmen's voices grow nearer and nearer. Deterministic fate closes in and seriously restricts the range of choices. Lennie and George are victims of harsh nature, of a destiny they had some hand in shaping but over which they now seem to have no control. But if nothing else—and, indeed, there is at that moment nothing else—they have each other, they can count on each other. The bond is both cementing and liberating. And then, through an heroic act of will, George demonstrates, with simple, unparalleled clarity, the transcendent power of love. In killing Lennie, thereby saving him from indignity and torture, George morally reverses (for the moment) the forces of fate and nature that have both of them in its grip. Nature controls *and* man is free. Hopelessness and courage exist side by side. Whichever way the pendulum swings is forever a part of the human drama, whether in art or in daily living.

In sum, the philosophical naturalism embodied in Steinbeck's early and best fiction reflects an understanding of and faith in both nature and man. It is a complex and sophisticated outlook that can, in Socratic fashion, assist in greater self-understanding (the Delphic oracle's most enduring command was "know thyself") while, in an ecological sense, illuminating our often unconscious attitudes toward nature and cultivating appropriate responses to present and future environmental challenges. Without doubt Steinbeck's ecological message—his desire to understand and cooperate with the environment rather than, like Hemingway, dominate it—was well ahead of its time. On this point, Steinbeck's biographer, Jackson J. Benson, has remarked: "As early as the mid-1930s he [Steinbeck] was talking about man living in harmony with nature, condemning a false sense of progress, advocating love and acceptance, condemning the nearly inevitable use of violence, and preaching ecology at a time when not even very many scientists cared about it" (Benson 1988, 196).[2] But as we know so painfully today, his pleas of almost sixty years ago fell on deaf ears. With hindsight, if Steinbeck's ideas about man and nature, man in nature, had been heeded rather than disparaged as Martian-like talk—attacked politically and ideologically—would we today be confronting the very real possibility of environmental calamity in the coming decades?

For Steinbeck, man is not just a cultural or political or economic animal but fundamentally a species in nature, a unique and hopeful part of the whole and never detached from it. Man suffers and makes mistakes when he rejects his biological identity, and his suffering is too often inflicted on everything around him. We today would do well to embrace the character of the hard-nosed scientific as well as the religious and philosophical in his richest ideas. At his most poignant moments, Steinbeck engenders a powerful, though naively unappreciated, divinity about nature and particularly man, as captured in the following lines that serve to close this essay:

Why do we dread to think of ourselves as a species? Can it be that we are afraid of what we may find? That human self-love would suffer too much and that the image of God might prove to be a mask? This could be only partly true, for if we could cease to wear the image of a kindly, bearded, interstellar dictator, we might find ourselves true images of his kingdom, our eyes the nebulae, and universes in our cells. (LSC 314)

Notes

Portions of this essay are included, but treated in a different context, in a previous paper of mine, "The Concept of Person in the Early Fiction of John Steinbeck," which appeared in a special issue of *Personalist Forum* 3.1 (Spring 1992): 67–73.

1. Naturalism in America of course has deep roots in nineteenth-century philosophical and literary thought (i.e., Emerson, Thoreau, Whitman). Here I offer in my own words a brief summary of some leading ideas about naturalism as addressed in the writings of such historical figures as John Dewey, F. J. E. Woodbridge, and Sidney Hook and in the highly influential work by George Santayana, *The Life of Reason.* Cf. also Ernest Nagel, "Naturalism Reconsidered" (1954).

2. My position in this essay has also been shaped by study of chapter 14 of the *Log from the Sea of Cortez* (1951), both editions of Warren French's Twayne book, *John Steinbeck* (1961, 1975), and the chapter "Some Conclusions," in Peter Lisca's *The Wide World of John Steinbeck* (1958).

Part Two:
The Grapes of Wrath

THREE

Turning Wine into Water: Water as Privileged Signifier in *The Grapes of Wrath*

David N. Cassuto

For the past century in the American Southwest, water's scarcity and its obvious utility have made it both a vital commodity and a powerful cultural symbol. In The Grapes of Wrath, *Steinbeck is keenly aware that to control water is to control the land. Powerful banking and farming interests in both Oklahoma and California dominated the land because they determined water use. Water and its absence therefore assume symbolic weight throughout the novel, informing its very structure and meaning. Steinbeck dismantles both the frontier myth of open land and the edenic promise of abundant yield through hard work.*

> Eastward I go only by force; but westward I go free.
> —Henry David Thoreau

The Old Testament describes wilderness as "a thirsty ground where there was no water." When the Lord wished to punish, He threatened to "turn the rivers into islands and dry up the pools and . . . command the clouds that they rain no rain upon it." When granting redemption in Isaiah, God promises instead that "waters shall break forth in the wilderness and streams in the desert" and that "the desert and dry land shall be glad" (Deut. 8:7, 15; Isaiah 5:6, 35:1, 6, 43:20). The Garden of Eden provided the antithesis of desert wilderness, a place where water flowed freely and bounty of all sorts lay ready to spring out of the ground. This is the legacy that spawned what Henry Nash Smith termed the "myth of the garden" in the American West. At the dawn of the common era, John offered Jesus his baptism in the river Jordan. Two millennia later, Casy baptized Tom Joad in an irrigation ditch.

I will argue that *The Grapes of Wrath* represents an indictment of the American myth of the garden and its accompanying myth of the frontier. The lever with which Steinbeck pries apart and ultimately dismantles these fictions is a critique of the agricultural practices that created the Dust Bowl and then metamorphosed into a new set of norms that continued to victimize both the land and its inhabitants. Both nineteenth-century homesteading (based on the Homestead Act of 1862) and agribusiness, its twentieth-century descendant (born from the failure of the Homestead Act), relied on the (mis)use of water to accomplish their respective goals. And both policies resulted in ecological disaster.

The Plains were called upon to supply grain for the international war effort in 1914 and to feed a hungry nation whose population continued to multiply exponentially. Throughout the nation, industrialization held sway as the isolationism of the nineteenth century gave way to the globalism of the twentieth. These transitions required great expenditures of resources, and, in the grain belt, the resource most in demand was water. As farmers poured their short-term profits back into land and seed, their fates depended ever more on the availability of water. When the climatic pendulum swung back toward aridity, Plains farmers had to declare hydrological bankruptcy, though neither they nor the federal government would abandon the myth of the garden. As the government scrambled to dam rivers and force water into the desert, farmers clung fast to their vision of uncountable abundance amid a green world.

Water was a commodity, symbol of wealth and expanding capabilities. Admitting its unattainability involved acknowledging the limited productive capabilities of the land. Such an admission also meant conceding the limitations of the nation and its people, a prospect that remained anathema to a culture steeped in the dominant myths. Myra Jehlen notes that "the conviction that farming brought reason and nature together (since man and nature had the same reasons) inspired cultivation . . . but made it particularly difficult, in fact, contradictory to contemplate basic changes in agrarian policy" (73). Instead of abandoning the American dream, the dream itself underwent an ideological shift. The myth of the garden remained intact, but its form evolved from an Edenic Xanadu to a neo-Baconian Atlantis that no longer awaited manna from heaven but wrested it instead from the grips of Nature.

Water's primacy as both commodity and signifier in the Southwest arose through a combination of its scarcity and utility. Its privileged place in the biotic schema predates its commodification by the state and corporate apparatus, but the two forces are by now inseparable in the history and mythology of the American West. The social and environmental conditions in the Southwest made water an ideal unit of exchange, and this led to its concurrent fetishization. As Gregory Jay characterizes commodity fetishism, "Capitalism structures symbolic exchange so as to elicit desire, manipulate its character, and teach it to find sublimity in prescribed objects" (167). Since water is necessary to human biology, in an arid region a dominant state apparatus would need to expend relatively little effort to transform water into a commodity whose scarcity would privilege it as well as its controllers. Once established as a commodity, any item of exchange value acquires symbolic value, connoting power and wealth and thereby enhancing the prestige of its possessor. In this sense, water becomes not just a measure of economic value but a culturally powerful symbol as well.

The class stratification depicted in *The Grapes of Wrath* arose from corporate control over the region's most precious resource. The region's aridity, however, made water an *absent* signifier. Both in the novel and in the desert itself, water's conspicuous absence is what makes it so powerful. The flooding that climaxes the novel is thematically situated to provide maximum counterpoint to the drought that originally forced the Joads to migrate west. Disenfranchised and dehumanized, the Joads can only curse the rising floodwaters even as they once prayed for a deluge to feed their parched crops.

The cycle of alienation appears complete; people whose humanity was once integrally tied to the land and the weather now care nothing for the growing season or the health of the earth. Their survival has come to depend on shelter from the elements rather than the elements themselves. They have become components of the factory-farming process, economically distant from their bourgeois oppressors but closely tied to the industrial ethos that rewards the subjugation of nature. The primary difference between the growers and the migrants now lies in their respective relationships with the privileged signifier. The growers—owners of the irrigation channels, centrifugal pumps, and watertight mansions, control it—while the Okies, starving and drenched, are at its mercy.

In *The Grapes of Wrath*, Steinbeck presents an archetypal Plains family caught in the modernization of the American dream. Forced to adapt to the realities of a closed frontier and a desert in the country's midsection, Americans retrofit their dominant myths to encompass corporate capitalism and, in so doing, accept water's scarcity and preeminence as commodity in the western region. This shift in ideology completed the antiquation of the Joads' way of life. Ecological realities had long ago proven their lifestyle quixotic, but it took the formidable alliance of the Dust Bowl and corporate agribusiness to dislodge the Okies from their land and homes. Later in his life, Steinbeck returned to criticize the America-as-Eden myth by writing *East of Eden*, a novel whose very title suggests alienation from paradise. It is in *The Grapes of Wrath*, however, that he is most concerned with the hydrological causes for that estrangement.

Steinbeck acknowledges water's primacy in the West by documenting the social ramifications of the ideology that permits its monopolization and waste. At the same time, his abiding affection for the yeoman agricultural ideal forms a strong undercurrent throughout the novel. Donald Worster believes that this nostalgia comes at the expense of a coherent critique of the water-based oligarchy primarily responsible for the ecological demise of the Southwest and its accompanying human suffering (Worster, *Rivers of Empire* 1985, 229). While Worster's criticism has substantial merit, it fails to address the symbolic power attached to water that pervades the novel. From the drought in Oklahoma to Noah's refusal to leave the river in Arizona to the raging floodwaters that climax the text, Steinbeck weaves water into the novel's structure as well as virtually every thematically significant event in the novel.

This tendency to privilege water, either by absence or surfeit, appears frequently in the Steinbeck canon. *Of Mice and Men*, for example, opens and closes on the banks of a river; *The Log from the Sea of Cortez*, showing a fascination with tide pools, offers the clearest presentation of Steinbeck's ecophilosophy; and *The Wayward Bus*, like *The Grapes of Wrath*, uses floodwaters in the desert to spur its characters to action and the acquisition of wisdom. That in *The Grapes of Wrath* Steinbeck chose to stress his affection for the yeoman tradition rather than explicitly condemn modern hydraulic society does not detract from the book's acknowledged success in subverting that same hydraulic apparatus. The reactions of the state and federal governments to the book's publication as well as that of the oligarchy-controlled media clearly demonstrate the novel's effectiveness. Vehement condemnations of the book and its author followed shortly after its publication in 1939 and continued for years afterward. That the most vociferous denunciations came from the water barons and their political allies demonstrates that, contrary to Worster's contention, Steinbeck did indeed understand the politics of water use and that his novel attacked it successfully.[1]

I

Water's dominance in the cultural and agricultural hierarchy of the arid region is neither new nor surprising. Not just in the Hebrew Bible but throughout history, the habitability of any region has traditionally been determined by the availability and accessibility of its water. The Spanish explorers who first traversed the Southwest deemed it an inhospitable wasteland, unfit for human settlement except by those savages already content to scrape an existence from the unforgiving rock. American trailblazers including Lewis and Clark and Zebulon Pike held little hope that the arid region could sustain American settlements (Reisner 1986, 20). Such criticism, however, quickly disappeared in the storm of patriotism that surged through the new United States. Parallel visions of world dominance and transcendental bonding with nature created a unique blend of ideologies that sought simultaneously to sustain an extractive economy and an unspoiled, untrammeled frontier. Not till near the turn of the twentieth century did the inexorable collision of these visions loom close enough to draw the notice of the nation's policymakers. The resulting tension between ecosystemic requirements and the modes of production caused a "transformation in consciousness and legitimating worldviews," a phenomenon Carolyn Merchant has termed an "ecological revolution" (5).

American history shows that people traditionally settled the Plains during periods of high rainfall. When the rains subsided to typical levels, people retreated or pressed on. But by the 1920s, the frontier was closed and Americans had bought solidly into the notion that technology and God would see to it that the Great Plains became the agricultural capital of the world. Unable to accept that meeting the grain demands of a global market economy in a region where annual rainfall fluctuated between seven and twenty inches made little ecological sense, Dust Bowl residents lashed out at the weather, believing it caused their woes. There was not enough water, they complained; the weather had failed them. Such an argument is analogous to blaming the mint for not making people enough money. I do not mean to belittle the very real human tragedy of the Dust Bowl or to deny the nobility of many of those who suffered through it. Nevertheless, the Dust Bowl's ecosystemic catastrophe was both avoidable and remediable except that neither option was palatable to the region's residents (Worster 1979, 28). It is precisely this sort of stubborn adherence to traditional values while implementing ecologically pernicious agricultural methods that brought on the "dirty thirties."

Early in the novel, Steinbeck establishes the fundamental conflict between the yeoman farmer and the land and then diagrams the imperialist maneuverings of corporate agribusiness:

Grampa took up the land, and he had to kill the Indians and drive them away. And Pa was born here, and he killed weeds and snakes. Then a bad year came and he had to borrow a little money. An' we was born here . . . our children born here. And Pa had to borrow money. The bank owned the land then. . . . Sure cried the tenant men, but it's our land. We measured it and broke it up. We were even born on it, and we got killed on it, died on it. Even if it's no good, it's still ours. . . . That makes ownership, not a paper with numbers on it. (TGOW 34–35)

The above passage reveals several of the guiding principles governing life in the Plains. First, the term "bad year" refers to inadequate rainfall and an accompanying water shortage, a cyclical reality of Plains life that formed one of the bases for the collapse of the yeoman lifestyle. Second, right of ownership was established through displacing the native peoples. That act in and of itself constituted (in the farmer's eyes) a right of title. Last, birthing and dying on the land created a blood right of succession that no financial transaction could negate. And most important, working the land formed the litmus test of possession. The quotation reveals the teller's sadness that the laws of the country conflict with the laws of the land. The agrarian ideology held that only those who work and love the land can truly own it: "If a man owns a little property, that property is him, it's part of him and it's like him. If he owns property only so he can walk on it and handle it and be sad when it isn't doing well, and feel fine when the rain falls on it, that property is him. . . . Even if he isn't successful he's big with his property" (39). Such feelings descend directly from the dual myths of the frontier and the garden. The frontier myth posited that land in the West was uninhabited by anybody with legal rights and that the strength of the nation lay in its boundless and unsettled western frontier.[2] The myth of the garden held that the land would yield bountiful harvests to any American willing to work it. Rain would fall in direct proportion to the farmer's needs. Any failure in these natural laws was necessarily transitory and had no lasting relevance. This supposed law of nature was disproven by the Okies' experiences in both Oklahoma and California. After a prolonged drought revealed the unsustainability of their farming methods and drove them from their homes, the wet/dry cycle in California nearly caused their demise.

Not only did meteorological laws conflict with the yeoman belief system, the Okies also found their way of life colliding with the policies of a nation committed to corporate capitalism. While for agrarians land constituted a part of themselves and their culture—something for which the term "market value" lacked a referent—banks and corporations translated it into assets on a balance sheet. Where the Joads spoke of "bad years," account managers acknowledged the reality of sparse rainfall and a semiarid climate. Historical climatic patterns decreed that "bad years" for rainfall were the norm for the Plains, a fact that made tenant farmers a poor investment. For banks, it became a matter of short-term profit at any cost. Years of drought and over-reliance on nutrient-draining cash crops had left the land ecologically devastated. Those keeping accounts looked to squeeze out every vestige of production before abandoning it for more lucrative investments: "But you'll kill the land with cotton. We know. We've got to take cotton quick before the land dies. Then we'll sell the land. Lots of families in the East would like to own a piece of land" (34). The sight of faceless corporate "monsters" intentionally destroying the land's fertility moved the tenants to violence. Yet the Joads and their neighbors had often planted cotton and were at present sharecropping in a frenzy so as to build up a stake to take west: "The whole bunch of us chopped cotton, even Grampa" (90). The differences between the Okies and the banks lay more in scale and philosophy than methodology and eventual result. Both sides participated in the capitalist mechanism, but the banks had better adapted to thrive within it.

Mining the land of nutrients and leaving it for dead demonstrate a new, production-oriented allegiance to the frontier myth. Treating the nation's breadbasket as an expendable resource necessarily assumes an infinite resource reservoir from which to replace it. Short-term profiteering, by its very nature, posits that the future will take care of itself. Such a position depends on a telos of inexhaustible plenty, a concept central to the frontier and garden myths. This pattern of behavior again shows that the onset of the Industrial Age and accompanying supremacy of corporate capitalism did not eradicate the dominant myths but simply adapted them to twentieth-century exigencies. Richard Slotkin offers an intriguing explanation for this transition. He argues that the systems of myth and ideology that developed in this country depended on a positive association with physical migration that revolved around two geographical poles: the "Metropolis" and the "Frontier." The Metropolis must have a negative association or no one would want to leave, while the Frontier needs to offer riches enough to satisfy all of our dreams. Emigrants suffer in the wilderness while temporarily regressing to a more primitive state. The results, though, more than compensate for the ephemeral loss of civilization's comforts: "The completed American was therefore one who remade his fortune and his character by an emigration, a setting forth for newer and richer lands; by isolation and regression to a more primitive manner of life; and by establishing his political position" (Slotkin 1985, 35).

This discussion offers striking parallels to the Joads' saga. Slotkin's analysis takes the city, or the "Metropolis," as the emigrant's point of departure, but we can substitute the Dust Bowl region without interfering with the argument. Since the trappings of the Industrial Revolution came late to the Plains, the region lacked the large, mechanized urban areas that pose such an effective antipode to the wilderness frontier. Instead, mechanization and factory farming—both consequences of industrialization—provided the major impetus that drove families like the Joads from their homes. In the Dust Bowl, wage slavery and the specter of starvation resulting from technological and economic displacement offered the negative contrast to the frontier. Not present was the traditional coupling of those factors with the dense population centers that characterized urban industry. The Okies' choices, in Steinbeck's view, were either to drive a tractor through their neighbors' homes while raping the land with machinery and cash crops or to leave.

When they attempted to settle in California, the geographical border of the once limitless frontier, they found themselves wage slaves on a privatized corporate fiefdom. Once more the Okies suffered primitive, dehumanizing conditions while attempting to exercise their supposedly inalienable human rights. The growers' cartel, however, had disenfranchised them even before they arrived, forcing them into a nomadic existence designed to destroy the homesteading instinct so central to the Frontier Myth.

Despite uncountable acres lying fallow, no land was available for the Okies, a reality Steinbeck often demonstrates (*TGOW* 225). Their dreams of subsistence farming were fundamentally incompatible with the market economy that allowed a select few to grow vastly wealthy from the toil of disenfranchised adherents to the old American dream. What ultimately kills Casy and exiles Tom is—just as in Slotkin's paradigm—an urgent desire to participate in the political process. They do not succeed, for the moment, because the growers' control over water rights allows them complete dominion over the local government and media. I will discuss this phenomenon at greater length later in the essay. Its relevance here stems from water's role in the third major cause for the Okies' westward migration: inadequate irrigation and a perceived drought.

II

Steinbeck's humanistic bent impelled him to focus on the human side of the agricultural morass that drove the Okies west. The underlying motivation for both the Okies' behavior and that of the agribusiness concerns, however, can ultimately be analyzed in hydrological terms. Rainfall in the Southwest in the 1930s fell well within historical norms; cycles of drought are more common than periods of heavy rain. Drought did not cause the Dust Bowl—a more accurate description of the region's troubles should instead focus on the Depression and local agricultural mismanagement. The Depression, though, did not seriously affect the Great Plains until the onset of the Dust Bowl. If local farmers had been able to continue planting and harvesting cash crops at the rate they had in the 1920s, the Plains might have escaped the worst of the Depression. Unfortunately, by the end of the decade, they had borrowed heavily and expanded their acreage to maximize annual yields. When the crops failed and the "black blizzards" came, the national plague of poverty and joblessness infected the Plains states as well.

By the 1930s, Plains farmers had plowed under virtually all the region's grasslands. Without sod and other vegetation to hold the topsoil in place, the land became extremely vulnerable to ecological disturbance. When the drought hit, the land had no natural defenses with which to keep its topsoil intact. The resulting dust storms stripped the land bare. Yet if the region had retained its indigenous vegetation, the drought would have had little long-term effect on the land. Profit-oriented agriculture and ecological ignorance turned a cyclical shortfall of water into a disaster.

High-yield monoculture is a dubious ecological proposition even in humid regions, but in the Southwest such methods become disastrous (Worster 1979, 13). When Grampa Joad cleared the land and put it to plow, he hoped to fulfill the traditional yeoman ideal. Barring precipitation shortfalls, the average homestead proved more than adequate for subsistence farming. The region could not, however, sustain the rigors of a capitalist-based agriculture, a task that the metamorphosis of the American dream soon demanded. Steinbeck condemns what he sees as a dissolution of the values so cherished by the people who settled the region. Reverence for the land became obsolete with the ascension of factory farming.

The driver sat in his iron seat and he was proud of the straight lines he did not will, proud of the tractor he did not own or love, proud of the power he could not control. And when that crop grew, and was harvested, no man had crumbled a hot clod in his fingers and let the earth sift past

his fingertips. No man had touched the seed, or lusted for the growth.
Men ate what they had not raised, had no connection with the bread. The
land bore under iron, and under iron gradually died. (TGOW 38)

Steinbeck mourned this change in values but could offer no viable
solutions. Even as they cursed the technology that drove them west,
the Okies traveled in cars bought through the trade of their mules
and watched with sadness as tractors did their work in a fraction of
the time. The Okies formed the pivot for the western land's transition from earth mother to degraded resource. As the yeoman ideal
gave way to the wages of capitalism, the Okies adapted their methods to meet the parameters of a market-based economy. Even as they
clung tenaciously to their preindustrial, terrestrial reverence, they
grudgingly accepted the new dominance of the capitalist shift.
Muley Graves, unable to relinquish his ties to the land, cannot go
with his family when they move west. Rooted to the place where he
was born, Muley rages against the dual inequity of bad land and evil
bankers: " 'Cause what'd they take when they tractored the folks off
the lan'? What'd they get so their margin a profit was safe? . . . God
knows the lan' ain't no good. . . . But them sons-a-bitches at their
desks, they just chopped folks in two. . . . Place where folks live is
them folks. They ain't whole, out lonely on the road in a piled-up
car. Them sons-a-bitches killed them" (*TGOW* 55).

For Muley, the link with the land still stained with his father's
blood is stronger than his ties to wife and family. He cannot leave
even as he acknowledges that he is a living anachronism ("You fellas
think I'm touched?"). Sadly, Muley's protestations held little weight
with a population caught up in the quasi-divine status allowed them
by technological advance. It did not matter if the land was poor because human ingenuity could and would transform it. No longer
need the land yield forth its bounty; it will instead be mined and
harvested. Modern agriculture provided the means to merge Henry
Adams's classic juxtaposition of the dynamo and the virgin. Through
this synthesis, the earth ceased to be a virgin and became a wife.[3]
Similar phenomena occur often both in the American landscape and
in the literary corpus. The masculine, aggressive machine assaults
and reshapes the idyllic, feminine landscape (Leo Marx 1976, 29).

As farmers were forced more and more to mistreat their holdings, they degraded the land further to sexual plaything and chattel. This ideological evolution progressed naturally from the dominant myths.[4] As industrialism began to dominate the West, the accompanying mindset fit a unique niche in the American dream of rugged individualism and merit-based achievement.

Bacon, anticipating the Industrial Revolution, advocated reclaiming Eden through industry and science; a century later, Americans embraced the challenge as their destiny.[5] Westerners could reclaim the garden, but doing so involved literally "reclaiming" their place in paradise through diligence and industry. Men would finish what Nature had begun. Eden, ideologues hastened to point out, was after all an irrigated garden. Adam fell; Americans will stand tall. The Reclamation Act of 1902 established the Bureau of Reclamation, intending to fulfill Powell's credo of "rescuing" and "redeeming" the land from its arid state. The true meaning of the word "reclamation" lost all significance in the technological assault on the region's hydrology. The verb "to reclaim" infers prior ownership; the people seeking to irrigate the desert could make no such claim. Nevertheless, whatever needed to be done would be done to get water to the land and restore it to its imagined, bountiful state.[6] Any water that ran into the sea without serving some agricultural purpose was "wasted," a Providential oversight correctable through human diligence.

Denying the hydrological realities of the Southwest while modernizing the dominant mythology permitted Westerners to reject the implication that all is not within the grasp of any perspicacious American. Henry Luce's *Time* magazine trumpeted the rediscovered limitlessness that irrigation technology brought to the frontier: "Irrigation experts are now convinced that the rapidly growing U.S. can expand indefinitely within its present boundaries" (qtd. in Worster, *Rivers of Empire* 1985, 266). This quotation is pregnant with the contradictions inherent in the American and specifically western dream of infinite abundance. The notion of indefinite expansion within acknowledged boundaries is fundamentally self-contradictory. Attributing this ability to accomplish the impossible to the calculations of irrigation experts beautifully underscores the incongruities within western water policy. Western land barons relied on irrigation to accomplish the impossible and ignored or destroyed anyone or any-thing that interfered with their pursuit of that grail. The Joads and their contemporaries were ill equipped for the ramifications of the growers' zeal. They clung fast to traditional yeoman values even while participating in the market economy. Caught between two worlds, they could not linger in Oklahoma and set out instead for the land where corporate growers had remanufactured the tradi-tional Myth of the Garden to entice exodusters westward.

As they traversed the migrant highway, the Joads met many who, like themselves, had readily believed the leaflets spread by agents of the California growers. "Why, I seen han'bills how they need folks to pick fruit, an' good wages. . . . An' with them good wages, maybe a fella can get hisself a piece a land an' work out for extra cash. Why, hell, in a couple a years I bet a fella could have a place of his own" (*TGOW* 160). That the Great Plains could no longer sustain the yeo-man ideal did not necessarily spell the death of the American dream for a dispossessed people, barely literate and ready to jump at any hope of salvation. The California growers' cartel, already enmeshed in a cycle of wage slavery, remained convinced that additional work-ers could only lengthen their profit margins. They recruited Dust Bowl refugees with promises of a vast, temperate paradise wherein they might re-create the homesteads they had been forced to leave.

This new myth of the garden presented an even more seductive exterior than the Plains by adapting the Jeffersonian ideal to a region where husbandry was allegedly secondary to the munificence of na-ture. Grampa, before becoming overwhelmed by his attachment to the land on which he had cleared and raised his family, fantasized about bathing in a washtub full of grapes where he would "scrooge aroun' an' let the juice run down my pants" (100). But this vision of unchecked abundance was less a cultural phenomenon than a calcu-lated product of the growers' propaganda mills. The agribusiness consortia dangled visions of their own wealth and massive land-holdings before the Okies in order to fuel their (the cartel's) hege-mony. And the irony of that vision, as Steinbeck depicts it, is that the growers were as alienated from their land wealth as they forced the Okies to be: "And it came about that the owners no longer worked their farms . . . they forgot the land, the smell and the feel of it, and remembered only that they owned it. . . . And the owners not only did not work the farms any more, many of them had never seen the farms they owned" (*TGOW* 257).

The California growers had become immensely wealthy and powerful as the result of an uneasy but mutually profitable alliance with the Bureau of Reclamation.[7] Having already incarnated themselves in the image of the new garden that depended heavily on the tools of the technocracy to subdue the land, they looked to consolidate their holdings by enacting the Social Darwinism that fueled their telos of industry. They had managed to consolidate the dual definitions of "garden" into one highly profitable vision of production and wealth. No longer could "garden" signify either a region of natural, providential splendor or an area of human-created agrarian abundance (Leo Marx 1976, 85); the Edenic garden propounded by Gilpin and his nineteenth-century allies was completely replaced by its opposing Baconian definition of a human-engineered paradise achieved through work and intellect. Humans—specifically men— had invented the tools necessary to subjugate nature. Those tools had brought water to the desert via centrifugal pumping and, more important, through the diversion of rivers.

By shaping the perceived objectivity of science to fit the needs of western agriculture, an elite group's control over the dissemination of knowledge led to dominion over the region's geography (Foucault 1980, 69). The men whose schemes created this technological garden stood to profit most from its enactment, and it was they who formed the powerful growers' cartel that enslaved the migrants. Those who controlled the water controlled the entire regional economy, and that domination bled into every other facet of life.

Californian agribusiness's command over nature required large temporary workforces, while the capitalist regime demanded that this transient labor force be paid very little. The growers had traditionally indentured immigrants and other disenfranchised groups because little public outcry arose from their mistreatment. Still, the arrival of the Okies, a large, skilled, English-speaking labor force whose migrant status left them bereft of any governmental protection, appeared to be a tremendous windfall to the growers' cartel. In the novel, however, the latent power of the oppressed becomes the looming threat to the water-based oligarchy as the Okies come to embody Marx's concept of alienated labor (Karl Marx 1964, 69). Their corporate oppressors force them to work ever harder and faster in order to eke out subsistence, yet each hour worked and each piece of fruit harvested bring them that much closer to unemployment and starvation. They must further compete against each other by under-bidding fellow workers in a futile attempt to participate in an exclu-sionary economic system. Conversely, growers must dehumanize the workers, degrading them as they do the land so that their acts of subjugation can be perpetrated on objects beneath contempt.[8] In *In Dubious Battle,* Steinbeck treats the worker/grower relationship as a matter strictly related to class struggle. In *The Grapes of Wrath,* he ele-vates it to the realm of epistemology, viewing the schism between workers and land barons as symptomatic of the larger issue of hu-man alienation from the earth and as a catalyst for the synthesis of humans and their surroundings into the all-encompassing organ-ismic one (Benson, *True Adventures* 1990, 268–69). "Three hundred thousand, hungry and miserable; if ever they know themselves, the land will be theirs. . . . And the great owners, who had become through their holdings both more and less than men, ran to their destruction, and used every means that in the long run would de-stroy them" (*TGOW* 263).

The cycle of poverty imposed on the Okies contained a sea-sonal period of starvation during the rainy season. Water again, this time through superabundance, became the immediate threat to the Okies' survival. When Rosasharn goes into labor, the men outside labor frantically to erect a dam to keep the boxcar shelters dry. Water, priceless commodity and building block of life, endangers the birth-ing process and threatens to starve an entire class of people. Both attempts—the birth and the dam—are unsuccessful. As the flood-waters force the Joads to flee, Uncle John is assigned the task of bury-ing the stillborn child. Rather than do so, he coopts the water, using it and the dead child to spread his message of despair and defiance: "Go down an' tell 'em. Go down in the street an' rot an' tell em that way. That's the way you can talk. . . . Go on down now an' lay in the street. Maybe they'll know then" (494). Driven from Oklahoma, where widespread refusal to acknowledge water's scarcity resulted in an unsustainable way of life, the Okies found themselves in a new region with an already intact and sophisticated capitalist infrastructure with water at its plinth. As a disenfranchised and powerless class, the migrants had no opportunity to gain control over water rights and consequently could not participate in the dominant discourse. John's act represented an ephemeral yet powerful appropriation of the preeminent unit of capital. Using water to convey a message of worker defiance strikes at the heart of the power structure: if the Okies were to gain actual control over the region's water, the growers' cartel would collapse. Legions of migrants could then seize power and redistribute the land according to need and fairness.

The dual hopes for the migrants, according to Steinbeck, are class alliance and worker control over the tools of domination. When Tom takes over the task of organizing the Okies from the martyred Casy, the class struggle takes a symbolic step forward. When Uncle John seizes control over the waters that enslave his people and threaten their lives, he takes another major step toward toppling the ruling class. Shortly after Uncle John's act of defiance, Rosasharn's gift of her maternal milk to another starving Okie demonstrates that both Tom's and John's acts will eventually bear fruit. Sheltered from the water by a barn, itself a potent symbol of the yeoman agricultural ideal, Rosasharn, by offering her breast to a fellow migrant, demonstrates the class cohesion that will ultimately topple the ruling class. While her stillborn infant rots in the town below, Rosasharn breastfeeds an old man whose advanced state of starvation has caused him to regress to a prelingual state. Her act and the old man's condition represent the succoring of the infant movement toward social change. Each act, while primarily symbolic, is also genuinely subversive. In these small acts of defiance and hope, suggests Steinbeck, lie the restoration of traditional ties between people and between people and the land. So despite their socialization into a culture in which water is both hoarded and feared, the Okies have not completely acquiesced to their role in the factory-farm mechanism. They retain their dreams of an idyllic land where the family farm reigns supreme and water and land are distributed according to need and connectedness to the land rather than according to amassed corporate capital and political dominance.

In the final analysis, however, the migrant dream of resurgent family farms reclaiming their place as the preeminent agricultural ideal cannot work in the arid lands. Water reclamation projects, because of their expense and complexity, require the participation of an elite, educated class. The projects therefore become political pawns. The family farmer, allied with a subsistence ideology and unwilling to exploit the land past its carrying capacity, cannot compete with wealthy, powerful corporate interests. For this reason, the novel, though hopeful, does not offer any quantifiable hope. Worster identifies this lack of an attainable goal as the novel's major failing. Decrying the system of land distribution without explicitly condemning the accompanying hydrological autocracy leads to the specious conclusion that simply putting the land in the hands of the migrants will solve the region's agrarian morass. In a section of *Rivers of Empire* titled "The Grapes of Wealth," Worster argues: "Nowhere in *The Grapes of Wrath* does Steinbeck draw attention to the elaborate hydraulic apparatus that has been required to create the California garden. . . . Grapes, carrots, cotton and the like are the products, it would seem, of spontaneous nature, not the contrivances of advanced water engineering and the social organization it has required" (229). Because Steinbeck failed to acknowledge the inherent oligarchic nature of irrigation-based societies, he creates the false impression that equitable land distribution and a classless society will return the region to ecological stability. Historically, there are no precedents for this vision being realizable. In fact, returning the family farm to the arid region without altering the national capitalist infrastructure will, given the Plains example, cause devastating ecological harm.

Worster's critique does raise the problematic issue of Steinbeck's unrepentant affection for the family farm but does not, as I mentioned earlier, address the powerful critique of hydraulic society implicit in the novel's structure.[9] That he used water throughout the novel as an absent signifier suggests that Steinbeck was well aware of its power and complicity in the region's power hierarchy. When, at the novel's end, Steinbeck suddenly introduces water as a tangible presence and powerful symbolic force, it empowers the migrants by demonstrating their class cohesion and latent strength. Structuring the novel in this manner permitted Steinbeck to criticize the extant hydraulic society more effectively than he could through overt polemics. Indeed, the novel's reception, both locally and nationally, bears witness to its powerful subversive nature, a fact that underscores the most crucial flaw in Worster's argument. If the novel caused both the government and the nation at large to reevaluate federal irrigation subsidies for corporate growers, clearly it must have effectively criticized the inequity and corruption infusing California's water-appropriation schema.

The migrants' struggle became a national cause célèbre, and the novel's verisimilitude was debated at the highest levels of government.[10] The Hearst-Chandler-Copley yellow press pilloried the novel and its author throughout California. Only after a *Life* magazine exposé and Eleanor Roosevelt's endorsement of the book's veracity did the tide of public opinion begin to turn in Steinbeck's favor.[11] The rage and furor from agribusiness conglomerates and their allies arose because *The Grapes of Wrath* shook the very foundations of the water-based oligarchy. Worster himself acknowledges this:

Up to the very end of the decade, both the Bureau [of Reclamation] and the Department of the Interior were placidly moving forward . . . avoiding any cause for alarm on the part of the growers in California . . . What changed all of that undoubtedly was . . . the publication in 1939 of The Grapes of Wrath. *. . . Suddenly, it became rather difficult for a liberal government in Washington to give subsidized, unrestricted water to groups like the reactionary Associated Farmers, to underwrite their labor policies and their concentration of wealth. (Worster,* Rivers of Empire *1985, 245)*

Nevertheless, despite a temporary surge in popular and governmental concern, neither the novel nor the reform movement it generated achieved any lasting change in western water policy. Pork barrel appropriations bills continued to subsidize corporate growers, who continued to couch their greed within the rubric of a technologically controlled Eden that they believed should form the destiny of the West. The migrants' struggle faded into the background with the outbreak of World War II. U.S. entry into the conflict stoked the fires of nationalism, and the nation turned to the West once again to fuel the American war machine. The Okies benefited from the wartime surge in production, finding work in munitions factories and other war-related industries. Relieved, the growers turned once again to immigrant labor, a class of people they could be relatively certain of keeping disenfranchised and powerless. The cycle of exploitation thus resumed after only a brief hiatus. Public interest in the issue peaked again two decades later when Cesar Chavez briefly managed to organize the Migrant Farm Workers Union into an effective national lobby.

Only in the 1990s, after a prolonged drought and numerous aborted attempts at reform, has the Californian agricultural machine seemingly run dry. Faced with a severe, unremitting drought and a recession-locked nation unwilling to finance any more quixotic reclamation projects, the growers in California now face a complete embargo on federally supplied water (Reinhold, *New York Times* 1992). Years of drought and insupportable agriculture in an arid land are seemingly on the verge of accomplishing what no individual person could accomplish alone: decanonization of the myth of the garden and its accompanying myth of the frontier. These two myths, dominant since the birth of the nation, eventually ran headlong into the realities of a closed frontier and a finite hydrology. Steven Goldstein, spokesman for interior secretary Manuel Lujan, aptly summed up the situation when announcing the curtailment of further water subsidy, saying: "We recognize . . . what a hardship this will be. But we cannot make it rain" (Reinhold, *New York Times* 1992).

Notes

1. One of the most effective techniques used by the press to discredit the novel involved letters to the editor from supposed "Okies" protesting that the conditions depicted in the novel did not really exist. The letters told of friendly treatment by the growers, clean living conditions, and enough work for everybody. The papers also spread rumors of Okies wanting to kill Steinbeck for telling lies about them. Little information defending Steinbeck's version of events reached the public at large until a number of other exposés (most notably Carey McWilliams's *Factories in the Field*) were released and photographs documenting the migrants' conditions gained widespread notoriety.

2. Frederick Jackson Turner's essay "The Significance of the Frontier in American History" (1892) (see Turner 1947) posited that the existence of the frontier allowed the nation's economy to expand constantly and thus allowed capitalism to dominate. His thesis was widely accepted until the middle of this century and is discernible in the literature as well as the governmental policies of the period.

3. In *To a God Unknown*, Steinbeck openly acknowledges the sexual bond between men and the land. After Joseph literally makes love to the earth, the narrator matter-of-factly notes that "for a moment, the land had been his wife"

(11). In *The Grapes of Wrath*, which postdates *To a God Unknown* by a decade, Steinbeck again acknowledges the sexual link—this time in the form of rape: "Behind the harrows, the long seeders—twelve curved iron penes erected in the foundry, orgasms set by gears, raping methodically, raping without passion" (37).

4. Kolodny argues that the progressive deterioration in cultural reverence for the land was an unavoidable by-product of viewing it as feminine while seeking to settle it: "Implicit in the metaphor of the land-as-woman was both the regressive pull of maternal containment *and* the seductive invitation to sexual assertion: if the Mother demands passivity, and threatens regression, the Virgin apparently invites sexual assertion and awaits impregnation" (67).

5. Jehlen argues convincingly that the uniquely American bond with the land and nature makes anything Americans choose to do necessarily right and natural: "The settlers' implementation of the continent's permanent contours and conditions . . . places the emerging social structures . . . in the realm of nature. Those who assist the emergence of those structures, moreover, wield the power of nature itself" (57). One of the ways Americans cast the conquest of the land within the current political climate was by classifying irrigation programs as a struggle between the forces of good and the forces of godless communists dedicated to subverting the American way of life. Robert Kerr, former governor of Oklahoma and head of the Senate's Select Committee on Water Resources, rhetorically asks: "Can a pagan Communist nation . . . make more efficient use of soil and water resources than the most advanced and enlightened nation in the world? Can ruthless atheists mobilize and harness their treasure of God-given wealth to defeat and stifle freedom-loving peoples everywhere?" (Kerr 1960, 323–24).

6. Worster offers this account of the Plains mentality during the mid-1930s: " 'You gave us beer,' they told Roosevelt, 'now give us water.' . . . 'Every draw, arryo [*sic*], and canyon that could be turned into a lake or lagoon,' wrote a clothing store manager, 'should be turned into one by dams and directed ditches & draws until there are millions of them thru these mid-western states.' A Texas stockman wanted to use natural gas to pump flood waters from the Mississippi River to the Plains. . . . An old soldier from Denver penciled his ideas on ruled tablet paper: stage sham battles with 40,000 Civilian Conservation Corp boys and $20 million worth of ammunition—the noise would be sure to stir up some rain. . . . 'Try it,' he finished, 'if it works send me a check for $5000 for services rendered' " (1979, 39).

7. California's water wars are far too complex to treat in this essay. Many excellent studies on the subject exist, and I have made extensive use of several, including Worster's *Rivers of Empire* and Reisner's *Cadillac Desert*. For a well-researched, highly critical history of the Bureau of Reclamation, see Berkman and Viscusi's *Damming the West*.

8. The women/nature, men/civilization duality linked women to the land, and so they shared in its degradation. By viewing the landscape as feminine, the patriarchy was traditionally able to construct the cultural paradigm both of

women and of the land in an image that suited its perpetuation. Damming rivers and mining aquifers in an attempt to reconstruct the landscape to fit a masculine ideal is analogous to girdling and reshaping women to fit the masculine concept of beauty. See Warren and Cheney, "Ecological Feminism and Ecosystem Ecology," and Catherine Roach, "Loving Your Mother: On the Woman-Nature Relation."

9. Louis Owens contends that Steinbeck does not romanticize the agrarian ideal. The novel's harsh depiction of Okie tenant farmers mitigates any endorsement of family farms and Jeffersonian agrarianism while demonstrating Steinbeck's awareness of their ecological impracticality: "By carefully and precisely placing the tenants within the historical pattern that has led to the destruction of the land, Steinbeck is making it obvious that agrarianism alone is insufficient. In fact, the ideal of the independent small farmer, the Jeffersonian image of the heroic individualist wresting an isolated living from the soil is firmly scuttled in *The Grapes of Wrath*" (54).

10. Congressman Lyle Boren of Oklahoma declared *The Grapes of Wrath* to be "a lie, a black, infernal creation of a twisted, distorted mind" (qtd. in *WD*, xxiv). Steinbeck also became the target of a whispering campaign by the Associated Farmers, including one rumor that Steinbeck was a Jew acting on behalf of a Zionist-Communist conspiracy to undermine the economy (Benson 1984, 420).

11. After visiting a series of migrant camps in 1940, Mrs. Roosevelt told reporters, "I have never believed *The Grapes of Wrath* was exaggerated" (qtd. in Benson 1990, 402).

FOUR

The "Great Mother"
in *The Grapes of Wrath*

Lorelei Cederstrom

Pagan cultures identify the earth, with its seasonal cycles of birth, growth, death, and renewal, with a feminine principle. Such cultures worship an earth goddess, on whose fecundity and compassion men depend, and depict her as a maternal figure, a "Great Mother." In The Grapes of Wrath, *the Joad family, with Ma Joad as matriarch, adopt the Great Mother's ethos and iconography. On the road to California, they become a matriarchy valuing family and nurture, a social system with roots deep in a primitive time when men lived in harmony with the land and in direct opposition to the patriarchal forces driving the Dust Bowl disaster. The novel's famous final image, in which Rose of Sharon gives her breast to a starving man, is not Christian iconography but the culmination of the pagan, earth-derived values of the Great Mother.*

In his depiction of the destruction of the fertile earth and the lives of those who have depended upon her abundance, John Steinbeck in *The Grapes of Wrath* presents a visionary foreshadowing of the universal ecological disaster that looms so prominently on the horizon today. Equally visionary is his evocation of the primordial alternative to the patriarchal structures and attitudes that are destroying the earth. Throughout the novel, he describes the reemergence of the archetypal feminine and asserts the importance of matriarchal cultures that understand the relationship between the cycles of their lives and the natural world. An archetypal analysis of Steinbeck's novel reveals that in assessing the economic problems of the 1930s he had, perhaps unconsciously, arrived at an alternative to the dominant structures of Western civilization.

This alternative surfaces among the people who are the first victims of the decline of the old order, the migrant families. The failure of Western civilization to provide the necessities for these disinherited wanderers leads them to establish a more primitive social order based upon feminine values and matriarchal structures. Concurrent with the development of the matriarchy is the irruption of images, patterns, and attitudes associated with the primitive and transformative forms of the matriarchal deities. Throughout the novel, patriarchal culture and its attitudes give way to manifestations of the presence of the archetypal "Great Mother."[1]

The powerful closing scene of the novel in which Rose of Sharon suckles a starving man at her breast provides an iconographic image of the Great Mother: "Rose of Sharon loosened one side of the blanket and bared her breast. 'You got to,' she said. She squirmed closer and pulled his head close. 'There!' she said. 'There!' Her hand moved gently in his hair. She looked up and across the barn, and her lips came together and smiled mysteriously" (501–2). The haunting power of this image indicates the presence of a powerful archetype. Sensing an archetypal pattern, critics have related Rose of Sharon to the Madonna, and her nurturing gesture has been seen as a manifestation of Christian love. One must keep in mind, however, that Rose of Sharon is not a mother suckling her child; her baby was born dead, "a blue shriveled little mummy" (489). At her breast is a starving stranger, a fellow refugee from a rising flood that has already destroyed many homes and families.[2] This archetypal gesture and mysterious smile are, nonetheless, the fitting conclusion to the novel, for it is in this affirmation of the power to give life and to take it, to nourish even while surrounded by the death and destruction she has wrought, that the full power of the Great Mother is evident. A detailed analysis of the archetypal Great Mother as she appears throughout the novel reveals more clearly the iconographic significance of this scene.

It is necessary to define the limits of this archetype as Steinbeck has used it, for in her many facets, the Great Mother encompasses virtually everything. "Woman=body=vessel=world," is the formula Erich Neumann[3] uses to define the all-inclusive quality of the archetypal feminine. In *The Grapes of Wrath*, the Great Mother appears in both her elementary and transformative characters. In the former, she can be seen as a primordial spirit behind both the positive and negative forces of nature, manifesting herself in soft sunlight and scourging drought, in gentle rain and destroying flood, in food and shelter as well as famine and deprivation. In her elementary character she is also present in the home and in the cultural activities that grow out of the establishment of facilities for sleep, food preparation, and so on. In her transformative character, the Great Mother is a force for change in the individual and society; this change may involve growth or destruction, rebirth or death, for both are within her domain.

This last point must be emphasized, for destruction is as much a part of the Great Mother as is creation; she who gives life can also bring death to the natural world or the individual. A well-known icon of the Great Mother, the nineteenth-century Indian statue of Kali dancing on Shiva,[4] indicates both aspects of her character; Kali holds a sword of destruction in her upraised hand and holds out a bowl of nourishment in the other. Similarly, among the dual mother goddesses of Central America we find the Mayan earth goddess who "gives all life, all food—and then cries in the night for human blood, her food" (Sjöö and Mor 170). Even the more familiar Near Eastern goddesses like Isis, Astarte, Ishtar, Artemis, and Diana have a dark face in which they represent the "womb-tomb, abysmally prolific with children and with death" (Sjöö and Mor 1987, 184). This same ambivalence is present throughout Steinbeck's novel and is profoundly expressed in the paradoxical situation of the final scene, when the man near death by starvation and flood, two disasters particularly associated with primitive earth goddesses like the Great Mother, is given the nourishing breast, the most elementary symbol of her life-giving quality.

On the most basic level, the Great Mother as the giver of life or death appears as a personification of the Earth itself. In Steinbeck's earlier novel, *To a God Unknown* (1933), the earth is constantly imaged as a female presence (6), a presence that like "an ancient religion" might "possess" (7) those who come to know her. The Indian, Juanito, shares with homesteader Joseph Wayne his understanding of this ancient power: "My mother said how the earth is our mother and how everything that lives has life from the mother and goes back into the mother" (26). Joseph spends his entire life trying to understand the Great Mother as she is manifest in the earth he tends. Indeed, he can be seen as a priest assisting in her mysteries, as he works to ensure the fertility of the earth. He views these priestly duties as "the heritage of a race which for a million years had sucked at the breasts of the soil and co-habited with the earth" (34).

It is apparent from the beginning of *The Grapes of Wrath* that man has lost awareness that the earth is both sacred and living. Mother Earth is still fertile, but the crops are covered with dust. The land has been raped, and growing the same crop year after year under these conditions has destroyed the ability of the earth to nurture those who treat her this way. The Joad family suffers because they too have been guilty of this kind of neglect: " 'Ever' year,' said Joad, 'Every year I can remember, we had a good crop comin' an' it never came. Grampa says she was good the first five plowin's, while the wild grass was still in her' " (37). The novel opens many years after the last of the wild grass; the land is not even owned by people any more but by banks or corporations.

The matriarchal consciousness has also been lost, for as Neumann notes, it is dependent upon man's "participation mystique with his environment" (293). The participation mystique has been replaced by an attitude of unemotional domination: "No man touched the seed, or lusted for the growth. Men ate what they had not raised, had no connection with the bread. The land bore under iron, and under iron gradually died; for it was not loved or hated, it had no prayers or curses" (*TGOW* 38). The land is worked by a "machine man" who sits on an iron seat on an iron horse. Steinbeck has embodied the lack of connection to the land in a number of small details as well. Tom Joad, returning to his home, discovers that all the artifacts that symbolize a life close to the earth are askew. The well is dry; there are no weeds under its trough. The house is aslant, all of the windows are broken, and there is a hole where there once was a stovepipe. The machine man's lunch is another detail of this kind. It is wrapped in waxed paper, and all his food is processed: Spam, white bread, "a piece of pie branded like an engine part" (38). The result of this process of alienation from the earth, the Great Mother, is separation and exile. The machine man "goes home, and his home is not the land" (126); the Joads have lost both home and land.

Both the male and female characters in the novel are depicted in terms of their relationship to the Great Mother. The women are divided between those who have no relationship to the earth, land, or a natural life and those whose lives demonstrate the many faces of the archetypal feminine. The female counterparts of the machine men are defined by the objects with which they surround themselves: big cars, cosmetics, clothing and potbellied husbands. Their feminine attributes are disguised: breasts are confined, "stomachs and thighs straining against cases of rubber" (169).

These women are also distinguished in terms of their relationship to time. The matriarchal consciousness is at work when a woman lives in tune with the cycles of nature. Mircea Eliade in *Cosmos and History* notes that primitive peoples experience the sacredness of life by living in tune with seasonal cycles and the recurrence of crops. In opposition, our contemporary world measures life linearly, as history, a progress from one point to another, stamping masculine measurements upon feminine cyclicality. Women, even in an industrial society, experience themselves at least in terms of biological cycles. Steinbeck's nameless women on the road, however, have accepted linear time and have lost the regenerative capacity that comes from recognizing oneself as part of an eternally recurring pattern. Steinbeck is explicit about this: the eyes of these women are "sullen, disliking sun and wind and earth, resenting food and weariness, hating time that rarely makes them beautiful and always makes them old" (169).

In contrast, the Joad women are linked to the cyclicality of the archetypal feminine. Granma, Ma, and Rose of Sharon manifest the three ages of the Great Mother: hag, mother, and nubile daughter. The youngest girl, Ruthie, remains outside; she has not yet achieved her initiation into womanhood, so she merely watches and learns. Granma is shrill, ferocious, and assertive, true to her mythical forebears, Hecate, or Athene as Crone. She once shot off one of Grampa's buttocks, an act that indicates her tendency toward matriarchal dominance. Her power is apparent; she outlasts her mate, without succumbing to grief. Her acceptance of death as a part of a pattern of renewal is indicated by Ma's assertion that Granma "always et a good meal at a funeral" (265). As her own death approaches, Granma becomes "like a little baby" (191). A sense of her involvement in the recurrent cycles of life is suggested by the mysterious whisperings between dying Granma and pregnant Rose of Sharon.

Tom describes Ma as the "citadel of the family, the strong place that could not be taken" (79). Neumann describes numerous instances in which the primordial Great Mother is similarly depicted as an encompassing shelter. Ma is the center and source of the family and its emotions; Tom sees her position as "great and humble" (80). Her beauty arises out of her services within the family: "From her position as healer, her hands had grown sure and cool and quiet; from her position as arbiter she had become as remote and faultless in judgment as a goddess" (80). At the center of the humble recurring cycles of family life, Ma continually reflects the many aspects of the nurturing force of the Great Mother.

The first time we see Ma she is cooking pork, food from an animal that is associated with her throughout the novel. Neumann notes that "the pig is a symbol of the archetypal feminine and occurs everywhere as the sacrificial beast of the Earth Goddess" (13). It is the pork that Ma has salted and prepared that keeps the family alive on the road. Like Granma, Ma lives in tune with recurrent cycles and is contrasted with the male characters. On the road, the men are concerned with maps, miles, and time: "From Sallisaw to Gore is twenty-one miles and the Hudson was doing thirty-five miles an hour. From Gore to Warner thirteen miles; Warner to Checotah fourteen miles; Checotah a long jump to Henrietta—thirty-four miles, but a real town at the end of it" (133). Ma sees the journey differently: "it's jus' the road goin' by for me. An' it's jus' how soon they gonna wanta eat some more pork bones" (134).

Before the journey, Ma was just one voice among many in making group decisions. As the novel progresses, Ma becomes more dominant. She forces the men to accede to the human needs of the family and decides when they will stop and go on. Pa threatens to reestablish patriarchal dominance with a shovel to the side of her head but acquiesces to her rule every time. Off the land, yet unable to relate to industrial society, the lives of the Joads are organized around primitive, matriarchal cultural activities. Preparing food and making shelter are their most immediate concerns, and Ma is the prime mover in creating the rituals of this primitive civilization. Ma also instructs Pa and the others about the importance of the family over property and the superiority of cyclic time over linear. A conversation between Pa and Ma establishes their separate priorities:

> "Funny! Woman takin' over the fambly. Woman sayin' we'll do this here, an' we'll go there. An' I don' even care."
>
> "Woman can change better'n a man," Ma said soothingly. "Woman got all her life in her arms. Man got it all in his head. Don' you mind. Maybe—well, maybe nex' year we can get a place."
>
> "We got nothin', now," Pa said. . . . "Seems our life is over and done!"
>
> "No it ain't," Ma smiled. "It ain't, Pa. An that's one more thing a woman knows. I noticed that. Man, he lives in jerks—baby born, an' a man dies, an' that's a jerk. Woman, it's all one flow, like a stream, little eddies, little waterfalls, but the river, it goes right on. Woman looks at it like that. We ain't gonna die out. People is goin' on—changin' a little, maybe, but goin' right on!" (467)

Ma is also a purveyor of matriarchal folk wisdom. She knows about burial rites, for example; Grampa is sewed neatly into his shroud, coins traditionally placed on his eyes. Ma also presides at births, acting as midwife, and she initiates Rose of Sharon into womanhood by piercing her ears: "Does it mean sompin?" Rose of Sharon asked. "Why course it does, . . . course it does," Ma replied (391). Everything Ma does is in accord with her function as an archetypal mother. She experiences herself as a provider of nourishment; others experience her as a source of strength. Her character has a positive effect on those around her for it is firmly rooted in the generating spirit of the Great Mother.

Rose of Sharon in her preoccupation with her pregnancy represents the transformative and life-giving power of the Great Mother. From the beginning of the novel, Steinbeck links Rose of Sharon to fertility: "The world was pregnant to her; she thought only in terms of reproduction and motherhood" (103). This pregnancy transforms her husband, Connie, as well. Steinbeck describes both Rose of Sharon and Connie as drawn together in contemplation of this central female mystery: "The world had drawn close around them and they were in the center of it, or rather Rose of Sharon was in the center of it with Connie making a small orbit about her. Everything they said was a kind of secret" (140). "Fecundation," Neumann notes, "makes the woman into a numinous being for herself and for the male" (270).

Removal from their home and land disrupts their relationship and focus on the child to be. Uprooted, Connie and Rose of Sharon both attempt to adjust to the patriarchal structures of the larger world. Connie begins to dream of a new life in the machine age, hoping to work in a store or a factory or to learn a technical trade, and eventually, he deserts the family in pursuit of these fantasies of power in the world of men's work. Rose of Sharon hopes to have her baby in a hospital, attended by doctors, rejecting traditional female wisdom by her willingness to accept male authority over female functions. Rose of Sharon's defection is strongly punished, however, for Connie abandons her, and her child is stillborn. Her recovery is directed by her mother as she reinitiates Rose of Sharon into the female mysteries of life and death: "Ma lay close to Rose of Sharon. Sometimes Ma whispered to her and sometimes she sat up quietly, her face brooding" (496).

It is at Ma's direction that Rose of Sharon transcends her individual suffering by giving her breast to the starving man. Neumann notes that the production of milk is an archetypal transformation mystery, involving a woman's transition from nubility to motherhood and focusing a woman's awareness of herself as a nurturing force. As she holds the starving man in her arms, Rose of Sharon develops into full womanhood. She moves from the inturned self-obsession of her adolescent passion for Connie to an understanding of selfless maternal love. Her smile reflects her recognition of the Great Mother within.

The male characters in the novel also experience the transforming power of the Great Mother. Speaking of the power of the feminine to act as a catalyst in men's lives, Neumann notes that "the male experiences . . . the feminine directly and indirectly as provocative, as a force that sets him in motion and impels him toward change" (32). The details that surround the various transformative experiences in the novel indicate clearly that the change is brought about as characters realign their former patriarchal attitudes in accordance with matriarchal values, rather than as the result of Christian conversion or the development of social consciousness. Steinbeck has created strong patriarchs in his other novels, but one looks in vain for sustained masculine attributes in either Pa or Grampa. Grampa, for example, was a force to be reckoned with until he left the land; it took only a few days of separation from his vital relationship to the earth for him to die. Pa, too, as we have noted, off the land becomes more and more an auxiliary of Ma, indicating a consistent dependence on the feminine whether manifested in land or woman.

Pa's attitude toward the archetypal feminine remains a troubled one, characterized by fear and misunderstanding, a fault for which he pays. Although Mother Earth fed him, he did not know how to ensure the fertility of his land; the constant raising of the same crop contributed to the failure of his farm and the removal of his family from their roots. In the scene that describes the birth of his first son, Noah, Pa is depicted as someone who fails to understand the fundamental transformation mystery of birth. Noah is sacrificed to his father's impatience and fear of the natural functions of the feminine:

For on the night when Noah was born, Pa, frightened at the spreading thighs, alone in the house, and horrified at the screaming wretch his wife had become, went mad with apprehension. Using his hands, his strong fingers for forceps, he had pulled and twisted the baby. The midwife, arriving late, had found the baby's head pulled out of shape, its neck stretched, its body warped; and she had pushed the head back and molded the body with her hands. But Pa always remembered and was ashamed. (85)

As a result, Noah is strange, aloof and alienated from the rest of the family. Halfway to California, however, Noah undergoes a symbolic rebirth, a baptism that brings him back into connection with the Great Mother. The rite of passage takes place in one of the domains associated with the feminine, a river where the men have come to wash and cool themselves. The river is too shallow to allow them to submerge their heads (223), signifying that their masculine consciousness will impede them from receiving the full benefit of their experiences in the female element and must be left behind. Noah's limited intelligence is a benefit in this case, and he is the first to respond to the call of the instinctual life promised by the Great Mother in the river. He tells the others: "I was in that there water. An' I ain't a-gonna leave her. I'm a-gonna go now, . . . down the river. I'll catch fish an' stuff, but I can't leave her. I can't" (229). Noah's use of the feminine pronoun is significant here. When told that Noah is gone, Pa does not understand, and his failure places him in the position of a child in the family, subservient to Ma, who seems to understand everything.

The case for the centrality of the Great Mother in the novel is challenged by the frequent and obvious association of Jim Casy with Christ.[5] It is obvious that Casy not only shares Christ's initials but also delivers the Christian message of love and professes a willingness to sacrifice himself for his fellow man. His relationships with women, however, reveal him as a truer disciple of the Great Mother than follower of Christian dogma. Casy tells Tom that he is no longer a preacher because love of God and religious ecstasy led him to express that love physically. "Tell you what," he said, "I used ta get the people jumpin' and talkin' in tongues, an' glory-shoutin' till they just fell down and passed out. . . . An' then—you know what I'd do? I'd take one of them girls out in the grass, an' I'd lay with her. Done it ever' time" (22). This combination of religious ecstasy and sexuality causes Casy to question how the so-called working of the devil could be present when a woman felt full of the divine spirit and leads to his abandonment of his ministry. Sexuality is, of course, perfectly compatible with the worship of the Great Goddess and has always played a part in her rituals.

Casy's concept of spirituality also departs from the narrow Christian view and emphasizes a unity between body and soul, in which sex and food reflect spiritual mysteries. His attempt to define a divine principle that includes both body and spirit leads to something akin to the oversoul of cosmic consciousness: "Maybe it's all men an' all women that we love; maybe tha's the Holy Sperit—the human sperit—the whole shebang. Maybe all men got one big soul ever'body's a part of" (24). He explicitly separates his spiritual ideas from Christianity, asking, "Why do we got to hang it all on God or Jesus?" (24).

Casy's views seem very similar to those that Steinbeck himself expressed. Robert Bennett, in *The Wrath of John Steinbeck; or, St. John Goes to Church,* reports that when Steinbeck was in college, he could not refrain, upon visiting a church, from responding to the minister's comments on the necessity of nourishing the soul: "A lot of crap," he remarked rather loudly. "If the soul is immortal, why worry about it—it's the body that—"[6] Casy, too, respects the body; although he expresses guilt at betraying his Christian principles through his sexuality, his experience of woman as a "holy vessel" leads him to take her to the grass time and again. Casy also feels alienated by the sexual prudery of Christianity and enjoys laughing at the old joke about the bull and the heifer.

Unlike the Father whom Jesus worshiped, Casy's god is a god unknown. Moreover, it is a divine principle that expresses itself through a feeling of unity with the natural world and an unqualified maternal love. Casy's rejection of formal religion is apparent in the scene when Granma asks him to bless their food. Here he explains his reluctance to participate in rituals of Christian tradition but agrees to present a more general blessing based upon a redefinition of holiness in terms of the central functions of the Great Mother, food, and love:

Sometimes I'd pray like I always done. On'y I coudn' figure what I was prayin' to or for. There was the hills, an' there was me, an' we wasn't separate no more. We was one thing. An' that one thing was holy. . . . An' then I got thinkin' I don't even know what I mean by holy. . . . I can't say no grace like I use' ta say. I'm glad of the holiness of breakfast. I'm glad there's love here. That's all. (88)

As Casy travels with the Joad family he becomes more and more closely attached to Ma and is initiated by her into some of the mysteries of the Great Mother. His first communal gesture is to help slaughter a pig, which is, as mentioned earlier, one of the Great Mother's sacrificial beasts. For the other men, this slaughter is simply part of their ordinary work, but Casy involves himself in the women's task of salting down the meat, thereby becoming an initiate in one of the fundamental mysteries of the Great Mother, that of food transformation. Ma is dubious about his participation at first: "It's women's work," she protests. "It's all work," the preacher replies. "They's too much of it to split it up to men's and women's work" (117).

In the final analysis, interpreting Casy as a Christ figure leaves out too much of his fundamental earthiness. If he is seen as the unconscious prophet of a primitive earth goddess, both his sexuality and his feeling that "all that lives is holy" (157) and "what people does is right" (233) can be taken into account. Nor do Casy's sacrifices of himself take him beyond the realm of the Great Mother, for she has always demanded sacrifices in her honor; pain and deprivation are associated with her most primitive rituals. Casy's first sacrifice was for the Joad family, the second for the family of man. Casy's last words are reminiscent of Christ's as he tells the men who are attacking him: "You don't know what you're a doin" (433). But his rationale for this remark is not that they do not know they are killing a son of god but that they do not know that they are "starvin' kids" (426), a basic concern of the matriarchs and the Great Mother.

Tom Joad is more nearly a Christ figure than Casy, but he is even more profoundly the son of his mother. He is badly abused by the patriarchy both before the novel opens and later in the work camps and rejects the hierarchies of patriarchal society as well as the violence toward the weak that sustains those structures. After each confrontation with men and authority, he returns to his mother for support and spiritual nourishment. Before he leaves the family, he undergoes an initiation into the mysteries of the Great Mother. The initiation begins with a symbolic reentry into the womb, as he hides in the maternal, cavelike darkness of a culvert. His mother brings nourishment to him, and he discusses with her his plans to aid the other migrants by organizing them. He envisions an apotheosis for himself, one in which he is absorbed into a maternal darkness, maintaining a transcendent presence at food rituals: "I'll be all aroun' in the dark. I'll be ever'where—wherever you look. Whenever they's a fight so hungry people can eat, I'll be there" (463). His transformation from bitter ex-con to fighter for humanity is the result of his developing matriarchal consciousness in which the needs of the family, the earth, and those who live close to it are primary.

Unlike Tom, Casy, and Noah, Uncle John has been transformed before the novel opens. He has been punishing himself with drink and celibacy for contributing to the death of his wife, suffering in atonement for his sins against the Great Mother. He remains in the background for the most part, a living reminder of the failure of patriarchal rule and values. Ma gives him a bit of appropriate and useful advice when she warns him not to burden others with his crimes against life: "Don't tell 'em," she warns. "Go down the river an' stick your head under an' whisper 'em in the stream" (295). John does not take her advice at this point, but at the end of the novel, he performs a ritualistic sacrifice in the river that can be seen as an act of reparation to the Great Mother for all of their sins. He takes Rose of Sharon's dead baby and casts it on the stream as a warning to others that they are betraying life: "Go down an' tell 'em. Go down in the street an' rot an' tell 'em that way. That's the way you can talk. . . . Maybe they'll know then" (493–94).

Beyond the manifestations of the transformative power of the Great Mother in the central characters, Steinbeck's descriptions of the migrant camps also indicate a strong matriarchal principle at work: "In the evening, a strange thing happened: the twenty families became one family, the children were the children of all" (213). The highlights of life in these camps, culminating in the Weedpatch camp, are the rituals that develop around the basic functional spheres of the feminine.[7] Birth and death incite community celebrations: "And it might be that a sick child threw despair into the hearts of twenty families, of a hundred people; that a birth there in a tent kept a hundred people quiet and awe-struck through the night and filled a hundred people with the birth-joy in the morning" (213).

Food preparation and laundry are social events on a smaller scale. Ma, for example, finds herself feeding twenty or more waifs in one campground. She is also told about the laundry rituals: "You wait till the women get to washing. . . . know what they did yesterday, Mrs. Joad? They had a chorus. Singing a hymn tune and rubbing the clothes all in time. That was something to hear, I tell you" (335–36). The principles on which families are established in the camps are based on the needs of women and children. The legal aspects of marriage, invented so that men can pass on their names and property, are no longer useful. The rules are simple: "a man might have a willing girl if he stayed with her, if he fathered her children and protected them. But a man might not have one girl one night and another the next, for this would endanger the worlds" (214).

This last custom, the development of a matrilinear principle, is responsible for Al leaving the Joads. Like Connie, Al had previously been a man of the new age. With his mechanical abilities he performed several small miracles in keeping the car on the road between Oklahoma and California. By the last scene of the novel, however, he has been absorbed by matriarchal principles and matrilinear necessities. His mechanical abilities fail at last, and he leaves his own family for the family of his wife, a custom demanded by the matriarchal world of migrant living. This is not regarded as a desertion of the family but a reestablishment of the basic principles on which the family can continue.

Steinbeck makes it clear that life in the migrant camps does not represent an emergent Christian communism. Rose of Sharon is frightened by a dour Christian woman who warns her against the sinful dances and wicked plays that are held in the camp, insisting that "they ain't but a few deep down Jesus-lovers left" (341). During the dancing, the "Jesus-lovers" remain aloof and keep their children under close scrutiny, safely protected from these pagan celebrations. Ma, however, urges husbandless Rose of Sharon to attend the festivities, telling her that she will be especially welcome because "it makes folks happy to see a girl in a fambly way" (372).

Thus, although the concluding scene has generated much debate, Rose of Sharon's nurturing of the starving man is the appropriate culmination of the many manifestations of the Great Mother throughout the novel. Critics who fail to see the importance of the developing matriarchal consciousness and to recognize the transformative power of the feminine interpret Steinbeck's final image in naturalistic terms, seeing the helpless humans at the mercy of the elements when the diminished family—Ma, Pa, Rose of Sharon, Ruthie, and Winfield—are driven from their boxcar home by the rising river. Other critics, unwilling to accept the implications of the ending for their theories about the Christian or communistic patterns, have tended to concur instead that "the ending is intentionally inconclusive" (French 1963, 93), albeit generally supportive of an optimism about the survival of the family of man (Chametzky in Donohue 1968, 234). In its poetic and paradoxical completeness, however, the image of Rose of Sharon nursing the stranger while the flood moves to engulf the family unites both the naturalistic and optimistic views.

Failure to recognize the culmination of the archetypal pattern in this has led to such realignments of the final message as John Ford's replacement, in the film version of The Grapes of Wrath,[8] of the powerful iconographic image of Rose of Sharon with Tom's farewell speech to his mother. Although the film's final scene, perhaps at Steinbeck's insistence, focuses on Ma Joad, the young Tom Joad, portrayed by rising star Henry Fonda, is the hero. Concluding the film with Tom's assertion of his ubiquitous, God-like presence "all around in the dark . . . ever'where—wherever you look" (463), with its echoes of Christ's "insomuch as you do it to the least of them you do it unto me" restores an emphasis to patriarchal values and Christian masculinist perceptions of spiritual power that the novel undercuts.

Steinbeck, however, had no ambivalence about the conclusion of the novel, feeling its correctness, although he did not fully express the reasons for his decision. He certainly intended to take the predominant social attitudes to task, and whether he articulated it intellectually or not, the archetypal alternative to Western patriarchal values comes to the surface in the novel. Each of the characters is forced to choose between patriarchal and matriarchal attitudes toward the natural world and each other. Muley Graves provides an example at the beginning of the novel when he refuses to be driven from the garden by the appearance of the man on the machine.[9] He will not leave the land that has been soaked by the blood of his father or the grass on which he first "laid with a girl" (54). So he remains, living in caves and eating wild rabbits, thereby aligning himself with the vestiges of the Great Mother in nature, as he haunts the machine men who ride unfeelingly over the living earth.

The Joads confront the Great Mother within: the women learn to understand themselves as a part of the natural cycles of life and death; the men are forced to atone for their sins against life and are either transformed or die in the process. In each case, the Great Mother is experienced as a dual power, a womb/tomb that can nurture or destroy. In a brief scene toward the end of the book, Steinbeck reinforces this message, as Ruthie teaches Winfield a stern lesson about the gifts of the Great Mother. When Winfield attempts to grab a flower from Ruthie, she bangs "him in the face with her open hand" (498). Winfield is learning early that the gifts of the Great Mother cannot be taken by force but must be earned by virtue of a reverent attitude toward nature and the feminine. He is also learning that she can withhold or bestow her gifts at will. The image of Rose of Sharon with the starving man at her breast expresses the paradoxical power of the Great Mother completely. Sword in one hand, bowl in the other, Kali, like Rose of Sharon, wears a smile.

Notes

1. The term "Great Mother" is universally used without etymological explanation. Although it is a translation of *Magna Mater,* used in connection with the virgin mother aspect of the archetype, the phrase predates the Christian virgin cult and is used in reference to such diverse mother goddesses as Isis, Ishtar, and Hera.

2. The most common images of the nursing mother are those of the Virgin Mary suckling the baby Jesus. The iconography of the primordial Great Mother, however, also includes images of a young woman giving her breast to miniaturized adult figures or even adult males. See the photographs of artifacts in Erich Neumann, *The Great Mother*—the Celtic Mother Goddess (45), the Goddess with Young God (46), and particularly the drawing of Sophia-Sapientia suckling two bearded males (174).

3. This discussion of the archetypal feminine is indebted throughout to Erich Neumann's thorough analysis in *The Great Mother.*

4. See *The Great Mother,* plate 65, and Manuela Dunn Mascetti, *The Song of Eve,* 35.

5. There are several Christian interpretations of *The Grapes of Wrath,* including Peter Lisca's *The Wide World of John Steinbeck* (1958), 174f., and Lester Jay Marks's *Thematic Design in the Novels of John Steinbeck* (1971), 76f.

6. In Robert Bennett, *The Wrath of John Steinbeck; or, St. John Goes to Church.* This pamphlet has no pagination. The quotation appears on the third-to-last page.

7. Steinbeck's discussion of the primitive matriarchal structures in the migrant camps is based on his readings in Briffault's *The Mothers.* Briffault, like Steinbeck, asserts that matriarchies are based not upon "artificial economic control" but rather upon "functional relations" (see Briffault 1927, vol. 1, 434).

8. To be fair, it is clear that Ford had several pressing reasons for changing the novel's ending, not the least of which was the censoring power of the Hayes Laws, which would have prevented the showing of a woman's breast. Economic reasons also contributed, for Elaine Steinbeck has pointed out that the studio intended the film to make Henry Fonda into a star, with the concomitant emphasis on Tom Joad as "hero."

9. See Leo Marx, *The Machine in the Garden* (1964). Although Marx's discussion of the prevalent image of the intrusion of the mechanical into the pastoral landscape of America suggests the terms of Steinbeck's imagery, Marx does not discuss the polarities of America in terms of the gender distinctions that are the subject of this essay.

FIVE

Steinbeck's Ecological Polemic: Human Sympathy and Visual Documentary in the Intercalary Chapters of *The Grapes of Wrath*

Peter Valenti

In the intercalary chapters of The Grapes of Wrath, *Steinbeck refines a unique ecological rhetoric characterized first by a polemical urgency typical of Aldo Leopold, second by a "high romanticism" of imaginative sympathy and outrage, and finally by a strong visual sense borrowed from Farm Security Administration photographers and filmmakers that linked the land and people. These verbal and visual models shaped Steinbeck's compelling prose in the intercalary chapters.*

As he neared the height of his creative powers in 1936 after completing *In Dubious Battle,* John Steinbeck worked increasingly with documentary material that revealed organized farming interests victimizing migrant farm labor in California. Feeling acutely the need to present the plight of the migrants in a rhetorically effective manner, he experimented with polemical stances; the early stages of what was to become *The Grapes of Wrath* reveal a political novel, virtually a text for activism, but not a traditional narrative representing a central character's progress (Benson 1984, 332–50, 361–63, 367–81, 385–92). The novel perhaps began with "L'Affaire Lettuceberg," a manuscript that Steinbeck later destroyed and that would have given vent to his outrage at the treatment of migrant workers in California. Like the articles written for the San Francisco *News* and later reprinted as *The Harvest Gypsies* and *Their Blood Is Strong,* much early work on *Grapes* resembled a documentary essay on the abuses perpetrated by agricultural employers, corporate interests, and local law enforcement agencies. Not until the final draft of the novel, when he used the title given him by his wife, Carol, did he discover the format that allowed him to present his case effectively. When Steinbeck added the fictional story of the Joads to the documentary material of the interchapters, he achieved the unity of human and physical worlds that constitutes his ecological rhetoric.

Thus the interchapters, or intercalary chapters, as they are also called, perform a vital function in Steinbeck's novel. Beginning with the first chapter, they continue throughout the novel to alternate regularly, or intercalate, with the fictional chapters describing the Joads' trials. The only exception to this alternation of documentary and fiction occurs at the end of the Joads' life in Oklahoma: chapter 11, an intercalary chapter describing the deterioration of a vacant house, is followed by another intercalary chapter opening the second section of the novel—the flight/journey to California along Route 66. Alternation of the Joad narrative with intercalary chapters resumes with chapter 13, telling of the deaths of Grampa and the family dog, as well as the beginning of the Joad-Wilson friendship, and chapter 14, describing the nervousness of the western states. Chapter 15, the novel's central chapter, is the only one to combine both intercalary and narrative material.

To suggest how Steinbeck gains effect from these two complementary modes, I will attempt to define what I see as Steinbeck's unique ecological rhetoric and then indicate how that rhetoric operates in *The Grapes of Wrath,* particularly with regard to the intercalary chapters, the application of Steinbeck's emotional polemic against forced misery and degradation. Steinbeck achieved huge success with *The Grapes of Wrath* because he successfully tapped the nation's need to understand the plight of the poor and dispossessed; he was not so much directly influenced by other texts, either visual or verbal, as responding to his culture and expressing some of its deepest needs. Steinbeck thus maintains the traditions of nineteenth-century naturalists, who present life as lived by the most downtrodden groups in society and suggest why such conditions exist; he continues in the imaginative mode of writers and photographers who understand the urgency of documenting human suffering and its contributory causes in order to create the resolve to end such misery. His desire to have readers experience the anguish he felt in the migrants' camps forces him to establish a visual, point-to-the-abuses style that contributes mightily to the success of *The Grapes of Wrath* as a novel.

Steinbeck's polemic derives its strength from ecology, emotional identification, and the visual. Exploring each of these three areas as they have been developed in twentieth-century American culture will reveal not specific influences on Steinbeck the writer but the sources of his power as a writer. More specifically, these are: the sense of ecology itself, most usefully as characterized by Aldo Leopold in the 1930s; the romantic sense of a democratic and transpersonal identification with all humanity; and the visual sense of immediacy, of suasive power, contained in photographic images. The power of these three combined influences is most obvious in the intercalary chapters, where Steinbeck's urge to provide a voice for the dispossessed fructifies in a unique artistic form. Examining the three will show how Steinbeck's artistry depends upon each of their unique strengths.

I

Writing from the early 1920s through the late 1940s, the early champion of conservation Aldo Leopold characterized three ages of human development in relation to the principles governing the conduct of human society: the first, or legalistic, rests on the Ten Commandments, on authoritarian rule; the second, or moralistic, depends on man's duties to the rest of society; the third, or environmental, focuses on man's obligation to interact profitably and responsibly with plants, animals, and the rest of the ecosystem. Though Leopold felt the third stage would not be achieved, I argue that Steinbeck is its first conscious champion in American narrative. *The Grapes of Wrath* offers clear and compelling support for Leopold's dream, though Steinbeck had almost certainly never heard of Leopold.

Unlike James Fenimore Cooper, who introduced his hero Natty Bumppo as a middle-aged outcast from a society already ferociously destroying its wildlife and habitat, Steinbeck ties human social needs to the requirements of a healthy earth; his method suggests that the two are interdependent. Though the balance is delicate (to use a metaphor given immediacy by Al Gore), Cooper is more concerned with the earth—the shallow landscape and its plant and animal inhabitants—being harmed by human activity. Steinbeck, on the other hand, is concerned with human welfare above all else. His language in *The Grapes of Wrath* extends the suggestions made earlier in *To a God Unknown*—for example, that digging in the earth with fingers and toes establishes a connection with the land vital to human beings.

Such ecological rhetoric emphasizes human considerations. In his 1935 essay "Land Pathology," Aldo Leopold states that "the properties of animal and plant populations are now to some extent known. Their interactions with environment are becoming predictable. Ecological predictions are made with such certainty as to be used daily in farm, factory, and hospital." He continues, however, "The properties of human populations and their interactions with land are still imperfectly understood. Predictions of behavior are made, but with much uncertainty, and hence are seldom used. Economists, conservationists, and planners are just beginning to become aware that there is a basic ecology involved" (Leopold 1991, 212). He continues to make his main point: "Philosophers have long since claimed that society is an organism, but with few exceptions they have failed to understand that the organism includes the land which is its medium. The properties of human populations, which are the joint domain of sociologist, economist, and statesman, are all conditioned by land" (212). To that list of thinkers, we should add the novelist as well.

Calling for conservation, Leopold offers what he calls a basic deduction about the relation between land and society, a relation explored in *The Grapes of Wrath*: "America presents the first instance of a society, heavily equipped with machines, invading a terrain in large part set on a hair-trigger. The accelerating velocity of destructive interactions is unmistakable and probably unprecedented. Recuperative mechanisms either do not exist, or have not had time to get under way. The mechanism of these interactions in such resources as soil, forests, ranges, and wild life has been traced, at least in its grosser aspects, and found to be strongly inter-connected" (213–14). In *The Grapes of Wrath*, chapter 1 tells of topsoil being blown away; traditional management practices cannot recoup its loss. Steinbeck's method of mingling intercalary with Joad family narrative chapters functions as a "recuperative mechanism" to bring together the people with the land they inhabit.

In emphasizing connections between land and society, Leopold pleads for a human ecology based on close inspection of the land. Steinbeck, on the other hand, sees the human side as more pressing. Clearly, the two examine different landscapes, but the principles involved parallel one another. The sense of faith driving both men told them that they could make a difference, that their ideas when presented to others could influence the ways society at large read and valued the message of pathology, both of land and of human beings. Both were polemic in their attempts to arouse sufficient outrage to ensure reform and changed behavior, but Steinbeck worked with more disparate materials more imaginatively presented. Of course, the narrative pull of fiction also fueled Steinbeck's success.

Leopold offers a final comment on human ecology:

Equipped with this excess of tools, society has developed an unstable adjustment to its environment, from which both must eventually suffer damage or even ruin. Regarding society and land collectively as an organism, that organism has suddenly developed pathological symptoms, i.e. self-accelerating rather than self-compensating departures from normal functioning. The tools cannot be dropped, hence the brains which created them, and which are now mostly dedicated to creating still more, must be at least in part diverted to controlling those already in hand. (217)

Pathology is an apt concept for humans as well as land; Pare Lorentz's 1936 documentary film produced for the Resettlement Administration, *The Plow That Broke the Plains,* for example, movingly shows causes of first land and next human pathology. When humans broke the grass sod of the Great Plains, they began a process of ever-increasing production that soon robbed the earth of its ability to produce. The Great Depression began with the stock market crash in the fall of 1929; the following spring and summer began a period of sparse rainfall that lasted until 1939. With the great droughts of the early thirties came dust storms that blew away first the topsoil and then the farmers who had depended on that soil to earn a living. In Lorentz's documentary film, as well as in Steinbeck's novel, the steady and unrelenting progress of the tractors admits no impediments.

II

The second characteristic of Steinbeck's ecological polemic is a certain high romanticism, or a desire to enshrine the individual's emotional investment in the lives of others. The power of the photographic image to arouse sympathy derives from a similar process of human identification with the subject. Furthermore, this quality of emotive power stands in contrast to the Darwinian naturalism of the documentary movement. Victor Hugo prophesied, "In the relations of man with the animals, with the flowers, with the objects of creation, there is a great ethic, scarcely perceived as yet, which will at length break forth into the light and which will be the corollary and complement to human ethics" (Passmore 1974, 3n). This ethic translates into a feeling of the importance of every human being as well as the landscape.

Victor Hugo's dream of a higher reality may still be an illusion, but similar hopes were shared by many during the dark hours of the Depression. The glorification of children and unfortunates—the better to see their unique gifts—translated into support for every human being. Walker Evans, in preparing to realize his goal of true communication as a photographer, wrote to himself: "These anonymous people who come and go in the cities and who move on the land; it is on what they look like, now; what is in their faces and in the window and the streets beside and around them; what they are wearing and what they are riding in, and how they are gesturing, that we need to concentrate, consciously, with the camera" (Evans 1982, 151). Like Coleridge's Ancient Mariner, Evans must establish contact and imaginative sympathy with those he meets. What wedding guest, the documentarists ask, could possibly refuse to hear and heed the stories told so wrenchingly?

Another romantic aspect of Steinbeck's intercalary chapters recalls William Blake's diatribes against the same sort of grinding down of humanity by the blind cogs of the great machine of state. Blake's chimney sweep muses that he has been made to suffer "Because I was happy upon the heath, / And smil'd among the winters snow" (Blake 1988, 22). Even a child's happiness in cruel conditions is an offense to "God & his Priest & King" and must not be allowed to continue. Similar malevolent forces operate in Steinbeck's world, where police stamp out vegetable seedlings grown secretly on disused land in an effort to kill the spirits of the migrants (*TGOW* 259–60). The workers, however, "know how a fallow field is a sin and the unused land a crime against the thin children" (*TGOW* 257) in another instance of Blakean outrage. Steinbeck fulfills Blake's definition of the great poet or prophet as a man who sees the truth clearly and selflessly and dares to preach it to his fellow men. This high romantic tradition combines indignation at seeing abuses perpetrated and the emotional identification of speaker with victim; it leads toward an ineffability, a feeling of the sad inadequacy of words to convey the depth of the emotion experienced.

III

The third area of the ecological polemic is its visual nature. Part of Franklin Delano Roosevelt's New Deal was the creation of the Resettlement Administration in 1935. Slightly rearranged in 1937 as the Farm Security Administration (FSA), it took as its main purpose to reveal the plight of farmers and migrants to the American public through thousands of different photographs. *The Grapes of Wrath* participated along with the FSA photographers in the most intense production of documentary America has seen. This tradition of visual human ecology perhaps originated with the work of Lewis Hine during the first three decades of the century; slightly later, the work of the FSA photographers and documentarists such as Pare Lorentz told similarly compelling stories. These potential models foreground the possibilities for Steinbeck's presentation; even if he knew none of them directly—a virtual impossibility, given their wide dissemination—as a literate middle-class American he was immersed in the same culture that produced these photographs.

Hine offered America a unique and lasting vision. He began a career as a teacher at the Ethical Culture School in 1901, started using a camera in his teaching in 1903, and soon learned the power of the photograph to present what he could not express in words (Gutman 1974; Kaplan 1988). Hine's work was so widely reprinted and available that the circulation of his images equaled that of the best-known FSA photos of the thirties. Working from a strong commitment to improve the world of the young, he championed their cause in his photos for *Charities and Commons*, later to become *Survey Graphic* and *Survey* magazines, and other publications, such as the *Child Labor*

Bulletin, in whose pages many of his photographs appear. He paired captioned photos of a normal child and mill child, for example, to show how drastically millwork affected a typical child. In another instance, he set up a composition to depict a social process; "Making Human Junk" shows a union of verbal and visual art for polemic purpose as he depicts normal children being adversely affected by their employment in a sweatshop. Normal children become "junk" as a result of their exploitation by employers. Even though such depictions might seem obvious or heavy-handed to a visually sophisticated late twentieth-century audience, they affected early twentieth-century consciousness to the extent that they helped in passing child labor legislation (Rothstein 1979, 29). Other photos by Hine show a pair of contrasting images, or at least centers of interest, that carry the reader/viewer back and forth. This method prefigures the success of Steinbeck's methods in *Grapes* where he modulates between intercalary and narrative chapters. In his photographic presentations, Hine is showing America how to see and understand. There is no unstated depth in the contrasting shots of children or even in the "Human Junk" presentation; we read as we are led in these photographs. It will remain for Hine's later work, and the work of Dorothea Lange and the other FSA photographers, to show us the power of the deeper significance of these visual texts. Reading from left to right or from top to bottom in Hine's illustrations shows clearly the sequence of the propaganda message, which is emphasized by arrows—as if the process were the production of a consumer good being illustrated on a corporate easel. Hine's method is of course to provoke his audience to see the human costs of manufacturing, of stoking the engines and tools of a system that pays inadequate attention to the children it victimizes.

Other visual documents of the period reinforce a polemic of human and vegetative interdependence. Photographs taken by the FSA photographers—including Dorothea Lange, Arthur Rothstein, Walker Evans, Ben Shahn, Marion Post Wolcott, and others—work as perfect visual counterparts to Steinbeck's nonfiction detailing the lives of migrant workers because they present humanity in the process of moving through the hostility of the landscape of crop harvesting; we do not need to know their names because we can read their stories in their faces. Dorothea Lange's most famous sequence, the five-shot "Migrant Mother" series taken in 1936, offers abundant evidence of this quality of emotion, which the viewer cannot choose but feel. Reproduced here as figure 1 is the "Migrant Madonna," her photo of a beautiful young migrant mother nursing a baby; this striking photo became the cover illustration for *Their Blood Is Strong* in 1938. Many of Lange's other California photos were also used to accompany Steinbeck's newspaper articles. Less well known but similarly effective are Arthur Rothstein's photographs of displaced black sharecroppers on the Missouri delta; figure 2 captures well the dilemma ("Where will we go?") facing the man and his child. Lange features other photographs of the Missouri evictions prominently in *An American Exodus*, a large book that provides full-size reproductions of many of her photographs along the migrant trails. As Lange and her coauthor husband Paul Taylor state in the foreword, "in the situations which we describe are living people who can speak. Many whom we met in the field vaguely regarded conversation with us as an opportunity to tell what they are up against to their government and to their countrymen at large. So far as possible we have let them speak to you face to face. Here we pass on what we have seen and learned from many miles of countryside of the shocks which are unsettling them" (Lange and Taylor 1939, 6; Stott 1986; Daniel 1987; Curtis 1989; Stange 1989). Ostensibly mute testimonies can ultimately provide the most eloquent of statements: displacement is pathology, of both landscape and human society.

The human ecology of land and its people inspired other artists as well. Margaret Bourke-White in 1937 assembled with her then-husband Erskine Caldwell the large-format photo-essay collaboration *You Have Seen Their Faces*. Implicitly suggesting that the reading public would be moved by such images, Bourke-White included a picture of used-up land surrounding a vacant farmhouse with the caption "It looks like God can't trust people to take care of the earth anymore" (Caldwell and Bourke-White 1937, 175). Another photograph by Lange, figure 3, depicts such a scene to inspire questions about stewardship of the land. Similarly, the work of Marion Post Wolcott and Walker Evans reveals parallel tendencies; as James Agee painfully phrases the intention to find a means of accurately telling what the life of a sharecropper is like, his prose in *Let Us Now Praise Famous Men* is "an effort in human actuality, in which the reader is

1. Dorothea Lange, "Migrant Madonna," 1938, California. Farm Security Administration, Library of Congress. Image used in 1938 for Steinbeck's newspaper articles collected as *Their Blood Is Strong*.

no less centrally involved than the authors and those of whom they tell" (Agee and Evans 1960, xvi). Seeing and reading these stories in the people's faces and lives, the authors and photographers feel compelled to retell, reprint, the accounts as partial fulfillment of their human obligation. Steinbeck's own phrase in the *Log from the Sea of Cortez* shows his determination to accomplish a similar task: " 'Let us go,' we said, 'into the Sea of Cortez, realizing that we become forever a part of it; that our rubber boots slogging through a flat of eel-

2. Arthur Rothstein, "Displaced Sharecropper," January 1939, New Madrid County, Missouri. Farm Security Administration, Library of Congress.

grass, that the rocks we turn over in a tide pool, make us truly and permanently a factor in the ecology of the region. We shall take something away from it, but we shall leave something, too' " (*LSC* 3). Working with the migrants was a taking away as well as a leaving for Steinbeck; his weaving of a tapestry of human need in the intercalary chapters presents his novel manner of arguing for human ecology.

Like Hine's photographs, Steinbeck's words suggest the power of sentiment behind the people and their haunting images. The first paragraph of the second installment of the *News* series called "The Harvest Gypsies" reveals this tendency:

3. Dorothea Lange, "Childress County, Texas," 1938. Farm Security Administration, Library of Congress.

The squatters' camps are located all over California. Let us see what a typical one is like. It is located on the banks of a river, near an irrigation ditch or on a side road where a spring of water is available. From a distance it looks like a city dump, and well it may, for the city dumps are the sources for the material of which it is built. You can see a litter of dirty rags and scrap iron, of houses built of weeds, of flattened cans or of paper. It is only on close approach that it can be seen that these are homes.
(THG *1988, 26)*

The "Let us see what a typical one is like" parallels the pull of the visual in Hine's photos of typical situations of industrial child abuse, visually and iconographically generalized to the point of perfect types of absolute categories. "Normal child" and "mill child" are not so much the individuals whose pictures are presented here as they are the representations of exploited and suffering youth. Hine's labels and arrows prefigure Steinbeck's insistent demonstrative pronouns, which I have italicized for emphasis: "*Here* is a house," "*This* is a family of six," "*There* is more filth *here*" (26–28). Longer statements allow Steinbeck to point to more complex issues: "*Here,* in the faces of the husband and his wife, you begin to see an expression that you will notice on every face; not worry, but absolute terror of the starvation that crowds in against the borders of the camp" (27). "*This* is the middle class of the squatters' camp" (29). "And if *these* men steal, if there is developing among them a suspicion and hatred of well-dressed, satisfied people, the reason is not to be sought in their origin nor in any tendency to weakness in their character" (31). This last remark concludes the essay; it moves away from a generalized view of the camp to a careful consideration of the innermost feelings of its residents. Like the projected audience for Hine's photos, the readers of Steinbeck's newspaper essays perceive a call for social action based on the most basic of shared human sympathies. Just as manufacturers made "human junk," so Steinbeck's words show how agricultural capitalism sucks the life out of its laboring poor. Given his focus on sanitary conditions as a clue to the migrants' state, "making human excrement" would be an apt title for this second chapter of "The Harvest Gypsies."

One final observation on this paragraph will help to demonstrate how the tradition of the social justice photograph works to help first the immediate cause of writing a successful newspaper piece and second the later purpose of building the intercalary chapter technique. Steinbeck moves from the entire state of California in his first sentence to the typical camp located at a source of water. He is carefully narrowing his visual field so that his verbal technique approximates a dolly-in shot as he moves closer to his specific subject: "From a distance it looks like a city dump." But he will tell us more specifically exactly what it is; as we get closer, we understand it better because we distinguish visual detail: "You can see a litter of dirty rags and scrap iron, of houses built of weeds, of flattened cans or of paper." The detritus captures the migrants forced to live in trash, but Steinbeck postpones the final knowledge: "It is only on close approach that it can be seen that these are homes." His craft takes us from "squatters' camps" at the head of the paragraph to "homes" at the tail so that we move in tight for a closeup, at which point we can begin to read the misery in the faces of the people. The man and baby in figure 2 suggest the uncertainty of their situation in their glances; their querying look makes the viewer wonder if these people too will one day find themselves in situations similar to those described in the *News* articles. That such concerns were crucial to Steinbeck is evident in his "Long Valley ledger," where late in 1936 he complains of his mind as "fat and sluggish. It hasn't emerged into the picture-making state so necessary" to be able to avoid "that old human trick of reducing everything to its simplest design. Now the designs of life are not so simple" (Benson 1984, 331). The work on the migrants, however, sharpened his visual capabilities to the point where he could use the intercalary chapters to show general patterns of human existence and the Joad family to illustrate an individual experience of suffering among the willows on the riverbank.

IV

Also during this period from late 1936 through 1938, Steinbeck had emotional assistance to push on to realization of the picture of migrant life. His marriage to Carol, his friendships with Ed Ricketts and Tom Collins, provided him with critical support and thus prepared him for the great surge of energy and inspiration needed to complete the final draft of the novel; no less critical was the actual work of observing the ecosystems of aquatic organisms and starving migrant families. Moving beyond a merely literary focus, such as Norris's intellectual studies of Darwinist theory and Zolaesque technique, Steinbeck discovers in the intercalary chapters the ideal means for fiction of uniting human ethics with the fate of the physical planet. He understood perfectly how instinctual identification with the suffering of others called forth an intellectual response that explained the sorrowful conditions but did not ameliorate them. Such work would, it could be hoped, come out of his prose. The sense of a polemic of human ecology, of a mode of writing that would convey to the world a sense of the tragedy being enacted in California in the 1930s, came to Steinbeck from a wide variety of sources, extending well beyond those I cover here.

The narrative chapters propel the story of the Joads plainly enough; the intercalary chapters, however, have unexplored power, offering Steinbeck's most crucial evaluations of the life lived on the road. Chapter 14 establishes the mood for this central core; Steinbeck uses snippets of the migrants' actual speech, very like the collection on the inside covers of *An American Exodus*, to establish the mood.

Lange reports migrants' comments such as "Burned out, blowed out, eat out, tractored out" and "Yessir, we're starved stalled and stranded" (Lange and Taylor 1939, inside covers). Steinbeck writes: "I lost my land, a single tractor took my land. I am alone and I am bewildered" (*TGOW* 165).

Taken together, these individual statements form a new whole; they articulate the possibility of a new society based on shared misery. The visual quality of Steinbeck's polemic—the absolute, driving need to make others participate in the migrants' misery—flashes forth in passages describing individual scenes of accessible moments, as in this one: "The two men squatting in a ditch, the little fire, the side-meat stewing in a single pot, the silent, stone-eyed women; behind, the children listening with their souls to words their minds do not understand" (*TGOW* 165). This sense of ineffability, of emotions felt so deeply that they lie beyond the power of language, charges the sharing in the darkness with sacredness.

Chapter 14 contrasts the attitudes of haves and have-nots—the nervousness of the western states grows as the desperation of the migrants increases—and offers preparation for the lessons of chapter 15. Mary Ellen Caldwell's essay on the intercalary chapters perceptively notes the importance of chapter 15 as a central point in the novel's development. She sees the chapter as a fiction complete in itself, a story of life on the road with both villains and heroes: the condescending wealthy couple who find fault with Mae and Al's diner and the truck drivers who reward Mae's reflexive generosity to migrants identical to the Joads. Caldwell views chapter 15 as binding together the two strands of narrative and intercalary chapters at the midpoint of the novel (in Davis 1982, 105–14; see also Owens, in Ditsky 1989, 109–10).

The most important points of Steinbeck's polemic of human ecology occur most strongly in chapters 17 and 19, where the banding together of individual migrants in their mutual poverty and dreams of a better future contrasts sharply with a thumbnail sketch of California's agricultural history, detailing the creation of an economy based on regular exploitation of workers: "In the evening a strange thing happened: The twenty families became one family, the children were the children of all" (*TGOW* 213). "Every night a world created . . . , every night relationships that make a world, established"

(*TGOW* 213)—such a feeling of the interdependence of individuals ensures that the forces operating against humanity can be withstood.

This feeling climaxes in chapter 19, where Steinbeck muses on the earlier residents of these California valleys and sees how the new migrants represent the latest group to suffer repression and injustice. The final victory of the people, however, is virtually assured as the outcome of this growing sense of interdependence, a revolutionary process. Steinbeck offers as an example the sharing of much-needed cash to pay for a child's funeral:

The men squatted on their hams, sharp-faced men, lean from hunger and hard from resisting it, sullen eyes and hard jaws. And the rich land was around them.

D'ja hear about the kid in that fourth tent down?

No, I jus' come in.

Well, that kid's been a-cryin' in his sleep an' a-rollin' in his sleep. Them folks thought he got worms. So they give him a blaster, an' he died. It was what they call black-tongue the kid had. Comes from not gettin' good things to eat.

Poor little fella.

Yeah, but them folks can't bury him. Got to go to the county stone orchard.

Well, hell.

And hands went into pockets and little coins came out. In front of the tent a little heap of silver grew. And the family found it there. (TGOW 263)

After noting this act of generosity, Steinbeck finishes the long chapter with a prayer: "Our people are good people; our people are kind people. Pray God some day kind people won't all be poor. Pray God some day a kid can eat" (*TGOW* 263). This prayer of the common people, of the ineffable, is not a prayer that comes through the conventions of organized religion, but rather a prayer that arises from the individual heart when it realizes a moment of true transpersonality. But Steinbeck's ultimate contribution lies in the last lines of this chapter, where he follows the prayer with the observations: "And the associations of owners knew that some day the praying would stop. And there's the end" (*TGOW* 263). His rhetoric moves a step beyond the joint photos and text of a book like *An American Exodus;* his is the true revolutionary alternative. Steinbeck knew that such statements endangered him because of the violence already used by growers' associations. But he knew as well that his statements of the situation were necessary to depict accurately the lives of migrants. The three-part movement from prayer, to cessation of prayer, to revolution hints darkly at the days ahead.

When Muley Graves argues for the ultimate ownership of his plot of land, sacred because it holds his father's spilled blood and his own sperm, or when Tom Joad scratches a crude outline of a woman's body in the earth's surface, he asserts a biological need every bit as pressing as the thirsty earth's appetite for water. When the women leave the sacred spot of earth, the farm/home, as exiles, they bring a strength that is also a part of the land. Like Antaeus, they will rest and refresh themselves at another spot of earth where they will build a new hearth fire. But the wrenching of humans from the land—even land so parched as that described in the first interchapter—carries the deep primordial threat of lapsed order in both the natural world and the society of humans.

The women attempt to ease this transition by leaving behind much of the old life; the tearing apart of the old households makes them ask, "How can we live without our lives? How will we know it's us without our past? No. Leave it. Burn it" (*TGOW* 96). Only when they burn into their visual memories the image of the dooryard willow because "the willow tree is you" are they are able to begin the journey (*TGOW* 96). Steinbeck's women understand the paradox verbalized by one of Lange's subjects, who stated, "A human being has a right to stand like a tree has a right to stand" (Lange and Taylor 1939, inside covers). But solely because one human has the right to stand does not mean that other humans will allow it. Fittingly, the willows reappear consistently: they guide the migrants to water in new surroundings and serve in the novel as a leitmotif, a constant in the background of the migrants' various stops.

Steinbeck's cinematic final image in chapter 9 captures the simple pathos of lives left behind: "The dust hung in the air for a long time after the loaded cars had passed" (*TGOW* 96). We are forced to contemplate the passing human caravan in a unique manner here; not only does this image recall the final sequences of *The Plow That Broke*

4. Dorothea Lange, "Interior of Migrant Tent," 1938, California. Farm Security Administration, Library of Congress.

the Plains with its images of groaning cars pulling out of a dying migrant camp, but it also demonstrates how Steinbeck has transferred the method of "The Harvest Gypsies" to his novel.

The pathos of this economical final sentence depicting overloaded cars laboring away through a veil of dust derives its strength from the structure of the chapter. The first sentence of the interchapter establishes the sense of loss: "In the little houses the tenant people sifted their belongings and the belongings of their fathers and of their grandfathers" (*TGOW* 93). The movement from the interior of the house, through the memories of the past and the pain of letting go the physical objects of the past, to the final scene of loaded autos, helps to explain how so simple an image can carry such an emotional weight.

The weight of significance carried by common details—the emotional, transpersonal power conveyed by simple material objects—infuses and empowers such visual documents as the photos of a table and a store interior in figures 4 and 5. Lange's photograph of a tent

5. Walker Evans, "General Store," 1936, Alabama. Farm Security Administration, Library of Congress.

interior with items on a battered table presents the textures of life in the migrant camps; Evans's photograph of the contents of a general store displays the beauty of symmetrical arrangements of common goods. Lange and Evans here have captured perfectly some aspects of the migrants' lives that make us understand them somewhat better; we come as close as we can to identifying with them when we imagine the humble table set far from the stores of goods available to the fortunate. Like Steinbeck's prose in chapter 15, these photos show the range of possibility. Pray God that the people living in the tent will have access to the goods in the store. Pray God that some day a hungry kid can eat.

The Grapes of Wrath argues for equilibrium between such needs and the means that can supply those needs. At times, however, the means take the form of tools that can be used to destroy human connections to the land, as is the case with the tractors and their goggled drivers. In focusing on "excess of tools," Leopold clearly shared

6. Dorothea Lange, "Migrants on the Road," 1938, California. Farm Security Administration, Library of Congress.

Steinbeck's view that those who made the tools that disrupted the sensitive relationship between human society and land must turn their attention to restoring the balance. Steinbeck's presentation of lives lived in forced dislocation, instances of human actuality, direct the tool builders to see that human ecology requires control in the sense of humane management not only of the land but of those humans living upon it.

Steinbeck manages irony effectively to the extent that the real tools, the hand plows and the harrows and the hoes, the means whereby humans established and maintained relationships with the land, became obsolete, piles of junk rusting in abandoned yards, replaced by tractors with their anonymous bug-eyed operators, moving in on houses such as that in figure 3, plowed up to the very door. A viewer might imagine the two families in figure 6 as Wilsons and Joads, helping one another in a new field of misery. The furrows plowed up to the door give way to muddy ruts on the much traveled migrant trail, leading the two families to their new dwelling places.

With similar technique and content, Steinbeck in the intercalary chapters has shown us what the human costs of making such a move must have been.

The anonymous farmer in intercalary chapter 9 warns the junk buyer of "a sorrow that can't talk" (*TGOW* 94), and the dispossessed poor find few to speak on their behalf. Even so, the expenditure of human life through the economic and ecological displacements pictured in *The Grapes of Wrath* evokes a strong response from readers. The artist's urge to capture the ineffable in human suffering, the truth behind the stony silences, finds a powerful resource in the intercalary chapters, whose documentary force deepens the resonance of the Joads' tragic story. For without such art to convey the moral weight of the story behind the abandoned fields and houses, both the world and our participatory roles as readers would suffer diminution.

SIX

Natural Wisdom:
Steinbeck's Men of Nature
as Prophets and Peacemakers

Marilyn Chandler McEntyre

Steinbeck's prophets, men of broad understanding and acceptance, draw their vision from the natural world. Jim Casy, a lapsed preacher and wise counselor to the Joad family, finds new faith in love of nature and renewed purpose through his involvement with the people of the earth. At the center of Cannery Row *is Doc, marine biologist, whose holistic vision and compassionate attention to human needs are similarly drawn from close observation of his environment and nature. Through a nonteleological acceptance of what is, both the rigorous scientist and the intuitive preacher recognize the interconnectedness of creation.*

Steinbeck's indebtedness to the American transcendentalists, particularly Emerson and Whitman, has been noted frequently.[1] That relationship lies partly in his way of looking upon the natural world as a source of knowledge, a text to replace or expand upon Scripture, which teaches those who have eyes to see and ears to hear. For Steinbeck, as for his predecessors, the wise man was above all else defined by his discerning relationship to the natural world, allowing it to inform his understanding of human relations and enterprises.

In several of Steinbeck's novels we encounter variations on the type of the wise man—a character whose self-knowledge, compassion for human frailty, and sharp intuitions come from close association with the natural world. Two of the most notable of these are Casy, the preacher in *The Grapes of Wrath,* and Doc in *Cannery Row.* Both are solitaries who take frequent "flights into the wilderness" but who live among people who rely upon them for guidance. Both understand themselves and others with an insight that at times seems prophetic, and indeed in the motley circles they frequent they are accorded special status as counselors and wise men. Both are more educated than those around them, but each in his way has rejected the institutional forms and frameworks that endowed him with professional credentials and lives as a maverick of sorts, moving easily among circles of people to none of which he belongs. Both are explicitly linked with images of Jesus, though neither is conventionally religious. Both are "nonteleological thinkers" in the sense in which Steinbeck claimed that he himself viewed the world: not in terms of defined purposes, but with what he called "is thinking"—acceptance without second-guessing of the divine plan.[2]

For each, the source of wisdom and virtue appears to lie in communion with nature. And each, communing with nature, assumes the status and role of prophet in his community. Indeed it might be said that in these characters Steinbeck is working out a definition of prophecy and the importance of the prophet in modern life, not as one who calls for specific acts of repentance and return to a covenantal tradition, but as one who sees into the heart of nature and speaks forth what lesson it teaches. In doing so he, in effect, issues a warning call to turn away from those forms of civilized life that remove us from what Robinson Jeffers, Steinbeck's contemporary and fellow Californian, called "the great humaneness at the heart of things." And like Jeffers, he writes as one who is himself a visionary trying to find a language for the ultimate interconnectedness of all creation as a means for understanding what as humans we must do.

Steinbeck's most explicit articulation of this vision is given in *Sea of Cortez*, where he describes "nonteleological thinking" as a way of understanding the natural and thence the social world independent of the causal relations and presumed purposes we so readily posit to satisfy our need for comprehensible meaning. Freeman Champney sums up nonteleological thinking as "a mixture of philosophical relativism, the rigorous refusal of the scientist to be dogmatic about hypotheses, and a sort of moral fatalism" (Robert Murray Davis 1972, 30). Steinbeck himself explains, "Nonteleological thinking concerns itself primarily not with what should be, or could be, or might be, but rather with what actually 'is'—attempting at most to answer the already sufficiently difficult questions *what* or *how*, instead of *why*" (SOC 135).

To think in such a way entails a kind of humility related to Jeffers's idea of "unhumanism"—a rejection of the myopic anthropocentrism that distorts our understanding of the functioning of whole systems, the large patterns of evolution, the nature of natural and human communities as organic wholes that transcend the life and purposes of any individual within them. This capacity for "whole sight," as well as what Champney sees as relativism, antidogmatism, and ultimate acceptance of what is, defines the prophet in Steinbeck's world. In *The Grapes of Wrath* it is Casy, the unpretentious fellow traveler in the Joads' pilgrim band and maverick Christian in self-imposed exile from institutional religion, who embodies the nonteleological or "is" thinker capable of prophesying and ultimately enacting a larger truth than those around him are able to grasp.

Casy, who was once a preacher, now makes it a point of honor to reject his status and its privileges, assuring the Joads, who receive him as a kind of family chaplain, that he doesn't pray any more. But the habit of prayer is as ingrained in him as the way of life he leaves behind on the road to California: " 'Fella gets use' to a place, it's hard to go,' said Casy. 'Fella gets use' to a way a thinkin', it's hard to leave. I ain't a preacher no more, but all the time I find I'm prayin', not even thinkin' what I'm doin' " (54). His prayer is no longer a petition to an omnipotent God but a way of being and a largeness of awareness that comes to him in moments of solitude in the wilderness. He recognizes in himself a natural kinship with the Jesus who fled the crowds and went up into the high desert to pray:

I been in the hills thinking, almost you might say like Jesus went into the wilderness to think his way out of a mess of troubles. I ain't sayin' I'm like Jesus, . . . But I got tired like Him, an' I got mixed up like Him, an' I went into the wilderness like Him, without no campin' stuff. Nighttime I'd lay on my back and look up at the stars; morning I'd set and watch the sun come up; midday I'd look out from a hill at the rollin' dry country; evenin' I'd foller the sun down. Sometimes I'd pray like I always done. On'y I couldn' figure what I was prayin' to or for. There was the hills, an' there was me, an' we wasn't separate no more. We was one thing. An' that one thing was holy. (88)

The idea of the holy has expanded for Casy since his rejection of the church. It springs from an awareness of nature honed and trained by his frequent retreats, his attitude of receptivity, and a habit of mind that links what he knows of the unconscious natural world to a deepening intuition about the ways of human nature. To be in the wilderness "without no campin' stuff" is to be in more direct sensual contact with the earth than those for whom the multilayered insulations of clothing and shelter dull the raw sensate experience of nature. Casy's reflection here also traces a line of thinking that begins in Christian typology and ends in a rejection of that tradition in favor of a universalistic mysticism removed from the claims of any institution. Like Emerson, the transcendentalist who left his pulpit and went out among the people, and like Thoreau, who turned eccentricity to high purposes, Casy opens his heart to a wider calling than the pulpit afforded—to return to the earth and live close to it and the people who till the soil and to learn from them:

I ain't gonna baptize. I'm gonna work in the fiel's, in the green fiel's, an' I'm gonna be near to folks. I ain't gonna try to teach 'em nothin'. I'm gonna try to learn. Gonna learn why the folks walks in the grass, gonna hear 'em talk, gonna hear 'em sing. . . . Gonna lay in the grass, open and honest with anybody that'll have me. Gonna cuss an' swear an' hear the poetry of folks talkin'. All that's holy, all that's what I didn' understand'. All them things is the good things. (101–2)

In both these speeches there are echoes of transcendentalism, Protestant theology, and Whitmanian democracy. Frederick Carpenter points out the rich soil and deep roots that underlie Casy's philosophical statements as he "translates American philosophy into words of one syllable" (324–25).[3] And Peter Lisca comments that in these same articulations, Casy moves "from Bible-belt evangelism to social prophesy" (Robert Murray Davis 1972, 98). As a social prophet, however, his task is to prophesy to a particular and peculiar people. It is in his shared life with the Joad family that he works out his destiny and mission, often in terms reduced to their own simpler way of understanding what he is about.

Despite Casy's protestations, the Joads and others continue to take him for a preacher. The title sticks, and in that assigned role Casy assumes a place in but not of the Joad family, increasingly committed to a vision of things and a version of action that might be described as natural Christianity. His models for prayer and action come from Jesus, but his epistemology emerges not from any organized doctrine but from observation of, trust in, and love for the natural world and the people who live close to the earth.

"I can see it like a prophecy," Casy says, prognosticating about the fate of the people when tractors have made work "so easy that the wonder goes out of work, so efficient that the wonder goes out of the land and the working of it, and with the wonder the deep under-standing and the relation" (126). Like his Old and New Testament prototypes he sees the broad connections among things, under-stands the ominous signs of destruction of the natural order, and longs to save "the people" from the legal and economic machinery that is devouring their lives and driving them off their land. "If ya listen," he says, "you'll hear a movin' an' a sneakin', an' a rustlin', an'—an' a restlessness. They's stuff goin' on that the folks doin' it don't know nothin' about—yet. They's gonna come somepin onto all these folks goin' wes'—outa all their farms lef' lonely. They's gonna come a thing that's gonna change the whole country" (190).

Casy knows these things because he watches and listens and un-derstands signs and portents. He stays awake nights, watching the stars and listening to the sounds of animals in their burrows. He frequently speaks what he knows in parables drawn from nature:

But they's somepin worse'n the devil got hold a the country, an' it ain't gonna let go till it's chopped loose. Ever see one a them Gila monsters take hold . . . ? Grabs hold, an' you chop him in two an' his head hangs on. Chop him at the neck and his head hangs on. Got to take a screw driver an' pry his head apart to get him loose. An' while he's layin' there poison is drippin' an' drippin' into the hole he's made with his teeth. (139–40)

Casy's sense of the enormity of the evil coming upon the people is commensurate with his great reverence for creation. At Grampa Joad's funeral he quotes, "All that lives is holy" (157). He has little respect for the laws of man, returning repeatedly to simple expres-sions of natural law as the only reliable guide for human action: "Law changes," he says, "but 'got to's' go on. You got the right to do what you got to do" (153).

His understanding of human nature as well as his rudimentary awareness of the profound involvement of human emotions and de-sires and needs in the life of the physical body as well as the body politic make him a healer. When Grampa falls sick, Ma finds Casy and asks him simply, "You been aroun' sick people. . . . Grampa's sick. Won't you go take a look at him?" (148). Significantly enough, he can't fix a car, though he can administer comfort, healing, and leadership. All he can do when the car breaks down is shine the light for Tom and Al to see by. His work is with matters of "the sperit."

As the awareness of evil grows on Casy, so does his sense of mission. "I hear the way folks are feelin'," he says. "Goin' on all the time. I hear 'em an' feel 'em; an' they're beating their wings like a bird in an attic. Gonna bust their wings on a dusty winda tryin' ta get out" (275). Casy eventually dies by the principle of natural law, leading a strike, telling his attackers, "You got no right to starve people," and then, "You don' know what you're a-doin' " (433)—final words that powerfully recall Jesus' words, "Father, forgive them, for they know not what they do."

Casy's homegrown natural theology has been the subject of much critical comment, especially the Emersonian echoes in his much-cited insight that "maybe all men got one big soul ever'body's a part of" (24). It is from this essentially pantheistic vision that his politics derive. Ownership makes little sense to him beyond the natural claim to what one needs. The arbitrariness of man-made boundaries seems not simply to ignore but to violate natural laws of distribution and interdependence. Frederick Carpenter in his essay "The Philosophical Joads" sums up Casy's story in this way: "Unorthodox Jim Casy went into the Oklahoma wilderness to save his soul. And in the wilderness he experienced the religious feeling of identity with nature which has always been the heart of transcendental mysticism. . . . the corollary of this mystical philosophy is that man's self-seeking destroys the unity or 'holiness' of nature" (324–25).

Casy's cosmic perspective on human affairs, his involvement in the immediacies of human needs, and his deep attention to the natural world as a source of wisdom are all reiterated in a new key in the character of Doc, the wise man of *Cannery Row*. Robert Benton has pointed out that the "ecological" cast of Steinbeck's thinking is reflected in his characterization of Doc—a way of thinking that "causes him to see man as an organism related to a vast and complex ecosystem" (Astro and Hayashi 1971, 133). In chapter 2 of that book, the narrator pauses characteristically to take a step back from the canvas on which he is painting the colorful local scene and take a cosmic perspective. He sees Lee Chong the grocer and Mack and the boys "spinning in their orbits" (125). The short chapter ends with a prayer: "Our Father who art in nature, who has given the gift of survival to the coyote, the common brown rat, the English sparrow, the house fly and the moth, must have a great and overwhelming love for no-goods and blots-on-the-town and bums, and Mack and the boys. Virtues and graces and laziness and zest. Our Father who art in nature" (125).

In light of this presentation of natural religion as the ideological backdrop to the narrative, Doc's close and attentive knowledge of nature endows him with not only professional but also prophetic credibility. In subsequent chapters the virtues of a good naturalist, as attributes of Doc's character, are manifestations of virtue in a much larger sense; Doc's patience in observing and collecting specimens for study, his steady commitment to objectivity, and his curiosity itself are seen as forms of compassion. He answers Hazel's desultory questions with more seriousness than they deserve because "Doc had one mental habit he could not get over. When anyone asked a question, Doc thought he wanted to know the answer. That was the way with Doc. He never asked unless he wanted to know and he could not conceive of the brain that would ask without wanting to know" (143). The simplicity and straightforwardness of his scientific habit of mind appear as an almost childlike innocence, a quality of guilelessness that wins him universal trust among the ragged crowd who surround him.

At times Doc's steadiness of focus is broken by a kind of whimsy, itself related to wider spiritual vision. When Hazel, observing a crowd of stinkbugs on the ice plant, asks "What they got their asses up in the air for?" Doc's first answer is, "I looked them up recently—they're very common animals and one of the commonest things they do is put their tails up in the air. And in all the books there isn't one mention of the fact that they put their tails up in the air or why" (147). Pressed further with "Well, why do *you* think they do it?" Doc answers, "I think they're praying," and to Hazel's shocked response adds, "The remarkable thing . . . isn't that they put their tails up in the air—the really incredible thing is that we find it remarkable. We can only use ourselves as yardsticks. If we did something as inexplicable and strange we'd probably be praying—so maybe they're praying" (147–48). The exchange speaks volumes about the way Doc brings together observation, research, deductive and inductive reasoning, contemplation, and a gentle humor that seems to proceed out of a detachment from the entangled human perspective that few men achieve.

Steinbeck's narrators take whole chapters to give voice and color to the natural environments the characters inhabit, embedding in those descriptions much philosophy about the right relation between earth and its creatures. But it is in these small exchanges that draw attention to the minute designs of the natural world that the novels reveal how nature shapes vision and character, how a place known intimately—a farm, a field, a tidepool—can become, as Casy puts it, "a way of thinkin'."

Doc's general wisdom, like Casy's, spills over the boundaries of professional definition. At various times he has to remind petitioners that he is neither a medical doctor nor a veterinarian nor a psychiatrist. Like the Joads with their proprietary expectations of Casy as personal chaplain, Doc's cohorts expect him to be all of these things as well as spiritual counselor, confessor, and source of ready money:

Now Doc of the Western Biological Laboratory had no right to practice medicine. It was not his fault that everyone in the Row came to him for medical advice. Before he knew it he found himself running from shanty to shanty taking temperatures, giving physics, borrowing and delivering blankets and even taking food from house to house where mothers looked at him with inflamed eyes from their beds, and thanked him and put the full responsibility for their children's recovery on him. When a case got really out of hand he phoned a local doctor and sometimes one came if it seemed to be an emergency. But to the families it was all emergency. Doc didn't get much sleep. He lived on beer and canned sardines. (207–8)

Doc maintains his own spiritual and mental health by means of frequent retreats into music, poetry, and nature. His scrupulously scientific habit of mind is a counterpart to Casy's broadly intuitive epistemology but expresses the same deep reverence for what can be learned from the natural world.

Doc had to keep up his collecting. He tried to get to the good tides along the coast. The sea rocks and the beaches were his stock pile. He knew where every thing was when he wanted it. All the articles of his trade were filed away on the coast, sea cradles here, octopi here, tube worms in another place, sea pansies in another. He knew where to get them but he could not go for them exactly when he wanted. For Nature locked up the items and only released them occasionally. Doc had to know not only the tides but when a particular low tide was good in a particular place. When such a low tide occurred, he packed his collecting tools in his car, he packed his jars, his bottles, his plates and preservatives and he went to the beach or reef or rock ledge where the animals he needed were stored. (210–11)

Doc doesn't even need a clock but lives by a tidal pattern: "He could feel a tide change in his sleep" (218). His knowledge has penetrated to his very body and bones. This kind of knowledge depends on humility, attentiveness, and long fidelity to the habit of patient contemplation—qualities that are also the basis of Doc's legendary compassion. But committed as he is to scientific accuracy and truthtelling, he has also had to learn that "people didn't like you for telling the truth" (213). Once, he recalls, on a walking trip through the South, he repeatedly encountered people who asked him why he was walking through the country but were disturbed by his honest answer:

Because he loved true things he tried to explain. He said he was nervous and besides he wanted to see the country, smell the ground and look at grass and birds and trees, to savor the country, and there was no other way to do it save on foot. And people didn't like him for telling the truth. They scowled, or shook and tapped their heads, they laughed as though they knew it was a lie and they appreciated a liar. And some, afraid for their daughters or their pigs, told him to move on, to get going, just not to stop near their place if he knew what was good for him.

And so he stopped trying to tell the truth. He said he was doing it on a bet—that he stood to win a hundred dollars. Everyone liked him then and believed him. They asked him in to dinner and gave him a bed and they put lunches up for him and wished him good luck and thought he was a

*hell of a fine fellow. Doc still loved true things but he knew it was not a
general love and it could be a very dangerous mistress. (214)*

The recognition in this passage that the solitary poses a subtle but
vividly felt threat to the community recalls some of well-known stories about the suspicions Thoreau encountered among his fellows
in Concord or, more dramatically, the association of intimacy with
nature with witchcraft and occultism. Hawthorne's Roger Chilling-
worth in *The Scarlet Letter* illustrates this latter point; an herbalist
whose compendious knowledge of the healing powers of herbs derives from long association with Indians and a solitary life dedicated
to this study appears as a practitioner of "dark arts." More benevo-
lent images like that of "Johnny Appleseed" still mark as an eccentric
the individual who forsakes community life and communes with
nature.

Doc understands this common suspicion, and with a diplomacy
that is the measure of his great charity he takes care to foster his own
needs in a way that does not threaten or alienate him from the community that depends on him. His understanding of the natural order,
like Casy's, informs his social behavior. Much of Doc's activity
among his cohorts on Cannery Row is a kind of pastoral subterfuge.
Like Casy he is a shrewd assessor of human nature and calculates
his demands and concessions accordingly. He also serves as a hub
that draws people together in a way that makes community possible.
He understands, like Casy, the wide web of interdependency that
binds the things of this world and makes a mockery of short-sighted
ideas of ownership. His generosity has a character of matter-of-fact
common sense to it; it is simply the way of nature.

We do get an occasional ironic comment on the effects of such
natural sanctity on the more commercially minded: "Lee was indebted to Doc—deeply indebted. What Lee was having trouble comprehending was how his indebtedness to Doc made it necessary to
give credit to Mack" (227). But Doc knows that somehow things even
out, like water seeking its own level. He trusts some principle of
natural distribution as a basis for all moral action: people do what
they can do, they act on what they can understand, and as long as
they act in harmony with their nature things even out and we learn

from one another. Thus his admiration for Mack and the boys escapes condescension because he understands the necessity of their presence in a world that needs just such a corrective. "Look at them," he says:

They are your true philosophers. I think . . . that Mack and the boys know everything that has ever happened in the world and possibly everything that will happen. I think they survive in this particular world better than other people. In a time when people tear themselves to pieces with ambition and nervousness and covetousness, they are relaxed. All of our so-called successful men are sick men, with bad stomachs and bad souls, but Mack and the boys are healthy and curiously clean. They can do what they want. They can satisfy their appetites without calling them something else. (251–52)

Chapter 31 of *Cannery Row,* which details the life and frustrated enterprises of a gopher, serves as a parable to describe Doc's solitary, industrious life in the face of the social changes and chances that defeat his human ambitions. The gopher, like him, is busy, solitary, in the prime of life. He burrows into rich soil "on a little eminence" where he could watch Mack and the boys (300). He prepares an elaborate place for a female to join him and raise a family, but no female appears. He goes out to court one but comes back bitten. Finally, "he had to move two blocks up the hill to the dahlia garden where they put out traps every night" (302). Doc is, finally, the gopher in the dahlia garden. He adapts to an environment diminished in natural richness, unsympathetic to his higher ends but livable. He is a prophet unhonored by a mechanized, commercialized, secular culture, quietly, stubbornly cherishing ideals that culture has begun to threaten.

In these two figures, Casy and Doc, Steinbeck incorporates a complex vision of wisdom derived from attentiveness to the natural world. The best of what we call human virtue—compassion, forgiveness, clarity, flexibility—comes from the habit of attention. And in characters like these he would seem to be suggesting that nature teaches us what we need to know—and that our best teachers are those who have learned her lessons.

Notes

1. See, for example, Shigeharu Yoshizu, "Emerson and Steinbeck: On the Oriental Concept of Being" (1974); Duane R. Carr, "John Steinbeck, Twentieth-Century Romantic: A Study of the Early Works" (1976); and J. Edward Shamberger, "Grapes of Gladness: A Misconception of *Walden*" (1972).

2. For an explanation of Steinbeck's idea of "nonteleological thinking," see also Robert Murray Davis's introduction to *Steinbeck: A Collection of Critical Essays* (1972).

3. See also Floyd Stovall in *American Idealism* (1943), 164, for comment on Casy's Emersonian character.

Part Three:
Sea of Cortez

SEVEN

Searching for "What Is": Charles Darwin and John Steinbeck

Brian Railsback

Steinbeck patterned his attitude and approach to the Sea of Cortez adventure on Darwin's Beagle *voyage and when he returned commented that the Western Flyer expedition had tried to bring back Darwin's broader view of the biological world. Like Darwin, Steinbeck went to "see what we see, record what we find, and not fool ourselves with conventional scientific strictures." Steinbeck actively sought the objective viewpoint that Darwin strove to achieve ("is" thinking) but like Darwin recognized that his own humanity would ultimately prevent his attaining total objectivity. Darwin's influence is seminal for* The Log from the Sea of Cortez, *and his "biological view of our species" pervades many other Steinbeck works as well.*

The Sea of Cortez was for John Steinbeck what the Galapagos archipelago was for Charles Darwin: a pristine panorama of the natural world, perfect for the illustration of profound interpretations of biology. Steinbeck clearly realized the parallels between his and Ed Ricketts's expedition aboard the *Western Flyer* and Darwin's aboard the *Beagle*. Yet Steinbeck's recognition of Darwin's achievement goes beyond the superficial comparison of voyages. Evolutionary theory underscores the power of inductive, objective reasoning; it represents the first thorough attempt at a holistic view of *Homo sapiens* and nature that successfully challenges theological or philosophical preconceptions. For a novelist fascinated by evolutionary progress, natural selection, and the inductive search for truth—all things of central importance to his version of "what is" thinking—we should not be surprised to find Darwin's name mentioned with feeling and reverence in Steinbeck's most important treatise: *The Log from the Sea of Cortez*.

Trying to determine Steinbeck's first contact with Darwin and his theories is impossible, but he had a formal dose of evolutionary theory when he took general zoology at Hopkins Marine Station in the summer of 1923. Of all the important naturalists and biologists with interpretations of Darwinian theory that Steinbeck learned from, the first was William Emerson Ritter. Richard Astro has shown that Steinbeck's professor at Hopkins was C. V. Taylor, who studied at Berkeley under Charles Kofoid, who in turn "undoubtedly had come under the influence of the ideas of William Emerson Ritter," so that "Ritter's ideas were transmitted via Kofoid and Taylor to the impressionable Steinbeck" (1973, 44). In his biography *The True Adventures of John Steinbeck, Writer,* Jackson J. Benson suggests Steinbeck may have read some of Ritter's *The Unity of the Organism; or, The Organismal Conception of Life* (240).

In discussing the great naturalists, who possess a wider view than modern specialized scientists, Ritter writes: "Three names that stand out with mountain like conspicuousness among those who in modern times have made the idea of evolution a household possession [are] Lamarck, Darwin, and Wallace" (I, 75). Later, Ritter applauds the inductive method of Darwin and examines the unfolding of the naturalist's discovery of evolution from the intense curiosity of a youth aboard the *Beagle,* to the long consideration of parts that became a theory years later. Ritter's reflections on Darwin, few as they are, set a trend of admiration typical of other evolutionary thinkers Steinbeck read at a crucial period in the writer's development. Because of Ritter's influence in the course at Hopkins, the positive view of Darwin in Steinbeck's mind was probably set even before he met Edward F. Ricketts in 1930.

As much as Steinbeck's experience at Hopkins Marine Station may have given him some of the foundations upon which he built his mature work, class really began at Cannery Row with Ricketts— who was less a teacher and more a fellow classmate. As Benson and Astro have demonstrated, Ricketts, proprietor of Pacific Biological Laboratories and an enthusiastic naturalist/philosopher, exposed Steinbeck to a number of ideas relating to biology. Steinbeck came to Ricketts with some of his own ideas, however, as Joel W. Hedgpeth writes: "Steinbeck's interest in marine biology did not arise out of his association with Ed Ricketts. . . . the friendship with Ricketts probably developed in part out of a common interest in biology" (Astro and Hayashi 1971, 96). In the makeshift library at the lab, Steinbeck encountered many of the scientific books he read between 1930 and 1940—the period in which most of his ideas concerning biology were formed. Looking through some of these books, a perusal now possible thanks to Robert DeMott's *Steinbeck's Reading: A Catalogue of Books Owned and Borrowed,* we can see where Darwin's name might have come up again and again in those days of reading and studying at Pacific Biological Laboratories. Darwin is sometimes debated and often revered in works on hand at the lab, such as John Elof Boodin's *Cosmic Evolution,* Henri Bergson's *Creative Evolution,* William Beebe's *Galapagos World's End,* and Mark Graubard's *Man the Slave and Master.*

One important evolutionary thinker who emerges early in Ricketts's and Steinbeck's investigations is Jan Christiaan Smuts. Hedgpeth observes that during the spring of 1932, Smuts's book was one of "Ed's principal household gods" along with W. C. Allee's *Animal Aggregations* and John Elof Boodin's *A Realistic Universe* (pt. 1, 12). Smuts is a votarist of Darwinian theory; he finds evolution a keystone of a wider vision, a holistic way of viewing nature, and is more explicit in linking Darwin to this way of thinking than Ritter. In the preface of *Holism and Evolution,* Smuts writes that "evolution in the mind of Darwin was, like the Copernican revolution, a new viewpoint, from which vast masses of biological knowledge already existing fell into new alignments and became the illustration of a great new Principle" (6). In several places throughout the book, he elevates Darwin and evolution, writing that the "view-point of Evolution as creative, of a real progressive creation still going forward in the universe instead of having been completed in the past, of the sum of reality not as constant but as progressively increasing in the course of evolution, is a new departure of the nineteenth century, and it is perhaps one of the most significant departures in the whole range of human thought" (89).

Smuts recognizes that Darwinian theory presents an examination of the whole and takes into account the interrelations of nature and how things in this larger view look different—and no doubt come closer to the truth—than things considered in the narrow, pre-Darwinian view of nature as static. In his enthusiasm for the creative aspects of evolution, Smuts interprets natural selection as a progressive force and the struggle for survival as a "form of comradeship, of social co-operation and mutual help" (218). In essence, we are all together in a great whole, and every struggle contributes—through selection—to the progress of all.

If Steinbeck did read these passages, and there is little reason to doubt that he did, he would have been given a picture of Darwin as a revolutionary thinker who broke through to a way of seeing that perceives an open, natural system of progress, interrelation, and co-operation. Steinbeck's fiction in many ways dramatizes such a holistic system; Smuts's book, like Ritter's, is significant because it links Darwin to that system and credits the naturalist's search for truth as largely originating the discovery of the whole of nature.

Having encountered many references to Darwin and his work, and considering the intense interest Steinbeck had in biology, he certainly encountered Darwin's famous *The Origin of Species* indirectly if he did not actually read it. The novelist does make reference to the work in *Sweet Thursday*. Discussing the "inductive leap" in which "everything falls into place, irrelevancies relate, dissonance becomes harmony, and nonsense wears a crown of meaning," Steinbeck credits Darwin with achieving this "greatest mystery of the human mind" along with such greats as Newton and Einstein (28). "Charles Darwin and his *Origin of Species* flashed complete in one second," Steinbeck writes, "and he spent the rest of his life backing it up" (28). Steinbeck seems to have done a bit of mythmaking here, for Darwin never claimed his theory "flashed complete" in such a way. The inductive process the novelist suggests, however, in which after a gathering of facts a theory emerges, does indicate his knowledge of Darwin's method. Furthermore, Steinbeck correctly states that Darwin spent the rest of his life "backing it up" (Darwin produced six editions, the last in 1872, ten years before his death).

If indeed Steinbeck read a copy of *The Origin of Species*, he would have seen a perfect illustration of the kind of inductive, wide-open method he and Ed so admired. In the first paragraph of *Origin*, Darwin summarizes his inductive process:

When on board H.M.S. "Beagle," as naturalist, I was much struck with certain facts in the distribution of the organic beings inhabiting South America. . . . These facts, as will be seen in the later chapters of this volume, seemed to throw some light on the origin of species. . . . On my re-

turn home, it occurred to me, in 1837, that something might perhaps be made out of this question by patiently accumulating and reflecting on all sorts of facts which could possibly have any bearing on it. After five years' work I allowed myself to speculate on the subject, and drew up some short notes; these enlarged in 1844 into a sketch of the conclusions . . . from that period to the present day [1859] I have steadily pursued the same object (Modern Library edition 35).

Also evident in *The Origin of Species* is Darwin's ability to use the method outlined above without the impairments of ego, preconceptions, or prejudices. As Peter Brent remarks in his biography, *Charles Darwin: A Man of Enlarged Curiosity,* "He could regard the world with an eye that saw only what was in front of it, unobscured by expectation. The only question was whether he had the courage to see with this childlike clarity. It was his lifelong gift and his intellectual salvation that he had" (169). In his great book, Darwin makes this capacity clear when he writes his discovery "that the view which most naturalists until recently entertained, and which I formerly entertained—namely that each species has been independently created— is erroneous" (*Origin* 38). In his determination to find what is true, Darwin has the courage to defy preconceptions that even he embraced (before his voyage on the *Beagle,* young Darwin was prepared—albeit halfheartedly—to be a clergyman).

The Origin of Species illustrates the kind of process Ricketts and Steinbeck made an ideal: it shows a man's attempt to find truth by abandoning popular beliefs, making observations firsthand, gathering the facts together, and making the inductive leap to discover a great principle. No wonder Darwin's name appears in the oft-quoted definition of nonteleological thinking that Ricketts passed on to Steinbeck for inclusion in *Sea of Cortez:* "Non-teleological ideas derive through 'is' thinking, associated with natural selection as Darwin seems to have understood it. . . . Non-teleological thinking concerns itself primarily not with what should be, or could be, or might be, but rather with what actually 'is'—attempting at most to answer the already sufficiently difficult questions *what* or *how,* instead of *why*" (*LSC* 160). As an observation of nature from an objective perspective of the whole that is as wide as possible, *The Origin of Species* provides a great example of "is" thinking. Steinbeck and Ricketts share the same view of "what is" in nature that Darwin not only saw but largely originated: the view of the whole, with humans as a part of all natural interrelations.

Ricketts and Steinbeck would not have missed the holistic perspective evident in Darwin's famous "tangled bank" metaphor in the concluding paragraph of *Origin:* "It is interesting to contemplate a tangled bank, clothed with many plants of many kinds, with birds singing on the bushes, with various insects flitting about, and with worms crawling through the damp earth, and to reflect that these elaborately constructed forms, so different from each other, and dependent upon each other in so complex a manner, have all been produced by laws acting around us" (131). Indeed, Smuts's book would have pointed this passage out to them, for he quotes it and then writes "[it is] the expression of a great selfless soul, who sought truth utterly and fearlessly, and was in the end vouchsafed a vision of the truth which perhaps has never been surpassed in its fullness and grandeur" (187). Darwin's metaphor demonstrates a way of seeing that takes in the many species, from simple to complex, and comprehends their interrelations; this perspective puts every individual organism in sync with all others—nothing, including *Homo sapiens,* can be so exalted as to be set aside from the biological realities of environment, heredity, selection, and evolution. *The Origin of Species,* by its conception and by its subject, illustrates much of what Steinbeck dramatizes in his writing.

For direct evidence of Steinbeck's comprehension of the essentials of evolution—that natural selection derived from the struggle for survival is the primary engine of species evolution—we need look no further than the *Log.* Steinbeck's fascination for the natural struggle is obvious in many of his entries that, significantly, do not appear in Ricketts's journal of the trip. Although Ricketts was certainly familiar with Darwin, he only mentions him once in his journal, in passing, while discussing dolphins (Hedgpeth 1978, pt. 2, 113). The only other mention of Darwin by Ricketts that ends up in *The Log from the Sea of Cortez* comes from the essay on nonteleology he passed on to Steinbeck. All other references to Darwin in the *Log* come from Steinbeck. Furthermore, the Darwinian emphasis on survival and species competition is Steinbeck's. Ricketts's journal has a tone of acceptance, perfectly summed up in Ed's comment that " 'Going along with' is merely an articulate expression for a process of relaxation whereby you go along with, rather than fight against, the pace of external events over which you have no control" (Hedgpeth 1978, pt. 2, 147). When observing animal life in the Sea of Cortez, Ricketts does not seem interested in the struggle for existence. Steinbeck delights in the great competition.

Peering into the sea near Magdalena Bay, Steinbeck notices the active food chain: "Everything ate everything else with a furious exuberance" (*LSC* 54). Nothing like this is found in Ricketts's account. Later, looking into the littoral at Cape San Lucas, Steinbeck observes "a vital competition for existence" where clinging to the rocks the starfish, urchins, and other animals fight back at the pounding sea "with a kind of joyful survival" (67). He adds, "This ferocious survival quotient excites us and makes us feel good, and from the crawling, fighting, resisting qualities of the animals, it almost seems that they are excited too" (67). This emphasis on survival comes entirely from Steinbeck; the only comment along these lines from Ricketts, observing the same scene, is "It seemed to me that life here is very fierce" (Hedgpeth 1978, pt. 2, 114). Throughout the *Log*, Steinbeck continues to make observations on this struggle, and near the end of the book he lets loose his own enthusiasm for what he has seen: "There would seem to be only one commandment for living things: Survive!" (287). In this same passage his understanding of the need for competition becomes clear: "This commandment decrees the death and destruction of myriads of individuals for the survival of the whole" (287). This general view is the one that Steinbeck, and not Ricketts, brought to *The Log from the Sea of Cortez*.

Steinbeck's fascination with competition often moves to observations of the human species. "It is difficult," he writes, "when watching the little beasts, not to trace human parallels" (110). Although he realizes that personification of animals can be a pitfall, Steinbeck cannot help but compare our species to others (Darwin never said the human *is* a monkey, only that we are subject to the same ecological laws—a viewpoint Steinbeck adopts when making human/animal parallels). The author goes on to note that a group of humans who dominate an area, driving all competitors out, will actually deteriorate because of the lack of competition. Meanwhile, the surviving remnants of the driven will toughen in their struggle to survive, finally becoming stronger than their atrophied conquerors—this particular dynamic is important in *The Grapes of Wrath*. From this discussion (*LSC* 111–12), Steinbeck reveals his belief that natural selection and evolution can be carried over to *Homo sapiens*. Whether the struggle is among crabs in a tide pool or among people in a lush farm basin, competition weeds out the weak, leaves only the vigorous, and selects the "strong blood" (a term Steinbeck uses in articles he wrote about migrants in 1936—reprinted in *The Harvest Gypsies*, 1988). He speaks of this process later in the *Log*, in his comments about the conquests of the Incas by Spaniards who, eventually atrophied in their conquest, are in turn overtaken by the native Peruvians. Clearly he links competition and natural selection to progress of *any* species: "Perhaps the pattern of struggle is so deeply imprinted in the genes of all life conceived in this benevolently hostile planet that the removal of obstacles automatically atrophies a survival drive" (*LSC* 269).

That Steinbeck understood and adopted the mechanics of Darwinian theory through his reading (even if he never saw the *Origin*) is certain; just as important, he must have become acquainted with Darwin, the man, from the naturalist's journal of the voyage of the *Beagle*. Steinbeck owned a copy of *Journal of Researches Into the Natural History and Geology of the Countries Visited During the Voyage of the H.M.S. "Beagle,"* which, considering the references to the book in the *Log*, he probably read in preparation for his the expedition to the gulf (DeMott 1984, 32). Clearly Steinbeck connects, perhaps romantically, his expedition to the Sea of Cortez and Darwin's voyage in the *Beagle*. The day the *Western Flyer* returned from the gulf and put in at San Diego, Steinbeck is quoted in a United Press release: "It seems that some of the broader, more general aspects of the tie-in of all animal species with one another have been lost since Darwin went out of the picture. We are trying in our small way to get back a phase of that broader view" (Hedgpeth 1978, pt. 2, 2). This quotation not only shows that Steinbeck had Darwin on his mind during the trip but also that the novelist credits the naturalist with a wider perspective. This view is also emphasized in the introduction to the *Log*: "Our curiosity was not limited, but was as wide and horizonless as that of Darwin or Agassiz or Linnaeus or Pliny" (2). The identification of

Darwin as a "wide and horizonless" thinker is one of Steinbeck's highest compliments.

From his reading of Darwin's journal, Steinbeck certainly admires the naturalist's method and writes nostalgically of it in the *Log*. He notes that the mission of the *Western Flyer* parallels that of the *Beagle* in terms of the collection of species on a sweeping scale. Where the *Beagle* could plod on for five years, the expedition to the gulf must conclude in just six weeks. Steinbeck laments the acceleration of his trip and envies the pace of Darwin's expedition. He begins a long passage on Darwin's methods by writing, "In a way, ours is the older method, somewhat like that of Darwin on the *Beagle*" (61). Traveling under sail or by horse, Darwin kept "the proper pace for a naturalist," for "we must have time to think and to look and to consider" (70). A key observation follows, which suggests Steinbeck's belief that Darwin's inductive method is indeed the way to capture the whole view that the novelist and Ricketts seek above all: "And the modern process—that of looking quickly at the whole field and then diving down to the particular—was reversed by Darwin. Out of long long consideration of the parts he emerged with a sense of the whole" (70). Although Steinbeck concedes that to imitate Darwin's pace, to take to a sailing ship or a horse, would be "romantic and silly," he finishes this passage on Darwin by noting, "We can and do look on the measured, slow-paced accumulation of sight and thought of the Darwins with a nostalgic longing" (71). His comments on Darwin here do suggest some firsthand knowledge of *The Origin of Species*, since the journal of the *Beagle* presents the trip that later inspired the theory of evolution—the "long long consideration of parts" commenced after the ship dropped anchor at Falmouth, England. Yet the journal documents the collecting of those parts from which the whole would emerge, as Steinbeck is keenly aware.

In many ways the expedition of the *Western Flyer* does parallel that of the *Beagle*. Although on colossally different scales, both are journeys of collection and observation, narrated by men uniquely humble and uniquely bent on recording what is true. Darwin's journal is an account of his observations as naturalist on a surveying voyage that circumnavigated the world. One of the many themes that emerges concerns the superiority of observation and experience over secondhand authority. For example, Darwin counters the Spanish geographer Felix de Azara's comments about the Agouti (a hare-like animal of South America) with observations of his own (*Beagle*, Penguin edition 86–87). He likewise overturns the notion that large animals require lush vegetation, a "prejudice [that] has probably been derived from India," from his observation of animal populations near Cape Town (98). Darwin notices that authorities on the Tahitians have misled him and dismisses with observations the belief that these Polynesians have become a gloomy people (301). After an arduous trip up the Santa Cruz River in Patagonia the naturalist wryly comments on the myth that going a little hungry can be a good thing: "Let those alone who have never tried it, exclaim about the comfort of a light stomach and an easy digestion" (170).

Pitting observation against authority, Darwin seems to delight in any discovery of truth that overturns an accepted falsehood. He augments this tendency with occasional comments upon the folly of ill-conceived theorizing. Encountering the half-buried remains of a Mastodon, he laughs at the locals' deduction concerning the fossil: "the necessity of a theory being felt, they came to the conclusion, that . . . the mastodon formerly was a burrowing animal!" (124). He also dismisses the supernatural explanation given by the inhabitants of Concepción, Chile, for the eruptions of a nearby volcano as a "silly belief" borne of a need "to apply the witchcraft to the point where their knowledge stopped" (233). In the conclusion of the journal, Darwin cautions about faulty theorizing, from making deductions without the proper observations: "I have found to my cost, a constant tendency to fill up the wide gaps of knowledge, by inaccurate and superficial hypotheses" (377).

The Log from the Sea of Cortez is also a journal of observations, and Steinbeck writes in the introduction that the goal "to observe the distribution of invertebrates" justifies calling the trip an expedition (2). The plan for the trip is to go wide open, as Steinbeck understood Darwin to do, and "see what we see, record what we find, and not fool ourselves with conventional scientific strictures" (3). The scientific strictures are those blinders that shut out a view of the whole. In the passage concerning Darwin's method, Steinbeck comments on the method of "our time" in which "the young biologists [are] tearing off pieces of their subject, tatters of the life forms, like sharks tearing out hunks of a dead horse, looking at them, tossing them away" (70). As a book with its basis in the observed world, the *Log*, like Darwin's journal, contains passages critical of deductions that defy reality. In a passage reminiscent of Darwin, Steinbeck discusses facts that offset a theory explaining the similarity among flora and fauna of the west and east coasts of Baja. From this discussion he writes of the scientific method in general, noticing the tendency to preserve a good hypothesis, which has become "a thing in itself, a work of art," despite facts that shoot holes in it (213). He cites the examples of a "leading scientist" trying to find a reef, despite no indicative soundings, because "his mind told him [it] was there" or the incident of an "institution of learning" that could not accept the existence of sea otters after it had determined that they were extinct (213). As Darwin would find when he advanced his theory of evolution on a creationist world, Steinbeck notes that "beliefs persist long after their factual bases have been removed" (214).

The two journals represent attempts to record the world in the truest way; these are books in which factual observations reign supreme, where no quarter is given to error. Yet both authors, meticulous in the desire to be honest, acknowledge the difficulty of being true and objective. Darwin not only recognizes his ignorance or inadequacies throughout the journal, he also occasionally comments upon the warp of the perceptions. After leaving the confines of the *Beagle* (where Darwin suffered horrible bouts of seasickness), the naturalist knows that he sees the "very uninteresting" country of Maldonado in South America with heightened affection (*Beagle*, Penguin edition 71). He notices how the experience of a bad earthquake in Chile destroys one's belief in the solidity of earth, therefore conveying to the mind "a strange idea of insecurity" (229). Darwin comments on the inadequacy of language or preserved specimens to convey the reality of his experience. After describing San Salvador, he finally admits that "to paint the effect is a hopeless endeavour" (367). He writes that "one wishes to find language to express one's ideas" but that "epithet after epithet is found too weak to convey . . . the sensation of delight which the mind experiences" (367). Clearly Darwin wants to get it all right, but he would also be the last man to say he has the last word.

Steinbeck recognizes that the *Log*, though an attempt to observe invertebrate distribution in a most objective way, will also be "warped, as all knowledge patterns are warped, first, by the collective pressure and stream of our time and race, second by the thrust of our individual personalities" (2). Steinbeck writes that one can pickle a Mexican sierra for species identification while the experience of the living fish in its natural habitat remains lost (a passage reminiscent of Darwin's comments on the preservation of exotic butterflies). Despite preserved specimens and accurate descriptions, the full sense of the gulf must elude the reader—in short, no objective, absolutely clear presentation is possible. Because Steinbeck and his companions enter the gulf, giving and taking from it, they can never "observe a completely objective Sea of Cortez anyway" and therefore will not "be betrayed by this myth of permanent objective reality" (3–4). Although striving to observe and record the truth, neither Steinbeck nor Darwin has an ego big enough to believe that he will write up the perfect picture.

Because of the relative similarity of the expeditions, at least in respect to naturalism, coupled with the similar attitudes of the authors (Darwin just discovering his inductive methodology and Steinbeck in full comprehension of it, thanks to his reading and to Ed Ricketts), both journals have the same point of view. In his comparisons of the expeditions of the *Western Flyer* and the *Beagle,* Steinbeck recognizes the similarities in approach as well as the differences in scope and Zeitgeist. An understanding of Darwin's methods and his theories, as well as the naturalist's contribution to holistic thought, would be enough to impress an amateur biologist like Steinbeck. Yet Steinbeck's reading of the *Beagle* journal also allowed him to be acquainted with Darwin's personality.

The tone of the following passage from the *Log* echoes the same kind of praise for Darwin that we find in some of the books Steinbeck read; Steinbeck writes about no one else in the *Log* with such unabashed enthusiasm:

On this day, the sun glowing on the morning beach made us feel good. It reminded us of Charles Darwin, who arrived late at night on the Beagle *in the Bay of Valparaiso. In the morning he awakened and looked ashore and he felt so well that he wrote, "When morning came everything appeared delightful. After Tierra del Fuego, the climate felt quite deli-*

cious, the atmosphere so dry and the heavens so clear and blue with the sun shining brightly, that all nature seemed sparkling with life." Darwin was not saying how it was with Valparaiso, but rather how it was with him. Being a naturalist, he said, "All nature seemed sparkling with life," but actually it was he who was sparkling. He felt so very fine that he can, in these charged though general adjectives, translate his ecstasy over a hundred years to us. And we can feel how he stretched his muscles in the morning air and perhaps took off his hat—we hope a bowler—and tossed it and caught it.

On this morning, we felt the same way at Concepción Bay. "Everything appeared delightful." (229)

Of all the biologists and scientists that Steinbeck read, only Darwin receives such personal affection. The novelist's identification with Darwin is presented with longing. Steinbeck would like to follow the naturalist's methods if it were possible, and from a passage in the *Beagle* journal the novelist not only wants to bridge a century by reading—he does so by imagining as well. Steinbeck's picture of Darwin "sparkling with life" or tossing a bowler is not only enthusiastic but rosy; he renders Darwin in the same tone he renders Ed Ricketts. Earlier in the *Log* he nostalgically pictures Darwin scooping up a jellyfish or staring into the sea over the ship's rail; Steinbeck praises this man whose thinking and writing possess "the slow heave of a sailing ship, and the patience of waiting for a tide" (70). From his reading, we can easily imagine how Steinbeck would come to admire the theories and methods of Darwin. Considering that the method and point of view of the journal parallel the *Log* in many ways, we need not wonder that Steinbeck enthusiastically compares his expedition to Darwin's—the naturalist pioneers a way of thinking that the novelist not only adopts but spends most of a lifetime depicting.

Steinbeck and Darwin certainly found their own version of "what is": a view of the whole. In his journal, Darwin comments that full comprehension of the beauty of a land is enhanced by knowledge of the whole—exotic lands and one's home appreciate in beauty by the possibility of comparison. Darwin writes, "As in music, the person who understands every note will, if he also possesses a proper taste, more thoroughly enjoy the whole, so he who examines each part of a fine view, may also thoroughly comprehend the full and combined effect" (*Beagle*, Penguin edition 373). When we consider the whole in regard to the natural scheme, we can realize our place in the world. As Steinbeck recognized, Darwin's conception of the whole of nature—his wide view—made the theory of evolution possible.

Of course, Steinbeck considers the wide view and the whole in the *Log*. Like Darwin, he considers things as they are, in their totality and interrelations. As Steinbeck writes, "The whole picture is portrayed by *is*" (178–79). An excellent example of Steinbeck employing this kind of thinking occurs in his discussion of Japanese fishing boats in the gulf, in which he tries to see the whole of the problem. These dredge boats scooped up the bottom for shrimp and killed about everything else caught. Steinbeck observes that the slaughter represents a terrible waste, particularly to the Mexican people who sorely need the squandered resource. Yet the author likes the Japanese fishermen, realizing that from their viewpoint they have no idea of what they are doing. Later, after Tiny (a fisherman crewing on the *Western Flyer*) complains of the waste, Steinbeck widens the view, recalling that while humans will suffer due to the loss, other creatures will benefit—from the seagulls gorging what they can from the water's surface to bacteria feeding on detritus at the sea bottom. This is the whole perspective at work: "To each group, of course, there must be waste—the dead fish to man, the broken pieces to gulls, the bones to some and the scales to others—but to the whole, there is no waste" (313).

We can see how this view of the ecosystem discovers the human as just another link in the food chain. Such thinking slips outside the limited wants of *Homo sapiens*. Steinbeck writes that our "most prized" understanding is "the attempt to say that man is related to the whole thing," a viewpoint that "made a Jesus, a St. Augustine, a St. Francis, a Roger Bacon, a Charles Darwin, and an Einstein" (257). So often when Steinbeck speaks glowingly of the whole viewpoint, the recognition of "what is," Darwin's name appears.

Steinbeck finds a kindred spirit in Charles Darwin. An important point, especially if we are to understand the biological slant of Steinbeck's fiction, is that the novelist appears to have been more interested in Darwin than Ed Ricketts. Of course, Ricketts and Steinbeck share many views, as Astro carefully demonstrates, and their holistic approach to nature is similar (Steinbeck's comments about the Japanese fisherman expand what Ricketts says about them in his journal, for example).

Yet the emphasis on Darwin and the struggle for survival is the novelist's own. Why? As Astro observes, Ricketts's approach to life dismisses all "goal-oriented activity" except the concept of breaking through, while Steinbeck "advocates a philosophy of action" (1973, 73). In Darwin, Steinbeck would see in many ways the kind of writer who would agree with his and Ricketts's inductive, holistic method; however, the naturalist's evolutionary theory presents a scheme of progress. Steinbeck uses this theory to dramatize a natural means of human progression. Add to this conception Smuts's view of natural selection as a creative force, anthropologist Robert Briffault's linking of evolution to human social improvement (particularly notable in *The Making of Humanity*, in Steinbeck's personal library [De-Mott 1984, 18]), and the result is a Darwinian process of development for *Homo sapiens* emphasized in Steinbeck's work, not Ricketts's. Evolution is a theory based on conflict and therefore naturally lends itself to dramatization in fiction (which, after all, feeds on conflict for dramatic tension). We do not have to analyze Steinbeck's novels and stories very deeply to see that most of his serious works derive from vigorous conflict, the same kind of fierce struggle for life he so admires in the tide pools.

To some extent, the parallel expeditions of Darwin and Steinbeck might even leave Ricketts behind. Darwin "translates over a hundred years" to Steinbeck indirectly through a range of writers like Ritter and Smuts and directly through the *Beagle* journal, if not *The Origin of Species*. The expeditions parallel in approach, as journeys of collection and observation, as inductive approaches to the whole. If we use Darwin as a pilot, an expedition through many of John Steinbeck's books reveals a biological view of our species that the novelist carefully charted in *The Log from the Sea of Cortez*.

EIGHT

"The Poetry of Scientific Thinking": Steinbeck's *Log from the Sea of Cortez* and Scientific Travel Narrative

Stanley Brodwin

Together with works by Cook, Humboldt, Forbes, and Darwin, The Log from the Sea of Cortez *belongs to literature's great scientific travel narratives. Like the best of its predecessors,* The Log *transcends simple narrative description by forming hypotheses and speculating on their relationship to broad natural functions. Steinbeck emulates Darwin in particular by exploring the aesthetic, romantic, and religious as well as scientific aspects of what he observed and felt. Thus Steinbeck rejuvenates the role of the poet-naturalist and recaptures the poetry in scientific thinking, exemplified by his vision of the hypothesis as a work of art "beautiful and whole" in its own right, capable of retaining that holistic beauty even when proved wrong.*

> They [Galileo, Einstein] were romantics, just as today the only true poets are found among the physicists, mathematicians and biochemists.
> —Steinbeck, cited in *The Steinbeck Newsletter*, 5, 1992

> I discovered long ago in collecting and classifying marine animals that what I found was closely intermeshed with how I felt at the moment. External reality has a way of being not so external after all.
> —*Travels with Charley*, 1961

Shortly after completing his first draft of *The Log from the Sea of Cortez*, subtitled *A Leisurely Journal of Travel and Research*, Steinbeck wrote to Pascal Covici on 4 July 1941:

This book is very carefully planned and designed Pat, but I don't think its plan will be immediately apparent. And again there are four levels of state-ment in it and . . . few will follow it down to the fourth. I even think that it is a new kind of writing. I told you once that I found a great poetry in scientific thinking. Perhaps I haven't done it but I've tried and it is there to be done. (SLL 232)

In this oft-quoted and challenging passage, Steinbeck gives us a re-vealing epitome concerning his artistic preoccupation with form and structure, so clearly reflected in his work as a whole.[1] The "four levels" statement still remains open to critical debate, although I would offer a provisional analysis that the *Log* does preoccupy itself thematically with four of the most fundamental questions central to the Darwinian "revolution" and the way they were reshaped or re-interpreted: the problem of "means and ends," the meaning of bio-logical and environmental "function," the crucial theological and scientific meaning of teleology, and, finally, a new apprehension of the nature of Time itself.[2] Yet whatever the final truth may be, what I am most concerned with here is the broader relationship and aes-thetic connection Steinbeck affirms between the poetry of scientific thinking and the complex ways they find formal literary expression in a work of art.

This question is trenchantly announced in the very first para-graph of the *Log*, where Steinbeck asserts not only that "the design of a book is the pattern of a reality controlled and shaped by the mind of the writer" but also that this is often unrecognized when it comes to "books of fact." Still, the essential point is that the "impulse which drives a man to poetry will send another man into the tide-pools and force him to try to report what he finds there. Why is an expedition to Tibet undertaken, or a sea bottom dredged?" (1).

Why, indeed? Steinbeck offers no definitive answer to an impulse that may spring from many factors but suggests one at least graced by both simplicity and common sense: "We were curious. Our curi-osity was not limited, but was as wide and horizonless as that of Dar-win or Agassiz or Linnaeus or Pliny" (2). But "curiosity" is the in-itiatory drive; in the end, there must emerge "some structure in modeled imitation of the observed reality" whose construct will in any case be "warped" by the "collective pressure . . . of our time and race" (2)—words that echo Hippolyte Taine's influential theory of literary naturalism.

This theory, first developed by Taine (1828–1893) in his *Histoire de la littérature Anglaise* (1864; Eng. trans. 1871–1872), is typical of the post-Darwinian impulse to explain cultural and social phenomena from a strictly "scientific" and deterministic perspective. For Taine, three major interrelated factors were responsible for the development and character of any national literature and its most distinctive writers: race, the historical "moment," and the "milieu," or predominant social and physical environment. These ideas became commonplace in defining, however loosely, literary naturalism, and Steinbeck here reflects their continuing presence. But Steinbeck significantly adds the unpredictable factor of "individual personalities" (2) to the equation. Thus, a "permanent objective reality" (4) is not, nor can ever be, the ultimate goal of a work whose form must somehow reveal the intrinsic poetry in scientific thinking so firmly based, as Steinbeck knew, on speculation, observation, and the formulation of hypotheses. A perfect illustration of Steinbeck's insight into the problem of poetry and "fact," hypothesis and art, comes in chapter 17 of the *Log*, when he mulls over an ecological "riddle" (210) concerning certain mollusks and crustaceans that are trapped in an ecological "blind alley" where they ought not to flourish. After considering the various answers given by scientists, Steinbeck concludes that the "literature of science is filled with answers found when the question propounded had an entirely different direction and end" (213). For

there is one great difficulty with a good hypothesis. When it is completed and rounded, the corners smooth and the content cohesive and coherent, it is likely to become a thing in itself, a work of art. It is then like a finished sonnet or a painting completed. One hates to disturb it. Even if subsequent information should shoot a hole in it, one hates to tear it down because it was once beautiful and whole. (213)

If a hypothesis can take on the finished form of a work of art, then a work of art itself can be—is—an aesthetic analysis of the "design" of nature or reality, both subject to criticism or interpretive revision. On their profoundest levels of epistemological organization, both scientist and poet teach us how to "know" physical or "spiritual" or "inner" reality. Their methods, superficially different, are, in essence, one. No matter how "revised," a good hypothesis and a work of art retain their ultimate value of being "beautiful and whole."

Surely, this understanding of the relationship between science and art lies at the heart of Steinbeck's relationship with Ricketts as well as the formal artistic tasks that confronted him in the writing of the *Log*. If the *Log* was to be a truly "new" form, a special genre, in fact, Steinbeck had to imbue its structure with a romantic tone of spiritual expansiveness, search and discovery, but without violating or distorting those "objective" elements of observed reality, be they the marine life in the tide pools or human social life in Tibet, Mexico, or America.

To explore the question of genre, therefore, seems to me crucial in order to understand the nature of Steinbeck's achievement in the *Log*, especially in the way he managed his collaboration with and transformation of the raw material of his and Ricketts's journals and in the way he imaginatively structured the essential linear pattern of the expedition itself and its episodic units into a narrative that not only is holistic and nonteleological in its thematic matter but also realizes in its action the organic relationship between aesthetic unity and scientific hypothesis. This approach may be what Steinbeck considered a "new kind of writing," although some of the literary "devices" he employed are those any sophisticated writer could use in transforming the reality of brute "fact" and direct experience into both a metaphoric and fresh philosophic statement about life and the laws of nature. The *Log* succeeds in doing just that but something more as well in its multilayered patterns of theme, tropes, and scientific speculation. It explicitly demands theological—indeed "mystical" perspectives and attitudes—in order to grasp the full import of what Steinbeck and Ricketts had to say about the laws of man and nature.

What the *Log* also succeeds in doing is to remind us that it is, in proper evolutionary fashion, a work that is a new species of the scientific-travel genre, a genre with its own acknowledged historical development and impact on Western thought, its own heroes and adventurers, whether on land or sea, its own masterpieces of "revolutionary" influence and lasting literary value. The *Log* reminds us too—especially through its allusions to great scientists, Darwin above all—that it is part of a history and that to understand its uniqueness or at least its special character and contribution, we have to acknowledge its predecessors and the problems of form and structure that earlier scientific adventurers confronted in fashioning their records of reality. For the *Log* does fall into a long and extraordinarily significant line of scientific-travel books of which Darwin's *Voyage of the "Beagle"* (1839) is judged the masterpiece. It is certainly the most relevant example of the genre for Steinbeck (and Ricketts) who alludes to it, as we shall see, in a number of thematically complex ways. It is important to note, too, that Darwin himself openly acknowledged that his book was profoundly influenced by the inspirational and methodological ideas of Alexander von Humboldt's *Personal Narrative of Travels* (trans. 1814–1829).

By discussing a few "standard" classics of this genre, therefore, we can perhaps grasp some of the essential structural problems inherent in the form and examine, however cursorily, each author's "spiritual" purpose in developing a scientific-adventure narrative beyond the obvious necessity of recording fresh information or titillating the reader with descriptions of exotic locales, though often the two are inextricably mingled, as indeed they are in the *Log*. But for the reader who sought more than surface description, the genre had to fulfill deeper needs; as a reviewer of Humboldt's *Narrative of Travels* insisted: "We toil through them with the certainty that some ingenious theory, some beautiful illustration, some curious facts will be brought to elucidate the point in question" (Kellner 98).

We may use this statement as a critical gloss on the works I have chosen to comment upon briefly: Captain Cook's three "Voyages of Discovery" (1768–1780), Humboldt's *Narrative,* Darwin's *Voyage of the "Beagle,"* and, finally, Edward Forbes's *The Natural History of the European Seas* (1859), the pioneering narrative of marine biology.[3] Each work is truly monumental in the history of scientific exploration as well as being a major exemplum of the genre. Of course, we will not find in these works the kind of transcendental poetry Steinbeck and Ricketts strove for in the *Log:* a vision of reality rooted in the observed facts of littoral and "primitive" Mexican village life employed to validate a nonteleological and holistic philosophy that can be expressed (in Ricketts's terms) only in the "imaginary" equation of the square root of minus one π, the mathematical metaphor for God, Nature, the Tao, or whatever transcendental term best expresses the Cosmic Pattern of Ultimate Reality on whose right hand man, as a "triumphant race" will finally "direct with pure intelligence the ordering of the universe" (103).[4] The poetry and rhetorical elevation in our other works rest upon radically different perspectives and stylistic techniques, although they have one technical problem in common: how to transform the normally prosaic everyday journal account into an aesthetically flowing and compelling narrative that offers the reader the sweep of an "epic" experience even as it limns an ingenious theory or beautiful illustration of the law of nature, the hypothesis or "point in question."

But the poetry of the genre is created by more than a sense of epic adventure; it resides more profoundly in "scientific thinking," the methodology of the scientific mind that controls the purposes of the narrator struggling to penetrate, if not resolve, questions of still greater mystery. Methodology is here what structure is to fiction; it determines perspectives, embodies tensions, creates order out of disorder; finally, through the organizing and yet suggestive power of the hypothesis-as-structure, our sensory experience and imaginations are challenged, and we must readjust our "vision" about the way the world functions. The end is always a thrill of liberation (or terror for some) in which the "real" and the "romantic" are bound together.

Method is, therefore, the underlying aesthetic dynamic of this genre. The basic unit of the form, the journal, is paradoxically wide-ranging within the time-imposed limits as it records a variety of events as a type of realistic reporting and allows an immense latitude for personal reflection. Ricketts exploited the form in this way for he knew, as he wrote in his essay "The Morphology of the Sea of Cortez," that "this little trip of ours was becoming a thing and a dual thing, with collecting and eating and sleeping merging with the thinking-speculating activity," leading to the perception that they were "all parts of a *larger whole* [his italics] and *we could begin to feel its nature but not its size*" (Hedgpeth 1978, pt. 2, 171). And on 15 March 1940, Ricketts concluded a journal entry concerned with all his legal and personal preparation for the trip with this observation: "An essay on life at sea would consider navigation, food, and living aboard small boats; all are special techniques" (Hedgpeth 1978, pt.

2, 111). For part of the power and fascination of the genre is to enable the reader to identify with the special problems or techniques of adaptation and survival within the experience that the science-travel narrative recounts.

But the responsibility for the narrative fell upon the novelists who had to dramatize their emotions, personal encounters, scientific techniques, and the arguments of the nonteleological thesis from their journals into a work of poetic art. "The structure is a collaboration, but shaped mostly by John," Ricketts tells us (Hedgpeth 1978, pt. 2, 171), and upon that fact critical analysis of the *Log* is based.

The other narratives I have mentioned do not pose the problem of collaborative effort, but they nevertheless adumbrate many of the formal literary questions Steinbeck had to solve. Frederick Bracher provides a succinct, if oversimplified, statement about Steinbeck's strategy: "Its form preserves the rhythm of the voyage—feverish collection and preservation of specimens, followed by periods of leisurely talk as the boat goes on to another station" (Tedlock and Wicker 183). This description could apply, with qualification, to most scientific-travel narratives whose authors faced the challenge of maintaining the "rhythm" of the expedition. In the cases of Cook, Humboldt, and Darwin, the expeditions cover so much time and geographical space and, in Darwin's case, many social encounters not related to scientific concerns, that creating a complex, flowing rhythm other than that dictated by strict chronology may seem impossible. Even the six-week voyage of the *Western Flyer* poses this problem.

But there are always unifying elements that structure the chronology of seemingly disparate incidents into a coherent ordering of relevant detail. In the separate journals of Captain Cook's three extraordinary voyages of exploration, we are always aware of the momentous scientific challenges and goals he and the scientists accompanying him were absorbed by amid a welter of nautical detail: the measurement of the transit of Venus across the Sun, the problem of scurvy, the charting of new continents, the description of new cultures, and, in the third voyage, the attempt to discover the Northwest Passage. Cook's various purposes had, ultimately, a profound political as well as scientific impact on Western culture. But the "inner" character of Cook himself, apart from his reputation for efficiency and leadership, appears in one remarkable entry of 30 January 1774, on his second voyage, when he was blocked by ice floes from penetrating to the then unknown continent of Antarctica; he reveals his "ambition not only to go farther than any one had gone before, but as far as it was possible for man to go." It is a revelation that would do justice to the most Promethean characters of romantic literature. His tragic death in Hawaii in 1779 has only added to his near mythic stature. His journals still stand as an "epic" account in the genre of scientific "Voyages of Discovery," matched, perhaps, only by Hakluyt's *Principal Navigations, Voyages, Traffics and Discoveries of the English Nation* (1598–1600), a work, incidentally, with which Steinbeck was familiar.

With the towering figure of Alexander von Humboldt, whom Darwin in 1832 called his "sun" that "illumines everything I behold" (Clark 1984, 34), we encounter narratives whose methodology, though superseded by his admiring disciple, was nevertheless "revolutionary" for the late eighteenth and early nineteenth centuries. Humboldt's travels resulted in his own conversion from being an adherent of Neptunism to Plutonism (or Vulcanism) in understanding the processes of geological change and its influence on terrestrial and marine life. As one of his biographers writes, Humboldt was essentially concerned with "interpretation of large-scale phenomena" involving everything from the origin of tradewinds, the influence of warm and cold sea currents, distribution of annual temperatures, and the total impact of climate on animal and plant species (Kellner 93). In Humboldt's words:

Before discovering the laws of nature, it is necessary to examine the causes of local perturbations and to obtain a knowledge of the average state of the atmosphere and the recurrent type of its variations. Of the whole picture presented to us by physics, only the facts are stable and certain. The theories, children of our opinions, are variable like them. They are the meteors of the intellectual world, seldom beneficent and more often harmful for the intellectual progress of mankind. (Kellner 93–94)

This remarkable metaphor of warning that theories without local fact can only be destructive lies at the very heart of the scientific process, and its principle bears, in every aspect, upon the composition and methodology of the genre itself.

Another statement crucially fuses science and philosophic adventure: "Nature is an inexhaustible source of investigation, and in proportion as the domain of science is extended, she presents herself . . . under forms which they have never yet examined" (*Personal Narrative*, II, 12–13). Thus Humboldt, according to his translator, has the power of "raising the mind to general ideas, without neglecting individual facts; and while he appears to address himself to our reason, he has the secret of awakening the imagination, and of being understood by the heart" (*Personal Narrative*, I, ix).

Here, then, is the recognition of a romantic ethos in Humboldt's work in which formal data and observation are woven into a pattern revealing "general laws" about creation that can stir a reader's heart and imagination. Captain Cook's literary method remained fixed on the journal entry and presented in rigid linear progression though obviously exercising discriminating selection; Humboldt's technique, on the other hand, was to merge his observations with the principle of "viewing Nature in the universality of her relations," which, while it might seemingly ignore the twin goals of "instruction and utility" traditionally associated with science travel, will avoid creating false ideas about the "ties which unite these phenomena" and to view the "Globe as a great whole" (*Personal Narrative*, I, 233). Finally, in *Kosmos* (Eng. trans. 1848–1858), Humboldt achieved his grand synthesis—what Ricketts might have described as an older "unified field" hypothesis or theory—by offering a metaphysical vision of cosmic unity emerging out of the immense variations of life and law in the natural world, charted and established by scientific methods. This was a major work that Emerson, for example, admired and that the artist Frederick Church used to inform the romantic interpretation of nature in his popular landscapes.[5] *Kosmos*, in fact, exerted a considerable influence in its time. Humboldt's work and method are, therefore, vital historical links in the general pursuit of a "unified" and even "holistic" perspective of life, however much theorists differed on their definition of the concept of cosmic unity and the law structuring it.

Curiously enough, the work that would seem most relevant to the *Log* as a historical model, Forbes's *The Natural History of the European Seas*, receives no mention, nor does the great 1871 oceanographic expedition of the *Challenger*, influenced by Forbes. Instead, Steinbeck's strategy enlists, with obvious relevance and logic, passages from Clavigero's eighteenth-century account of Lower California for speculations about the origin of the name California and dramatic incidents about the shipwrecks and travails of the Spanish monks and priests in the region (60–63, 275–77).

Yet while such passages help to romanticize the relationship between past and present in the *Log,* it was Forbes's scientific achievement that laid the historical foundation for most marine expeditions. Considered the "pioneer of oceanography," Forbes was the first observer to define the various zones of water depth and the particular kinds of marine life distributed in each. In his fine popular account of the history of oceanography, Ritchie Ward writes that Forbes—like Humboldt, we can assume—searched for "generalizations from which he might see some central logic relating apparently random facts" (Ward 69). Forbes's methodology is further defined by Charles Wyville Thomson, the director of the *Challenger* expedition: "To Forbes is due the credit for having been the first to treat these [marine ecological] questions in a broad philosophical sense, to point out that the only means of acquiring a true knowledge of the rationale of the distribution of our present fauna, it is to make ourselves acquainted with its history, to connect the present with the past" (Ward 70). Vital as this latter principle is in all evolutionary thought, both in its pre- and post-Darwinian development, Forbes, nevertheless, insists on that sense of wonder he experienced during his observations. He writes: "To sit down by the sea-side at the commencement of ebb, and watch the shore gradually uncovered by the retiring waters, is as if a great sheet of hieroglyphics—strange picture writing—were being unfolded before us" (*Natural History* 12–13). This quasi-Emersonian mood and language would not be out of place in Steinbeck and Ricketts, nor would Forbes's continuing rhapsody over how the "commonest of the sea-snails creeping over the wet sea-weed and other marine phenomena" lead to the "mystery (deepest of mysteries) of their first appearance—the changes of the outline of continents and oceans" (13). Yet Forbes nobly asserts that even if he cannot resolve the mystery, it is there to be confronted: "the rejection of a mystery, because it is a mystery, is the most besotted form of human pride" (13). These sentiments surely suggest a disposition, a stance or point of view so crucial to the genre that it would not be an exaggeration to call it a form of genetic linking transmitted consciously or unconsciously as each scientist forges a narrative account in which the "mystery" and the methodology of inductive and deductive reason are held in tension.[6]

Perhaps, for all its weighty significance in the history of ecology and marine biology, Forbes's work was finally either too prosaic or "technical" a model for Steinbeck and Ricketts, if indeed, they had read the book, although it seems unlikely they would not at least have been aware of its importance. Of course I do not mean that our authors were searching for a model that they could consciously imitate structurally or thematically. Rather, as the *Log* itself makes clear, they were drawn to those figures—philosophers, scientists, poets, and theologians—for whom they felt a profound spiritual connection and whose historical influence could somehow illuminate their own undertaking they define as an attempt to show that "man is related to the whole thing, related inextricably to all reality," a "religious . . . mystical outcrying" (257). Life is so relational we learn, each species "only the commas in a sentence" creating the "point and base of a metaphoric pyramid," that an "Einsteinian relativity seems to emerge" (256–57). This "profound feeling" makes a "Jesus, a St. Augustine, a St. Francis, a Roger Bacon, a Charles Darwin, and an Einstein" (257). To gain this perspective and feeling for ourselves, "it is advisable to look from the tide pool to the stars and then back to the tide pool again" (257).

Like other critics, I take this passage as the core principle of the *Log,* a structural and philosophical concept enabling us to achieve what is, at last, a theological knowledge about the holistic character of God or Nature. And that is why Darwin's name on that list is at once so challenging and yet problematic. At first glance the name of Darwin, the dragon slayer of Creationism and the subverter of Faith, linked to that of Jesus and St. Augustine, might seem to be a grand blasphemy.

All this is true, of course, but for Ricketts and Steinbeck (and, with certain qualifications, for the "household gods" who directly shaped their thought—Ritter, Smuts, Boodin, and Allee), Darwin was the ultimate Holist, the thinker who demonstrated the interrelatedness of all life and nature's ecosystems, the grand mechanisms of adaptation and natural selection upon which the validity of philosophic naturalism rests. Ricketts cited Darwin as the key to nontheological thinking, a way of "attempting . . . to answer the already sufficiently difficult questions of *what* or *how,* instead of *why*" (160), and Steinbeck announced the centrality of Darwin to his quest, when, in a United Press release about the forthcoming expedition of the *Western Flyer,* he claimed that "the more general aspects of the tie-in of all animal species with one another has been lost since Darwin went out of the picture. We are trying in our own small way to get back to a phase of the broader view" (Hedgpeth 1978, pt. 2, 2).

The evidence is compelling that Darwin was a seminal figure for both Steinbeck and Ricketts and that the force of his thought implicitly and explicitly informs their purposes in the *Log.* Most recently, Brian Railsback has offered a thorough demonstration of Darwin's influence on Steinbeck's work as a whole, and I am indebted to his study.[7] The question at hand now is to investigate just how Steinbeck used Darwin and the *Voyage of the "Beagle"* to fashion his own contribution to the genre. Surely by invoking Darwin in his press release, Steinbeck was counting on the power of the great scientist's name to alert his audience to the scientific validity of the enterprise as well as to the principle—the "tie-in"—that would inform the future narrative.

Into this web of enthusiasms and perspectives, Steinbeck does present a Darwin compatible with his own artistic purposes and, while obviously reflecting in general the ideas of *The Origin of the Species,* ignores the later figure, who believed that the contradiction between science and religion, Cosmic Benevolence and endless suffering or predation could never be adequately resolved. These were subjects Darwin wrote about to Asa Gray in 1860, subjects "too profound for the human intellect . . . let each man hope and believe what he can."[8] Steinbeck's Darwin will be the image of the young naturalist, explorer, and passionate social observer. This image will be artistically deployed in four distinct ways to provide a spiritual and scientific link between past and present. The four ways I have constructed to understand Darwin's presence in the *Log* fall into the categories of identification, the problem of time and travel, the question of method, and the aesthetic of the romantic image.

The first extended image of Darwin comes following Steinbeck's description of collecting along the littoral "ferocious with life" and in a "vital competition for existence" (67). But he is oppressed with his haste, lack of time, and inadequate equipment, although he remains enthralled by the "incredible beauty of the tidepools" (69). Before him lies the drama of distribution and the changes in species "under varying conditions" (69). These Darwinian reflections lead naturally to an image of Darwin himself on the *Beagle*. "In a way," Steinbeck writes, "ours is the older method, somewhat like that of Darwin on the *Beagle*. He was called a 'naturalist.' He wanted to see everything, rocks and flora and fauna; marine and terrestrial" (69). The evocation of the term "naturalist" in a society where it has become virtually old-fashioned at best, is crucial, for it binds through language a conception of the *lover* of nature in contradistinction to the specialized scientist who has lost the central concern of biology: life itself.

Steinbeck admits to "envy" of the young Darwin who was allowed the "proper pace for a naturalist" with time to "think and to look and to consider." The modern method of "looking quickly at the whole and then diving down to a particular" is summarily dismissed. Only Darwin "emerged with a sense of the whole." Above all, it was the "pace" of the *Beagle* that makes all the difference to Steinbeck, and even Darwin's prose style reflects the "slow heave of a sailing ship, and the patience of waiting for a tide" (70), thus fusing style with time, purpose with expression. He imagines Darwin staring into the water in a contemplative manner, unaffected by time, but must reject any attempt to imitate this as "romantic and silly," for this would only produce a "philosophical costume piece." And so he must satisfy himself with "nostalgic longing" alone (70–71).

In this context, the "romantic" is a synonym for the artificial, a false mimesis, an unoriginal costume no longer relevant to the modern world. By contrast, a "true" romantic lives into the Whole in which acceptance of what "is" vivifies the soul into transcendental experiences like those of figures as diverse as St. Augustine, Emerson, Bacon, Jung, and Einstein. The identification here is with Darwin as a *naturalist*, with all the spiritual value that venerable title confers. This is a title Steinbeck deems vital to his scientific enterprise without in any way compromising the need for disciplined scholarship. The true naturalist responds to the sublime, the mysteries embedded in the structures and purposes of life. This, then, is the crucial point of identification, a gesture that mitigates the purely physical and temporal limitations with which Steinbeck felt burdened, in contrast to Darwin's experience.

But if the name *Western Flyer* could never resonate like the name *Beagle*, it nevertheless embodies a poetic power and meaning of its own. Steinbeck establishes this at the very start of his narrative when he describes the *Western Flyer* pushing toward the southern tip of the Bay of Monterey, picking up the winds as squadrons of pelicans follow them in the troughs of the waves, an old sea lion crosses its bow and, finally, the ship itself begins to sing under the wind, "a deep and yet penetrating tone like the lowest string of an incredible bull-fiddle" (35). Here is Steinbeck's version of the *Western Flyer* as symbol of romanticism, a nautical Aeolian harp. Like the *Beagle*, the *Western Flyer* has embarked on its own voyage of the imagination, where the mind can contemplate tidal theories of cosmogony as well as Jungian archetypes of sea serpents and the Old Man of the Sea while collecting sea cucumbers or tunicates, a veritable "harvest of symbols" (39). All this quasi-mystical speculation entwined with scientific effort is clearly necessary to Steinbeck's own sense of being a poet-naturalist in an age when the two roles have become disassociated. And in this way the *Western Flyer* establishes its own identity while acknowledging the *Beagle* as its source of "envy" and inspiration.

A second significant passage occurs again later in the text in relation to similar problems of time, work, and pace. Members of the crew have developed a "good leisurely state of mind" as they go from station to station, and at last, on 29 March, they experience "the sun glowing on the morning beach," making them "feel good." This experience triggers a memory of Darwin on the *Beagle*, who enjoyed a similar moment one morning in Valparaiso, "the heavens so clear and blue . . . that all nature seemed sparkling with life" (229). Steinbeck comments that, "being a naturalist, [Darwin] said 'All nature seemed sparkling with life,' but actually it was he who was sparkling." More important, perhaps, is that Darwin, the naturalist, was also a writer who could "translate his ecstasy over a hundred years to us. And we can feel how he stretched his muscles in the morning air and perhaps took off his hat—we hope a bowler—and tossed it and caught it" (229). Again there is emphasis on that charged word "naturalist," which connects Steinbeck to Darwin as an *artist*. Now, like any gifted writer, Steinbeck must also be able to re-create the living emotion—"the way it was"—at a certain moment of time. Thus, a wide range of emotions, troubling and exalting, become identified with Darwin: literary challenge, envy, nostalgia, contemplation, anxiety, and pleasure in methodology, the triumph of the artist who reaches over the centuries to make living contact with the future.

The category of the problem of time is a particularly fascinating one that goes well beyond the simple disparity of calendar time between the two expeditions, the difference between years and weeks, as Steinbeck remarks. The artistic challenge is to overcome this disparity by infusing into the structure of the *Log* that Rickettsian "breakthrough" over the barriers of linear time.

A key passage states that man can dig back to electrons and leap into space and so "fight out the moment into non-conceptual time. The ecology has a synonym which is ALL" (99). Like the Indians who do not use time as "medium of exchange" (290), we inhabit a dual world of the temporal and Eternal and necessarily leap from one mode to another, the micro- to the macrocosm.[9] The *Log* is, therefore, a flight into time, giving it a sense of "epic" voyage, intellectual and spiritual rather than spatial or linear. Perhaps the best image in the book reflecting this duality is the description of the Mother-of-Christ plaster and paint statue whose putatively eternal spiritual force is one of the "strongest ecological factors" in a worldly Mexican town, no more possible to ignore than a "granite monolith in the path of waves" (207–8). Cook, Humboldt, Forbes, and Darwin were essentially unburdened by time in their narratives—at least philosophically speaking—but Steinbeck fashioned his account to suggest a constant movement to overcome the limits of time and so made a special contribution to the genre.

My third category concerning method is, therefore, bound up with the question of the uses and perception of Time, the link between past and present, evolution itself. But the problem of Time for Steinbeck was not only a metaphysical one; he also needed to locate and to penetrate imaginatively Darwin's own past "milieu"—to obliterate the historical time separating their respective ventures and at the same time to recognize and understand the changes in scientific method and culture now before him. For Steinbeck, Darwin's was the "older method" as we have noted, a way of perceiving how the particular leads to the whole and the mechanisms that propel the process. But this generalization leaves open the very complex problem of Darwin's methodology, which scholars still explore and debate.

For Michael T. Ghiselin, Darwin is a great "system-maker" whose hypotheses are at once the product of a profound imaginative construct using both Baconian principles of induction and the process of deduction (15). Ernst Mayr calls Darwin a "speculator" of a special kind who, apart from his observational skills, was "first and foremost a naturalist" and also (unlike many other naturalists) a "great theoretician" and "indefatigable experimenter" (Mayr 10), surely the type of scientist Steinbeck and Ricketts admired most. Ghiselin also calls Darwin a "speculator" but adds that he "was not concerned with method as such . . . his approach was basically intellectual, depending on abstract thinking to an extreme degree. His interest in facts lay not in the illustration of principles but in the testing of hypotheses." As a result, Ghiselin concludes, Darwin's "reasoning tended to be obscure, and his ideas have been exceedingly controversial, almost as a rule" (Ghiselin 15).

With these generalizations in mind, we can never be quite certain how well Steinbeck (and Ricketts?) penetrated the complexities of Darwinian methodology, beyond the conviction, as we have seen, that he was essentially a holist, seeing the "tie-in" between all life and the environment and arriving at his revolutionary principles of evolution by studying the "particular" first in order to grasp general laws. Thus, when Steinbeck writes that the *Origin of the Species* simply "flashed" into Darwin's mind, we must agree with Railsback[10] that he is indulging in mythology—poeticizing his hero rather than analyzing the tortuous process that led to Darwin's formulations.

Yet the *Log* contains many reflections and examples suffused with the spirit of Darwin and his methodology as Steinbeck understood it, lending the book some of its most trenchant insights and conceptual tensions about the relationship between life and theory. For example, Steinbeck warns that the "greatest danger to a speculative biologist is analogy," the mistake of drawing tenuous and false parallels between animal and human behavior (110). Again, man has evolved into an "ethical paradox" who would rather be "successful than good" (112). In fact, words like "good" and "bad" ultimately imply Darwinian values, "good" meaning "weak survival quotient" and "bad" with "strong survival quotient" (112–13). Steinbeck's conclusion, fraught with meaning for all his work, is that man paradoxically "admires the power and forms which will lead to extinction but which are contradicted by his natural urge to survival." Man is still in a state of "becoming bound by . . . physical memories to a past of struggle and survival, limited in his futures by the uneasiness of thought and consciousness" (113). Such an interpretation of Darwinian thought by Steinbeck into a personal statement about the paradoxes that lie at the heart of the "human condition" seems to me one of his penetrating uses of his hero's vision.

But in the end, the *Log* remains a fully romantic work, its theological explorations maintaining a meaningful tension with its search for hard scientific information in the tide pools and shores of Baja California. For God, Steinbeck writes, "sees in a non-mystical sense, sees every sparrow fall and every cell utilized" (313). The "final" perspective is that "yet our history is as much a product of torsion and stress, as it is of unilinear drive" (313). These concluding statements of belief embrace all the dynamics of teleology, competition, and struggle as well as the logic, harmony, and purposefulness of the Whole to which we can "break through" in our life of *becoming*. God, after all, is the true nonteleologist who apprehends the ALL of His Creation in, presumably, one Eternal Moment when all relationships and contingencies are seen as part of a necessary Unity requiring no "mystical" faculty for human beings to grasp. The goal of the quest into the Sea of Cortez and its world was somehow to test and explore these assumptions in scientific collection, encounters with nonindustrial cultures, and metaphysical hypothesizing. Nor is traditional Christianity wholly excluded, for the image of God watching every sparrow fall echoes directly a Christian affirmation of a Divine, a plenary Providence.

The vital point, however, is that this final vision, absorbed by the nonmystical and mystical "eyes" of both God and humankind, is an imaginative poetic theology, a spiritualizing hypothesis bearing its own aesthetic harmony of form and meaning. And the *Western Flyer* carried its small crew into those physical and metaphysical waters, a twentieth-century version of the *Beagle* taking up the song of a Divine Musical Wind blowing through its guy wire like the "low pipe on a tremendous organ. It sang its deep note into the wind" (321). The poetry of "scientific thinking" and life vivified by Steinbeck's lyrically reconciling vision thus at last triumphs.

Notes

1. The standard work on the relationship between Steinbeck and Ricketts and its impact on the *Log* is Richard Astro, *John Steinbeck and Edward F. Ricketts: The Shaping of a Novelist* (1973). Jackson J. Benson, in his biography *The True Adventures of John Steinbeck, Writer* (1984), provides a fine account of their relationship, reminding us that Steinbeck remained an "agnostic, and, essentially, a materialist—but Ricketts's religious acceptance did tend to work on his friend, moderating . . . his rage and persuading him in his daily life to take a larger perspective" (248). Also see Benson's seminal article, "John Steinbeck: Novelist as Scientist," which demonstrates the "split" in Steinbeck between romance-adventure and the "dark imagery of fundamental religion" (252–53). In some ways, the *Log* seeks to reconcile this split or tension through the fusion of "organismic" and holistic thinking into a "new kind of writing." Indispensable, too, is Joel W. Hedgpeth's insightful commentary in his edition of Ricketts's journals. See *The Outer Shores, Part 1: Ed Ricketts and John Steinbeck Explore the Pacific Coast* and *The Outer Shores, Part 2: Breaking Through—From the Papers of Edward F. Ricketts.* Other brief but excellent commentary on the *Log* is in Peter Lisca, *The Wide World of John Steinbeck*, 178–85; and Joseph Fontenrose, *John Steinbeck: An Introduction and Interpretation*, 84–97.

2. I am indebted for these generalizations, which I see evident in the *Log*, to John Herman Randall, Jr., "The Changing Impact of Darwin on Philosophy" (1961).

3. I have chosen these works as only the most famous works of the genre. Obviously, there are many others worth studying, e.g., Chamisso's *A Voyage Around the World in the Romanzov Exploring Expedition . . . 1815–1818*; Johann and George Forster's separate accounts of their experience on Cook's ship *Resolution* (the second voyage); and those of T. H. Huxley, Hooker, Wallace, and Haeckel, all of whom, William Irvine remarks, "had embarked on seas of ripe and boundless possibility, where every ability and strength won a fabulous reward." Indeed, Darwin "high on a peak in theoretical Darien, had glimpsed . . . his own particular Pacific" (Irvine 15). See also Ritchie Ward, *Into the Ocean World: The Biology of the Sea* (1974), an excellent popular account of the development of oceanography and the history of the many important expeditions that marked it. There is a good discussion of both Forbes and Ricketts.

4. An important analysis of the scientific knowledge and capabilities of Steinbeck and Ricketts in the *Log* is Peter A. J. Englert's "Education of Environmental Scientists: Should We Listen to Steinbeck and Ricketts's Comments?" included in this anthology. While generally giving high praise for the *Log*, Englert points out that Rickett's knowledge of physics was shaky and that his use of the "imaginary" equation to explain oscillations in waves or other phenomena is inaccurate. Modern quantum physics and molecular biology in particular have

challenged and even destroyed the assumptions of biological (and philosophical) holism.

5. See Stephen Jay Gould, "Church, Humboldt and Darwin: The Tension and Harmony of Art and Science" (1989).

6. Like many of his predecessors in the genre, Darwin recognized the element of mystery in the scientific quest. In viewing "aboriginal beings" on the small and isolated islands of the Galapagos, he writes: "Hence, both in time and space, we seem to be brought somewhat near to that great fact—the mystery of mysteries—the first appearance of new beings on this earth." *Journal of Researches into the Natural History and Geology of the Countries Visited During the Voyage of the H.M.S. "Beagle"* (1899), 373. Of course, after the *Beagle* voyage was over, Darwin developed a methodology and hypothesis to unlock the "mystery of mysteries."

7. See his *Parallel Expeditions: Charles Darwin and the Art of John Steinbeck* and his article "Darwin and Steinbeck: The 'Older Method' and the *Sea of Cortez.*" Railsback's analysis of Steinbeck's reading and frame of mind during the period of preparation for the collecting trip is especially important for showing how vital Darwin was to the enterprise.

8. Cited in Stephen Jay Gould, *Hen's Teeth and Horses' Toes: Further Reflections in Natural History,* 44, in the essay "Nonmoral Nature," an analysis of Darwin's skepticism about the "benevolence" of nature and the futility of seeking any absolute ethical imperatives from the theory of evolution itself. An article by D. Kohn, "Darwin's Ambiguity: The Secularization of Biological Meaning," analyzes the difficulty of interpreting Darwin's language about the relationship between biology and theology.

9. See Betty L. Perez's fine study, "The Form of the Narrative Section of the *Sea of Cortez*: A Specimen Collected from Reality," in *Steinbeck's Travel Literature: Essays in Criticism,* ed. Tetsumaro Hayashi (1980), for an analysis of the brilliant structural use Steinbeck makes of the idea of time and images of a micro- and macrocosm in the *Log*.

10. See Railsback's dissertation, p. 27. Steinbeck wrote in *Sweet Thursday:* "Darwin said his *Origin of the Species* flashed complete in one second, and he spent the rest of his life backing it up, and the theory of relativity occurred to Einstein in the time it takes to clap your hands. This is the greatest mystery of the human mind, the inductive leap. Everything falls into place, irrelevancies relate, dissonance becomes harmony" (28). Here, perhaps, Steinbeck is talking not so much about inspired science as about inspired art—the moment when form and meaning, or whatever the writer needs to achieve a coherent vision of his work, suddenly "flashes complete" into the mind. But then, the two modes of creation, the scientific and the artistic, spring from the same deep source.

NINE

Revisiting the Sea of Cortez with a "Green" Perspective

Clifford Eric Gladstein and
Mimi Reisel Gladstein

This essay places Sea of Cortez: A Leisurely Journal of Travel and Research *in the context of nineteenth- and twentieth-century "philosophical streams" of American environmental thought and compares Steinbeck's ecological reasoning to that of 1990s "ecowarriors." With one or two exceptions,* Sea of Cortez *proves to be a work ahead of its time, with a holistic view of nature approaching the Gaia hypothesis. Both prescient and prophetic,* Sea of Cortez *is especially notable for its early recognition that the ocean's resources are finite and cannot withstand for long the pressures of wasteful and destructive fishing practices.*

Modern environmentalism was presaged by several philosophical streams whose headwaters can be traced in the conservationist, preservationist, and transcendentalist movements of the nineteenth and early twentieth centuries. On the one hand, thinkers such as John Wesley Powell and Gifford Pinchot viewed nature as a finite resource that had to be managed effectively to bring about more efficient development and to conserve it as a source for human profit.[1] In a related but different evolution, preservationist and transcendentalist thinkers such as William Cullen Bryant, Ralph Waldo Emerson, and Henry David Thoreau romanticized the natural environment, believing it to be a source of refuge, rejuvenation, and purification for the human spirit oppressed by a "world that is too much with us." John Muir, who founded the Sierra Club more than one hundred years ago, sought to conserve wilderness in its natural state, not necessarily for the use of humanity, but as a reserve from people's corrupting influence.[2] These were the forebears who contributed to the course of much that is the contemporary environmental movement.[3]

Still, what we define as contemporary environmentalism has characteristics that distinguish it from what came before. The preservationist, transcendentalist, and conservationist movements were at least a century old before they merged, in the years following World War II, in the writings of Rachel Carson and the activism of David Brower to become the collection of ecological ideologies subsumed under the umbrella of today's environmentalism.[4] The sages of the present movement integrated the ideas of their predecessors with new knowledge from the postwar world of plastics, pesticides, and profligate consumption into a more comprehensive ideology, recognizing not only the challenge of preserving natural resources, but also the threat created by industrial society's exploding use of unnatural substances. In doing so, contemporary environmentalism moved forward from its fountainhead philosophies. The ethic of Pinchot and Powell focused on the productive value that could be sustained from conserving natural resources, while the ideology that is the mainstream of the contemporary environmental movement stresses the interconnectedness of all things. Whereas Muir and his acolytes resolved to preserve patches of nature and set them apart to prevent abuse by people, contemporary ecology emphasizes that humans are a part of nature, not apart from it.

Contemporary environmentalism differs from its roots in that it recognizes nature as a finite resource and seeks to address the complex natural relationships upon which humanity depends for survival. It moves beyond the notions of conservation for more efficient use or preservation in order to maintain intrinsic value. As environmental historian Samuel Hays explains: "The conservation movement was an effort on the part of leaders in science, technology, and government to bring about a more efficient development of physical resources. The environmental movement, on the other hand . . . stressed the quality of the human experience and hence of the human environment" (13). Modern environmentalism is further distinguished from its predecessors, in the words of John McCormick, by "a broader conception of the place of man in the biosphere, a more sophisticated understanding of that relationship and a note of crisis that was greater . . . than it had been in the earlier conservation movement" (48).

Literary works often precede and foretell the articulation of philosophical concepts. And lovers of the natural world have been among the most devoted readers of John Steinbeck. Maybe it is because they see in his works strong identification with and respect for tillers of the soil and harvesters of the sea as well as an abiding reverence for the earth in its pristine state. Maybe it is because Steinbeck's appreciation for nature and his concern regarding humanity's relationship with it is more complex than a simple awe for the power and beauty of creation. Although Steinbeck wrote in a period of transition between the era of conservationism and the evolution of modern environmentalism, his ideas, as articulated in *Sea of Cortez*, reflect both the influence of the past and a vision of the future. A generation before such ideas were popularized, Steinbeck exhibited an ecological understanding and environmental sophistication both rare and unusual.

The pivotal role of the natural environment in the fictional writings of John Steinbeck is well established. From the pantheistic premises of *To a God Unknown,* complete with human sacrifice as a propitiation to the rain gods, to the Edenic function of the thicket in *Of Mice and Men,* where the safety and peace of the "fresh and green" pool and trees are juxtaposed with the rough, unpainted, and whitewashed bunkhouse, where the society of other human beings promises problems and the destruction of dreams, Steinbeck has presented Nature as touchstone and theme. Echoes of Thoreau are evident not only in Tom Joad's "maybe . . . a fella ain't got a soul of his own, but on'y a piece of a big one" but also in the Walden-like refuges his characters seek but seldom retain. Still, whereas any uses he makes of the natural environment in his fictional works are subject to the interpretations of readers, in *Sea of Cortez* Steinbeck blends the colorful and image-filled language of the creative writer with the observations of a scientist to make a clear and direct statement about his attitudes toward the natural world. And it is in this narrative that Steinbeck's writing augurs the philosophy that would not be popularly articulated for another generation.[5]

To the environmental activist of the 1990s, the most striking thing about Steinbeck's account of the Sea of Cortez expedition is what Richard Astro calls his "holistic" vision, a clear manifestation of an understanding of the systemic nature of the environment. This earth-embracing philosophy, although clearly influenced by his relationship with marine biologist Ed Ricketts, is also very much Steinbeck's own. Astro points out that "there are a half dozen statements about the holistic approach to life in the published narrative for every one in Ricketts's journal" (1973, 30), underlining its importance to Steinbeck. For his day, the author exhibited a surprising level of appreciation and respect for the notion that the activities of humanity, benign and/or exploitative, have a significant impact on the world we inhabit.

This worldview is evident throughout the narrative of the trip and first surfaces in the introduction, when Steinbeck reminds the reader that, once the expedition arrives at the Sea of Cortez, it will "become forever a part of it; that our rubber boots slogging through a flat of eelgrass, that the rocks we turn over in a tide pool, make us truly and permanently a factor in the ecology of the region" (SOC 3). Toward the end of the narrative he articulates what he identifies as the "Einsteinian relativity" of both the inanimate and the animate world, explaining: "One merges into another, groups melt into ecological groups until the time when what we know as life meets and enters what we think of as non-life: barnacle and rock, rock and earth, earth and tree, tree and rain and air. And the units nestle into the whole and are inseparable from it" (SOC 216). Here Steinbeck's observations of the tide pool echo a perception that did not become part of public culture until after his death. It would be not until over a generation later, in The Closing Circle (1971), that Barry Commoner, one of contemporary environmentalism's best-known champions, enunciated a similar message about this interconnectedness. For him it is the first law of ecology: "Everything is connected to everything else."

Steinbeck's clear understanding of the interconnectedness of the most minute and the largest components of the world is illustrated by his example of the limitations individuals bring to their visions of reality. As he explains, when one "has strength and energy of mind the tide pool stretches both ways, digs back to electrons and leaps space into the universe and fights out of the moment into non-conceptual time." He sums up his vision of the "wide and colored and beautiful" picture of both tide pool and universal observation, with the categorical statement that "ecology has a synonym which is ALL" (SOC 85).

What's more, Steinbeck's observations about the hazy boundaries between the animate and inanimate anticipate one of the more lively and provocative debates in the contemporary environmental movement, that surrounding the Gaia hypothesis. Proponents of Gaia, in the same way that Steinbeck connects rock and earth, earth and tree, "have observed that the boundary line between life and the inanimate environment that most of us assume to be resolutely engraved somewhere cannot be clearly drawn. Just as matter and energy are radically different yet ultimately interchangeable phenomena, so too are the environment and living organisms ultimately functions of one another" (Joseph 53). Like Steinbeck, J. E. Lovelock, the originator of the Gaia hypothesis, understood the natural wisdom of people untouched by the complexities of urban society. Explaining his choice of the name Gaia, after the Greek Earth Goddess, he muses about the difficulty urban dwellers and institutional scientists have with the theory that the planet is a living entity while "country people still living close to the earth often seem puzzled that anyone should need to make a formal proposition of anything as obvious as the Gaia hypothesis. For them it is true and always has been" (Lovelock 1979, 10–11). In *Sea of Cortez*, Steinbeck compares the "Our Lady of Loreto" statue in the church of the small village with "the Virgin Mother of the world," or the Magna Mater (*SOC* 175), seeing in the figure the archetypal concept of the earth as a living female being.

Steinbeck's recognition of the interconnectedness of humanity and its environment and the possibility of irrevocable change was not in keeping with the prevalent ecophilosophies of his day. Conservation was the dominant concept in the period prior to World War II. The New Deal policies of Franklin Roosevelt reflected the president's belief that the land and its treasures needed to be husbanded for human use. The programs conceived and implemented by Roosevelt and his lieutenants sought to harness nature for human good. Their form of environmental concern was well grounded in the Pinchot tradition of harnessing nature to improve the human condition. The Civilian Conservation Corps used the legions of unemployed to plant trees, dig reservoirs, build dams, and prevent soil erosion. The interconnectedness of nature was set aside in the 1930s in order to lift a depressed nation out of the worst of economic times.

Necessary to a holistic view of the world, a view predicated on the interconnectedness of the living and nonliving entities on this planet, is the concept of human beings as a species, subject to the same kinds of categorization and description as other species. Steinbeck understands the average person's inability to conceive of human beings in that way. In his contemplation of the issue, he characterizes human blindness: "We have looked into the tide pools and seen the little animals feeding and reproducing and killing for food. . . . We completely ignore the record of our own species" (*SOC* 16–17). This, he explains, is because "we do not objectively observe our own species as a species" (*SOC* 17).

Steinbeck's ruminations about the parallels between the human species and other species lead him to speculate about the genesis of humanity's bent for destructive behavior. He identifies the foundation of this behavior as a tendency peculiar to *Homo sapiens*. It is Steinbeck's observation that "man is the only animal whose interest and whose drive are outside of himself" (*SOC* 87). For him, the human desire for "property, houses, money, and power" is evidence of that external drive. All other species need only that which is necessary to survive: shelter, nourishment, and the opportunity to procreate. According to Steinbeck, though they may burrow in the ground, weave nests, or spin webs, create their habitat out of the "fluids or processes of their own bodies," other species leave "little impression on the world" (*SOC* 87). Humanity, on the other hand, is a species that injures the natural order and has "furrowed and cut, torn and blasted" the world. Human beings level mountains and litter the world with the debris of living. Once again, the images Steinbeck's text calls forth are amazingly contemporary. From the deck of the *Western Flyer*, over half a century ago, Steinbeck critiqued the modern "whole man," whose existence required the material paraphernalia created by runaway technical ability (*SOC* 87).

Steinbeck sees the results of this externalization as evidence of harmful mutation. Whereas other species experience mutation in self, our species, with its strong drive for possession and domination, exhibits its mutation in the direction of its drive. Hypothesizing in *Sea of Cortez* that both the Industrial Revolution and collectivization were mutations, Steinbeck worries about the future of humanity. His syllogism develops from a major premise of paleontology, that ornamentation and complication precede extinction, and from the minor premise that the human species' assembly lines, collective farms, and mechanized armies are the equivalents of the thickening armor of the great reptiles. He is thus led to the conclusion that the human mutations he has observed will eventually lead to extinction.

A half century later, the Sea of Cortez stimulated similar thoughts in naturalist John Janovy. Explaining that "paleontologists tell us that our planet has experienced several massive extinctions; in each the diversity of life was greatly diminished" (150), Janovy speculates that the world is experiencing its third major reduction in global diversity even as the reader peruses his words. The tropical rainforests that are being cleared contain about 70 percent of the genetic information that, according to Janovy, spell "life on earth" (150). Nor did Steinbeck hold out much hope that the destructive tendencies or mutations would be stemmed. In his opinion, "conscious thought seems to have little effect on the action or direction of our species" (*SOC* 88).

Steinbeck's experience with environmental conflicts in 1940 is eerily prescient of an ecological tragedy that continues to be played out in contemporary ocean waters. The *Western Flyer's* encounter with the Japanese shrimpers off of Guaymas is the subject of a graphically poignant chapter. Steinbeck describes the Mexican fishermen complaining bitterly about "the Japanese shrimpers who were destroying the shrimp fisheries" (*SOC* 246). Curious about this situation, the men of the expedition decide to pay the Japanese a visit. Steinbeck observes the operations of their fleet, commenting that "they were doing a very systematic job, not only taking every shrimp from the bottom, but every other living thing as well" (*SOC* 247). This practice, through which "the sea bottom must have been scraped completely clean," brought onto the decks of the Japanese dredge boats, not only their quarry, the bottom-dwelling shrimp, but tons of other mortally wounded sea creatures as well, which the usually frugal Japanese simply threw overboard. Steinbeck found the "waste of this good food appalling" and predicted that unless limits were imposed which maintained balance between catch and supply, "a very short time will see the end of the shrimp industry in Mexico" (*SOC* 248).

Steinbeck's dire prediction may have been forestalled by an event that his narrative could not anticipate. Late in the year that *Sea of Cortez* was published, the Japanese bombed Pearl Harbor, and the ensuing war kept Japanese draggers out of the area for the better part of a decade. Shrimping in the northern Sea of Cortez continues to be the single largest fishery of the entire Mexican economy. Many of the problems that Steinbeck encountered continue, however. Like the villagers who complained to Ricketts and Steinbeck, the fishermen of the small coastal communities remain concerned about the activities of large commercial vessels. Though studies show that the large boats are not energy-efficient, requiring twelve times the energy to harvest the same amount of shrimp as the small boats, their large catches and the necessities of a world market ensure their continued prevalence in the area. Furthermore, the wasteful by-catch policies of the large boats make their presence in the Sea of Cortez a concern for environmentalists. The Delegación Federal de Pesca en Sonora estimated that the by-catch (everything pulled up with the shrimp) is often twice the weight of the shrimp, and most of it dies before it can be returned to the gulf. The same is not true in the small boats, where much of the by-catch finds its way into the local economy.[6] The practices Steinbeck deplored continue, as he predicted, to the detriment of marine life and the local economy.

Steinbeck's book is full of expressions of admiration for the people he encountered in the small coastal villages of the Sea of Cortez. Though he tries hard not to sentimentalize them, his descriptions leave the reader with a strong sense that Steinbeck found their way of life markedly saner than that of industrialized countries. He fabricates the thoughts of an Indian of the gulf: "It would be nice to have new Ford cars and running water, but not at the cost of insanity" (*SOC* 242). He writes of their kindness, their calm, and the "invasion" of "good roads and high-tension wire" (*SOC* 244). Steinbeck was concerned about the impact of such invasions on the lives of the kind people he met, and in the chapter about the Japanese draggers, he categorically states that "catch limits should be imposed, and it should not be permitted that the region be so intensely combed" (*SOC* 249).

Steinbeck suggests that a study be made to ensure that "there might be shrimps available indefinitely" (*SOC* 249–50). Obviously, his advice was not heeded. As recently as the fall of 1991, University of Texas at El Paso researchers reported local shrimpers' complaints about the depletion of the shrimp beds. Present-day vessels drag the shrimp grounds an average of seven times per year. Steinbeck's prophecy that dragging would bring an end to the shrimp industry seems to be coming to pass. Fewer locals are able to make a living from the sea. Puerto Penasco, once a shrimping village, now sees tourism as its chief economic prospect. Shrimpers, who in the past could make enough in fishing season to survive for the whole year, now must seek other work to make a living. Not only are the shrimp being depleted, but large birds, such as pelicans, who depend on marine life, are also dying off. Indiscriminate collecting continues and pollutants are poisoning the upper gulf.[7]

Steinbeck does not want to brand the Japanese fishermen or Mexican officials who permitted the dragging as criminals. Yet while calling them "good men," he is quick to extrapolate the universal from the particular. Steinbeck saw that what was happening to one group of fishermen could happen worldwide. He proved prophetic. Today, the debate over fishing practices employing these and similar methods still rages. The world's fisheries have been severely depleted by technologically advanced techniques of capturing and processing marine resources into commodities for human consumption. The use of driftnets that, when strung between two ships sailing as much as forty miles apart, can literally sweep the ocean clean of all living things is a practice much disputed by nations and abhorred by environmentalists. Reacting to the practice much as Steinbeck reacted to what he saw a half century earlier, Charles Bowden, a 1990s ecowarrior, writes: "Think of it, 35,000 miles of nets go down each night, the nets 40 miles long, 30 feet deep, the weave invisible monofilament, the death by entanglement and suffocation. Nothing gets through; the technique is perfect. Curtains of death" (41). The state of California recently banned the use of these nets within its waters, as have the states of Washington and Oregon. Again, it is the Japanese "with their industry and efficiency" (249) who are most insistent on their use of these ecologically unsound methods. Steinbeck's concerns for the future of the Mexican shrimp industry fifty years ago are now voiced for all the world's fisheries.

Ironically, his ominous observations regarding the Mexican shrimp supply came to pass about a marine industry closer to home. During the early 1940s Ed Ricketts began work analyzing the shrinking supply of sardines in Monterey Bay. In 1936, the sardine catch brought to the Monterey canneries peaked at a billion and a half pounds, making it the largest fishery in the United States. The catch declined progressively from that point until the entire industry was destroyed by 1960. Astro's biography of Ricketts indicates that among the biologist's unpublished material and notebooks was information for a project to be titled "The California Sardine: An Ecological Picture" (1976, 37). Although Ricketts attributed only part of the shrinking sardine catch to overfishing, he did believe that a rational conservation program "based upon sound scientific knowledge of the ecology of the marine environment" would have stabilized the sardine production at about 400,000 pounds per year and established a "smaller but streamlined cannery row" (Astro 1976, 37). The conservation program that he envisioned was never put into effect. A lesson may have been learned from the Monterey Bay disaster; in April 1992, the federal government forbade the annual salmon catch for northern California and central Oregon fisheries because of the serious depletion of that resource.

In Monterey today, Ed Ricketts, John Steinbeck, and an aquarium are the principal resources for the economic viability of an area that once housed great sardine canneries. Tourism is the chief industry. A similar fate may await the Sea of Cortez. As the abundance of the fisheries is depleted, a factor no less dangerous to the environment has come into play. The quiet and deserted beaches that Steinbeck and Ricketts admired are now lined with condos. Tourism and developers may complete what the draggers and driftnets began.

While the environmentalists of today read much of Steinbeck's narrative with admiration for the modernity of his ecological thought, there are also instances where the reader is brought up short at his descriptions of behavior paradoxical in terms of his stated philosophy and/or disturbing in terms of present-day ecological mores. Perhaps the most troubling images, especially for those who dive, are the descriptions of many of the collecting trips. The section that portrays gathering specimens at the Pulmo coral reef is illustrative. Steinbeck notes that El Pulmo is the "only coral reef" found on the entire expedition (SOC 78). Certainly, anyone who knows about coral knows how much time is involved in the development of a reef. Novice divers are instructed not to touch coral, as a touch may kill it, and breaking off pieces of coral is taboo. Even though Steinbeck expresses wonder at the complexity of life's pattern on the reef, recording that "every piece broken skittered and pulsed with life" (*SOC* 76), he is seemingly untroubled by his destruction of that life, although some of his language does suggest sensitivity to the carelessness of the collectors. He writes of feet put down "injudiciously" (*SOC* 77), of a large fleshy gorgonian, or sea fan, the only one of this type found in the area, in fact on the whole trip, "pulled" up, and of the "rush of collecting" that makes the party "indiscriminate" (*SOC* 78).

Perhaps Steinbeck does not express overt reservations about this behavior because the injudiciousness often results, when going over the pieces of coral and rubble, in the discovery of "animals we had not known were there" (*SOC* 78). He complains that a lack of diving equipment prevented the collection of "concealed hazy wonders" on the undercut shoreward side of the reef, and as he describes diving "again and again for perfect knobs of coral" (*SOC* 79), contemporary diver/readers can only feel relief that the expedition lacked the requisite equipment.[8]

Still another disquieting impression is left by some of the anecdotes about Tiny's harpooning of large sea creatures. Initially one is relieved, when following the gruesome mutilation of the tortoiseshell turtle, Tiny decides never again to harpoon one: "In his mind they joined the porpoises as protected animals" (*SOC* 46). This relief is short-lived, however, as Tiny then decides to hunt manta rays. Though they have "no proper equipment" for this enterprise, the lack does not deter the crew from tormenting the majestic creatures, described by Steinbeck as being "twelve feet between the 'wing' tips" (*SOC* 251). The ecologically sensitive reader is horrified as Tiny harpoons ray after ray, for no defensible reason. Steinbeck's narrative expresses concern mainly about the fact that the method of hunting was not working as each stricken ray fades to the bottom of the sea and eventually breaks the harpoon line. Even Tex is unable to devise a workable system, though his trident spear comes up with a "chunk of flesh on it" (*SOC* 252). In his description, Steinbeck's tone is one of amusement at Tiny's hysteria, at his being "heart-broken." When the crew, trying to soothe Tiny, points out that there is nothing worthwhile to do with a ray once it is caught, Tiny explains that he wants to have his picture taken with it.

Steinbeck's ideas are also not in line with present thought on the subject of the importance of rare species and biodiversity. Discussing wealthy amateur collectors who seek immortality by having their names attached to a newly discovered species, Steinbeck proclaims: "The rare animal may be of individual interest, but he is unlikely to be of much consequence in any ecological picture" (*SOC* 216). Although he understood that the disappearance of such a common species as plankton "would probably in a short time eliminate every living thing in the sea and change the whole of man's life," Steinbeck also concludes that the extinction of one of the rare animals "would probably go unnoticed in the cellular world" (*SOC* 216).

Today's researchers in the pathology of the "cellular world" are learning of the healing effects of some of the rarest of species. One example is the Rosy Periwinkle. A plant native to the island of Madagascar, it is the main source of a drug used to combat cancer. Jay D. Hair, president of the National Wildlife Federation, whose daughter was cured by this drug, bemoans the fact that the natural habitat of this plant, the forested area of Madagascar, is almost totally destroyed. Taxol, which is derived from the rare yew tree, is another natural source of the life-saving drugs used effectively in the cure of ovarian and breast cancer. The habitat of this species is also gravely threatened by the clear-cutting practices of the nation's northwest timber industry. These are but two examples of obscure species whose extinctions could have harmful effects on the rate of progress with which humanity conquers some of its most vexing and destructive health hazards.

Still, although a few items in Steinbeck's account of the Sea of Cortez expedition may give pause, given the historical context and the requirements for scientific collecting at the time, the overriding impression is of an avant-garde and enduring achievement. Just as most well-documented stories about the problems of migrant workers refer to *The Grapes of Wrath*, so all thorough studies of the bay of Baja California mention *Sea of Cortez*. For naturalists, the work has achieved mythic status. In the words of John Janovy, Jr., it is a "parable" that is "now a part of the scriptures of marine biology" (7). For him, a field trip to the area was a trip "to a place made sacred by a book published in 1941" (8).

In *The Grapes of Wrath*, Ma Joad, despite all the hardships her family endures, speaks optimistically about the future: "Why, we're the people," she proclaims, "we go on" (310). A few years later, in his own voice, Steinbeck made a less positive assessment: "We in the United States have done so much to destroy our own resources, our timber, our land, our fishes, that we should be taken as a horrible example and our methods avoided by any government and people enlightened enough to envision a continuing economy" (*SOC* 250). He was also aware of the mistakes being made by other countries and the reverberating implications of their acts. In his horror at what he saw in the Sea of Cortez, Steinbeck noted that the Mexican official, who permitted the ecologically unsound practices, and the Japanese captain who pursued them, were good men, but men who were committing a "true crime against nature and against the immediate welfare of Mexico and the eventual welfare of the whole human species" (*SOC* 250). Revisiting the Sea of Cortez a half century later with a "green" perspective, we are struck by both how prophetic and how contemporary an environmentalist Steinbeck was.

Notes

1. John Wesley Powell is best remembered for his surveys of the Colorado River basin and the Grand Canyon in the 1850s and 1870s and for his efforts to convince Congress and the American people that the deserts of the western United States could be tamed through planned development. His ideas, revolutionary at the time, sought orderly and thoughtful settlement of the arid regions of the country through government management. His 1878 *Report on the Lands of the Arid Region of the United States* is widely regarded as establishing the conceptual framework upon which so much of this country's land management philosophy is now based. Two sources for more information about Powell are Wallace Stegner, *Beyond the Hundredth Meridian: John Wesley Powell and the Second Opening of the West* (1954), and John U. Terrell, *The Man Who Rediscovered American: A Biography of John Wesley Powell* (1969). Gifford Pinchot is the founder of the Forest Service and is generally recognized as the first to incorporate successfully the concept of scientific management of natural resources into public policy making. He differed from some of his contemporaries, such as John Muir, in that he viewed the forests as resources to be developed rather than preserved for their own sakes. Although he favored public control of the nation's natural resources, he consistently opposed as wasteful the setting aside of land in wilderness areas or parks. For a good discussion of the differences between Pinchot and Muir, see Roderick Nash, *Wilderness and the American Mind* (1982).

2. John Muir is regarded as the founder of the modern preservation movement. His lectures, writing, and activism around the turn of the century are credited with creating modern environmentalism, the idea that nature should be pre-

served and protected because of its intrinsic beauty and value for recreation. He sought the development of wilderness areas where land would be set aside and left untouched by grazing or logging. His books, *The Mountains of California* (1894) and *The Yosemite* (1912), were the most widely read books on nature and the environment of their day.

3. Two helpful sources for information about these nineteenth-century conservationalists are Stephen Fox, *The American Conservation Movement: John Muir and His Legacy* (1981), and Douglas H. Strong, *Dreamers and Defenders: American Conservationalists* (1971).

4. Rachel Carson is the author of perhaps the most influential of all contemporary environmental treatises, *Silent Spring* (1962). In it, Carson warns of the insidious and pervasive adverse impact on the natural environment of insecticides, suggesting that if broadcast unchecked, chemical poisons can cause the extinction of whole species. She is credited with opening a new chapter in the history of understanding the consequences for the natural world of humanity's activities. A marine biologist by training, she wrote other books—*The Sea Around Us* (1951) and *The Edge of the Sea* (1955)—that became international best-sellers. David Brower was the first executive director of the Sierra Club (1952–1969) and transformed the group from a small, California-oriented hiking club to an influential national organization. Brower is credited with developing a modern environmental lobby that could compete with the resources of big business through the mobilization of millions of voters. After he left the Sierra Club, he founded Friends of the Earth and the Earth Island Institute; the former has become one of the world's largest environmental organizations. For more information see Stewart L. Udall, *The Quiet Crisis and the Next Generation* (1988), and David Brower, *Work in Progress* (1991).

5. We are aware that in writing the narrative portion of *Sea of Cortez*, Steinbeck was using Ed Ricketts's journal. Both Richard Astro, *John Steinbeck and Edward F. Ricketts: The Shaping of a Novelist* (1973), and Jackson J. Benson, *The True Adventures of John Steinbeck, Writer* (1984), demonstrate that the ideas reflected in Steinbeck's narrative were generally shared by both men. Benson explains that Steinbeck "wanted to make the account a true reflection of the joining of their two minds" and of the "ideas they shared and developed together" (1984, 481). Astro concludes that in situations where Steinbeck greatly amplifies Ricketts's notes, it is probably because Steinbeck had greater interest in, or belief in the validity of, the concept in question (1973, 30). We are not interested in which man originated which idea but will assume, for the purposes of this essay that, as the author of the narrative, Steinbeck held the views he articulated and published.

6. Information about the fishing industry in the present Sea of Cortez is contained in "Energy Analysis and Policy Perspectives for the Sea of Cortez, Mexico," prepared by Mark T. Brown, Stephen Tennenbaum, and H. T. Odum (1991). It is originally a report prepared for the Cousteau Society.

7. Interview with Dr. Lillian Mayberry and Dr. Jack Bristol, Department of Biology, University of Texas at El Paso, El Paso, Texas, 30 September 1991.

Dr. Mayberry has been conducting research trips to Puerto Penasco for seven years. The bay there has the second highest tide differential in the world, making it an ideal location for tide pool research.

8. We want to reiterate our "green" perspective, complete with its 1990s sensibility. Steinbeck and Ricketts were following correct procedures for good marine biological collecting of the 1930s. They lacked the photographic, video, or SCUBA equipment for a more judicious collection behavior.

TEN

Education of Environmental Scientists: Should We Listen to Steinbeck and Ricketts's Comments?

Peter A. J. Englert

Nuclear chemist Peter Englert explores Steinbeck and Ricketts's scientific thinking as expressed in The Log from the Sea of Cortez. *Their knowledge of physics was deficient, even for the 1940s, and fairly frequent physics references and analogies in LSC suffer accordingly. But by striving to be "good" scientists by their own philosophical and holistic standards, the two men managed to approach some very modern ecological ideas regarding the interactions of organisms and the dynamics of populations. Englert laments the lack of broad, cross-disciplinary thinking in today's overspecialized and "goal-oriented" training of environmental scientists. He points out that, although flawed, Steinbeck and Ricketts's generalist or naturalist approach still has validity for training today's scientists.*

There are many reasons to study John Steinbeck and Ed Ricketts's *Log from the Sea of Cortez.* Perhaps most urgent is the fact that today the study of "nature" seems the exclusive privilege of "environmental scientists." "Environmental science" has recently been vehemently "introduced" into the academic world as if it were something radically new. Social, physical, and life science departments are rushing into the education of "environmental scientists" because society has suddenly recognized a need for them. This development could not have been foreseen more than fifty years ago, when *Log from the Sea of Cortez* was published, although major environmental problems began at that time.

In *Log from the Sea of Cortez,* Steinbeck and Ricketts developed a sensitivity for nature and environment that, could it be shared in academic and political worlds, might prevent many harmful developments. The two men, a successful writer and a scientist, study a selected part of nature and environment. They are limited in time, but their vision is unlimited. They claim to be free of prejudices, and they stretch, but sometimes also overstretch, their scientific and philosophical capacity. Steinbeck and Ricketts demonstrate to us an unconventional way of looking at the environment. Their comments on science, the scientific process, and the study of nature are highly relevant to the education of today's environmental scientists and warrant further investigation.

Although not always firm in their scientific knowledge and application of hypotheses to their thoughts and study, Steinbeck and Ricketts recall a type of scientist that ceased to exist with the start of modern industrialization. They show that the "Darwinian naturalist," rather than the modern specialist, is most likely to understand nature and note that scientists educated in their time are too specialized to understand the interconnectedness of all things in nature—a problem still afflicting today's scientific community. They imply that a modern "naturalistic" approach would bring progress to our understanding of nature's complexity. Taken as one person, Steinbeck and Ricketts, the scientifically interested writer and the open-minded scientist, exemplify the qualities needed to be a truly understanding environmental scientist.

Throughout the Log from the Sea of Cortez, Steinbeck and Ricketts make significant comments about scientists, teachers, and students in their field. Both authors were educated at quality institutions of higher education—Stanford University and the University of Chicago were, then as now, considered excellent undergraduate and research universities. Although neither author completed his studies, the college experience seems to provide the background for the many comments made by both on science, teaching, and the scientific process. Sometimes even the language used comes very close to undergraduate jargon.

Nostalgia for the Darwinian method influenced the Sea of Cortez expedition. A natural scientist typical of his time, Darwin was the product of a long-standing tradition of nonspecialization.[1] When criticizing modern scientists and their behavior, Steinbeck and Ricketts tend to emphasize the loss of Darwinian style: "And the modern process—that of quickly looking at the whole field and then diving down to a particular—was reversed by Darwin" (*LSC* 70). More than once they try to describe their methodical approach to the subjects of their expedition as "Darwinian," although they can only envy Darwin the ample time he had to make and ponder his observations. Contemplating their own first day of collecting activities on the shores of the Gulf of California, they write:

In a way, ours is the older method, somewhat like that of Darwin on the Beagle. He was called a 'naturalist'. . . . And in the writing of Darwin, as in his thinking, there is the slow heave of a sailing ship, and the patience of waiting for the tide. . . . This is the proper pace for a naturalist. Faced with all things he cannot hurry. We must have time to think to look and to consider. . . . We can look with longing back to Charles Darwin, staring into the water over the side of the sailing ship, but for us to attempt to imitate that procedure would be romantic and silly (LSC 69, 70)

Steinbeck and Ricketts hold very idealistic and high standards for those they call true scientists: individuals with an all-embracing curiosity about the measurable and nonmeasurable components of the world around them, for whom "an answer is invariably the parent of a great family of new questions" (*LSC* 197). In addition to curiosity and breadth—as opposed to specialization—Steinbeck and Ricketts attribute another characteristic to "great scientists": the ability to communicate scientific ideas and principles with great clarity. Indeed, many excellent scientists are excellent teachers to the degree that they can communicate very complex ideas to peers, to their students, and to the general public. And so "it is usually found that only the little stuffy men object to what is called 'popularization,' by which they mean writing with clarity understandable to one not familiar with the tricks and codes of the cult" (*LSC* 84).

Even the famous "dry-ball" paragraph in *Log from the Sea of Cortez* describes two extreme types of biologists, bad and good. The bad, or "dry-ball," biologists "are not really biologists. They are the embalmers of the field, the picklers who see only the preserved form of life without any of its principle. Out of their own crusted minds they create a world wrinkled with formaldehyde" (*LSC* 33). Joel Hedgpeth has probably revealed the specific target of these acidic remarks, Professor W. K. Fisher, director of the Hopkins Marine Station. Fisher's sin was a less than academically correct review of *Between Pacific Tides*, a book coauthored by Ricketts and Calvin. According to Hedgpeth: "Suspiciously this tirade against overly academic minds was linked to a reference to starfish, Fisher's specialty: 'The dry-balls cannot possibly learn a thing every starfish knows in the core of his soul and in the vesicles between the rays.' It must be confessed that it is difficult to conceive of W. K. Fisher as a tenor of the scientific world" (1978, pt. 1, 33).

By contrast, the good biologist or scientist is a well-rounded person who loves life and is willing to learn from it: "The true biologist deals with life, with teaming boisterous life, and learns something from it, learns that the first rule of life is living" (*LSC* 33). Steinbeck and Ricketts make remarks about some contemporaries who may meet these criteria, and they give us a nineteenth-century example, John Xántus:

Sent down by the United States Government as a tidal observer, but having lots of time, he collected animals for our National Museum. . . . We wonder what modern biologist, worried about titles and preferment and the gossip of the Faculty Club, would have the warmth and the breadth, or even the fecundity for that matter, to leave a "whole tribe of Xántuses." We honor this man for his activities. He at least was one who literally did proliferate in all directions. (LSC 71–72)

To be considered a scientist in the eyes of Steinbeck and Ricketts, an individual must possess a number of criteria: all-encompassing interest in the physical world, time to observe carefully, ability and will to communicate research results to all people, energy, and love for life. The opposites of these characteristics, however, were almost as prevalent in Steinbeck and Ricketts's time as they are today. At the start of World War II, the industrial influence on the development of science was vehement. The specialist, rather than the generally educated scientist, was needed by society to accelerate industrial development amid keen international competition. The idealistic perception of scientists as true naturalists, prevailing since the eighteenth century, now conflicted with industrial society's need for an extremely specialized and highly trained workforce.

The academic world has not changed significantly since the World War II era. The specialist, interested only in his or her own small area, is the rule rather than the exception. Very few look beyond the limits of their fields. Scientists are not encouraged to do so; there are no rewards. Although teaching evaluations keep most university professors apace with their students' demands for entertainment, passing such tests does not constitute the ability to communicate that Steinbeck and Ricketts valued. How can a frequently over-worked and frustrated specialist develop enthusiasm for life, the universe, and everything unless he or she leaves work at five and forgets about the job (*LSC* 98)? And on the other side of the lectern, are the students exposed to these role models, students who will carry their example into the world of science and discovery?

Steinbeck and Ricketts think of the ideal teacher when they think about their ideal scientist. But they refer to universities as institutions that want to "turn out" students; they talk about "brittle jerky curricula": "We have thought in this connection . . . that the brittle jerky thinking of the present might rest on the brittle jerky curricula of our schools with their urge to 'turn them out.' To turn them out. They use the phrase in speeches; turn them out to what?" (*LSC* 70). This ingenious way of describing the situation hits on one of the signal traits of the American university system in the early 1940s (a trait European countries did not try to emulate until much later, in the 1960s and 1970s): the effort to tie universities into the process of industrial production and public need. Clyde Barrow, in his analysis of the American university system's development, describes the phenomenon as follows:

These administrative developments have been accompanied by the appearance of an ideology of higher education which explicitly defines the university as merely another business organization. University expenditures are defined as a social and educational investment that must efficiently yield some tangible return in the form of usable knowledge, technical innovation, and marketable skills for white collar and professional labor. Return on educational investment is now one of the chief measures for judging whether a university has successfully performed its public service mission or offered a quality product to its consumers (students and taxpayers). (253)

It is at least remarkable that Steinbeck and Ricketts point to exactly those things—specialization and the production of a skilled workforce—that a university of Darwinian (or Humboldtian) style would never have agreed to.

The description of Steinbeck and Ricketts's joint expedition places their Sea of Cortez endeavor squarely in the tradition of Darwin's voyage of the *Beagle:* "We came to envy this Darwin on his sailing ship" (*LSC* 69). Although Steinbeck and Ricketts were aware of the differences between their expedition and this particular past endeavor, they frequently invoke the *Beagle* when describing their journey and research goals: "It reminded us of Charles Darwin, who arrived late at night on the *Beagle* in the Bay of Valparaiso" (*LSC* 229).

Darwin's voyage and subsequent analysis of his observations laid the foundations not only for the theory of evolution, one of the most important discoveries in biology, and for nonteleological thinking but also for one of the most questionable developments in philosophy—Social Darwinism (Clark 1985, 152, 177). The *Beagle* was only one of many expeditions during the eighteenth and nineteenth centuries, some of them exclusively seagoing, some of them combination sea-land expeditions.[2] Yet it is not surprising that, with the exceptions of Xántus and Clavigero, Darwin is the only major scientific explorer mentioned by Steinbeck and Ricketts. The voyage stands out because of Darwin's subsequent results, and a brief survey of the history of science books available during Steinbeck and Ricketts's time shows that the *Beagle* expedition is usually the only one mentioned and discussed (Gore 603; Libby 197). Steinbeck and Ricketts are, therefore, following "general knowledge" rather than more detailed study of their naturalist predecessors.

The scientific scope of the *Beagle* expedition was very broad, its duration almost five years, and its results scientifically overwhelming. The scope and duration of the Sea of Cortez expedition were much narrower than those of the voyage of the *Beagle*. While Darwin was dedicated to observing many aspects of the physical and living world around him, Steinbeck and Ricketts focused more consciously on the "littoral," a well-separated and defined environment, and the distribution of species within it. Such a focus, however, was broad when compared to those of contemporary specialists:

Our collecting ends were different from those ordinarily entertained. In most cases at the present time, collecting is done by men who specialize in

one or more groups. Thus one man interested in hydroids will move out on a reef, and if his interest is sharp enough, he will not even see other life forms about him. . . . Collecting large numbers of animals presents an entirely different aspect and makes one see an entirely different picture.
(LSC 69)

While the *Beagle* did not sail to discover evidence for evolution, the *Western Flyer* sailed with an agenda, novel and very open—I suppose—but possibly ready for confirmation (although expedition participants made many claims to the contrary): the applicability of holistic approaches for describing and understanding ecological systems. The *Beagle* and the *Western Flyer* are connected by Steinbeck and Ricketts's nostalgic attachment to the great mind that provided the world with evolution and nonteleological thinking, central themes in *Log from the Sea of Cortez*.

Underlying these central themes is Steinbeck and Ricketts's basic philosophical orientation—biologically founded holism—imported by Ricketts via his teacher in Chicago, Warden Clyde Allee. According to Hedgpeth:

Ed studied these papers [the material of some of Allee's lectures] very carefully [and] used them as guides in his own observations on the Pacific coast, for he considered them to be "applicable anywhere." The impression of the professor upon his student was reciprocated. Even twenty-nine years later, W. C. Allee remembered Edward F. Ricketts as "a member of a small group of 'Ishmaelites' who tended sometimes to be disturbing, but were always stimulating." (1978, pt. 1, 5)

Hedgpeth's account of Ricketts's educational background also assures us that he was familiar with Jan Christiaan Smuts's *Holism and Evolution* (1926), the major work of holistic philosophy at this time.

Steinbeck and Ricketts's philosophical approach and their field of interest, practical marine biology, generally complement one other. Only occasionally do the two men stray into a modified form of metabiological holistic political thinking. Holistic, nonteleological philosophy is otherwise coherently presented throughout the *Log from the Sea of Cortez*. Steinbeck and Ricketts formulate the major holistic assumption, that the whole must be more than the sum of its parts, and in numerous observations, descriptions, and discussions give evidence for this assumption. As early as the introduction to *Log from the Sea of Cortez* they present their holistic ideas: " 'Let us go,' we said, 'into the Sea of Cortez, realizing that we forever become a part of it; that our rubber boots slogging through a flat of eelgrass, that the rocks we turn over in a tide pool, make us truly and permanently a factor in the ecology of the region. We shall take something away from it, but we shall leave something too' " (*LSC* 4). And again, near the end of the expedition, they write:

This is a simple thing to say, but the profound feeling of it made a Jesus, a St. Augustine, a St. Francis, a Roger Bacon, a Charles Darwin, and an Einstein. Each of them in his own tempo and with his own voice discovered and reaffirmed with astonishment the knowledge that all things are one thing and that one thing was all things—plankton, a shimmering phosphorescence on the sea and the spinning planets and an expanding universe, all bound together by the elastic string of time. It is advisable to look from the tide pool to the stars and then back to the tide pool again. (LSC 257)

Steinbeck and Ricketts's choice of the tide pool as a relative microcosm to juxtapose against the ultimate all-encompassing macrocosm, the universe, may suggest that anything below the symbiotic multitude of that special coastal environment was not important to their holistic considerations. Yet even that basic constituent of any biological or physical material, the molecule, is made up of atoms, and the atom itself is a composite of nuclear particles, or nucleons, in their turn composites of other parts, elementary particles such as quarks, muons, pions, and so forth. Steinbeck and Ricketts, as well as their teachers (Smuts, Allee), must have had sufficient information at hand to understand the substructure of the atom and radioactivity. But they seem to have had difficulties handling the new discoveries using their philosophical theorems.

Steinbeck and Ricketts do write in some detail about one elementary particle, the electron. It even appears as if the electron will be their synonym for the structured atomic, subbiological, physical world, but throughout the entire book only one other hint appears that indicates Steinbeck and Ricketts's familiarity with subatomic structures—a brief discussion of radioactivity. The role of electrons in nature, however, and Steinbeck and Ricketts's understanding of their importance, although definitely not as parts of the atom, is illuminated in the section on nonteleological thinking. Here they write:

Statistically the electron is free to go where it will. But the destiny pattern of any aggregate, comprising unaccountable billions of these same units, is fixed and certain, however much that inevitably may be slowed down. The eventual disintegration of a stick of wood or a piece of iron through the departure of the presumably immortal electrons is assured, even though it may be delayed by such protection against the operation of the second law of thermodynamics, as is afforded by painting and rustproofing. (LSC 160)

Steinbeck and Ricketts definitely do not accept the "statistically free" electrons as part of atomic matter's substructure. It may seem that on one occasion they included the subatomic world into their picture of the whole: "[A] man looking at reality brings his own limitations to the world. If he has strength and energy of mind, the tide pool stretches both ways, digs back to electrons and leaps space into the universe and fights out of the moment into non-conceptual time. Then ecology has a synonym which is ALL" (*LSC* 99). But this all-encompassing stretch from "electron to universe" does not reach from one infinity to the other, i.e., from the ever-extending border of the inner structure of matter to the ever-extending border of the universe.

One other passage shows that Steinbeck and Ricketts's knowledge of the subatomic world was rather sketchy and influenced by metaphysical and metabiological thinking rather than by scientific analysis. This passage concerns radioactivity associated with barren locations on the West Coast and in the Gulf of California, areas they call "burned." They write:

Might there not be a mild radio-activity which made one nervous in such a place so that he would say, trying to put words into his feeling, "This place is unfriendly. There is something here that will not tolerate my kind?" While some radio-activities have been shown to encourage not only life but mutation (note experimentation with fruitflies), there might be some other combinations which have an opposite effect. (LSC 210)

In 1940, at the time of the Sea of Cortez expedition, the nature of almost all types of ionizing radiation was known, and the scientific groundwork for weapons from nuclear energy was well under way. Radioactivity had long before been identified as a property of the atomic nucleus; and a specific kind of radiation emitted from unstable atomic nuclei, beta radiation, had been connected with electrons, about which Steinbeck and Ricketts know so much. By assigning anthropomorphic qualities to radioactivity, just because they do not have enough interpretable information, Steinbeck and Ricketts cross the border to speculation.

Today molecular biology and biotechnology are predominant branches of the life sciences, and we understand much more about such complex entities as whole organisms and the functions and interactions of their substructures, even down to molecular/atomic levels. This is the success of nonholistic, "reductionist" approaches. In a short but valid critique of holistic points of view, based on the success of molecular biology, the scientist Jacques Monod writes in *Le hazard et la nécessité:*

Certain schools of thought (all more or less consciously or confusedly influenced by Hegel) challenge the value of the analytical approach to systems as complex as living beings. According to these holist schools which, phoenixlike, spring up anew with every generation, only failure awaits attempts to reduce the properties of a very complex organization to the 'sum' of the properties of its parts. A most foolish and wrongheaded quarrel it is, merely testifying to the 'holist' profound misappreciation of scientific method and of the crucial role analysis plays in it. (79)

Monod then describes the achievements of the analytical approach and identifies the weakness of holistic thinking in the light of modern microbiology: "Lastly, from the study of these microscopic systems we come to see that for complexity, for richness, for potency, the cybernetic network in living beings far surpasses anything that the study of the overall behavior of whole organisms could ever hint at" (80).

Holistic philosophy as it developed in the 1940s and 1950s did not remain either nonteleological or politically innocent and is, therefore, questionable. The political consequences of holistic thinking are, insofar as they were used in practice, at least remarkable: Smuts was prime minister of the South African Union and, under the banner of holism, defended racism and colonialism in Great Britain's interest between 1939 and 1948. And it does not astonish that German Fascist ideology was very much in favor of holistic principles: "Du bist nichts; Dein Volk ist alles" ["You are nothing; the people are everything"]. If the part, the individual, is considered to be subordinate to the whole, and is governed by it, there is nothing to prevent the oppression of individuals and minority groups in the interest of the whole.

Although holistic philosophy seems to be the chosen vehicle of modern environmentalists, it is not the only philosophical approach to recognize the interconnecting and contradictory properties of matter. Steinbeck and Ricketts's holism has quite a few holes, and insofar as holistic philosophy contributes to coherence of the *Log from the Sea of Cortez*, it does not comprise the most valuable aspect of the narrative.

Related to the general lack of information on the subbiological world is Steinbeck and Ricketts's questionable extension of the discoveries of physics into the realm of the life sciences. Their use of terms borrowed from quantum mechanics, relativity theory, and field theory is doubtful in many respects. Steinbeck and Ricketts frequently merely adapt key words attached to the world of atoms, fields, and waves to the world of day-to-day experience, as well as to biological theories and hypotheses. Several statements show that they had problems comprehending the inherent limitations of these highly abstract physical science subjects.

For instance, Steinbeck and Ricketts quote a unified-field hypothesis for anything and everything. During their first night aboard the *Western Flyer*, after observing Tony, "the master" of the boat, they write: "There is probably a unified-field hypothesis available in navigation as in all things" (*LSC* 42). And in the long passage on nonteleological thinking: "We doubt that there are any truly 'closed systems.' Those so called represent kingdoms of a great continuity bounded by the sudden discontinuity of great synapses which eventually must be bridged in any unified field hypothesis" (*LSC* 169).

And "in a unified-field hypothesis, or in life, which is a unified field of reality, everything is an index of everything else" (*LSC* 306).

Here is clear evidence that Steinbeck and Ricketts misunderstood a concept of physics they used for describing by analogy other realms of reality. A field is a physical state of space, a property of matter, conditioned by the presence of mass, magnetic poles, electric charges, or currents. It transduces the influence of the forces exerted by these entities. There are electric, magnetic, and gravitational fields; and in the nuclear environment, meson, electron-positron, and neutron fields are postulated. In physics, a unified-field theory, one that would explain the connection and interaction between all of these fields, has not yet been found. Either simple misunderstanding or wishful thinking led Steinbeck and Ricketts to speculate about how a nebulous unified-field hypothesis could possibly be attached to all and everything. In the light of popular, holistically interpreted interconnectivity (everything is connected to everything), the word "field" might be an acceptable new creation, but its difference from the "physical field" should be stated or described. This does not happen.

Steinbeck and Ricketts were also interested in another physical phenomenon, oscillations or waves. Oscillations are important and ubiquitous in atomic and subatomic physics, in the physics of waves and fields, and elsewhere. The mathematical apparatus that describes waves makes use of complex numbers. But the complex numbers are not physical reality; they are only used to describe this reality. According to Steinbeck and Ricketts, "The mean levels of the extreme ups and downs of the oscillations symbolize opposites in the Hegelian sense. No wonder, then, that in physics the symbol of oscillation, $\sqrt{-1}$, is fundamental and primitive and ubiquitous, turning up in every equation" (*LSC* 43). And later, with an ironic twist: "For in spite of overwhelming evidence to the contrary, the trait of hope still controls the future, and man, not a species, but a triumphant race, will approach perfection, and, finally, tearing himself free, will march up the stars and take his place where, because of his power and virtue he belongs: on the right hand of the $\sqrt{-1}$" (*LSC* 103).

Richard Feynman, like no other teacher of physics, had the gift of expressing the difference between physical reality and descriptive apparatus:

*We are going to apply complex numbers to our analysis of physical phe-
nomena by the following trick. We have examples of things that oscillate;
the oscillation may have a certain driving force which is a certain constant times cos ωt. Now such a force, F = F$_0$ cos ωt, can be written as a
real part of a complex number F = F$_0$ e^{iωt} because e^{iωt} = cos ωt + i sin ωt .
The reason that we do this is that it is easier to work with an exponential
function than with cosine. So the whole trick is to represent our oscilla-
tory functions as the real parts of certain complex functions. The complex
number F that we have so defined is not a real physical force, because no
force in physics is really complex; actual forces have no imaginary part,
only a real part. We shall, however, speak of the "force" F$_0$ e^{iωt}, but the
actual force is the "real part" of that expression. (Feynman, Leighton, and
Sands, 1, chap. 23–1) [Note: i = $\sqrt{-1}$]*

In contrast to Feynman, Steinbeck and Ricketts have focused their
attention on an unimportant aspect of waves and oscillations. They
apparently did not distinguish between physical reality and the convenient describing apparatus and so imply that the "square root of
minus one," which appears in the imaginary part of complex numbers, is ubiquitous, but it is by no means primitive or fundamental
in physics. The mathematical description using complex numbers is
a mere convenience; the square root of minus one "has no physical
meaning."

Nor does quantum theory go unmentioned in *Log from the Sea of
Cortez*. In the long chapter on nonteleological thinking, Steinbeck
and Ricketts discuss the universality of quanta:

*Chiefly, however, we seem to arrive occasionally at definitive answers
through the workings of another primitive principle: the universality of
quanta. No one thing ever merges gradually into anything else; the steps
are discontinuous, but often so very minute as to seem truly continuous.
If the investigation is carried deep enough, the factor in question, instead
of being graphable as a continuous process, will be seen to function by
discrete quanta with gaps and synapses between, as do quanta of energy,
undulations of light. (LSC 168)*

Again Steinbeck and Ricketts transfer the realities of a physical
property and behavior of matter and light from their realm of validity by analogy into the general world. The word "quantum" sounds

good, but their use of the word does not hold water in physics. Again, Feynman, the great physics teacher, warns of false prophets:

Let us consider briefly some philosophical implications of quantum mechanics. As always, there are two aspects of the problem: one is the philosophical implication for physics, and the other is the extrapolation of philosophical matters to other fields. When philosophical ideas associated with science are dragged into another field, they are usually completely distorted. Therefore we shall confine our remarks as much as possible to physics itself. (Feynman, Leighton, and Sands, 2, chap 2–8)

Steinbeck and Ricketts's use of Einstein's name is another demonstration of careless reference to the principles of physics: "Our own interests lay in relationships of animal to animal. If one observes in this relational sense, it seems apparent that species are only commas in a sentence, that each species is at once the point and the base of a pyramid, that all life is relational to the point where an Einsteinian relativity seems to emerge" (*LSC* 256). Einstein's theories of relativity (there are two) are based on physical observations and are valid, despite their depth and subtleties, only in the physical world. Einstein's relativity theory, however, has influenced the lay philosophers of his and later times like no other. "Einstein's theory says all is relative" is one of the most common and convenient misinterpretations and misquotations of physical findings. Opines Feynman: "So the fact that 'things depend upon your frame of reference' is supposed to have had a profound effect on modern thought. One might well wonder why, because, after all, that things depend upon one's point of view is so simple an idea that it certainly cannot have been necessary to go to all the trouble of physical relativity theory in order to discover it" (Feynman, Leighton, and Sands, 1, chap. 16–1).

Steinbeck and Ricketts show awareness of the pitfalls into which they often seem to step: "The greatest danger to a speculative biologist is analogy. It is a pitfall to be avoided" (*LSC* 42). But they then use analogies uncritically and frequently. The few shortcomings resulting from their false analogies to the world of physics, however, should not distract us from the real importance of and wealth of thoughts presented in *The Log from the Sea of Cortez*.

In their time, only minds as independent and strong as those of Steinbeck and Ricketts could produce such a unique and over-whelming work, including expedition, adventure, science, parties, philosophy, and, finally, excellent prose. *Log from the Sea of Cortez* could not possibly be the work of narrow academic minds. Steinbeck and Ricketts may not have done their homework in physical sciences. They may have used popular adaptations of new physical theories to describe their day-to-day and biological world. They may have been attached to a holistic philosophy almost unquestioned by biologists of their time, somewhat like a religion, a philosophy that nowadays has faded as a result of the progress of molecular biology. But these are not the major criteria for evaluating their potential contribution to the current debate about who should study nature and how he or she should go about it. Rather, their major contribution is a very careful look at and meditation on what a scientist who wants to understand nature has to do and to be.

The present-day definition of "environmental science/scientist" is very confusing. The "naturalist" is not considered to be an "environmental scientist" any more. Environmental sciences and the individuals working in them range from university-bound social scientists to gainfully employed physical scientists at private companies who are "influencing" the environment within the limits of discharge and emission imposed by the Code of Federal Regulations, with all kinds of shades and hues in between.

Just within the university "environment," an amazing flood of supposedly new areas of environmental study is occurring at minor, major, certificate, master's, and doctoral levels. Name changes for existing programs in natural sciences, however, predominate without significant changes of content—although new curriculum developments including mixtures of physical, life, social, and political sciences do pop up occasionally. Excellent new ideas surrounded by recycled old curricula with new and fancy titles indicate the lack of coherent scientific discussion about the subject. In addition, what little discussion is going on is very parochial; that is, whichever science, social science, or engineering program wants to decorate itself with the new "environmental" label tries to ensure that its individual subject area is most important and therefore must comprise the major part of a curriculum. Political and social aspects are actually the driving forces of the new "environmental sciences," while philosophy, ethics, humanities, arts, and solid basic science are frequently overlooked.

There are several reasons for this urgent rush into the "environmental sciences." The first is obvious: society's increasing awareness of undisturbed nature as mankind's greatest resource. This concern in itself radically contradicts the traditional values of the Western world, whose ideology is built upon the use and exploitation of nature. Unfortunately, the new awareness is not the predominant "reason" for the "environmental science" fad. The teaching of "environmental sciences" and the unreflecting inflation of programs is being driven instead by the university's need to lure students into programs with attractive names and society's need for a workforce that can compete successfully within the framework of environmental regulation. The goal of educating students in the best possible way to understand the interrelation of all components, properties, and forms of matter in nature, including a clear recognition of science, scientific procedures, and philosophical and humanistic aspects of man's interaction with this nature, is rarely found.

Some expansion on the less altruistic motives for program inflation in the "environmental sciences" may be necessary. The first, attracting students into a program with a name or label, rather than content, is a mercantilistic, and an academically questionable, approach. It is, however, driven by the economic necessities of the American educational system, where enrollment and faculty-student classroom hours may override academic quality. The second, creating a workforce educated to handle environmental regulation, is tied not so much to "environmental awareness" as to implementing laws and regulations passed over the last thirty years to moderate human impact on the environment. As controversial and as complex as these rules and regulations may be at local, state, and federal levels, enforcement of the law and control of hazardous substances and processes require a well-educated workforce. A good foundation in physical and life sciences and a satisfactory education in the regulatory process will provide society with the hazardous materials specialists it needs. But note that these are specialists, not environmental scientists and by no means naturalists.

Steinbeck and Ricketts have a very strong opinion about who can be called a real scientist. A real scientist cannot be a specialist, cannot be narrowly focused. They do not ignore the fact that a scientist may be engaged in difficult and highly complicated work (e.g., Einstein), but they ask that he or she be wide open and willing to step beyond academically established boundaries in the attempt to understand nature. They do not believe that a scientist who sits day in, day out in a laboratory will be able to contribute to understanding the complexities of nature, because he or she obviously cannot appreciate the subject in its many manifestations.

A real scientist in the process of acquiring knowledge must perpetuate his or her curiosity, for each new answer must necessarily create new questions. A real scientist cannot and will not retire into pure didacticism and will always be enthusiastic about many subjects of study. A real scientist must communicate answers and questions about nature to the general public and is willing to do so as a matter of principle. A real scientist must be close to the open-minded naturalists of the past century.

Steinbeck and Ricketts have demonstrated that by staying outside the academic world, with its rules and requirements, one can cross boundaries of traditionally separate subject areas with an ease that facilitates innovative discussion. Such openness can lead to speculation as well as to simplified analogies rather than carefully researched statements, but the risk is worthwhile. Understanding nature as a whole, inseparable entity is the best foundation for learning how to live in it without destroying it. Steinbeck and Ricketts demonstrate that all forms of matter, from the tide pool to the stars, are interrelated, connected. In asking the reader to think about interconnectivity, they provide insight and guide their audience away from particularized and parochial thinking.

To be a natural scientist of Steinbeck and Ricketts's standard seems to be possible today only outside the academic mainstream. Forced to produce a qualified workforce, the majority of institutions of higher learning will continue in their present path. The legitimate demand for specialists is high, and so universities will continue to "turn out" specialists to meet the consumer/taxpayer's demand. The specialists will be well trained, of course, and able to understand chemistry or nuclear sciences perfectly, as well as laws and regulations.

Such specialized "environmental scientists," however, may not be able to cross boundaries and think the radical new thoughts that might be needed. Steinbeck and Ricketts's *Log from the Sea of Cortez* provides a strong argument that academia must provide curricula and learning environments for the education of classical naturalist-scientists. Both the sciences and humanities are called upon to create such an education for the few that want to engage in it. Society needs naturalist-scientists as well as specialists.

Notes

1. Alexander von Humboldt, who wrote "Kosmos, Versuch einer Physikalis-chen Weltbeschreibung," a work highly appreciated by Darwin, was one of the English naturalist's most important predecessors (Clark 1985, 22).

2. Darwin himself confirmed his enthusiasm for a position on the *Beagle* after reading an English translation of Alexander von Humboldt's "Vom Orinoko zum Amazonas" in addition to Sir John Herschel's "Preliminary Discussions on the Study of Natural Philosophy" (Clark 1985, 25, 29). More relevant to Steinbeck and Ricketts was Tshirikov, Bering, and Steller's exploration of the Alaskan Coast (1741–1742), with seagoing expeditions originating from Petropavlovsk. But Ricketts, in earlier writings related to his later expedition to Alaska, mentions prior expeditions only in a general and very brief paragraph: "The British Co-lumbia–S.E. Alaska shore is interesting biologically in that it has received scant attention recently, although it was one of the first areas on the Pacific Coast to be carefully examined (Brandt, the Russian, in 1835). . . . In the groups treated, the reports of the Columbia Puget Sound Expedition, the Harriman Alaska Expedi-tion, and those of the Canadian Arctic Expedition are illuminating, and there are various other scattered papers (Verrill, etc.) and from the marine stations at Friday Harbor and Nanaimo. Thus a good many systematic surveys have been made and reported on by specialists; but seldom in a general way or ecologi-cally—the point of departure having been specific rather than general" (in Hedg-peth 1978, pt. 1, 16). Humboldt's voyage and Steller's expedition must have es-caped Ed Ricketts.

ELEVEN

The Pearl in the *Sea of Cortez:* Steinbeck's Use of Environment

Kiyoshi Nakayama

While the Western Flyer *was docked at La Paz, Steinbeck heard a story of a young boy who found a pearl of great value, could not sell it for a fair price, and so threw it back into the sea. This sketch from* Sea of Cortez *became the germ of Steinbeck's novella,* The Pearl. *But connections between* The Pearl *and* Sea of Cortez *go deeper—to a shared philosophic stance. Steinbeck's biological holism and environmental sensitivity are reflected in both works.*

In the "Narrative" section of *Sea of Cortez*, John Steinbeck notes that "on the water's edge of La Paz a new hotel was going up, and it looked very expensive. Probably the airplanes will bring week-enders from Los Angeles before long, and the beautiful poor bedraggled old town will bloom with a Floridian ugliness" (*SOC* 118). He was prophetic. Fifty years later, in the early summer of 1989, a Mexicana jet brought me and dozens of tourists from Los Angeles to La Paz. The city I found had grown to a population of 180,000 people. The hotel where I stayed, Steinbeck's "new," "expensive" Hotel Perla, was only one of many high-rise luxury units along the beach. Even though I knew that the La Paz of the 1990s would be a far different place from that of the 1940s, I had long wanted to visit the old city—the setting of *The Pearl*—as well as the Sea of Cortez that Steinbeck delineates so attractively in the novella. Also, I had long wished to learn about the rise and fall of pearl industry in the area and, with luck, also about the Indian boy's story that Steinbeck had heard in 1940.

The present essay materialized from this "leisurely" research trip in search of "The Pearl in the Sea of Cortez," tracing closely how Steinbeck made use of what he saw in the Gulf of California in the spring of 1940 to write his own version of the "pearl" story. Accordingly, I will discuss how Steinbeck's organismic biology and philosophy as well as his use of the environment—the sea, the land, and the people of La Paz and the Sea of Cortez—relate to Kino's life and the theme of *The Pearl*.

The Historical Background

From 11 March through 20 April 1940, John Steinbeck and Edward F. Ricketts made a scientific expedition to the Gulf of California aboard a chartered purse seiner, the *Western Flyer*. On the night of 20 March, waiting for a pilot to lead the boat through the channel to La Paz Harbor the next morning, Steinbeck and the crew "wanted very much to get to La Paz," because they "were out of beer" and found "the water in [their] tanks stale-tasting" (*SOC* 101). Steinbeck continues:

But there were other reasons why we longed for La Paz. Cape San Lucas had not really been a town, and our crew had convinced itself that it had been a very long time out of touch with civilization. . . . In addition, there is the genuine fascination of the city of La Paz. Everyone in the area knows the greatness of La Paz. You can get anything in the world there, they say. . . . It is a proud thing to have been born in La Paz, and a cloud of delight hangs over the distant city from the time when it was the great pearl center of the world. The robes of the Spanish kings and the stoles of bishops in Rome were stiff with the pearls from La Paz. (SOC 101–102)

The history of La Paz dates back to the sixteenth century. A brochure available at the Tourist Information Center reads:

La Paz . . . was founded by Hernan Cortes in May 1535. The conqueror called it "Puerto de Santa Cruz" (Port of the Holy Cross), but in 1596 Captain Sebastian de Vizcaino, referring to the beautiful bay as "Bahia de La Paz," baptized it with that name. . . . It was a coveted prey of English pirates for the best pearls of the world found here, and its beaches served them as solid shelter after their raiding the galleons cruising the Pacific Ocean. (La Paz N. pg.)

La Paz was permanently settled in 1811 and twenty years later became the capital of all of Baja California. In the course of its history, there was brutal bloodshed, even in this peninsula of Baja California, remote from the more volatile population centers of Mexico proper. A pamphlet titled *Guia Que Hacer A Donde Ir* [*What to Do, Where to Go*], notes, "After many years of war between the natives and Spanish troops, this place was named by the Spanish when the permanent settlement was established. The city of La Paz was called 'The Capital of the Pearls' due to the vast exploitation of pearls over the centuries" (Diaz de Sandi, N. pg.).

Steinbeck's *The Pearl* is based upon an ostensibly true story the author heard during his stay in La Paz. He nursed the story in his mind for four years before writing his own version, "The Pearl of the World," which appeared in the *Woman's Home Companion* (December 1945) before the novel was published by Viking Press in 1947. The story Steinbeck heard at La Paz was, as described in *Sea of Cortez*, about an Indian boy who found a great pearl, was unable to sell it for the amount he had expected, and, hurt and tortured, became angry. Finally he cursed the pearl, threw it into the sea, and laughed a great deal about it. After recounting the folklorelike story, Steinbeck comments that it "seems to be a true story, but it is so much like a parable that it almost can't be. This Indian boy is too heroic, too wise. He knows too much and acts on his knowledge. In every way, he goes contrary to human direction. The story is probably true, but we don't believe it; it is far too reasonable to be true" (*SOC* 103).

Steinbeck expanded on the simple story he heard at La Paz, thinking of making it into a movie script, hoping that his own version would be as "true" as the seed story, but at the same time a parable not "far too reasonable to be true." The principal alterations he made were to convert the heroic figure of the unnamed Indian boy to a young married man named Kino,[1] who has a wife, Juana, and a first-born son, Coyotito. They represent the whole family of man.

César Piñeda Chacon, director of the Museum of Anthropology, has commented on the background of the story: "The native inhabitants in the La Paz area, consisting originally of the three tribes—Pericues, Guaycuras, and Cochimos—had come from the South Seas, and one of these tribes engaged in pearl fishing. The pearls they took from the sea were so-called 'black' pearls, and the most flourishing era dates back to the 1890s. The pearl oysters died off, however, in an epidemic that began around 1940."[2]

Chacon's statement suggests that the pearl of the world found by the Indian boy in the germinal story might not have been of "silver incandescence" or "gray" (*TP* 19, 89) as in Steinbeck's fictional descriptions, but with a "blackish" quality. And the story itself might not have been as "recent" as Steinbeck claims in *Sea of Cortez*. The epidemic mentioned by Chacon took place in the 1930s,[3] with pearl oysters in the Sea of Cortez dying out just as the sardines in Monterey Bay disappeared. Significantly, Ed Ricketts's *Sea of Cortez* journal, "Gulf of California Trip: March–April 1940," mentions only one pearl oyster found at Puerto Escondido on 25 March 1940: "a pearl oyster" is brought by a local fisherman and his son together with "a gigantic scallop" and "a small hacha, several giant conches, and much other stuff" (in Hedgpeth 1978, pt. 2, 120). Similarly, Steinbeck notes in *Sea of Cortez*: "[A man and a little boy] had also some of the hacha, the huge fan-shaped clam; pearl oysters, *which are growing rare*; and several huge conchs" (*SOC* 158; emphasis added).

The Sea

Steinbeck begins chapter 2 of *The Pearl* with a description of the estuary at La Paz based on what he actually saw in 1940:

The town lay on a broad estuary, its old yellow plastered buildings hugging the beach. And on the beach the white and blue canoes that came from Nayarit were drawn up. . . . The beach was yellow sand, but at the water's edge a rubble of shell and algae took its place. Fiddler crabs bubbled and sputtered in their holes in the sand, and in the shallows little lobsters popped in and out of their tiny homes in the rubble and sand. The sea bottom was rich with crawling and swimming and growing things. The brown algae waved in the gentle currents and the green eel grass swayed and little sea horses clung to its stems. Spotted botete, *the poison fish, lay on the bottom in the eel-grass beds, and the bright-colored swimming crabs scampered over them.* (TP 13)

La Paz and its estuary appear to be as calm and peaceful as the town's Spanish name suggests. But Steinbeck reminds the reader that man is not free from such poisonous creatures as botete (or scorpions). Of all the marine flora and fauna Steinbeck and Ricketts collected during their expedition, botete drew their curiosity most strongly, and *Sea of Cortez* includes a comprehensive explanation of the poison fish, reading in part: "we found botete everywhere in the

warm shallow waters of the Gulf. Probably he is the most prevalent fish of all in lagoons and eel-grass flats. He lies on the bottom"
(SOC 122).

After describing the estuary, Steinbeck in chapter 2 of *The Pearl*
introduces the ambiguous and uncertain vision associated with atmospheric haze in the Gulf of California and, in particular, the La
Paz area. He writes:

> *Although the morning was young, the hazy mirage was up. The uncer-
> tain air that magnified some things and blotted out others hung over the
> whole Gulf so that all sights were unreal and vision could not be trusted;
> so that sea and land had the sharp clarities and the vagueness of a dream.
> Thus it might be that the people of the Gulf trust things of the spirit and
> things of the imagination, but they do not trust their eyes to show them
> distance or clear outline or any optical exactness. . . . There was no cer-
> tainty in seeing, no proof that what you saw was there or was not there.
> And the people of the Gulf expected all places were that way, and it was
> not strange to them. (TP 14)*

In *Sea of Cortez*, Steinbeck had already written: "The mirage shook
the horizon and draped it with haze, distorted shapes, twisted
mountains, and made even the bushes seem to hang in the air. Until
every foot of such a shore is covered and measured, the shape and
extent of these estuaries will not be known" (SOC 254). And Ricketts,
also describing the area of Estero de la Luna, noted in his journal:
"Mirage is very very bad here. A strange region. You can't see the
shores of these lagoons. No wonder the charts show dotted lines.
Everything so strange and indefinite, and wind always on the water.
No wonder the Yaqui fishermen (if it was Yaquis that I talked to) have
such a bad reputation. They live in an uncertain land" (in Hedgpeth
1978, pt. 2, 143).

Steinbeck uses the mirage in *The Pearl* to emphasize the dual quality
of the landscape; to describe, rather symbolically, how the local people trust things of the spirit and things of the imagination but not
the appearance of reality. In the novella, everything seems to possess
this duality, a duality Steinbeck sees embodied in the history of
Mexico as a country. He notes, "As with all retold tales that are in
people's hearts, there are only good and bad things and black and

white things and good and evil things and no in-between any-where" (*TP* ii). When a scorpion moves delicately down the rope to baby Coyotito, Kino hears in his mind "the Song of Evil" on top of "the Song of the Family," while Juana "repeat[s] an ancient magic to guard against such evil, and on top of that she mutter[s] a Hail Mary between clenched teeth" (*TP* 5).

Likewise the great pearl is beautiful only when gazed upon by a person of pure heart. In the last scene of the story, when Kino looks into the surface of the pearl just before throwing it back into the sea, "it was gray and ulcerous. . . . And the pearl was ugly . . . like a ma-lignant growth" (*TP* 89). "Evil faces peered from it into his eyes" (89), because Kino has killed the trackers and sees his infant son with the top of his head shot away. Once the pearl settles into the water, how-ever, after Kino has released it, "The lights on its surface were green and lovely" (*TP* 90).

In chapter 3, the novella turns to deadly fights for survival taking place mostly in the darkness of night: "Out in the estuary a tight woven school of small fishes glittered and broke water to escape a school of great fishes that drove in to eat them. And in the houses the people could hear the swish of the small ones and the bouncing splash of the great ones as the slaughter went on. . . . And the night mice crept about on the ground and the little night hawks hunted them silently" (*TP* 32–33). This paragraph falls between the doctor's two night visits to Kino's house, so that readers cannot miss the sym-bolic application of the "law of the jungle" to the Indians—the mem-bers of the Kino family are destined to be eaten as the weak. The estuary, where marine animals live and kill each other for survival, is a microcosm of the sea, just as a town is a microcosm of the human world. The motif recurs throughout the Steinbeck canon, for in-stance, in *Cannery Row*, where the animals of the tide pool kill and eat one another to live and where the human community also func-tions as a microcosm of a larger ecosystem. And Steinbeck never fails to describe how, in the estuary or elsewhere, the strong consume the weak.

Steinbeck's phalanx theory, a thesis describing the group behavior of the schooling fishes and of man, was first introduced in a letter to Carlton A. Sheffield dated 21 June 1933:

For a number of years I have been very much interested in certain reactions and phenomena which seemed to indicate a racial physiology. I have a good many hundreds of notes. Certain groups of human units, their boundaries usually topographical, react to stimuli much as though they were a unit much more close-knit than is generally thought. . . . The larger unit, and it may contain any number of the biological units, has a nature entirely different from its parts as different in fact as a man is from the single cells of which he is composed. As an example—the biologic unit has a mechanism which allows him to profit by experience. If he follows a course and is hurt, no[thing] changes his process. The larger unit has not this mechanism. The group unit never learns by experience, in fact has not such a faculty. The group unit is so strong that it can change the nature of its biologic units.[4]

And in an undated letter to George Albee, probably written in July 1933, Steinbeck notes:

We know that man seems to be a physical entity and, to some extent a spiritual entity. . . . And there have been mysterious things, inexplicable things which could not be explained if man is the final unit. Now a man while he is made of cells which in turn are made of atoms and electrons and so forth, by no means has the nature of his parts or small units. So man is not the final unit. He also arranges himself into larger units, which I have called the phalanx. . . . And just as man's nature is not the nature of his cells, so the phalanx by no means has the nature of man. For indeed the phalanx has its own memory—memory of the great tides when the moon was close, memory of starvations when the food of the world was exhausted.[5]

In *Sea of Cortez* Steinbeck uses colonies of pelagic tunicates to illustrate the phalanx theory: "Each member of the colony is an individual animal, but the colony is another individual animal, not at all like the sum of its individuals" (*SOC* 165). Later in the book he discusses the idea more fully in reference to fish:

And this larger animal, the school, seems to have a nature and drive and ends of its own. It is more than and different from the sum of its units. If we can think in this way, it will not seem so unbelievable that every fish heads in the same direction, that the water interval between fish and fish is identical with all the units, and that it seems to be directed by a school intelligence. (SOC 240)

And in *The Pearl*, Steinbeck uses his phalanx theory to describe La Paz as a closed and self-contained community with a rigid structure, noting: "A town is a thing like a colonial animal. A town has a nervous system and a head and shoulders and feet. A town is a thing separate from all other towns, so that there are no two towns alike. And a town has a whole emotion. How news travels through a town is a mystery not easily to be solved" (*TP* 21). As this passage clearly shows, Steinbeck expresses in terms of organismal biology his contention that a town, like a colonial animal, is an independent entity different from and foreign to other towns. Furthermore, he uses this favorite motif in the story to give a mysterious quality to news spreading quickly across a community.

Many have noted that Steinbeck uses the phalanx theory as a recurrent theme in *Tortilla Flat, In Dubious Battle, The Grapes of Wrath,* and *The Moon Is Down*. He also uses it in *The Pearl*, as noted above, but not as a dominant theme. The conflicts between the Indians and the descendants of the Spanish are used as historical background in the story, but there are no battles between the mob and the oppressors as in *In Dubious Battle* or *The Moon Is Down*.

The Land

Another significant landscape description, analyzed by Louis Owens in *John Steinbeck's Re-Vision of America*, is of the mountainous inland area where the Kino family arrive after a two-day exodus, driven by the dark trackers just as Pepé Torres is driven by anonymous dark pursuers in the short story "Flight." It would have been almost impossible for the Kino family to walk to Loreto, located 220 miles from La Paz by today's highway. The walking distance may be shorter, but the trail is through wild mountains, arid and hot throughout the year, and barren except for cacti and a few shrubs. Kino and Juana would surely die unless they found an oasis, and so Steinbeck writes:

High in the grey stone mountains, under a frowning peak, a little spring bubbled out of a rupture in the stone. It was fed by shade-preserved snow in the summer, and now and then it died completely and bare rocks and dry algae were on its bottom. But nearly always it gushed out, cold and

clean and lovely. . . . It bubbled out into a pool, and then fell a hundred
feet to another pool, and this one, overflowing, dropped again, so that it
continued, down and down, until it came to the rubble of the upland, and
there it disappeared altogether. (TP 78–79)

Undoubtedly, this is the place that Steinbeck visited when he and
Ed Ricketts were invited on a two-day hunting trip by a rancher, a
schoolteacher, and a customs man at Puerto Escondido, just beneath
Loreto. Steinbeck and Ricketts "accepted immediately" because
they "wanted to see the country" (*SOC* 159). At one campsite is a
pool, an oasis, just like the one Kino and Juana "came utterly weary
to" (*TP* 80) in their flight. Steinbeck notes in *Sea of Cortez:*

We came at last to a trail of broken stone and rubble so steep that the
mules could not carry us any more. . . . After a short climb we emerged
on a level place in a deep cleft in the granite mountains. In this cleft a
tiny stream of water fell hundreds of feet from pool to pool. There were
palm trees and wild grapevines and large ferns, and the water was cool
and sweet. This little stream, coming from so high up in the mountains
and falling so far, never had the final dignity of reaching the ocean. The
desert sucked it down and the heat dried it up and on the level it disap-
peared in a light mist of frustration. (SOC 161–62)

Then Steinbeck and Ricketts look into the pool and make further
observations as biologists:

We had sat beside the little pool and watched the tree-frogs and the horse-
hair worms and the water-skaters, and had wondered how they got there,
so far from other water. It seemed to us that life in every form is incipi-
ently everywhere waiting for a chance to take root and start reproducing;
eggs, spores, seeds, bacilli—everywhere. Let a raindrop fall and it is
crowded with the waiting life. Everything is everywhere; and we, seeing
the desert country, the hot waterless expanse, and knowing how far away
the nearest water must be, say with a kind of disbelief, "How did they get
clear here, these little animals?" And until we can attack with our poor
blunt weapon of reason that causal process and reduce it, we do not quite
believe in the horsehair worms and the tree-frogs. The great fact is that
they are there. (SOC 164)

Also interesting is Ed Ricketts's impression of the area recorded in his *Sea of Cortez* journal:

We six rode until too steep, then led horses to flat, maybe 1500' up, near 300–400' drop waterfall. Little water, but good pools. And such an oasis around it; known probably and loved for hundreds of years. Fresh and cool. [G]reen; the shadow of a rock in a weary land. Or, rather, in a fantastic land, since the plains and hills over which we came were rich with xerophytic plants, cacti, mimosa, brush and small trees with thorns. . . . The little waterfall canyon up in the mountains was steep, unapproachable from below because of cliffs; we got in from a side canyon above. It had palms . . . , some tree with edible fruit . . . , maidenhair fern (infusion used on women after childbirth), bracken, lichens. Tree frogs about pool, tadpoles, water striders and horsehair worms within. Doves. (in Hedgpeth 1978, pt. 2, 120)

The wetland Steinbeck pictures in *The Pearl* is quite similar to that encountered on the *Sea of Cortez* hunting trip:

Beside this tiny stream . . . colonies of plants grew, wild grape and little palms, maidenhair fern, hibiscus, and tall pampas grass with feathery rods raised above the spike leaves. And in the pool lived frogs and water-skaters, and waterworms crawled on the bottom of the pool. Everything that loved water came to these few shallow places. . . . The little pools were places of life because of the water, and places of killing because of the water, too. (TP 79)

The only species encountered on the actual trip left out of *The Pearl* is the dove, defined in *The Dictionary of Mythology, Folklore, and Symbols* as "a symbol of gentleness, peace, and divine guidance, as in the legend of Noah" (Jobes 466). Although Steinbeck's descriptions of flying doves proved quite effective in the first chapter of *Of Mice and Men* and the eighth chapter of *The Grapes of Wrath,* he must have felt that there was no place for a bird of peace in *The Pearl* or in the Baja California landscape where Kino and his family are hunted like wild animals.

To Steinbeck, the little pools where the Kino family and the dark trackers arrive are, like the Great Tide Pool in *Cannery Row,* not only "places of life" but "places of killing." In "Some Philosophers in the Sun: Steinbeck's *Cannery Row,*" Robert S. Hughes argues that "the two most important strands of Steinbeck's thinking in *Cannery Row*" are "the moral and the ecological" (in Benson 1990, 119). His argument is basically true of *The Pearl* as well. Just as Jackson J. Benson calls *Cannery Row* "an ecological parable" ("John Steinbeck's *Cannery Row*" 25), so we may call *The Pearl* "an ecological parable." The two stories are only superficially different from one another. *The Pearl* is not only a symbolic parable with moral lessons but also a realistically told, humanistic novella with ecological and sociological viewpoints.

People

In his Mexican novella Steinbeck reveals the keen economic antagonism between the poor exploited pearl fishermen (native Indians) and the rich, greedy, Spanish professionals (the doctor, the priest, and the pearl brokers). The former live in primitive brush houses in an isolated community on the fringes of the town; the latter lead a luxurious life in the stone houses of the wealthier section. In *Sea of Cortez*, Steinbeck recollects what he found at Pulmo Reef—how the Indians' dwellings looked and what their lives are like. The Indians in *The Pearl* lead similar lives in indigent circumstances:

On the shore behind the white beach was one of those lonely little rancherias *we came to know later. Usually a palm or two are planted near by, and by these trees sticking up out of the brush one can locate the houses. There is usually a small corral, a burro or two, a few pigs, and some scrawny chickens. The cattle range wide for food. A dugout canoe lies on the beach, for a good part of the food comes from the sea. Rarely do you see a light from the sea, for the people go to sleep at dusk and awaken with the first light. (SOC 74)*

As Kino and Juana usually do, the Indians habitually hold their "blankets carefully over their noses and mouths" to protect themselves from the white men (*SOC* 74). Steinbeck explains:

So much evil the white man had brought to their ancestors: his breath was poisonous with the lung disease; to sleep with him was to poison the generations. Where he set down his colonies the indigenous people withered and died. He brought industry and trade but no prosperity, riches but no ease. After four hundred years of him these people have ragged clothes and the shame that forces the wearing of them; iron harpoons for their hands, syphilis and tuberculosis; a few of the white man's less complex neuroses, and a curious devotion to a God who was sacrificed long ago in the white man's country. (SOC 74)

At the outset of *The Pearl*, when Coyotito is stung by a scorpion, Kino and Juana take the baby to a Spanish doctor for immediate treatment. But it is a desperate and reckless idea for an Indian to go to the doctor without money. The greedy doctor complains, "I am a doctor, not a veterinary" (*TP* 11). Kino has no money but "eight small misshapen seed pearls, as ugly and gray as little ulcers, flattened and almost valueless" (*TP* 11). Similarly, in *Sea of Cortez*, Steinbeck delineates a meeting at Pulmo Reef with three Indians who sit in a dugout canoe: "One of the men at least offers us a match-box in which are a few misshapen little pearls like small pale cancers. Five pesos [one U.S. dollar] he wants for the pearls, and he knows they aren't worth it. We give him a carton of cigarettes and take his pearls, although we do not want them, for they are ugly little things" (*SOC* 75). Kino's pearls too prove valueless, although he holds them in "a paper folded many times" kept in "a secret place somewhere under his blanket" (*TP* 11). Refused by the greedy doctor who longs for "civilized living" in France, all Kino can do is strike "the gate a crushing blow with his fist" (*TP* 12), making the blood flow down between his fingers.

The Indians had always been cheated by the white men and the mestizos, as Steinbeck writes in *The Pearl*. At one time the old Indians, resisting unfair treatment by the brokers, conceived the idea of selling their pearls for better prices, and to this end they sent an agent to the capital. It was a vain effort: "He was never heard of again and the pearls were lost. Then they got another man, and they started him off, and he was never heard of again. And so they gave the whole thing up and went back to the old way" (*TP* 45–46). A common understanding among the Indians was that "it was against religion. . . . The loss of the pearl was a punishment visited on those who tried to leave their station" (*TP* 46). This is the position the priest repeats at least once a year in a sermon. In La Paz, perhaps as in any town in Mexico, social rank was established during the Spanish conquest, and continuing subjugation was sanctified by religion.

Kino's attempt to sell his great pearl in the capital is in vain; his journey turns out to be a mere flight from the enemy. In the novella's final impressive scene, after Kino throws the great but cursed pearl back into the sea, the only thing remaining to him is a rifle taken from one of the trackers. At the outset of the story, Kino and Juana had a brush house, a canoe, and most of all their beloved son, Coyotito. At the end they have lost everything but have gained a rifle.

Puzzled critics and readers naturally question the ending. How will Kino and Juana use the weapon after all their tragic losses? Will they be able to live when their only possession is a rifle?[6] But Kino has long coveted a rifle, and ironically, it is the only one of his dreams to come true. Earlier in the story, when Kino, watching his great pearl, adds a rifle to the list of things he wants, Steinbeck notes prophetically that "it was the rifle that broke down the barriers. This was an impossibility, and if he could think of having a rifle whole horizons were burst and he could rush on" (TP 25).

Now that Kino has symbolically broken down the barrier, he may be able to "go running about" against the priest's teaching to "remain faithful to his post" (TP 46) but toward what end? Nothing meaningful and productive can be accomplished by violence only. Kino will always be in danger of being shot by another "dark thing," even though the people see that "there was almost a magical protection about [Kino and Juana]" (88). As Roy S. Simmonds contends in "Steinbeck's 'The Pearl': Legend, Film, Novel": "The logical ending to the story is future tragedy and death" (in Benson, Short Novels 1990, 182).

Another possible interpretation of the ending, however, is that Kino will contribute to his people. The Indians need someone to protect them or at least someone to prevent them from being cheated. To work for the betterment of society seems to be Kino's only recourse. It is, as Harry Morris suggests in "The Pearl: Realism and Allegory," "the third journey, the journey still to be made, the journey that Dante had still to make even after rising out of Hell to Purgatory and Paradise, the journey that any fictional character has still to make after his dream-vision allegory is over" (in Davis 1972, 160).

Such a journey would resemble the one the historic Emiliano Zapata made. In fact, as his brother Juan Tomás says, Kino has already "defied not the pearl buyers, but the whole structure, the whole way of life" (*TP* 54). He can be a Zapata of La Paz, the leader of the people Steinbeck and Ricketts define in *Sea of Cortez*: "the people we call leaders are simply those who, at the given moment, are moving in the direction behind which will be found the greatest weight, and which represents a future mass movement" (*SOC* 138). Steinbeck does not make Kino "laugh a great deal" against modern capitalism, social injustice, and human greediness, as the young boy of the germinal story did; rather, Steinbeck emphasizes his protagonist's seriousness (*TP* 88–89).

In short, Kino may be destined for self-sacrifice in the fight against oppression, like Jim Nolan of *In Dubious Battle* or Jim Casy in *The Grapes of Wrath*. He can be, if he wishes, a person like Friend Ed in *Burning Bright*, a "leader of the people" like Jody Tiflin's grandfather in *The Red Pony*. Or he could be, in Oriental terms, a "dogan," the "wild goose that takes the role of the watch and safeguard of the flock."[7] Or in Steinbeck's own terms from *In Dubious Battle*, Kino could be the "head" or the "eyes" of the "group-man" or "phalanx." What Lester Jay Marks calls the Steinbeck hero, a Ricketts-like figure, is always such a great individual who willingly sacrifices himself for the whole (30).

Conclusion

I have examined how Steinbeck uses the environment—the sea, the land, and the people of the Sea of Cortez region—to incorporate organismic biology and philosophy as undercurrents in *The Pearl*. He exuberantly exploited what he really saw in the Gulf of California in 1940 to make his own version of the pearl story "believable" rather than "far too reasonable to be true." In his 1953 article, "My Short Novels," Steinbeck disclosed that he "tried to write it as folklore, to give it that set-aside, raised-up feeling that all folk stories have" (Tedlock and Wicker 1957, 40). Some may call *The Pearl* "folklore," as Steinbeck suggests, and others may call it a parable, a symbolic tale, a realistic novella, or humanistic short fiction. And yet such labels are always unsatisfactory. The novella surpasses any classification—it is a well-combined, multilayered novella, created by what John Clark Pratt calls "Steinbeck's use of syncretic allegory" (14).

Steinbeck's depiction of the environment and his holistic world view correlate the protagonist's life and the themes of the novella. In

The Pearl, the environment appropriately functions as a microcosm in which the protagonists live as a family of the world and in which Kino as hero could act as "dogan," a guardian of the people like Emiliano Zapata.

Notes

1. He is named after the seventeenth-century Jesuit, Eusebio Francisco Kino (1645?–1711), a missionary and explorer in the gulf region who visited La Paz on 1 April 1683.

2. César Piñeda Chacon, interview with the author, 31 May 1989, La Paz, Mexico (interpreter, Eliza Ruiz de Page, secretary of the Museum of Anthropology).

3. Sparky Enea notes in his recent book, *With Steinbeck in the Sea of Cortez* (1991): "The oysters had a disease eight or so years before that and had just petered out. The oyster shells were thick with disease" (34).

4. "Steinbeck: A Life in Letters 'Original Unrevised MS, Chapters I–VI,' " II–37, 38. The duplicated letters donated by Elaine Steinbeck are kept at the Special Collections of the Bracken Library, Ball State University. The published letter included in *Steinbeck: A Life in Letters* (1975), pp. 74–77, is heavily edited.

5. "Steinbeck: A Life in Letters 'Original Unrevised MS, Chapters I–VI,' " II–48 (Bracken Library, Ball State University). See also *Steinbeck: A Life in Letters,* 79.

6. Warren French notes in his *John Steinbeck* (1961): "Steinbeck leaves the impression at the end of *The Pearl* that all is forgiven and will be forgotten. But is it? . . . There are too many left here. Kino has killed several agents of his pursuers. Can he expect to go unpunished? Even more important, can he really suppress his ambitions and accept his former humble place?" (142). Roy S. Simmonds in "Steinbeck's *The Pearl:* Legend, Film, Novel" also reveals his dissatisfaction with the ending: "Steinbeck leaves his readers perplexed and unbelieving. . . . We cannot believe that Kino would be content to return to the environment from which he thought he had escaped, nor can we believe that he would have been unreservedly welcomed back by those he had, in his briefly assumed position of superiority, been forced to leave behind in his obstinate search for wealth. And what of the three men he had killed? Are not the pearl dealers going to exact some sort of revenge, even if they cannot now get their hands on the pearl? . . . Kino will have to defend himself with [the rifle]. There is more blood to be shed, ultimately Kino's own" (in Benson 1990, 182).

7. Yukichi Fukuzawa, the founder of Keio Gijuku University in Tokyo, Japan, defines a dogan as "a wild goose in a flock, while they are eating in the field, that takes the role of the watch and safeguard of the flock in case that they should be suddenly attacked." He adds, "A scholar is a dogan of the nation" (in Ishikawa, 3–4).

Part Four:
Later Works

TWELVE

"Working at the Impossible": *Moby-Dick*'s Presence in *East of Eden*

Robert DeMott

Certain environments are forever haunted by the great works of literature that have imagined them for us. John Steinbeck, writing East of Eden *on the island of Nantucket in* Moby-Dick's *centennial year, composing his own massive novel atop Sankaty Bluff, where Herman Melville himself had stood a century before to overlook the Atlantic swell, underwent just such a haunting. "Sailor, can you hear the Pequod's sea wings, beating landward, fall headlong and break on our Atlantic wall off 'Sconset?" inquired Robert Lowell in "The Quaker Graveyard at Nantucket." Here Robert DeMott demonstrates that sailor Steinbeck indeed heard those sea wings, and that much of* Moby-Dick *crept into* East of Eden *with the Nantucket fog.*

For Maggie and Bob Cook

> A good writer always works at the impossible. There is another kind who pulls in his horizons, drops his mind as one lowers rifle sights. And giving up the impossible he gives up writing. Whether fortunate or unfortunate, this has not happened to me.
>
> —*Journal of a Novel: The "East of Eden" Letters*

I

On Wednesday, 15 August 1951, John Steinbeck might easily have traveled the six miles or so from Footlight, his rented cottage on Baxter Road next to the Coast Guard's Sankaty Lighthouse in Siasconset, to the Unitarian Church in Nantucket for the Historical Association's "Melville Memorial" observance, marking the 100th anniversary of the publication of *Moby-Dick*. It would have been a fitting endeavor—part business, part leisure—for Steinbeck on that "muggy and thick and foggy" (*SLL* 428) afternoon, because he was playing hooky from the manuscript of *East of Eden*, which he had been composing daily since February, first in New York City, then from June 18 onward, in 'Sconset, where he was summering with his wife, Elaine, and sons, Thom and John.

Since Steinbeck's arrival on the island, he had written obsessively each working day in the cottage's small upstairs back study. The window of his writing room faced inland, away from the inviting panorama of the Atlantic Ocean (their cottage was no more than thirty feet from the high-flown edge of Sankaty Bluff). Steinbeck worked on his "big book" right through Sunday, 12 August. Then he took "the longest layoff" since starting the novel (*JN* 145) to prepare for Elaine's birthday party on Tuesday (Benson 1984, 689–90). On Thursday, 16 August, Steinbeck made a fairly long entry in his working journal indicating that his plan for the novel's final section would "concentrate" on developing "powerful new people . . . , Cal and Abra and a new Adam" (*JN* 146), though he did not actually compose any fiction that day. In fact he took several more days off before launching into book 4 on Monday, 20 August. This much is known and recorded; he said nothing at all in his journal or his letters about his whereabouts on August 15.

Now comes my speculation, which concerns that conspicuous silence, upon which even his biographer and his widow could shed no light (Benson 1984, 691; E. Steinbeck 1992). On 15 August, I imagine, still tired from having completed the third book of *East of Eden*, Steinbeck, unmoored from his manuscript, and in a receptive mood, visited—in thought, if not in deed—the Historical Association's dual celebration of *Moby-Dick*'s centenary of *Moby-Dick*, and the ninety-ninth anniversary of Melville's only visit to Nantucket (Melville published *Moby-Dick*, with its eighty-eight references to Nantucket, before he had ever set foot on the island).

Steinbeck was already attuned to the significance of Nantucket as an historical, cultural, and literary site, for as early as 21 May, he had written to his agent, Elizabeth Otis, to discuss the feasibility of doing a "pet project—a set of informal but informative articles about the island of Nantuckett [*sic*]" (Special Collections, Stanford University Library). His curiosity about the place and its cultural history was matched by his energetic sense of belonging: "This island is wonderful. I feel at home here. I wonder if it is my small amount (1/4) of my

New England blood operating. . . . I never felt better about working"
(*JN* 107).[1] He was well on his way to becoming a Melvillean "fast
fish."

Steinbeck might have been aware of the Melville meeting since at
least Saturday, 4 August, when the Nantucket *Inquirer and Mirror* ran
this notice: " 'Melville Memorial' To Be Held on Wednesday, Aug.
15th" (1). The event, featuring talks by Wilson Heflin and Edouard
Stackpole, was covered in the newspaper on Saturday, 18 August
1951; it makes no mention of Steinbeck's being present, though he
could have slipped in unnoticed (3). All in all, the historical celebration of Melville and his relations with the very island Steinbeck was
then visiting, and especially the praise of Melville's greatest book,
had a redoubled effect on Steinbeck when he began chapter 34 of *East
of Eden* on 20 August.

Although it is not possible to tell precisely when Steinbeck first
encountered *Moby-Dick*, he appears to have discovered it with full
force a year or so before its centenary, when between 1949 and 1950
a spate of Melville biographies and critical studies (Chase 1949,
Stone 1949, Vincent 1949, Arvin 1950) and editions of *Moby-Dick*
(Howard 1950, Paul 1950) attracted public attention.[2] These works
advanced the relatively recent rediscovery of Melville, extolled his
struggle for native authorship, and elevated the uniquely "American" genius of his greatest fiction. *Moby-Dick* circulates throughout
East of Eden.[3] Steinbeck's reading of Melville was a profound happening, a gifted presence, that entered the environment of his awareness, "the warp and woof of . . . consciousness" (*EOE* 541). Thomas
Steinbeck, the novelist's eldest son, recalled his father's introducing
him to *Moby-Dick* during the centennial year by reading aloud. He
pointed specifically to his father's continued enthusiasm for the
novel's "elegant form"—its dazzling layered construction and multiple voices; its bold, rhythmic, energetic language; and its abundant symbolic technique, characterization, philosophy, and setting
(T. Steinbeck 1985).

This essay focuses primarily on *East of Eden* as a recipient of some
influential Melvillean resonances, parallels, and strategies and seeks
to extend a conversation already partially begun (French 1961,
McCarthy 1980, Zane in Hayashi 1989). Keeping in mind the inevitable distortion that occurs in creative impact and appropriation,

East of Eden, like *Moby-Dick*, is a "speculative" fiction (Benson, "Novelist as Scientist" 1977, 249) that points up the tribulations of positing a coherent national experience and of the representational power of American literary modes. Melville's ship of state (presented through his inflating rhetoric of democratic tragedy) and Steinbeck's Garden of Eden (presented through its conflating drama of sexual pathos) function as powerful ironic tropes of fallen worlds that fit the temper of Melville and Steinbeck's uneasy negotiations with their respective historical, political, and cultural eras (Rogin 107–9; Timmerman 1986, 211–18). And yet ironically beneath—or in spite of—the overarching mythology of corrupt national and personal identity (expansionism and capitalism, tyranny and dynastic destiny) that imbues both works, Melville and Steinbeck arrive at a notable humanistic (and hermeneutical) consensus. Just values, they suggest, reside in independent gestures of sacramental communication, however tenuous or incomplete. Creating a world elsewhere proves to be both a liberating and constraining act.

In seeking out some of these dynamic textual (and intertextual) affinities with Melville, and in proposing ways in which they endure in Steinbeck's work, my purpose is interpretative and descriptive rather than valuative, holistic and ecological rather than critical. Many American novels—Steinbeck's included—pale in comparison to the sheer imaginative brilliance of Melville's audacious (and blemished) masterpiece. I hasten to add, though, that *East of Eden* is a far stronger, more engaging book than it has generally been credited for being. This experimental text—Steinbeck's last major work of fiction—has much to recommend it and deserves the earnest revisionist scrutiny it has lately attracted (Ditsky 1977, 13–14; Buerger 1981; DeMott 1992, 17–18).

II

When, on 29 January 1951, after several years of gestation and false starts, John Steinbeck sat down to begin concentrated work on *East of Eden*, he took a headlong dive into uncharted waters by consciously abandoning many of the dictates and underlying assumptions of prevailing literary realism that had marked his most successful earlier novels. Sporadically, beginning with *Cannery Row* (1945), and again in the play-novelette, *Burning Bright* (1950), he deliberately turned away from the "squeemish" [*sic*] mimetic mode, "the modern fashionable method" (*JN* 43) that emphasized tightly controlled movement, circumscribed characterization, seamless omniscient narration, and fidelity to the aesthetic illusion of verisimilitude.

Even though Steinbeck used the term "novel" almost exclusively to describe *East of Eden*—he was turning toward the romance tradition of American fiction initiated by Nathaniel Hawthorne and Herman Melville (Brodhead 20–25). While the legitimacy of romance as an exclusive, American literary project is now currently undergoing intense debate (see Ellis), the term is still viable for describing an alternative fictional stance, exemplified by mythopoesis, philosophical dualism, verbal opulence, self-referential artifice, processive narration, multiple authorial roles/voices, and symbolistic action, setting, and characterization (Chase 1980, 13; see also Dryden). Steinbeck never abandoned realism entirely, but like Melville leaving behind the stylized successes of *Redburn* and *White-Jacket* and launching into the treacherous metaphysical depths of *Moby-Dick,* he too gave up his secure routine and embraced a naked presentation of self and world in a comparatively loose, expressive mode of fiction.

East of Eden is a partly historical, partly fictional epic tale, based on the Cain-Abel story, of several generations of fictional Connecticut Trasks (Steinbeck took their name from "a friend of my father's— a whaling master named Captain Trask") and quasi-real-life Hamiltons (Steinbeck's matrilinear family) whose lives run parallel, then contiguously, in a sixty-year period from 1862 to 1918, mostly in California. Each successive generation of Trasks is fated to repeat the sins of its fathers.

At one pole Steinbeck has situated his semifictional, larger-than-life grandfather, Samuel Hamilton, who stands, like Ishmael, for everything potentially sacramental in the fallen world. Against this humane yeoman philosopher (William James is his favorite writer)— and against everyone else in the novel, for that matter—Steinbeck poses Adam Trask's wife, Cathy Ames Trask, the mother of their two children, Caleb and Aron (whom she abandons after she shoots Adam and leaves him for dead). Kate, as she comes to be known, is a seducer, murderer, vicious madam of a Salinas brothel, and moral "monster" of the first order, who dominates the book.

Adam Trask is ranged between Samuel and Kate. This patently American Adam (conceived several years before R. W. B. Lewis gave the type a name) is naive, guileless in the ways of heterosexual love, and fatally determined to create a dynastic farm on his land. If Kate is the linchpin of the novel, Adam is its axle. He fails the Edenic ideals of his quest, but, through the ministrations of Sam Hamilton and Lee (the Trask family's Chinese servant/savant), Adam becomes the instrument through which emphasis on free will—symbolized by the Hebrew word *timshel* (translated as "Thou mayest")—grants human beings (his wayward son Cal first and foremost) the potential to triumph over sin and to return to the wellsprings of their integrity.[4]

If this quick plot sketch, however, does little to capture the unresolved paradoxes between fatalism and free will, it does even less to portray the technique of Steinbeck's initial enterprise. In its original form, *East of Eden* boldly departed from tradition. In fact it was a startlingly innovative, double-voiced, cross-referential work. On the left-hand page of a large lined ledger book Steinbeck wrote daily warm-up letters—a running workshop journal—addressed to Pascal Covici, his esteemed Viking Press editor. These entries formed an informal, personal commentary on Steinbeck's daily artistic process and his intentions for the novel. Across from the journal, so that both kinds of entries "will be together" (*JN* 5), on the right-hand page of the ledger book, Steinbeck composed the chapters of his novel, initially addressed specifically to his sons, Thom and John, aged six and four. Steinbeck recorded his purpose in the opening entry: "I am choosing to write this book to my sons. . . . They have no background in the world of literature, they don't know the great stories of the world as we do. And so I will tell them one of the greatest, perhaps the greatest story of all—the story of good and evil, of strength and weakness, of love and hate, of beauty and ugliness. I shall try to demonstrate to them how these doubles are inseparable—how neither can exist without the other and how out of their groupings creativeness is born" (*JN* 4). The novel's essential dualism, then, was purposely thematic and formal.

Unfortunately, the published novel represents a truncated version of Steinbeck's "inseparable" conception. All of the journal entries were dropped (published posthumously as *Journal of a Novel*), and many of the direct homilies to his children were dropped as well, so *East of Eden* is a good deal tamer than Steinbeck planned (Govoni 15). Nevertheless, the published version and the integrally linked journal (also edited for publication) retain enough traces of Steinbeck's initial informing vision and spirit to show that he was working at a level of discourse far different from that of his previous fiction.

"In considering this book and in planning for it I have thought of many great and interesting tricks. I have made new languages, new symbols, a new kind of writing: and now that the book is ready to go, I am throwing them all away and starting from scratch" (*JN* 6). In the process of reexamining the ontological ground of his past work, Steinbeck tried to achieve a multiple perspective with *East of Eden*, combining "all forms, all methods, all approaches" into a hybrid order. "I am not going to put artificial structures on this book," he said. "The real structures are enough. I mean the discipline imposed by realities and certain universal writers" (*JN* 118), of whom Melville—with his deep sense of Manichaeism, his abiding awareness of philosophical and aesthetic dualism, and his use of alternating narrative and cetological chapters in *Moby-Dick*—was surely one. Not for nothing, then, Steinbeck claimed, "Great writing has been a staff to lean on, a mother to consult" (*JN* 115–16).

Throughout 1951, as Steinbeck worked at his "impossible" task of finding "symbols for the wordlessness," Melville's masterpiece was a type of his bold experiment: "The admired books now were by no means the admired books of their day. I believe that Moby Dick, so much admired now, did not sell its small first edition in ten years. And it will be worse than that with this book" (*JN* 29). Though *East of Eden* fared spectacularly, Steinbeck was intuitively correct in calling up *Moby-Dick* as a model for his "huge" effort.[5] *Moby-Dick* exemplified the nonlinear narrative and dramatic "pace" (*JN* 29), the resilience and flexibility of the romance form Steinbeck sought to revive in contemporary dress. Steinbeck's newly adapted technique would allow him to develop his characters not only through the contemporary realistic means of dialogue and exposition but through the older interpretive method of personal analysis as well (*JN* 43). The technique would allow the writer to be both subject and object by slipping in and out of his triple role as implied narrator, editorial speaker, and actor in his own novel: "For many years I did not occur in my own writing. . . . But in this book I am in it and I don't for a moment pretend not to be" (*JN* 24). Following Melville's lead, Steinbeck produced in *East of Eden* the closest thing to a self-portrait of the artist that he had ever written.

III

Moby-Dick and *East of Eden* do not fit like hand and glove. It is not true that "*Moby-Dick* is referred to repeatedly in the *East of Eden* letters" (Owens 1985, 240). There is only one direct reference in *Journal of a Novel*, and more often than not, Melville's book is latent in *East of Eden*, lurking in the shadows behind and below Steinbeck's private and public texts, at the informing edges of his consciousness. It is enough, however, to color a great deal of Steinbeck's novel on everything from the pursuit of artistic form to the achievement of enabling beliefs.

Both books enact a retrospective view of their authors' pasts filtered through the symbolic distance created by memory. *Moby-Dick* and *East of Eden* rise essentially from autobiographical ground, acute personal awarenesses, spatial and geographic memories. Melville reprised his *Acushnet* whaling experience of a decade past; Steinbeck recreated his native California from Manhattan and Nantucket, two eastern islands a continent away from the main physical setting of his book. The opening chapters of *East of Eden* function like Melville's "Loomings" because they evoke through memory Steinbeck's generative past, his link with the place of his birth and youth. As with the conflicting "wild conceits that floated" into Ishmael's "inmost soul" (7), Steinbeck's "rich" past introduces the book's bittersweet action. As surely as *Moby-Dick*'s "Call me Ishmael," Steinbeck's incantatory refrain—"I remember"—announces on *East of Eden*'s first page a journey into a world of imaginative proportions vivified by the shape-shifting teller of the tale (who continually defies narrational propriety) and into spatial/geographic settings that reinforce symbolic aspects of characterization and psychology.

Indeed, Thomas Steinbeck singled out *Moby-Dick*'s shipboard setting as one of the book's chief attractions for his father (T. Steinbeck 1985). Melville had achieved a double interpretive feat: he made the unfamiliar cosmos of the globe-circling *Pequod* "real" at the very same time he invested it with mystery, wonder, and terror. Thus imaginative orientation is important, because for Ishmael "true places" are never "down in any map" (55), while for Steinbeck, the narrator "must name a thing before you can note it on your hand-drawn map" (*EOE* 7). By setting most of *East of Eden* in California's agriculturally rich Salinas Valley, Steinbeck foregrounded its small town past and sought to give "a semblance of real experience" (*JN* 27) to a rural social world where he, too, located qualities of wonder and evil, sacredness and profanity.

These intensely felt books are also enriched by literary artifice and allusions. "No one," Melville quipped in a letter to Evert Duyckinck in March 1849, "is his own sire." The "truth is," he explained, "we are all sons, grandsons, or nephews or great-nephews of those who go before us" (78).[6] Both Melville and Steinbeck read to write, so that each book reflects its author's literary researches and preferences (DeMott 1984; Sealts 1988). Melville ransacked more extensively than Steinbeck but probably no more shamelessly. Melville's inspired transformation of his cetological sources—Beale, Bennett, Browne, Cheever, Scoresby—is but one example of Ishmael's contention that he "swam through libraries" (136; see also Howard Vincent 126–35). Steinbeck's borrowings were similarly functional and aesthetic. *East of Eden*—his "culling of all books plus my own invention" (*JN* 31)—draws upon works by Herodotus, Plutarch, Marcus Aurelius, Dr. John Gunn, Lewis Carroll, William James, and Erich Fromm (DeMott 1984, xxxii–xliii). In this vein, both novels center on and exploit embedded biblical texts for their own ends—the typological parables of Jonah and of Cain and Abel are central to plot, theme, and characterization in each.

Both writers create characters who strain plausibility and therefore require our willing suspension of disbelief. Melville's Ahab, Queequeg, and Fedallah; Steinbeck's Sam Hamilton, Cathy Trask, and Lee, are more often allegorical or exotic than physically or socially normative. Many characters have crippled or missing body parts (Ahab's leg, Moby Dick's deformed lower jaw, Captain Boomer's arm, Cyrus Trask's leg, Kate's hand, "wrinkled as a pale monkey's paw" [*EOE* 425]). Or they are scarred in significant, emblematic ways: Ahab's lightning scar, Queequeg's tattoos, Charles Trask's and Kate's Cain-marked foreheads underscore their links to the netherworld of grotesque experience—Melville's "speechlessly quick chaotic bundling of a man into Eternity" (37) and the hell of the Trask family's conflicted relationships.

Kate is Steinbeck's most diabolical example. She is a demented isolato, a female tyrant, who sometimes out-Ahabs Ahab in her cold-heartedness, selfish pursuit of power, and calculating disregard for the sanctity of human life. Kate is far more motiveless in her evil than Ahab, but otherwise similarities between these two sensational Gothic characters run deep. Ahab's inordinate pride, his overbearing hubris, the "sultanism" of his brain—"I'd strike the sun if it insulted me. . . . Who's over me?" (164)—is echoed in Steinbeck's portrayal of Kate: "I'm smarter than humans. Nobody can hurt me," she says (*EOE* 424). Both Ahab and Kate are driven by fate—Ahab's soul, grooved to run on iron rails, has its equivalent in Steinbeck's statement that "Whatever she had done, she had been driven to do" (*EOE* 713). Both are reclusive and isolated—bearlike Ahab in his "caved" cabin "sucking his own paws" (153); catlike Kate in the "cave" lean-to of her brothel feeding on her own enmity, anger, and silence (*EOE* 615). Both dissemble to advance their secret agendas, and both necessarily employ Ahab's "external arts and entrenchments" (148) to consolidate their power over underlings.

In this vein, both debase the process they are in charge of fostering. Ahab selfishly undermines the economic purpose of the *Pequod*'s owners. In the world of Steinbeck's novel, where "the church and the whorehouse arrived in the Far West" at the same time (*EOE* 283), prostitution purportedly provides some redeeming social value except at Kate's brothel, where bondage, sadomasochism, and blackmail make it a dirty commercial venture, fit for revenge and extortion only. Ahab's dream of revenge—to get even with Moby Dick for dismasting him, is analogous to Kate's admission to Adam (questionable in its total veracity) that her deepest purpose is to get even with Mr. Edwards, the New England whoremaster who once disfigured her and left her for dead (*EOE* 425).

Like Ahab, a twisted latter day Prometheus who vows to spit his heart's hot shell at Moby Dick for mankind's sake, Kate is totally consumed by hatred—ostensibly for Adam but also for the human race in general, which, in an equally perverse way, she hopes to disabuse of hypocrisy. At key points before their deaths, Kate and Ahab both perform litanies of affirmation to demonic sources: Ahab's address to the "clear spirit of clear fire" in chapter 119 ("The Candles")—"To neither love nor reverence wilt thou be kind; and e'en for hate thou canst but kill" (507)—finds its cunning duplicate in Kate's gleeful assertion that only hatred, evil, and folly exist in the world (*EOE* 422–28).

Somewhat like Ahab, somewhat like Moby Dick, then, Kate is central to the dramatic and moral action of the book. She is a vivid, almost unbelievable symbol of malevolence, so that, like Ahab's doubloon, the depth of each person's character is judged by his reaction to her. But confrontation can lead to spiritual or psychological redemption: just as Ishmael is saved from his nightmare vision of complicity, first Adam is reborn from his "nightmare dream" and escapes Kate's cruelty, then their son Cal is set on a path toward redemption by knowledge of his mother's tainted nature (*EOE* 604–5) and by his father's deathbed blessing (*EOE* 778).

Both Melville and Steinbeck believed that their capacities to uncover life's deepest truths were necessarily limited in an indeterminate world, but artistic duty demanded they try. Melville's operative belief in "Hawthorne and His Mosses," that "in this world of lies, Truth is forced to fly like a scared white doe . . . and only by cunning glimpses will she reveal herself" (in *Piazza Tales* 1987, 244), has its parallel in Steinbeck's statement that only "a little" of what the artist tries to do "trickles through" (*JN* 4) the elusive "great covered thing" (*JN* 42). Their narrators' pronouncements are often marked by honest self-doubt, denial, or forgetfulness. Furthermore, where Ishmael must "explain" the compelling and indefinite "phenomenon of whiteness," otherwise all his "chapters might be naught" (188), Steinbeck's narrator seeks to plumb the equally mysterious phenomenon of sexuality, the heart of mortal inscrutability: "What freedom men and women could have, were they not constantly tricked and trapped and enslaved and tortured by their sexuality!" (*EOE* 99). Feline Kate becomes the focus of the narrator's didactic expositions—and increasingly indeterminate resolutions—on public and private evil, human fate, and the haunting specter of genetic determinism. As much as Steinbeck wanted to be positive, getting at the truth "secreted in the glands of a million historians" (*EOE* 168) remains such a puzzling and elusive task that Steinbeck reverses direction in chapter 17: "When I said Cathy was a monster it seemed that it was so. Now I have bent close with a glass over the small print of her and reread the footnotes, and I wonder if it is true" (*EOE* 242). In this self-immolating fiction, even the vaunted certitude of the author's role is undercut.

This kind of flip-flopping appalled some early critics of both *Moby-Dick* and *East of Eden* (Peterson in Hayashi 1979, 81). But such improvisation was especially relevant for Melville's wandering act of composition. His letters reveal that he first conceived of *Moby-Dick* as "a romance of adventure, founded upon certain wild legends in the Southern Sperm Whale fisheries" (109), and while the *exact* chronology of the evolution of his masterpiece is not known, it is true that the book evolved substantially—even drastically—through at least three "distinct periods," and that during those phases from August 1850 through the following summer, Melville was constantly adding, elaborating, and revising his text in a sometimes frenzied and haphazard way (Hayford 655–59; Barbour and Quirk 40–47).

Steinbeck did not build in such patchwork manner, but he too continually modified his novel (Simmonds 1992, 62–64), giving way to new impulses, especially in regard to characterization (his Cain/Abel paradigm did not hold up in all the ways he envisioned) and plot (his alternate story lines became blurred and attenuated). "Dam it, this book gets longer, not shorter. Everything has pups. I never saw anything like the way it grows" (*JN* 79). His working titles reflect the vicissitudes of his method. The book was called "Salinas Valley," then "My Valley," then "Cain Sign" (each title valorized a different fictive aspect). After he fully realized the psychological significance of the first sixteen verses of Genesis, Steinbeck found his permanent title, *East of Eden:* "My discovery of yesterday is sure burning in me. . . . I think I know about the story finally after all this time," he noted on 12 June 1951 (*JN* 104).

Both novels exist simultaneously on multiple planes of dramatic, expository, and narrational engagement (McCarthy 119). Plenitude is further encoded in the many literary styles and discourses: although Melville resorts far more frequently than Steinbeck to puns, jokes, and extravagant metaphors, both writers mix graphic realism with soaring philosophical flights and discursive exposition with rapturous, lyrical passages. The books resist constitutive conventions, easy formulations of plot; rather, they are heterogeneous creations, kinetic dances between teller and tale, even if rough-hewn, unsymmetrical, and unfinished. From Arrowhead, his Pittsfield home, Melville told Hawthorne on 29 June 1851, "I have been building some shanties of houses . . . and likewise some shanties of chapters and essays" (132). Steinbeck, too, imagined that houses and books grew in similar ways (*JN* 20). Even their distrust of a perfectly finished product was similar: "God keep me from completing anything," Melville wrote in chapter 32. "This whole book is but a draught—nay, but the draught of a draught" (145). And Steinbeck claimed flatly at one point, "I do not ever intend to finish it" (*JN* 14).

In *Moby-Dick*, Melville embraced the organic method—"Out of the trunk, the branches grow; out of them, the twigs. So, in productive subjects, grow the chapters" (289)—paralleling Steinbeck's position not as an objective recording consciousness, but as a convincing fabricator of characters and events from competing "hearsay," "stories told," and "memories" (*EOE* 10), all of which allowed the book to take "its head" and go "as it wishes and I learn from it rather than being taught by it" (*JN* 29). Tracing out the multitudinous "growth and flowering" of such sources takes the narrator in a variety of unpredictable directions surprising both to himself and, he guesses, to his audience (*JN* 39, 116). For both authors, then, process was all (Bezanson 193; Zane in Hayashi and Moore 1989, 5).

Clearly, *Moby-Dick* gave Steinbeck the courage to experiment with form, structure, and point of view. I emphasize the word "experiment" because even though *Moby-Dick* was written midway in the nineteenth century it displayed a number of daring technical features that have only recently—in the past thirty years or so—become assimilated into postmodernist contemporary fiction (Lee 103–5). In updating Melville's inventive romance strategies—symbolism, organic form, artful digressions, and self-reflexivity, including frequent commentary on the process of making a book, especially important for the original version, Steinbeck was attempting to create a fabular, metafictional novel (Mulder 109) that belonged less to his own time than to the future of the children for whom he was writing the book in the first place.

I don't think it is too much to claim that, because they turn so often on the metaphor of reading (Leviathan as text, Queequeg as a puzzling hieroglyphic volume, Father Mapple's sermon on Jonah; Samuel and Lee's central act of interpreting Genesis and the narrator's own attempt to decode the "indecipherable" language of Kate's life), both *Moby-Dick* and *East of Eden* first challenged, then taught, their respective audiences to learn (or relearn) the act of reading. In performing this feat, both are prophetic books that have required the passage of time for audiences to catch up with them, to consider them not merely "hideous and intolerable" allegories but writerly texts requiring suitably imaginative—even aggressive—responses to complete the "careful disorderliness" of their method.

In *Moby-Dick*, Ishmael's conversion narrative (which reaches its psychological climax in chapter 96) and his ongoing cetological divagations cannot be subordinated to the dramatic trajectory of Ahab's quest for revenge against the white whale, because they are all part of the same "warp and woof" (215) of consciousness, to be treated with "equal eye" (374). In *East of Eden* Steinbeck showed that the story of his country and the story of himself were so deeply intertwined that they were one and the same. Just as Herman Melville repeatedly crossed into the persona of fictive Ishmael, for instance in dating the composition of chapter 85 at "(fifteen and a quarter minutes past one o'clock P.M. of this sixteenth day of December, A.D. 1850 [370])," so Steinbeck did not curb his desire to break through to the other side of the artist's mirror. How else can we willingly accept that the fictional Adam Trask actually visits the real-life John Steinbeck at his parents' home on 132 Central Avenue in Salinas (*EOE* 505)? Whether we call such effects magical realism, metafiction, performative postmodernism, or deconstruction, in *Moby-Dick* and *East of Eden* Melville and Steinbeck were practitioners, well ahead of their times.

In their zigzag tack toward an ever-receding horizon of truth, both writers expressed their experiences in candid, brutal, and often shockingly irreverent terms. In a letter written 12 [?] September 1851, Melville warned his genteel Pittsfield neighbor, Sarah Morewood, not to read *Moby-Dick* because a "polar wind blows through it, & birds of prey hover over it" (138); the emerging diabolism in Cathy Trask prompted Steinbeck to warn Covici that she would "worry a lot of children and a lot of parents" (*JN* 46). It should come as no surprise that the former believed *Moby-Dick*—whose motto, trumpeted by blaspheming Ahab in chapter 113, was "Ego non baptiso te in nomine patris, sed in nomine diaboli" (489)—to be a "wicked book" ([*Letters*] 142), while the latter felt *East of Eden* was "a terrible book" (*JN* 156). When their labors were done, both writers felt similar reactions: each doubted the efficacy of his work, each admitted an enormous sense of relief, and each spoke of a suitable follow-up (Melville's "Kraken" *Pierre;* Steinbeck's unwritten sequel, intended to cover 1918 to the 1950s).

IV

For whatever reason, if not on August 15, then sometime during that seven-day hiatus from his manuscript, Steinbeck dove back into his copy of *Moby-Dick* (Thorp's edition or maybe Howard's), perhaps by reading passages to his son Thom. When Steinbeck resumed writing *East of Eden* again on Monday, 20 August, *Moby-Dick* made its presence palpably known in chapter 34, one of Steinbeck's major discursive chapters. It concerns the world's central story—the battle of good and evil—also one of *Moby-Dick's* main themes. There is an interior signature at work that shows Steinbeck imitating Melvillean discourse in the penultimate paragraph of his newly penned chapter: "In uncertainty I am certain that underneath their topmost layers of frailty men want to be good and want to be loved" (*EOE* 543). That paradoxical diction ("uncertain certainty") and that hierarchical valuation ("topmost layers") are, like "warp and woof" (*EOE* 543), Melvillean syntactical constructions, signifying that Melville's latent text had emerged into Steinbeck's present moment.

Even Steinbeck's organizing strategy in chapter 34 simulates Melville's. In chapter 96, "The Try-Works," Ishmael's warning on the deadening effects of fire ("Look not too long in the face of fire, O man! Never dream with thy hand on the helm!"), is supported by his pointed reference to a classic text—Solomon's *Ecclesiastes*—whose "fine hammered steel of woe," underscores the chapter's theme of human vanity and accountability (424). These elements, substantially grounded and enriched by the sad tale of Perth, the *Pequod's* blacksmith (chapter 112), are paralleled in Steinbeck's literary allusions to Herodotus's story in *The Histories* of Solon and Croesus, a cautionary tale that concerns the apocryphal issue of human vanity and good fortune and mirrors Steinbeck's own idea of universal accountability: "It seems to me that if you or I must choose between two courses of thought or action, we should remember our dying and try so to live that our death brings no pleasure in the world" (*EOE* 543).

In Steinbeck's drive toward resolving these knotty issues, the final paragraph of chapter 34 corresponds to the final paragraph of Melville's chapter 105, "Does the Whale's Magnitude Diminish?—Will He Perish?" In Steinbeck's line—"And it occurs to me that evil must constantly respawn, while good, while virtue, is immortal" (*EOE* 543)—there are resonances of Melville's belief that "wherefore, for all these things, we account the whale immortal in his species" (462). After completing his novel-writing stint that August Monday, Steinbeck commented approvingly on the result: "I have ranged the changeable with the continuing. . . . I have set down some things which I believe and some things which have not been said for a long time" (*JN* 147). *Moby-Dick* and *East of Eden* are hymns to the persistence of beneficence in whatever form it is found.

Ahab's final lament in chapter 135—"Am I cut off from the last fond pride of meanest shipwrecked captains? Oh, lonely death on lonely life!" (571)—presages the demise of Kate, who repents her actions just minutes before her untoward suicide. Here we read Steinbeck revising Melville. Where Promethean Ahab perishes in his unmediated final effort to penetrate the whale's imprisoning "wall" of "inscrutable malice," to thrust through the pasteboard mask of reality (believing he can still revenge himself—and therefore mankind—against the evil symbolized by the White Whale's agency), Kate penetrates her "wall" of self and finds a horrifying emptiness on the nether side. If Kate gains a modicum of sympathy, it is quickly subverted by her ironic legacy: her son Aron will live "all his life on the profits from a whorehouse" (*EOE* 752), a figuration ultimately no less ironic and far-reaching than Ishmael being saved from drowning by Queequeg's coffin.

After harpooning Moby Dick in the final chapter, Ahab dies a terrible death—partly willed, partly fated (in a sense, he too commits suicide)—garroted by the very whale line he has just thrown; yanked from the small boat, he disappears "ere the crew knew he was gone" (572). First Ahab, then the *Pequod*, dissolve into nothingness, pass "out of sight" into the spinning vortex of the ocean. In much the same way Kate shrinks in terror to nothingness: "The gray room darkened and the cone of light flowed and rippled like water . . . as she grew smaller and smaller and then disappeared—and she had never been" (*EOE* 715). Both Ahab and Kate seem in the end to have been consumed by a similar kind of monomania (French 1961, 153); in their lust for destruction both can be said to deconstruct their identities before our eyes.

East of Eden reveals that Steinbeck was alive to the implications of Melvillean theme, style, technique, and characterization. In the wondrous geography of the storytellers' world, anything can happen in the net of narrative: characters can be utterly good or blatantly evil; a ghostly Parsee can prophesy the future, and aged Chinese savants can undertake the study of Hebrew in order to interpret a single word; a man, grievously insulted by the universe, can search the oceans of the world to find the lone whale upon which to vent his vengeful heart, while another man, laid low by treachery for ten years, can find the courage to redeem himself and his son by granting the gift of free will (like Ahab, Adam lacks the "low, enjoying power" and, through most of Steinbeck's novel is "damned in the midst of Paradise!"); and finally, authors can perform narrative sleights of hand that astound, instruct, and delight us.

If *East of Eden* fails to be completely convincing (Pratt 24–25; Owens 1985, 141), it is nevertheless a magnificent undertaking because, like *Moby-Dick*, it is a book whose scope of vision, risk-taking technique, and assault on the impossible is large, compelling, brave, and "impressive" (McCarthy 123). And while both books have obvious inconsistencies and flaws (both are full of anomalies, factual contradictions, and lapses), we need to remember that their narrative logic is often internal, metaphoric, and poetical, so that to read either of these books in the right spirit of faith demands that we emulate the "archangel" Hawthorne of Melville's letters, look past "the imperfect body, and embrace the soul" (142).

Notes

1. Although *East of Eden* privileges the Hamilton clan, Steinbeck's matrilinear family, and his California roots, he did have a significant connection to New England. The Dicksons, Steinbeck's paternal great-grandparents, hailed from Groton and Dunstable, Massachusetts. In the 1850s, Walter and Sarah Dickson

went to Palestine to work as independent missionaries. In one of those historical moments so uncanny it might have been invented, the Dicksons were visited by Herman Melville, on 26 January 1857, during his tour of the Holy Land. Steinbeck learned of the visit in 1966 when, on a trip with Elaine, a staff member of the American Embassy in Tel Aviv showed him a copy of Melville's *Journal of a Visit to Europe and the Levant*, where the event is recorded (DeMott 1993).

2. Steinbeck's discovery might have occurred prior to 1949 or 1950, but I have not found documentary evidence to support an earlier date. Some time around the centenary year, Steinbeck acquired at least these four works—Thorp's edition of *Moby-Dick* (1947), Leyda's *The Melville Log* (1951), Howard's *Herman Melville* (1951) (DeMott 1984, 79), and Howard's edition of *Moby Dick* (1950). Although it is a topic that requires further investigation, the intellectual climate of late 1940s Cold War politics (which helped authorize *Moby-Dick* as a triumphant expression of American exceptionalism) was a contributing influence in Steinbeck's radical turn in *East of Eden* toward unfettered individualism (*SLL* 359–60; *JN* 15, 31–32; *EOE* 171).

3. Parenthetical citations from *Moby-Dick* refer to the Northwestern-Newberry edition (Hayford, Parker, Tanselle 1988).

4. Steinbeck's improper spelling of the Hebrew term is one of his novel's gaffes. Steinbeck had been "misinformed" (Benson 1984, 687) about the proper spelling of the imperfect form, *timshol*; his choice of "Thou Mayest" (rather than "Thou Canst") to show free will is within the word's interpretive range (Nakayama, Pugh, and Yano 1992, 81–83). More to the point, in his etymological investigations Lee replicates the task of Melville's "sub-sub librarian." Like Queequeg's hieroglyphic coffin, *Timshel* has the capacity to save lives by preserving free choice and moral duty, restoring love and integrity, and allowing characters to enter the full sacrament of their humanity, their mutual "joint stock company," to use Melville's apt phrase. No one symbolizes this tendency more than Lee, Steinbeck's androgynous man, his feminized man, who, in the tradition of Ishmael's "marriage" to Queequeg, remains committed to constancy in human relationships, not in an exotic world elsewhere, but in the common frontier of human endeavor, the family of man, the place Ishmael himself prophesied as the sphere of "attainable felicity" (416).

5. *East of Eden*'s initial print run was over 112,000 copies; the novel has never been out of print (DeMott 1992, 19). The first print run of the British edition of *The Whale* was 500 copies, and of *Moby-Dick*'s American edition, 2,915. Overall, *Moby-Dick* sold about 3,700 copies in both editions between 1851 and Melville's death in 1891 (it was out of print during his last four years) and earned its author a little over $1,200 (see Tanselle's "Historical Note" in the Northwestern-Newberry edition of *Moby-Dick*, 686–89). Steinbeck's comments about *Moby-Dick*'s publishing history, repeated again in 1966 in *America and Americans*, thematically resemble the introduction to Leon Howard's edition of *Moby Dick* (1950).

6. Parenthetical citations from Melville's correspondence refer to the Yale University Press edition of *The Letters of Herman Melville* (1960).

THIRTEEN

At Sea in the Tide Pool: The Whaling Town and America in Steinbeck's *The Winter of Our Discontent* and *Travels with Charley*

Nathaniel Philbrick

The eastern towns of Nantucket and Sag Harbor, where Steinbeck chose to spend his later years, were first jumping-off places for exploitation of the American West, for the harvesting of the Pacific's whales and of California's goldfields, then tourist attractions for the harvesting of visitor dollars. In his final novel, The Winter of Our Discontent, *Steinbeck uses the history and development of a whaling town to achieve an overarching vision of the American psyche, a vision corroborated by his investigations in the nonfiction* Travels with Charley, *and elaborated in* America and Americans. *Throughout these late works, Steinbeck's ecological understanding of the tide pool's teeming and competitive life informs his fears for the future of a people whose "predatory nature" must confront the "terrible hazard of leisure" (AAA 138–39).*

John Steinbeck's *The Winter of Our Discontent* (1961) is a novel that seems almost calculated to be critically unpopular. Certainly, the book's setting, an old whaling town on the East Coast, is a highly improbable one for an author so strongly associated with his native California. For those who adhere to the theory that it was his Gatsby-esque reverse migration to the East that destroyed him, *Winter* exemplifies what went wrong with Steinbeck in the 1950s and 1960s. By living the life of a famous writer on a foreign soil, he cut himself off from the nourishing wellsprings of his past; instead of Salinas and Monterey, he now turned to Nantucket Island and Sag Harbor—whaling towns turned summer retreats for the well-to-do. How could the author of *The Grapes of Wrath* (1939) dare look to a place so far removed, both geographically and economically, from his own beginnings?

This essay is written with the conviction that the charges I have just repeated overlook an important point of continuity throughout Steinbeck's life on both coasts. While for most Americans in the second half of the twentieth century, the whale fishery was a distant part of the nation's past, Steinbeck had a more immediate connection to whaling, which was very much alive during his youth in California. Once we recognize that his engagement with the old whaling towns of Nantucket and, most important, Sag Harbor opened a kind of cultural conduit to his past, we can begin to appreciate *The Winter of Our Discontent* as the novelistic culmination of a career in which his philosophical and ecological interest in the tide pools of *The Log from the Sea of Cortez* (1951) evolved into the social and cultural preoccupations of *Travels with Charley* (1962) and *America and Americans* (1966). By fusing his own background with that of a nation, the whaling town provided the setting with which Steinbeck would begin the exploration of his final great theme: the meaning of America.

I

In *Travels with Charley* Steinbeck quotes from a "rude poem" describing how the California of his youth came into being:

> *The miner came in forty-nine,*
> *The whores in fifty-one.*
> *And when they got together,*
> *They made a Native Son.*
> *(174)*

As it turns out, a significant number of these miners were from Nantucket. The combination of a disastrous fire in 1846 and a sandbar at its harbor mouth sent the island into a terminal decline well ahead of most other whaling ports on the East Coast, and many Nantucketers left to seek their fortunes in California. In 1850, 650 Nantucketers were reportedly either sailing for California or already there. In just nine months, the island lost a quarter of its voting population to the goldfields, causing a portion of San Francisco to be called "New Nantucket" (Guba 1965, 212; Macy 1970, 291–92). As the goldfields lost their allure, the San Francisco whale fishery entered into an era of remarkable expansion in the 1880s with the outfitting of a new class of steam whalers designed to exploit the arctic whale fishery (Bockstoce 1986, 213). Thus as whaling ceased to be an economically viable endeavor in the East (the last whaler left Nantucket in 1869), it acquired a new lease on life in the West.[1]

One hundred miles to the south of San Francisco, Steinbeck's native Monterey had its own distinct whaling identity. In 1854, it became the site of the first shore whaling station on the California coast (the same form of whaling with which both Nantucket and Sag Harbor had started more than a century and a half before) when Captain J. P. Davenport from Rhode Island began the Monterey Whaling Company; a year later the Portuguese Whaling Company began operation (the owners and operators of which may have been the forefathers of Big Joe Portagee in *Tortilla Flat* [1935]). With the virtual extinction of the gray whale in the late 1850s and the increased use of petroleum products, shore whaling slowly declined until the last humpback whale was brought into Monterey Bay in 1905. In 1919, when Steinbeck was seventeen years old, a new form of whaling station began operation in Monterey that machine-processed the whales into fertilizer, bone meal, and soap. In 1925, after harvesting over 700 humpbacks, the company went out of business (Gordon 1991, 22–26).

That his native region's whaling culture was of no small interest to Steinbeck and that it may in turn have contributed to his interest in Nantucket Island (where he wrote much of *East of Eden* during the summer of 1951) is suggested by an early passage from *Journal of a Novel: The East of Eden Letters,* in which he discusses the genesis of the name of the novel's protagonist, Adam Trask: "The name is so important that I want to think about it. I remember a friend of my father's—a whaling master named Captain Trask. I have always loved the name. It meant great romance to me" (7).[2] In keeping with Steinbeck's identification of whaling with the romantic dreams of his youth is the fact that his favorite place to play as child was a cliff overlooking Whalers Bay on Point Lobos that would become the site of his funeral service (Benson 1984, 1038).

At about the same time that he was remembering Captain Trask, he wrote to his agent Elizabeth Otis concerning a "pet project—a set of informal but informative articles about the Island of Nantucket." In an unpublished letter dated 21 May 1951, he continued, "It has a fantastic history, its own language and it seems to have developed a culture and an outlook quite different from the mainland." Even though he was already in the midst of *East of Eden*, Steinbeck said that he had "decided to go to the Island of Nantucket, make the research for such a series, even to the extent of recovering the kind of speech and doing the pieces."[3]

Although he would never write the proposed articles, he did spend the summer of 1951 on Nantucket. Undoubtedly contributing to his enthusiasm for the place was his recent discovery of *Moby-Dick* (DeMott 1984, 163). Echoing Ishmael's statement that "there was a fine, boisterous something about everything connected with that famous old island, which amazingly pleased me" (Northwestern-Newberry edition 1988, 8), Steinbeck would write Otis from Nantucket, "I feel excited and good. Never knew a place with more energy than here. The air is full of it" (*SLL* 423). Even though he remained immersed in *East of Eden*'s evocation of his own family's history as well as that of the Salinas Valley, Steinbeck displayed a keen interest in Nantucket's past throughout the summer, often speaking with local historian Edouard Stackpole about the island's whaling history (personal interview, 25 October 1991).[4]

Steinbeck's association of an East Coast whaling town with his own past experiences in California is even more strongly indicated by his purchase in 1955 of a house in Sag Harbor, Long Island—another old whaling community cut from the same cultural cloth as Nantucket. But Steinbeck was apparently attracted to Sag Harbor less by its similarity to the island on which he had written *East of Eden* than by the way in which the town reminded him of Monterey. According to the editors of *Steinbeck: A Life in Letters*, "It was for him an East Coast equivalent of the Monterey Peninsula. . . . It marked his complete acceptance of the East Coast as his permanent home" (505).

It was a "complete acceptance" that had, in one sense, been forced upon him. After he began to feel no longer welcome in Monterey in the 1940s,[5] Steinbeck became convinced that he would never again be able to feel "the old nostalgia" (*SLL* 285) for a specific location, commenting to Pat Covici: "I've made my tries at 'places' and they don't work" (335). In Sag Harbor, however, he discovered a "place" that evoked his past but in a new and invigorating context. In 1956 he wrote Covici, "Out here I get the old sense of peace and wholeness," finally proclaiming: "I seem to be reborn" (521–22). In latching on to what the biographer Jackson J. Benson has called "a Cannery Row East" (1984, 771), Steinbeck had found a kind of bicoastal cultural constant that would inevitably involve him in issues and concerns that transcended any one region.

II

In lieu of the usual disclaimer, *The Winter of Our Discontent* begins with this epigraph: "Readers seeking to identify the fictional people and places here described would do better to inspect their own communities and search their own hearts, for this book is about a large part of America today." By insisting that the old whaling village of New Baytown—which is later described as "one of the first clear and defined whole towns in America" (47)—is a nation in miniature, Steinbeck places *Winter* in a long-standing literary tradition that includes Ralph Waldo Emerson, who in 1847 referred to the island that was Sag Harbor's whaling precursor as the "Nation of Nantucket" (Emerson 1973, 63).[6]

But it is in Herman Melville's famous "Nantucket" chapter in *Moby-Dick* (1851) that whaling receives its perhaps definitive identification with America, the ironic reverberations of which are noticeable throughout *Winter*. In Melville's view, the Nantucket whalemen epitomized the hyperactive spirit of conquest that was then motivating America's push to California: "Let America add Mexico to Texas, and pile Cuba upon Canada...; two-thirds of this terraqueous globe are the Nantucketers. For the sea is his; he owns it, as Emperors own empires" (Northwestern-Newberry edition 1988, 64). In *Israel Potter* (1855), Melville expands upon this identification of whaling with America, commenting that the protagonist had "unwittingly prepared himself for the Bunker Hill rifle" by "darting the whale-lance." It is in Melville's depiction of Ethan Allen's "barbaric disdain of adversity," however, that *Israel Potter* most explicitly takes up where *Moby-Dick* left off, describing the "spirit" that would define America as a new, ocean-to-ocean nation. Just as the Nantucketer is in essence landless in his globe-girdling acquisitiveness, so does

Ethan Allen—whom Melville describes during his imprisonment in England—embody a spirit that knows no regional home: "Though born in New England, he exhibited no trace of her character. . . . His spirit was essentially Western; and herein is his peculiar American-ism; for the western spirit is, or will yet be (for no other is, or can be) the true American one" (Northwestern-Newberry edition 1982, 149).

In *The Winter of Our Discontent*, Steinbeck also uses the name of Ethan Allen to signify the new direction the country has taken. But whereas Melville looked to Allen and whaling to evoke the raging vitality of a new, western-oriented nation in the nineteenth century, Steinbeck uses the combination to describe an eastern community in a state of suspended animation in the twentieth. Ethan Allen Hawley is an overeducated grocery store clerk obsessed with the legacy of his whaling ancestors, a backward orientation that also applies to his town as a whole: "Other towns not too far away grew and prospered on other products and energies, but New Baytown, whose whole living force had been in square-rigged ships and whales, sank into torpor. The snake of population crawling out from New York passed New Baytown by, leaving it to its memories" (206). As a community stuck in a cultural cul-de-sac, New Baytown exemplifies what Steinbeck would describe five years later in *America and Americans* as a nationwide malaise: "We have reached the end of the road and have no path to take, no duty to carry out, and no purpose to fulfill" (140).

Although he may be preoccupied with it, Ethan Hawley is hardly at ease with his own and his town's past. Unlike his father, whom he describes as a "high amateur ancestor man" infatuated with a romanticized image of the past, Ethan recognizes that his ancestors were "sailing, whale-killing men," who reveled in just the kind of money-grubbing, survival-of-the-fittest world for which his "gentle, well-informed" father was so ill-adapted: "They successfully combined piracy and puritanism, which aren't so unalike when you come right down to it. Both had a strong dislike for opposition and both had a roving eye for other people's property. Where they merged, they produced a hard-bitten surviving bunch of monkeys" (47). His grandfather, who had experienced firsthand the old whaling days, is the one who sets Ethan straight on what the past was truly like: "Old Cap'n remembered the fights over shares, the quibbling with stores, suspicion of every plank and keelson, the lawsuits, yes, and the killings—over women, glory, adventure? Not at all. Over money" (60).

Although he appreciates the essential ruthlessness of his whaling ancestors, Ethan cannot help but be tempted by his father's conviction that the old days were somehow better than the present. At one point he lapses into a reverie inspired by one of his father's "heritage lessons":

the docks, the warehouses, the forests of masts and underbrush of rigging and canvas. And my ancestors, my blood—the young ones on the deck, the fully grown aloft, the mature on the bridge. No nonsense of Madison Avenue then or trimming too many leaves from cauliflowers. Some dignity was then for a man, some stature. A man could breathe.
   That was my father talking, the fool. (60)

Ethan's tortured ambivalence toward the past is perhaps best illustrated by his ancestral home. With its attic of easy chairs and ancient books, it is a virtual shrine to a vanished age, but it is the "glass-fronted cabinet" in the second-floor hallway that most fully evokes the museumlike nature of the Hawley house. Although Ethan dismisses its contents as "worthless family treasures," he also acknowledges that "the cabinet had always been the holy place of the *parenti* to me" (160–161). Besides scrimshaw, models of boats, artifacts from the Orient, and some other objects, the cabinet contains what Ethan describes as "a kind of mound of translucent stone"—"a magic thing" or talisman particularly prized by his daughter Ellen. In that it exists behind a pane of glass, this collection of artifacts is a fitting emblem of Ethan and New Baytown's whaling past, a defunct culture that can be examined and admired but that has little relevance to the day-to-day world of the living.

Ethan's ultimate decision to pursue economic success ruthlessly, to make a buck out of the inevitable transformation of his town into a summer retreat, is not a betrayal of his forefather's heritage; rather, it marks his clear-eyed acceptance of their way of doing things. No longer a hand-wringing "ancestor man" luxuriating in a past that never was, Ethan becomes a committed, albeit covert, member of New Baytown's business world, who is prepared to do just about anything (as were New Baytown's "hard-bitten" whalemen) if it will gain him the financial security and social standing he craves.[7]

Ethan's transformation from a morally upright observer to an amoral, even immoral participant marks a return not only to the ways of his ancestors but to an even more basic, animalistic level of existence. For Steinbeck, who had dealt with the aftermath of *The Grapes of Wrath* by leading the slap-dash collecting expedition described in *The Log from the Sea of Cortez*, the tide pool provided the ultimate metaphor for man's relationship to his surroundings.[8] In *Winter* Ethan has his own personal tide pool, a wave-washed hideaway at the end of his family's abandoned wharf that he calls "the Place." If the Hawley house is the symbolic repository of New Baytown's cultural identity, the Place is where Steinbeck evokes the underlying biological imperatives at work in the community. Early in the novel, the Place is a refuge where Ethan can observe and enjoy the tide pool much in the same way that he indulges in fanciful visions of New Baytown's whaling past: "Now, sitting in the Place, out of the wind, seeing under the guardian lights the tide creep in, black from the dark sky, I wondered whether all men have a Place, or need a Place, or want one and have none. . . . What happens is right for me, whether or not it is good" (57).

For Ethan, the Place is a "an inevitable world of cycles of life and time and of tide" (341), in which he can escape what Steinbeck called in *The Log* the "ethical paradox" of his own humanity. Indeed, in this earlier work, Steinbeck established the crux upon which Ethan's relationship to New Baytown's past and present would be based: "In our structure of society, the so-called and considered good qualities [wisdom, tolerance, kindliness, generosity, humility] are invariable concomitants of failure, while the bad ones [cruelty, greed, self-interest, graspingness, and rapacity] are the cornerstones of success" (*LSC* 112). Ethan is what Steinbeck called in *The Log* "a viewing-point man" who "while he will love the abstract good qualities and detest the abstract bad, will nevertheless envy and admire the person who through possessing the bad qualities has succeeded economically and socially" (112). Ethan's eventual determination that "a man must carve and maul his way through men to get to be King of the Mountain. Once there, he can be great and kind—but he must get there first" (*WOD* 195) reflects an uneasy attempt to reconcile what

Steinbeck earlier saw as the central "paradox" of the human species, in which man's need for success, which in the Darwinian world of the tide pool is equated with a "strong survival quotient," inevitably overrides the "weak survival quotient" (*LSC* 112–13) of his need to do good.

When Ethan finally trades a weak for a strong survival quotient (a transformation that is described as a "deep-down underwater change" [79]), he becomes a predator in what Steinbeck increasingly compares to a tide pool. Instead of the peaceful waters of the Place, this is a tide pool red in tooth and claw. When Ethan receives a hand-written will from a friend who is about to drink himself to death with the money Ethan has given him, he tells us, "The skin on my face felt as hard as a crab's back" (200). Mr. Baker, the scheming banker who ultimately becomes the victim of Ethan's own machinations, is compared to an anemone casting off the "shell of a sucked-clean crab" (234). Ethan's wife, Mary, on the other hand, is "a great granite rock set in a tide race" (354).

This identification of Mary with a symbol of stability is significant. Even as he secretly surrenders himself to the tide race, Ethan hopes to shelter his family and especially his children from its pernicious undertow.[9] When he discovers that honorable mention of his son Allen in a "Why I Love America" essay contest resulted from his having plagiarized the great books in the attic, he finally realizes that no matter how good his final intentions may be regarding his own children, it is already too late as far as his son is concerned. For Ethan, who has betrayed virtually everything he believes in, the only alternative is suicide.

Given Steinbeck's use of tidal imagery throughout *Winter*, it is almost inevitable that the novel's final scene occurs at the Place. A rising tide has transformed what was a spot of quiet contemplation at the novel's beginning into a hostile and dangerous environment, marking Ethan's total immersion in the Darwinian world of the tide pool. Buffeted by incoming waves and stung by jellyfish, he reaches in his pocket for a razor blade but finds instead the glass talisman so treasured by his daughter. Ethan's sudden determination to live is made possible by his realization that humanity's only hope rests not with a group but with the individual: "It isn't true that there's a community of light, a bonfire of the world. Everyone carries his own, his lonely own" (357). Only after he has connected this insight with his own daughter (through the intervention of the talisman) does Ethan find the will and the strength to emerge from the tide pool's carnivorous waters, an almost evolutionary progression in which his self-centered obsessions with the past and present give way to one final, truly altruistic act directed toward the future.

III

In many ways, *Travels with Charley*, Steinbeck's account of the journey across America he began soon after finishing the first draft of *Winter*, begins where his novel left off—in the tide pool. Whereas we last see Ethan wading through the chest-deep waters of the Place, Steinbeck starts *Travels* with a stormy baptism off Sag Harbor. After singlehandedly reanchoring his boat, the *Fayre Eleyne*, in the middle of Hurricane Donna, the fifty-eight-year-old author is left with a dilemma:

Well, there I was, a hundred yards offshore with Donna baying over me like a pack of white-whiskered hounds. No skiff could possibly weather it for a minute. I saw a piece of branch go skidding by and simply jumped in after it. There was no danger. If I could keep my head up I had to blow ashore, but I admit the half-Wellington rubber boots I wore got pretty heavy. It couldn't have been more than three minutes before I grounded and that other Fayre Eleyne [Steinbeck's wife] and a neighbor pulled me out. It was only then that I began to shake all over, but looking out and seeing our little boat riding well and safely was nice. (16)

While this might seem like an incongruous way to begin the account of a journey across America in a camper-equipped truck, it offers a dramatic and imagistically appropriate transition between two books about America, taking us from the fictional waters of The Place to the real-life tide pool that initiates Steinbeck's description of a nation in *Travels*.

Although his stated objective is to rectify what he feels is a twenty-five-year estrangement from America (lending credence to the charge with which this essay began), there is another, very personal dimension to this quest that underlies Steinbeck's battle with the elements: his need to reassert the "violence" in his life in spite of the inevitable encroachments of old age. Early on he tells us, "I did not want to surrender fierceness for a small gain in yardage" (20). Thus his trip across America becomes the means by which he not only reacquaints himself with what he calls the "wild and reckless exuberance" (26) of the American people but also reasserts his own personal vitality—a very Melvillean sort of "peculiar Americanism" through which he ultimately discovers that the nation is "the macrocosm of microcosm me" (209).

Indeed, what astonishes Steinbeck is that no matter where he goes in "this monster of a land" (209), he finds people who are all very much like himself:

If I found matters to criticize and to deplore, they were tendencies equally present in myself. If I were to prepare one immaculately inspected generality it would be this: For all of our enormous geographic range, for all of our sectionalism, for all of our interwoven breeds drawn from every part of the ethnic world, we are a nation, a new breed. Americans are much more American than they are Northerners, Southerners, Westerners, or Easterners. . . . The American identity is an exact and provable thing. (210)[10]

Although some critics have called *Travels with Charley* "the record of a failed venture" (Ditsky 1975, 45), it actually marks Steinbeck's validation of his own continued connection with America, describing a journey that proved, if the previously quoted epigraph to *Winter* is any indication, the authenticity of the novel he had written (but not yet published) the previous summer. Even if it had been twenty-five years since he had explored the nooks and crannies of the country, he now realized that no matter where he lived in America, even if it was three thousand miles from where he had grown up, he was still living in his native land.

It is a cultural insight that corresponds closely to Steinbeck's cosmic worldview as stated more than twenty years earlier in *The Log*: "All things are one thing and . . . one thing is all things—plankton, a shimmering phosphorescence on the sea, and the spinning planets and an expanding universe, all bound together by the elastic string of time. It is advisable to look from the tide pool to the stars and then back to the tide pool again" (257). In an important sense, *Travels with Charley* is the journal of Steinbeck's journey through the tide pool of America—a journey that is bracketed, fittingly, by the fishing villages of the author's present and past: Sag Harbor and Monterey.

Equipped with the realization that America, East or West, is all essentially one entity, he is able to see Monterey in much the same terms as he had depicted New Baytown. Just as all that is left of the whalers of New Baytown are the artifacts in the Hawley cabinet, so has Steinbeck's Monterey "ceased to exist except in the mothballs of memory" (206). At one point he tells his old friend Johnny the bartender, "What's out there is new and perhaps good, but it's nothing we know" (203).

What Monterey has become is what Steinbeck had earlier described as the imminent fate of his fictional New Baytown—an old fishing village turned into a tasteful tourist trap:

In my flurry of nostalgic spite, I have done the Monterey Peninsula a disservice. It is a beautiful place, clean, well run, and progressive. The beaches are clean where once they festered with fish guts and flies. The canneries which once put up a sickening stench are gone, their places filled with restaurants, antique shops, and the like. They fish for tourists now, not pilchards, and that species they are not likely to wipe out. (205)

If the "proportionality" (Ditsky 1975, 47) of *Travels* is skewed toward the first half of the journey, it is because once he has visited Monterey, the most vital connection has been made—Steinbeck's past and present in coastal fishing towns have come together in the cultural context of America.

Whereas Steinbeck's imaginative ties to a past that had "ceased to exist" made it difficult for him to have any enthusiasm for Monterey's new identity as a tourist mecca, he apparently did not have the same problem with his adopted Sag Harbor and served for several years as honorary chairman of an annual "Old Whalers Festival."[11] Instead of the sense of mourning and loss for old Monterey that dominates *Travels,* his introduction to the Whalers Festival's program of events is a hilarious and irreverent take on Sag Harbor's whaling heritage, describing a whaleboat race in which participants pursue "a genuine artificial whale" known as "Mobile Dick" and a beach buggy contest. Concerning the beach buggies, he comments, "No one can foresee what will happen here but the prospects are dreadful and beautiful to contemplate. But after all, the Old Whalers whom we celebrate lived dangerously, and we cannot let them down" (*Old Whalers Festival* 4).

Steinbeck's enthusiasm for the event was so large that he repeatedly invited the president of the United States to the festival (Benson 1984, 965). The idea that Lyndon Johnson, a Texan, might preside over an Old Whalers Festival in Sag Harbor is a supremely American conception, particularly when we remember Ishmael's linking of the country's western ambitions ("Let America add Mexico to Texas") with the conquests of the Nantucket whalemen in *Moby-Dick*. Under the umbrella of Melville's "peculiar Americanism," whaling and the West were intimately involved with one another as part of what Steinbeck describes in *America and Americans* as "a new society" in which "all these fragments of the peoples of the world . . . became one people" (13–14).

And yet, as *Winter, Travels,* and *America and Americans* all make clear, the country had moved beyond this dynamic state of becoming and entered into a deeply troubled era: "The roads of the past have come to an end and we have not yet discovered a path to the future" (*AAA* 142). In his portrayal of a community still clinging to an outworn identity rather than forging a new one, Steinbeck's final novel effectively uses an old whaling town to describe a nation that has come to the end of one line and has not, as of yet, found another. Besides bridging the cultural gap between Steinbeck's two lives in California and New York, the whaling town also provided a deeply personal connection between his own beginnings and that of America as a bicoastal nation. Despite the pessimism and uncertainty he might have felt concerning that nation's future, Steinbeck was able to affirm at least one thing during his cross-country journey in *Travels:* He had not, as he had once feared, lost touch with his native land.

Notes

I thank Susan Shillinglaw of the Steinbeck Research Center, David Hull and William Kooiman of the National Maritime Museum in San Francisco, George A. Fickenor of the Sag Harbor Whaling and Historical Museum, Mary Jean S. Gamble of the John Steinbeck Library, Jacqueline Haring and Amy Rokicki of the Nantucket Historical Association's Research Center, and Elaine Steinbeck, Edouard Stackpole, Robert DeMott, and Susan Beegel for their help in researching this article.

1. Not until 1911 did the whale fishery in San Francisco go into a terminal decline (Hare 1960, 105).

2. In a letter to the author, Mary Jean S. Gamble from the John Steinbeck

Library in Salinas states, "In a 1976 interview, Mildred K. Hargis said Captain Trask was a Paso Robles man who knew the Steinbecks when they lived in Paso Robles, and he later visited them in Salinas. In a 1977 interview, another Salinas resident, Lucille G. Hughes, mentioned meeting Captain Trask. She said she thought he was a sea captain but was not sure." In a phone conversation, Susan Shillinglaw, director of the Steinbeck Research Center, mentioned the existence of several letters to Steinbeck's father written between 1907 and 1910 by D. P. Trask from Paso Robles, who was apparently godfather to Steinbeck's older sisters, Esther and Beth. Trask appears to have been a close family friend whose tales of the whaling life deeply impressed the young Steinbeck.

3. My thanks to Robert DeMott for bringing this unpublished letter to my attention.

4. Stackpole also commented that Steinbeck "only seemed happy when he was sailing his catboat."

5. In a letter to Pat Covici, he commented, "This isn't my country anymore. And it won't be until I am dead. It makes me very sad" (281).

6. See Burke's famous speech, "Conciliation with the Colonies" (1775); Crèvecoeur's *Letters from an American Farmer* (1782), of which approximately a third is about Nantucket; Jefferson's *Observations on the Whale-Fishery* (1788); Cooper's *The Pilot* (1821), in which he creates the Natty Bumppo–like archetype, Long Tom Coffin from Nantucket; and Emerson's May 1847 *Journal* entries about his stay on the island.

7. Although Ethan uses the alleged burning of the *Belle-Adair* by Baker's ancestors as justification for his actions against him, his reasoning is highly suspect and self-serving—a desperate attempt to dodge any moral responsibility for his actions. At one point Ethan admits to the ghost of his grandfather, "I'm looking for a real hate to take the heat off" (317).

8. In *The Log* he states, "the tide pool stretches both ways, digs back to the electrons and leaps space into the universe. . . . Then ecology has a synonym which is ALL" (99).

9. This attempt to insulate his domestic life from his business life accounts for the often jarring dissonance created by Ethan's use of two languages throughout *Winter*—the almost embarrassingly cute conversations between Ethan and Mary versus the hard-bitten, Hemingwayesque exchanges between Ethan and almost everyone else in New Baytown.

10. In *America and Americans,* he would expand upon this insight, commenting: "With our history, every law of probability forecast a country made up of tight islands of ethnic groups. . . . In spite of all the pressure the old people could bring to bear, the children of each ethnic group denied their background and their ancestral language. . . . America was not planned; it became" (16).

11. The Whalers Festival may have reminded Steinbeck of the festivities that once marked the end of the sardine season in Monterey, to which he refers at the beginning of *The Log* (28).

FOURTEEN

"The Scars of Our Grasping Stupidity" and the "Sucked Orange": John Steinbeck and the Ecological Legacy of John Burroughs

H. R. Stoneback

Today almost as thoroughly forgotten as John Steinbeck is celebrated, John Burroughs was, during the youths of Steinbeck and Ricketts too, America's best-known and most prolific nature writer. "Scars of Our Grasping Stupidity" explores the high probability that Steinbeck was familiar with Burroughs's work and the many shared resonances between Steinbeck's ecological thought and that of the earlier writer. H. R. Stoneback introduces to Steinbeck studies a potentially important and hitherto unnoticed influence and in the essay's appendix generously provides bibliographical information to facilitate future research on a Burroughs-Steinbeck connection.

I

I Love Nature, but Nature does not love me.
    John Burroughs, *A Sharp Lookout*

While this essay is not exactly an exercise in source study, one of my main concerns here is to decode the presence of John Burroughs in the life and work of John Steinbeck. In order to do that, it will be necessary to pay close attention to Burroughs at the outset, to restate the case for Burroughs's pervasive importance, to remind readers that although John Burroughs may now have some claim to the title—Most Neglected Major Literary Figure—nevertheless, in Steinbeck's formative years, Burroughs was arguably *the* best-known American writer. Most certainly he was the best-known American writer on nature; indeed, he was the most celebrated "literary naturalist" (to employ the usual, if somewhat misleading label) in American history. It is curious, given the burden of critical commentary on Steinbeck and nature, that the name and work of Burroughs has not once, as far as I am able to discover, has *never*, been linked with Steinbeck.

I may as well confess at the outset that I write more as a student of Burroughs than as a student of Steinbeck; that I serve as a director of the John Burroughs Association (with offices at the American Museum of Natural History); that I live, as it were, in John Burroughs's backyard, in the middle of the Hudson Valley, in the shadow of Burroughs's beloved Catskills; and that this essay has roots in a conversation with my friend and neighbor, Elizabeth Burroughs Kelley, granddaughter of John Burroughs. Some time ago, I felt one of those tremors of intuition, I had a hunch about Burroughs and Steinbeck. I asked Elizabeth Burroughs Kelley, who is a writer and a former English teacher, if she had any notions about her grandfather and Steinbeck. She said: "Oh well—Steinbeck? I don't know, I just don't know. Do you really think he knew nature and cared about the land the way my grandfather did? Do you think Steinbeck was a real naturalist? Do you think he read my grandfather?" It seemed clear enough that her answer to these questions was no. It was her skepticism, in part, that spurred me on to pursue this complex matter, to arrive at the point where my answer could be yes, oh most certainly Yes.

Who was John Burroughs? No, he did not write "Tarzan and Teleology." Nor did he write "Naked Non-Teleological Lunch." Recently, when I encouraged a student to write a research paper on Burroughs she went to bookstores and several libraries, on the trail of Burroughs. She came to my office with books by Edgar Rice and William Burroughs and nothing by John Burroughs. It is not only our bookstore clerks and librarians but our contemporary literary scholars and environmentalists who are all too often guilty of abysmal ignorance of Burroughs, *the nature celebrity* in American literature.

Burroughs lived (1837–1921) a long and productive life as a writer and public figure, and his works included the following books: *Notes on Walt Whitman as Poet and Person* (1867), *Wake-Robin* (1871), *Winter Sunshine* (1875), *Birds and Poets* (1877), *Locusts and Wild Honey* (1879), *Pepacton* (1881), *Fresh Fields* (1884), *Signs and Seasons* (1886), *Indoor*

Studies (1889), *Riverby* (1894), *Whitman: A Study* (1896), *The Light of Day* (1900), *John James Audubon* (1902), *Literary Values* (1902), *Far and Near* (1904), *Ways of Nature* (1905), *Bird and Bough* (1906), *Camping and Tramping with Roosevelt* (1907), *Leaf and Tendril* (1908), *Time and Change* (1912), *The Summit of the Years* (1913), *The Breath of Life* (1915), *Under the Apple Trees* (1916), *Field and Study* (1919), *Accepting the Universe* (1920), *Under the Maples* (1921), and *The Last Harvest* (1922).

For decades, Burroughs was front-page news; his camping trips and expeditions with Theodore Roosevelt, Henry Ford, Thomas Edison, and others made him one of our earliest charismatic media figures. Thousands of pilgrims came to Riverby, his Hudson River farm, and Slabsides, his bark-covered cabin in the woods, to consult the man known worldwide as the "Sage of Slabsides." Writers, students, naturalists, farmers, politicians, and presidents came; Roosevelt, Ford, Edison, Walt Whitman, and yes, even Oscar Wilde and Theodore Dreiser came to the Hudson Valley to see John Burroughs.[1] Henry Ford gave him a Model-T, which Burroughs promptly wrecked on the country road by my house; it seems driving got in the way of his nature observation. Ford pronounced Burroughs the greatest writer in *world* history—the greatest ever, anywhere—a view that caused Burroughs to remark: "Ford's taste in cars is better than his taste in literature" (Stoneback, "Conservation Ethic," S2).

At the very time that Steinbeck was attending school in Salinas, special school editions of Burroughs's essays were required reading from Maine to California. Burroughs Nature Clubs were the vogue nationwide. It is arguable that no other American writer was ever so widely read and so beloved by such a broad public. What other American writer was publicly and privately consulted at his cabin in the woods by presidential candidates? Did any other writer receive state visits from a president? People in West Park still talk about the day in 1903 when the presidential yacht brought Roosevelt and his party up the Hudson to the obscure home village of Burroughs and how the famous writer introduced every man, woman, child, and dog in the village to the president by name. And Burroughs's extraordinary fame did not fade immediately with his death in 1921. When Fred Eastman, in the 1930s, published the biographies of twenty crucial figures in world history, a five-volume set entitled *Men of Power*, volume 4 included biographies of Lincoln, Tolstoy, and

John Burroughs, the man who "had learned what was essential and inessential to the art of living. . . . Men and women who had been battered and bruised in the noisy scramble of American cities heard in Burroughs a call to the simple life. Here was a man who had kept his soul. They would seek him out." What many people sought to find in Burroughs were the qualities they attributed to nature, which was "a beneficent mother," as Eastman said, "to be cherished" (Burroughs 11).

The beneficence of Nature, however, is hardly the primary nature signal that Burroughs sends. Readers willing to penetrate behind the iconic image of the genial bearded Sage of Slabsides, to read Burroughs truly, would get an education in everything from Emerson to Whitman, from Darwin to Huxley, from Ernest Haeckel's new notions about Oekologie (a term coined by Haeckel in 1866) to Bergson's *Creative Evolution* and beyond. The true reader of Burroughs would get a thorough grounding in the dangers and sentimentalities of anthropomorphism, of "nature fakers," of all the traps of teleological thought. Such a reader would also find in Burroughs the best early literary criticism of Emerson, Thoreau, and Whitman. And the attentive reader of Burroughs would learn much about weather, land, mountains, rivers, farming, gardening, and the numinousness of place (all matters that figure importantly in Steinbeck's work). Finally, in all Burroughs essays, whether concerned with science or travel, literature or bird-watching, farming or fishing, his primary concern is a concrete sense of the natural world and his place in that world. He writes in lucid straightforward prose, a "natural" style attained after much deliberation and effort to rid nature writing of the quaint and affected as well as the thudding scientist jargon that had so pervaded the genre until Burroughs purified it. Indeed, as a master for an apprentice writer much concerned with nature, Steinbeck could not have found a better model than Burroughs. Even, it might be added, for lessons in narrative, in storytelling techniques, since especially in Burroughs's camping and fishing essays there is mastery of narrative thrust and design.

The March 1992 issue of *National Geographic,* in an article on Lake Tahoe, reminds us that the "apprentice novelist John Steinbeck put up a business sign saying 'Piscatorial Obstetrician' " at the barksided fish hatchery in Tahoe City, where he was caretaker in the 1920s

(Furgurson 118). This reminder, together with Jackson Benson's commentary in passing about Steinbeck's trout fishing (e.g., Benson 1984, 88), helps to establish a resonant image of a Burroughs-Steinbeck affinity. Burroughs was, of course, a "piscatorial obstetrician" of some renown, a man so well versed in trout midwifery (i.e., delivering them *from* the streams) that, as I have suggested elsewhere, perhaps we should forget his famous nickname "John O'Birds" and rechristen him "John O'Trout." Trout fishing was, for Burroughs, the most enduring and endearing form of pilgrimage to the very heart of nature (see Stoneback "Compleat Quest . . . "). And it is worth adding that neither Burroughs nor Steinbeck was piscatorially correct in the L. L. Beanified, vermiphobic catch-and-release fashion of these latter days. The two men were not cultic fly fishermen; they did not scorn the lowly worm or spinner; they held no Beanie-weenie Orvis-nervous niggling views of the hungry catch-and-eat fisherman. (This aside might stand as an "environmental" cameo of Burroughs and Steinbeck.)

What *evidence* is there that Steinbeck was aware of Burroughs? If we ask for evidence, not resonance, this is not an easy question to answer. Reading carefully Benson's biography, the Burroughs scholar sees the resonance on nearly every page. For example, Benson's very first paragraph stresses young Steinbeck's "impulse to get away" from the house that "brought him so close to nature so young"; this "childhood communion with nature"; these "secret experiences and private discoveries" stayed with Steinbeck for the rest of his life. Then Benson cites a passage from *East of Eden* that evokes the trees and flowers and ferns, the "mossy banks of the water courses," the sense of connection "so rare and magical that a child . . . felt singled out and special all day long" (1984, 7). This is the essence of Burroughs. Indeed this entire passage sounds so much like Burroughs, in content, in the texture and rhythm of the prose, in the fixing of the observing eye and the other participating senses, that I searched for the verbal source for this passage—and many others—in Burroughs. This kind of search is a formidable task, since Burroughs published more than *five hundred* essays. For the student or critic of Steinbeck more interested in this kind of investigation, for the scholar with the will, patience, and a project of sufficient scope (perhaps a dissertation), I am willing to guarantee that such source passages are there to be found, and the discoveries will be rich with implications regarding Steinbeck's views of nature *and* his prose style.

Uncanny resemblances and affinities continue to echo throughout the Benson biography. For example, the stress on Steinbeck's country ways and his love of gardening—Burroughs, born a farmer, gardened and farmed all his life; the affection Steinbeck felt for his maternal grandfather, Samuel Hamilton, whose bearded visage bears a striking resemblance to Burroughs (they were both born in the 1830s); the description of the various cabins and shacks that Steinbeck lived in during his apprenticeship years, from his woodshed shack when he was at Stanford to the slabsided caretaker's cottage at the Brigham Estate at Tahoe to the slabsided fish hatchery in Tahoe City. In all these places, Benson observes, Steinbeck cultivated the image of the outsider, the recluse, the literary hermit-who-was-not-really-a-hermit. Taken together, all this provides an exact *constatation* of the iconic Burroughs: in the first three decades of this century there was not, anywhere in the world, a more famous, available, and compelling example of the writer as ostensible hermit living in a slabsided retreat than John Burroughs.

Indeed the very vogue for slabsided lodges and camps and rustic twig-and-tree furniture that created at least two of the dwellings in which Steinbeck resided was due in large part to the fame of Burroughs's cabin, Slabsides, as a literary hermit's retreat in the wilderness. Of course, since the whole world sought out Burroughs at Slabsides—sometimes, for example, as many as one hundred Vassar and New Paltz students in one day—he was anything but a hermit. (And as Benson notes, neither was Steinbeck.) In short, if Steinbeck had a model for his apprenticeship role of literary outsider, immersed in the concrete details of nature, studying nature in a rustic retreat, it had to be John Burroughs. The reader who objects here, raising perhaps the banner of Thoreau, is reminded that Thoreau (who lived, of course, in a highly civilized New England townscape never too far from Emerson's dinner table) was not nearly as well known in the early decades of this century, that he was a distinctly minor figure *then*, in comparison with the now-neglected Burroughs, and that it was in large part due to Burroughs's essays that Thoreau became better known. It was Burroughs, more than any other, who clearly identified Thoreau as the often erroneous observer of nature that he was and Burroughs who tagged Thoreau with the label "transcendental supernaturalist."

These, then, are just a few of the many Burroughs-Steinbeck resonances. And yet, in spite of all the attention paid to obscure naturalists, zoologists, and biologists (in Benson as in other Steinbeck studies), in spite of detailed study of Ed Ricketts—who, by the way, sounds as if he sprang full-blown from the heart of Burroughs's work—there is *no* mention of Burroughs, neither in Benson nor in any other study of Steinbeck that I have been able to uncover. It is unthinkable that men of Ricketts's and Steinbeck's generation and inclination would not have known well the Burroughs myth and method, the Burroughs books and nature studies. Still, I acknowledge that the scholar has a certain duty to provide more than suggestion and resonance.

Evidence? Very well, then, since Benson tells us that the Steinbeck family "always subscribed" to such magazines as *Century* (1984, 18), let us note that between 1903 and 1918 Burroughs published nine essays in *Century*, including such titles as "Ways of Nature," "The Divine Abyss," "The Gospel of Nature," "What Do Animals Know?" and "On Humanizing the Animals" (later retitled "Animal Communication," when collected in *Ways of Nature* 1905). This last essay was his follow-up to his famous piece in the *Atlantic*, entitled "Real and Sham Natural History" (March 1903), which initiated the most heated nature controversy of the early 1900s. There Burroughs attacked the "nature fakers," the sentimental writers on nature and animals who presented "anthropomorphic absurdities" as scientific observation.

Burroughs condemned, for example, Ernest Thompson Seton's *Wild Animals I Have Known* and retitled the volume "Wild Animals I Alone Have Known"; as Burroughs noted, the crows, foxes, horses, and rabbits in Seton's book are creatures that, "it is safe to say, no other person in the world has ever known" (*Sharp Lookout* 51–56, 525–48). The "nature faker" controversy set in motion by Burroughs went on for a good many years, whipping some writers (such as Seton) into more precise observations and formulations and banishing other writers and their quaint "wild friends" into the outer anthropomorphic darkness. It is hard now to recover a sufficient sense of the fame of this controversy, which even elicited the sustained attention and literary participation of the president. When Roosevelt read Burroughs's first essay on the subject, he wrote him a letter, praising the article. When Burroughs and Roosevelt made their media-blitzed trip to Yellowstone, Burroughs was as sought after and cheered by crowds at whistle-stops as was the president. Roosevelt, following Burroughs's lead, wrote several essays on the controversy. This must be the only literary controversy in American history that involved the vigorous participation of a president. Surely, Steinbeck knew of it in his youth and would have gleaned many of his best intuitions and attitudes about real observation of natural facts from such a cause célèbre. Just as surely, students of Steinbeck's uses of animal imagery, for example, would profit from close reading of Burroughs's many essays on animals. One instance of a possible source for Steinbeck's phalanx notions might be found in "Animal Communication," where Burroughs speculates on the "community of mind" in animals, as well as on those occasions of fear, anger, or other excitements when human groups behave like a single organism.

This is just the tip of the Burroughs iceberg, and all of this the young Steinbeck could have followed just in the issues of *Century* that were in his home as he grew up. If the other magazines in Steinbeck's childhood home, or in other homes and libraries to which he had access during his youth, included *Atlantic, Cosmopolitan, Country Life, Critic, Current Opinion, Harper's, Independent, Ladies' Home Journal, McClure, North American Review, Outing, Outlook, Scribner's,* and *Yale Review,* then Steinbeck might have seen, by the time he turned twenty, more than *seventy-five* essays by Burroughs in these magazines alone. To list just a few of these titles is to sketch a road map of Steinbeck's career: "Literary Treatment of Nature," "Literature and Science," "The Arrival of the Fit," "Life and Chance," "Shall We Accept the Universe?" "Emerson and His Journals," "A Critical Glance into Darwin," "Another Word on Thoreau," "The Hit-and-Miss Method of Nature," "The Reds of Literature," and "The Hazards of the Past." Most of these essays are readily accessible in the twenty-three-volume Riverby Edition of *The Writings of John Burroughs.* Since future students of Steinbeck may wish to consult these Burroughs essays as they appeared in periodicals, however, and since the pertinent bibliographical information is not available elsewhere, I have gathered here the names, dates, and places of publication of essays that appeared between Steinbeck's birth and Burroughs's death, between 1902 and 1921 (see appendix). For future students of Steinbeck, there are riches to be mined here—sources, stylistic echoes, affinities, analogues, and philosophical, scientific, and literary observations and attitudes.

II

One cannot but reflect what a sucked orange the earth will be in the course of a few more centuries. Our civilization is terribly expensive to all its natural resources.
—John Burroughs, "The Grist of the Gods"

We in the United States have done so much to destroy our own resources . . . and our country will not soon lose the scars of our grasping stupidity.
—John Steinbeck, *Sea of Cortez*

Given the limited scope of this essay, perhaps it would be most useful merely to list several established rubrics in Steinbeck criticism and to suggest the possible influence, presence, and resonances of Burroughs in these matters. All of these rubrics, however obscure the connections may at first seem, have a good deal to do with that much abused term "environmentalism," have everything to do with an ecological sense of things.

1. *Steinbeck and Emerson.* Since Frederic I. Carpenter's seminal essay, "The Philosophical Joads," many commentators have noted Emersonian motifs and patterns in Steinbeck's work. As Carpenter has it, Emerson's "mystical transcendentalism," individualism and self-reliance, and his notion of the "transcendental oversoul" are crucial for Steinbeck, especially in *The Grapes of Wrath* (in Donohue 81, 89). It should be noted here that Emerson was the earliest mentor for Burroughs, that when Burroughs published his first major essay, James Russell Lowell, editor of the *Atlantic Monthly*, felt that the essay was so much like Emerson that it must have been plagiarized. This 1860 essay, "Expression," was published unsigned, and in some bibliographies, it is still attributed to Emerson. Indeed there are many Emersonian echoes in Burroughs, but the more important fact is that Burroughs rejected much, perhaps most of the Emersonian package. As Frank Bergon puts it:

Burroughs depicts the boy as part of nature, rather than presenting na-
ture as part of the boy. We don't read nature, he frequently noted; nature
reads us. Burroughs felt that both Emerson's distance from physical na-
ture and his passion for analogy frequently betrayed him into seeing the
whole of nature as only a metaphor for the human mind. . . . Burroughs
did not accept such a dualistic view of the universe, especially a view that
made nature auxiliary to man. (in Burroughs 1987, 18)

Burroughs, as I see it, makes available to Steinbeck a rigorously revised and downsized Emersonian vision, much qualified by a more
scientific view of nature. If, as Benson says, "there is no evidence that
Steinbeck was particularly fond of Emerson" and if Steinbeck "was
not, even in part, a Transcendentalist" (1984, 233), then maybe he got
what little Emerson he had through Burroughs, who was anything
but a transcendentalist.

2. *Steinbeck and Whitman.* Once again, Carpenter and others make
much of the presence of Whitman in Steinbeck's work. For Carpenter, Whitman's "earthy democracy" and his "religion of the love of
all men" (in Donohue 81, 89) signify immensely in Steinbeck. The
formula reads something like this: Emerson Plus Whitman Divided
by Pragmatism Equals The Philosophical Joads. Perhaps there is
something to this. For the rest, we know that Steinbeck "did share
with Ed Ricketts an admiration for Whitman's poetry, particularly
its lustiness and celebration of the natural" (Benson 1984, 233–34).
Both Benson and Richard Astro note Ricketts's admiration for Whitman; and Astro writes that Whitman was, for Ricketts, one of those
rare poets who "reflect a heightened consciousness . . . which en-
ables them to move non-teleologically . . . , beyond right and wrong
to an acceptance of what is" (1973, 40–41). If Steinbeck shared that
view of Whitman, he certainly didn't have to wait until he knew
Ricketts to learn it: it is precisely what Burroughs had been saying
about Whitman since at least 1866. It was, of course, Burroughs who
wrote the first real literary criticism of Whitman (a review of *Drum-
Taps* in 1866 and *Notes on Walt Whitman as Poet and Person* in 1867)—all
told, more than two dozen essays and two books on Whitman. It has
often been said that without Burroughs as his champion, Whitman
might have been "undiscovered," might now be just another forgotten poet, or at least a writer as much neglected as Burroughs is today.

They were close friends and literary allies; it was Burroughs who gave Whitman the song of the hermit thrush as a key voice and symbol for "When Lilacs Last in the Dooryard Bloomed" (a favorite Ricketts poem), and it was Whitman who gave Burroughs the memorable title for his first book, *Wake-Robin*.[2]

In sum, for Burroughs, Whitman was *the* great interpreter of nature, a poet and prophet of oneness and acceptance, and it is this vision of Whitman's "procreant urge," his nonteleological embrace of an ur-ecological sense of allness, that Burroughs passed on to thousands of readers through six decades of writing about Whitman. It would be difficult to gainsay the likelihood that Steinbeck or Ricketts or any reader in the early 1900s got their Whitman filtered through Burroughs. Thus perhaps Burroughs is the essential missing link for Steinbeck criticism that invokes Whitman.

3. *Steinbeck and Agrarianism.* At least since Chester E. Eisinger's 1947 essay on "Jeffersonian Agrarianism in *The Grapes of Wrath*" agrarianism has figured importantly in many discussions of Steinbeck. I know that when I first read Steinbeck, *The Grapes of Wrath* followed by *The Long Valley*, it was the vision of the farmer and the land that I found most compelling. Perhaps, by some strange historical twist, it was my thirteen-year-old's sense of Steinbeck's version of agrarianism that ultimately got me, long years later, to Vanderbilt University, where I studied a radically different yet mysteriously similar version of agrarianism with Allen Tate, Donald Davidson, and other neo- and postagrarians. In any case, if Eisinger and others are right about the importance of agrarianism in Steinbeck, if the "noble" ideal of the farmer "standing as an anachronism in the midst of the machine-made culture of twentieth century America— a culture sick and foundering in depression" (in Donohue 143) is somewhere near the center of Steinbeck's vision, then this may indicate one more area of Steinbeck's indebtedness to Burroughs. For Burroughs was nothing if not an agrarian—in work, in image, and in life he remained to the end the Catskill farm boy that he was by birth. The core image of the farmer and his shadow self, the dispossessed and deracinated farmer, haunts the work of both Burroughs and Steinbeck.

4. *Steinbeck and Regionalism.* Steinbeck is often associated with various notions that fall under the rubric of regionalism. Surely, when

we think of that California known as "Steinbeck Country," we are thinking of him as a kind of regionalist. Just as surely, in much of his work from *The Long Valley* to *East of Eden,* Steinbeck is a kind of regionalist, and his work demands more careful and thoroughgoing consideration than it has had, for its strengths and qualities, which are rooted in the very best senses of regionalism. I employ the term here in much the sense that the Nashville agrarians did, Donald Davidson, Allen Tate, Robert Penn Warren, and others; regionalism, as they saw it, is not a term of limitation, is not quaintness and local color and folklore, not the charm-mongering picnic regionalism of certain urban sensibilities. It has much to do with rootedness, with certain deeply felt senses: sense of place, past, community, family— and, too, a sense of *pietas,* a sense of the numinous that is very much bound up with the land. Regionalism means that a writer writes out of, not necessarily *about,* a profound sense of place; that he sees in and through and because of a kind of intense localism. Regionalism is, above all, a way of seeing, a vision that has been purged by a kind of ongoing sacramental relationship with near and common things.

Burroughs exemplifies this kind of regionalist and, I think, a good deal more than has been noted, so does Steinbeck. I have carefully defined elsewhere the ways in which Burroughs seems to me to be our preeminent New York regionalist (see "John Burroughs: Regionalist"). Burroughs has much to tell us about the kind of rootedness Steinbeck invokes, for example, in *Travels with Charley:* "One of our most treasured feelings concerns roots, growing up rooted in some soil or some community" (100). Burroughs insists that this "home feeling," as he calls it, is the "private door" that admits one "behind the scenes" of things (Burroughs 1904–1922, 1–3). Perhaps echoing Burroughs explicitly (since he puts the phrase in quotations), Steinbeck also has much to say about this curious "home" feeling, even in a place where he had never been before, as when he evokes the "home" feeling of La Paz in *Sea of Cortez* (126). Burroughs and Steinbeck have a deeply shared sense of this kind of regionalism, this "home feeling." I would hasten to add that, in my view, and perhaps in theirs, to be at home in one place is to be at home in all places, to be at home in the world. And it is this kind of true regionalist who makes the best "environmentalist," the best ecologist.

5. *Steinbeck and Nonteleological Thought.* It may be de rigueur in a

Steinbeck volume, especially one dealing with Steinbeck and nature, to be teleologically correct, or nonteleologically fashionable. Yet I must say that the entire question of Steinbeck's "nonteleological thought" seems to me a bit overcooked, overdone. To some degree, Richard Astro's study of Steinbeck and Ricketts illuminates the question, but insofar as Astro's reader is asked to believe that Ricketts's nonteleological vision is particularly striking or original, this reader is not convinced. Nor am I convinced that, as Astro says, "it was largely through Ricketts' eyes that Steinbeck learned how to see natural beauty and . . . fundamental truths about the relational unity of all life" (1973, 218). Also illuminating, to a degree, is Benson's contention with certain points made by Astro, a contention which turns on just how thoroughly nonteleological Steinbeck and Ricketts were; or which man deserves the Oscar for Dysteleology? Of course, we know from the Ricketts-Steinbeck Easter Sunday sermon on nonteleological thought in *Sea of Cortez*, and from much of Steinbeck's fiction, that dysteleology is an important matter for students of Steinbeck.

But if a Burroughs scholar may be permitted the observation that both the structure and the terms of this debate sometimes seem a bit rickety, I will simply record here my modest proposal that we turn to Burroughs as a source for both Steinbeck and Ricketts in this matter. Nearly everything that pertains to the question may be found in Burroughs, where both the terms and the concepts are pervasively present in scores of well-known essays that were published in major periodicals during the time that both Ricketts and Steinbeck were children. Benson is right, I think, to say that Steinbeck was probably a "nonteleological thinker" very early on, "from his high school days or before" (1984, 242); Benson does not venture a "precise source of these ideas." Again, I suggest Burroughs. More important, perhaps, Burroughs is also a source for a sense of what John Timmerman calls the "philosophical insufficiency" of nonteleological thought (23); and an absolutely vital source for what Benson sees as Steinbeck's central creative "tension of counterbalancing between a scientific or naturalistic view of the world and a poetic-idealistic one" (1984, 645).

There are other rubrics under which Steinbeck scholars might usefully examine the Burroughs legacy, including genre study of the nature essay. Although I have never heard any of my Burroughs colleagues, or any of my naturalist colleagues at the Museum of Natural History or elsewhere, take Steinbeck seriously as a nature writer, most of them know very well that Burroughs is the acknowledged master of the nature essay in American literature. And reading that very distinguished contribution to the genre, Steinbeck's *Sea of Cortez*, I sense behind every page the tough and genial presence, the solid example, of Burroughs.

III

Conservation came to us slowly, and much of it hasn't arrived yet.
  —John Steinbeck, *America and Americans*

What, then, is the environmental legacy of Burroughs and Steinbeck? Perhaps the greatest difficulty is with that tricky popular word: environmentalist. Recently a student of mine, an avowed "radical environmentalist" if not a card-carrying friend of the earth, set out to write, at my suggestion, a term paper on Burroughs, Steinbeck, and the Environment. I told him what sources to consult; he came back to my office a week later, enraged. He was appalled that on pages 27 and 28 of *Sea of Cortez* Steinbeck reports on the boozy bon voyage party of the *Western Flyer* and talks, without righteous ecocommentary, about the bobbing beer cans tapping against the hull of the boat and washing on the Monterey shore. He would read no further. He was equally outraged with Burroughs: how, he asked, could a true Sage of Nature cavort with those "Machine Age Anti-Christs" Thomas Edison and Henry Ford? Burroughs must be a "phony," he declared; the car was the ultimate enemy, the worst of all the machines in the ruined garden. He was also mad about Steinbeck's love of big gas-guzzling cars. This may say something about the legacy of Burroughs and Steinbeck to radical young environmentalists today. It may not. In any case, no amount of urging suspension of disbelief, no amount of ludic banter on my part, would penetrate or soothe his Luddite rage. He would read no more Steinbeck, no more Burroughs. (He did a term paper on Hemingway in Paris.)

What kind of ecologists, what kind of environmentalists were Burroughs and Steinbeck? Take one instance: the national parks. Burroughs influenced Teddy Roosevelt as much as anyone did, and

Roosevelt "created" the national parks. When Roosevelt invited Burroughs to accompany him on that 1903 trip to Yellowstone, a journey that was front-page news, Burroughs wanted to stay home and work in his garden. After the trip, he remarked: "The most interesting thing in that wonderful land was, of course, the President himself." Neither the Yellowstone trip nor Burroughs's journey to the Grand Canyon with John Muir in 1909 elicited any ringing declarations from Burroughs regarding national parks or conservation or wilderness preservation. The Burroughs-Muir trip to the Canyon, it seems, is best remembered for the humorous anecdote told by one of their companions: "The last day at the Canyon, as we stood looking into the vast abyss . . . , I said to a companion: 'To think of our having the Grand Canyon, and John Burroughs, and John Muir thrown in!' 'I wish Muir *was* thrown in sometimes,' retorted Mr. Burroughs, who had overheard" (Stoneback, "Conservation Ethic," S3).

The point, of course, is the tension between the quiet non-crusading Burroughs and the wilderness-manifesto-raving Muir, or, the tension between a quiet pastoral-centered vision and a vociferous wilderness-centered vision. As for Steinbeck's attitude toward the national parks, it may be best summed up by his confession of "laxness in the matter of National Parks," which he offers in *Travels with Charley:* "It is my opinion that we enclose and celebrate the freaks of our nation. . . . Yellowstone National Park is no more representative of America than is Disneyland" (161).

For another instance, consider that although both Burroughs and Steinbeck lived in big cities at various times, they were both essentially countrymen. Steinbeck rages in *Travels with Charley* against the "new American" who loves "traffic-choked streets, skies nested in smog, choking with the acids of industry," where the "air smells of chemicals" and the "rivers are choked and poisoned"; he is sure that the "swollen cities" will rupture and "disperse their children back to the countryside" (72). In *America and Americans* he bemoans our "irresponsibility," which has produced poisoned rivers, "reckless dumping of sewage and toxic industrial wastes," city air that is "filthy and dangerous," towns "girdled with wreckage and the debris of our toys—our automobiles and our packaged pleasures" (127). Distaste for the city is also pervasive in Burroughs; amazingly enough, as early as 1875, he gives us an image of the city as a "purgatory of heat and dust, of baking, blistering pavements . . . , of dead, stifling night air . . . [and] all diffusing privy and sewer gases" (Burroughs 1904–1922, 1–4).

Both Burroughs and Steinbeck long for escape from the city to where they can see a clear sky; where, to cite one shared example, they can see the Aurora Borealis. Burroughs, camping in the Catskills, sees the "phantasmal waves of magnetic light" and stands in awe as "the sky shook and trembled like a great white curtain" (Burroughs 1987, 246). Steinbeck, similarly awed, echoes Burroughs as he tells how the sky "hung and moved with majesty in folds like an infinite traveler upstage in an infinite theater" (*TWC* 48).

Both Burroughs and Steinbeck explicitly bemoan the abuse of the planet and the waste of natural resources. In an extraordinary and visionary 1908 essay, "The Grist of the Gods," Burroughs renders his essential ecological vision of the "earth as a living entity covered by a thin film of soil where the organic and inorganic blend together and the biosphere and atmosphere merge"; in this essay, as Bergon notes, Burroughs "celebrates the oneness of life found in the earth's natural processes" (in Burroughs 1987, 551–52). Then, in one of his best-known passages, Burroughs laments: "One cannot but reflect what a sucked orange the earth will be in the course of a few more centuries. Our civilization is terribly expensive to all its natural resources; one hundred years of modern life doubtless exhausts its stores more than a millennium of the life of antiquity." It won't be long, Burroughs fears, before the coal and oil will be used up, all "mineral wealth greatly depleted," the fertility of the soil "washed into the sea through the drainage of its cities," the wild game "nearly extinct," the forests gone, "and soon how nearly bankrupt the planet will be!" (Burroughs 1987, 558).

Steinbeck shares Burroughs's vision of the "sucked orange," and he writes about such crimes "against nature" in *Sea of Cortez,* for example: "We in the United States have done so much to destroy our own resources, our timber, our land, our fishes, that we should be taken as a horrible example. . . . With our own resources we have been prodigal, and our country will not soon lose the scars of our grasping stupidity" (250). Steinbeck saw this as early as 1940, and maybe he saw it much earlier, through the eyes of Burroughs. Maybe he contemplated Burroughs's "sucked orange" metaphor in his boyhood.

Maybe, in one of those last winters of his life that Burroughs spent by the Pacific Ocean, the Scripps' guest at La Jolla, studying the behavior of seals and the creatures of the reef and the tidal pool—just maybe the octogenarian Burroughs might have encountered a young Stanford student, nineteen-year-old John Steinbeck. Burroughs's journals record random encounters with unnamed young men who had a curiosity about nature. And science professors and naturalists, even in California, knew who Burroughs was, and many of them paid court when he made his annual visits to California. Some of them must have been Stanford professors. And even if they didn't meet in person, I think the young Steinbeck would have felt a powerful resonance in those national headlines that reported John Burroughs's death in 1921. He died on a train, headed home from California to his New York farm. The headlines proclaimed his last words: "How far are we from home?"

If Burroughs and Steinbeck were alive today, what kind of environmentalists would they be? Would they be environmentally correct? Would they be P.C.? Would they be PCB-fighters? Burroughs loved the Hudson River that flowed by his door—that same Hudson, or perhaps a very different Hudson flows by my door; would Burroughs join my fishermen friends and environmentalist neighbors who are fighting now to improve the condition of the Hudson? And Steinbeck loved the redwoods: would he chain himself to a great tree and resist a chainsaw-crazed logger? Would they, both in some way champions of the small farmer, make guest appearances at a Willie Nelson Farm-Aid Concert? I will not even guess at the answers.

Not long ago, revisiting my former career as an entertainer, a folksinger, I was a guest performer at a special gala concert in Austin, Texas. Many stars were there. Some had just come down the road from Willie Nelson's Farm-Aid Benefit. Ecosensitivity was much in evidence, in the talk and the songs front stage for the packed house and in the conversation among performers backstage. The rich and the powerful were there, the small farmers and the oilmen, the students and the fans. The governor was there. As at many such occasions there was a lot of envirotenderness and radical greenpreening. In the course of the long evening somebody said backstage: "You know, it was Steinbeck who first taught us to care about the small farmer." This was in response to a new song about a dispossessed farmer. Then another country-folk star said: "Taught us to care, yeah.

And so did old John Burroughs." Though now publicly identified with Texas, this star is also, like Burroughs, a native of the Catskills.

Yes indeed, there was much environmental concern in the air that evening and on all the other evenings like it. There seemed to be some core image to contemplate, rich with implications for my research for this essay; moreover, there was a numinous sense, a creative energy that was nodding to us, making some obscure demand or command. But it did not escape my notice that most of the stars there owned three or five or seven cars; and I knew that they lived in resource-devouring pleasure domes, surrounded by Tinker-techno-toys and state-of-the-art consumption devices. Of course, they all proudly live in what they are pleased to call "the country." And in the backstage alley where the automobiles of the stars were parked, there was not one vehicle that cost less than $50,000. I do not pretend to know what all this adds up to, nor do I protest my innocence.

On the plane on the way home I was reading *Sea of Cortez* and thinking about modes of ecological awareness. I read Steinbeck's words: "Ecology has a synonym which is ALL" (85). Yes, somehow we had always known this, and Burroughs and Steinbeck have helped us to know it more truly. Then, as we flew in low over the Chicago suburbs and landed at one of the great "sucked orange" airports, I was nodding in agreement with Steinbeck's view of how the Virgin, Our Lady of Loreto, was "one of the strong ecological factors" of the place (175), thinking, yes, and some of us have learned this only lately, though many had such knowledge long ago. Back in the air again, on the time and space and sky and resource-devouring way to New York, looking down at what did not really look much like a "sucked orange" at all, flying in over John Burroughs country too high to see many of the "scars of our grasping stupidity," I was nearing the end of *Sea of Cortez*:

And it is a strange thing that most of the feeling we call religious, most of the mystical outcrying . . . , is really the understanding and the attempt to say that man is related to the whole thing, related inextricably to all reality, known and unknowable. This is a simple thing to say, but the profound feeling of it made a Jesus, a St. Augustine, a St. Francis, a Roger Bacon, a Charles Darwin, and an Einstein. Each of them in his own

tempo and with his own voice discovered and reaffirmed with astonish-
ment the knowledge that all things are one thing and that one thing is all
things. . . . It is advisable to look from the tide pool to the stars and then
back to the tide pool again. (216–17)

While this would not suffice on some days, Easter and Christmas, say, or certain other saint's days and movable feasts, it was sufficient for an airport landing in 1992. And then we had landed, and I drove through John Burroughs country to my home, past the old stone Episcopal church next door to Burroughs's farm, the church *he* would not attend, where his son had been vestryman for decades, and over the bridge his son built that spanned the stream he fished, and I did not even ask "How far are we from home?" I knew. For weeks, certain passages of *Sea of Cortez* ran through my head, passages that suggested a Steinbeck I could not locate in Steinbeck criticism, and much of the time I was thinking that Burroughs wrote these passages. He could have. And of course, it was exactly what both Steinbeck and Burroughs were always saying, always singing.

Knowing all this—their environmental and ecological legacy—we must act. And act we do, in various senses. Some write, some protest, some create, some resist, some sing. Perhaps we act most authentically when we act daily and locally in our own gardens. Like Burroughs and Steinbeck, we can still be passionate gardeners. And sometimes we also act efficaciously, as did Burroughs and Steinbeck, on a larger stage. We stand in the ruined theater, a sucked orange in one hand, the scars of our grasping stupidity scoring the other outstretched hand, our voices breaking through at least momentarily into perfervid oneness and allness, and we sing the old song again, because the song *is* and we *have* to sing it.

Notes

1. For biographical information about Burroughs, see Clara Barrus, *The Life and Letters*. Barrus, who wrote or edited four more Burroughs books, was his authorized biographer, and although her *Life* is somewhat marred by her closeness to her subject (she was his amanuensis-disciple until his death), it remains the most comprehensive treatment. See also Elizabeth Burroughs Kelley, *John Burroughs: Naturalist* and *John Burroughs' Slabsides*. The best recent brief treatment of Burroughs is Frank Bergon's introduction to *A Sharp Lookout*; this volume also has useful bibliographical notes. Wherever possible, parenthetical references to

Burroughs essays are to Bergon's edition of them, the most recent selection of Burroughs essays; otherwise I cite the Riverby Edition of the complete *Writings*. Additional sources for material in this essay include countless conversations with Burroughs family members and scores of persons who knew Burroughs; these conversations—not dated academic "interviews"—have occurred over the past twenty-three years. In addition, since this writer has long been immersed in the life of the community—a small rural settlement—where Burroughs lived, I draw on the oral traditions of the community. Finally, it should be noted that the charge of grievous neglect of Burroughs, over roughly the last fifty years, is more applicable to literary scholars and historians than to naturalists. In the community of nature students and scholars, Burroughs's reputation remains reasonably secure. Burroughs thought of himself from the beginning of his career to the end as a *writer*, however, not a naturalist, and it was as *writer* that he made his vast impact on American literature and culture. Thus the act of historical recovery of the Burroughs legacy must be made by literary scholars, not by naturalists.

2. That Burroughs and Whitman had a close friendship, and influenced each other's works, is common knowledge among Burroughs scholars and not very well known among literary scholars. Documentation of such matters—for example, Burroughs's gift of the song of the hermit thrush to Whitman for use in his poetry—is ample and includes unpublished correspondence and journals (in the Burroughs Archives at Vassar College) as well as readily available published materials. For the most widely accessible brief account of the hermit thrush question, see Perry D. Westbrook, 17–19; for a brief but adequate account of Burroughs's role as proselytizer for Whitman, also see Westbrook, especially 16–49; see also Barrus, passim, and Burroughs, *Writings* (23 vols., passim).

Appendix

The essays listed here are those by Burroughs that appeared in periodicals in the years 1902–1921. Most, if not all, of these essays were subsequently collected—some with title changes—in the various collected editions of Burroughs's works. None of the various collected editions, however, gives bibliographical information regarding original periodical appearance of the essays. The information that follows is intended to be of use for further investigation by Steinbeck scholars on what Burroughs essays Steinbeck might have seen in his apprenticeship years. Of course, it is manifest that Steinbeck might also have seen Burroughs's work in various books, collections, and editions. That information is readily available. What follows is not. I record my gratitude here to Gregg B. Neikirk, research assistant, and to William Consiglio, warden-naturalist of the John Burroughs Sanctuary, for their assistance in the preparation of this appendix.

The list is arranged alphabetically by periodical and chronologically per periodical.

Art World
1916 March "The Good Devils"
1917 November "Emerson and His Journals"

Atlantic
1904 July "The Literary Treatment of Nature"
1905 June "Gay Plumes and Dull"
1907 August "Nature and Animal Life"
1908 April "The Divine Soil"
1909 April "The Long Road"
1910 May "Through the Eyes of the Geologist"
1910 November "The Animal Mind"
1911 December "The Hit-and-Miss Method of Nature"
1912 May "The Summit of the Years"
1912 September "In the Noon of Science"
1913 April "The Breath of Life"
1913 October "A Hay-Barn Idyll"
1914 January "A Prophet of the Soul"
1916 March "The Still Small Voice"
1918 April "The Spring Bird Procession"
1919 June "Another Word on Thoreau"
1920 August "A Critical Glance into Darwin"
1920 September "The Flight of Birds"

Bookman
1920 October "What Makes a Poem?"

Century
1903 June "Ways of Nature"
1904 March "Animal Communication"
1904 August "What Do Animals Know?"
1910 November "The Spell of the Yosemite"
1911 January "The Divine Abyss"
1912 September "Holidays in Hawaii"
1913 October "In the Circuit of the Summer Hills"
1918 June "Nature Lore"

Cosmopolitan
1905   June "A Beaver's Reason"
1906   April "An Outlook upon Life"

Country Life
1911   January "Wild Life in Winter"
1911   April "Bird-Nesting Time"
1911   August "Intensive Observation"
1912   August "The Bow in the Clouds"

Current Opinion
1921   April "The Reds of Literature"

Harper
1913   March "A Barn-Door Outlook"
1913   November "The Friendly Rocks"
1914   March "Under the Apple-Trees"
1914   August "A Bird of Passage"
1915   April "A Wonderful World"
1915   December "Old Friends in New Places"
1916   March "The Master Instinct"
1917   May "Fuss and Feathers"
1917   July "The Familiar Birds"
1919   April "Each After Its Kind"
1920   May "Bird Intimacies"
1920   August "A Midsummer Idyll"
1921   May "The Pleasures of a Naturalist"
1921   August "New Gleanings in Field and Wood"

Independent
1910   July 14 "The Worm Striving to be Man"

Ladies Home Journal
1920   September "Near Views of Wild Life"

McClure
1910   July "The Key to Animal Behavior"

North American Review
1912   September "The Phantoms Behind Us"
1914   March "Literature and Science"

1914   October "Life and Mind"
1915   February "The Arrival of the Fit"
1915   August "Life and Chance"
1916   March "Life the Traveler"
1916   August "Manifold Nature"
1919   January "Shall We Accept the Universe?"
1919   November "The Faith of a Naturalist"
1920   May "Men and Trees"
1920   September "A Sheaf of Nature Notes"

Outing
1906   December "Human Traits in the Animals"
1907   December "Animal and Plant Intelligence"

Outlook
1907   December 14 "The Reasonable but Unreasoning Animals"
1908   May 2 "Untaught Wisdom"
1911   February 25 "Scientific Faith"
1912   June 15 "The Hazards of the Past"
1921   May 25 "With Roosevelt at Pine Knot"
1921   November 2 "The Falling Leaves"

Scribner's
1920   October "Under Genial Skies"

Yale Review
1915   April "The Journeying Atoms"
1920   January "The Universal Beneficence"

It should be noted that this bibliographical appendix does not purport to be a complete listing of Burroughs's pieces that appeared in the years 1902–1921. Burroughs essays appeared in such popular boys' magazines as *St. Nicholas* during these years, for example, and these items are not included here. In addition, it is obvious that if Steinbeck had access to more or less complete runs of the above journals and others, he might well have seen hundreds more of Burroughs's essays that appeared in the above journals, and others, before 1902.

FIFTEEN

Steinbeck under the Sea
at the Earth's Core

Robert E. Morsberger

Robert Morsberger relates the surprising and whimsical story of John Steinbeck and the Mohole project. Named for the Mohorovicic Discontinuity, the junction between the earth's lighter crust and denser mantle, the Mohole Project sought to drill a hole through this boundary, located some two to three miles beneath the ocean floor. Steinbeck was chosen as historian for the venture, whose objectives were scientific information about the earth's crust and possible economic exploitation of the mantle. After preliminary success, Congress abandoned the Mohole project as too expensive, although its cost was a fraction of the current space program's funding. Nevertheless, Steinbeck's articles about Mohole reaffirm his fascination with the "inner space" of our own planet and the process of studying it.

What lies beneath the surface of the earth? In 1818, John Cleve Symmes, a veteran of the War of 1812, speculated that the earth is hollow and that there are immense apertures at the North and South Poles through which explorers could venture into another world underground. Symmes tried in vain to raise support for an expedition into the north hole, though he actually got twenty-five Congressmen to vote for it. Symmes's hole aroused the imagination of Edgar Allan Poe, who corresponded with Symmes's disciple Jeremiah N. Reynolds and ended two of his tales of terror, *The Narrative of Arthur Gordon Pym* and "MS. Found in a Bottle" with a ship being swept over a vast waterfall or being sucked into an immense whirlpool at the south hole. Elaborating on this notion, science fiction writers from Jules Verne to Edgar Rice Burroughs, Roy Rockwell, and A. Conan Doyle all wrote extravagant narratives about adventures underground in the center of the earth. Reynolds actually succeeded in persuading the navy to launch the celebrated Wilkes Expedition, which, exploring the South Pacific from 1838 to 1842, discovered numerous unknown islands and archipelagos, disproved the idea that there was a warm sea containing a vast temperate continent behind the Antarctic ice barrier, and established that Antarctica is the southernmost continent. Some crackpot pseudoscientists maintained well into the twentieth century that the earth is hollow, but no reputable scientist now thinks so.

Rather, in 1909, Andrija Mohorovicic, a scientist from the University of Zagreb analyzing earthquake vibrations, found that the center of the earth consists of an inner core, above which is a dense mantle, some 1,800 miles thick, upon which rests the earth's crust. The boundary where the comparatively light layers of the earth's crust meet that much denser mantle is named the Mohorovicic Discontinuity, in honor of its discoverer. What mysteries and what mineral resources lie within the mantle? No longer do we expect to find alien races and prehistoric monsters at the earth's core. Instead, scientists have attempted to explore the mantle by drilling a hole through the earth's crust into the mantle itself. The Mohorovicic Discontinuity has been nicknamed the Moho, and naturally, the hole through the Moho came to be called the Mohole.

The project to drill such a hole was conceived by the American Miscellaneous Society, or AMSOC, which was founded in 1952 to explore ideas that the scientific establishment would not consider seriously. The informal and whimsical AMSOC stated that its only divisions were in Triviology, Calamitology, Etceterology, Phenomenology, and Generalogy (Greenberg 1964, 115). In 1957, Gordon Lill, the chairman of AMSOC, discussed with Dr. Walter Munk of the Scripps Institution of Oceanography a proposal to drill into the mantle of the earth. Together, they formed a committee that included additional members of the Scripps Institution, Princeton University, the U.S. Geological Survey, the Office of Naval Research, and Columbia University's Lamont Geological Observatory (Matthews 694). In turn the National Academy of Sciences annexed the AMSOC-Mohole Committee, enabling it to get funds from the National Science Foundation, despite public paranoia that a hole through the earth's crust on the deep sea floor would drain all the water from the oceans, unleash suboceanic volcanoes, or blow up the entire world like popping a balloon (Matthews 694).

Why drill through the crust in the deep ocean rather than on land? On land, oil companies had already drilled almost five miles deep

(Matthews 692). But the earth's crust varies widely in thickness. On land, the Moho lies from eighteen to forty-five miles deep, whereas at sea, it is only two and a half to three miles beneath the ocean floor. Though the deep ocean is one of the earth's most mysterious, difficult, and dangerous environments, it is the most accessible location for drilling into the earth's core. When in 1960, five holes, one 1,035 feet deep, were drilled into the ocean floor 3,100 feet deep in the San Diego trench about eighteen miles off the California coast near La Jolla, it seemed to demonstrate the plausibility of the Moho project ("Mohole Job Up for Grabs," 144).

Still, why drill through the Moho? Scientists hoped to learn more about the formation of the earth as well as the mineral content of the mantle. According to Samuel W. Matthews of the *National Geographic*, in November 1961, Project Mohole might become one of the most significant scientific achievements of the century: "It will offer geologists their first direct contact with the earth's mantle; it will shed new light upon the history of our planet, perhaps even upon the beginnings of life itself" (Matthews 689). Even before reaching the Mohole, the digging could uncover some of the history of the earth by exploring layers of sediment in the earth's crust that would contain the record of silts, sands, volcanic debris, and fossil remains beneath the ocean floor. The project would be the first to explore the strata beneath the sea. The oil industry hoped to find new and rich pools of oil and gas as well as to obtain a great deal of information on techniques and equipment for deep sea oil drilling. Other industries were eager to learn about the mineral content of the earth's core: "We are in it for the experience," said one oil company executive. "It is a real research project and not one motivated by profit" ("Mohole Job Up For Grabs," 144).

Though there was indeed little likelihood that the Mohole would yield any immediate profits, over fifty companies attended a briefing held in July 1960 by the National Science Foundation to contract for the job, and over twenty-five more sought to serve as subcontractors. Not only were all the major oil companies and oil industry suppliers interested, but thirty-four nonoil companies, in such fields as electronics, chemistry, and aircraft, attended the briefing ("Mohole Job Up for Grabs," 142). For the San Diego trench exploration, the Mohole project was carried on mainly with borrowed or rented equipment, but now a new ship would have to be built with equipment especially designed for the drilling. So far, the drilling had been done by the Global Marine Exploration Company. At this point, the National Academy of Sciences, which had provided about $1 million, asked to be excused, as the project was expected to take three to five years and cost between $15 million and $20 million. Thus many drilling and drilling equipment firms were eager to bid for the contract. The Mohole might be a scientific gamble, but Continental, Union, Shell, and Superior Oil all paid to play and funded a drilling barge named the *CUSS I*, an acronym for the name of the oil companies. A few weeks after the tests in the San Diego Trench were completed, the *CUSS I* prepared to move southwest to a position seventy miles northeast of Guadalupe Island off Baja California, where the water was nearly four times as deep, two and one-fifth miles.

At this point, Willard Bascom, the project's director, invited John Steinbeck to come aboard as historian. About ten years earlier, Steinbeck had been invited to be historian on a survey of the Marianas and the Great Barrier Reef, but he had just married Elaine Scott and reluctantly declined (Benson 1984, 893). This time, he accepted with enthusiasm, commenting that "I was picked . . . not because I am a superb oceanographer but simply because I seem to be the only American writer who is one at all" (*SLL* 694). Hemingway, the only other modern American novelist to be associated with the sea, had died in July 1961, and he had been a killer of giant marlins rather than a marine scientist. Steinbeck conceded, "Maybe I'm too old, and surely I'm too ignorant but I'm the best they've got because my mind can look ahead" (Benson 1984, 893). Struck as much with the drama and poetry as with the scientific details of the project, Steinbeck considered the drilling "a fascinating job, a whole new world being discovered for the first time. With these cores and some more in the future, we will know much more about what the earth is made of, how old it is, and what has happened to it during its five billion years, how long life has existed and very possibly how it came to be at all" (*SLL* 694).

Just back from a working vacation on Barbados, Steinbeck flew in March 1961 to San Diego, where the Bascoms welcomed him and put him up for two weeks at their home in La Jolla until the *CUSS I* was ready to sail. "Sailing is a laugh," Steinbeck wrote to his wife and sons. "We are going to be towed by a navy tug and when we turn across the waves we wallow like you couldn't believe" (*SLL* 695). "Sailing is a status word for what we did," he commented wryly; he called the *CUSS I* "an oil rig" with "the sleek race lines of an out-house standing on a garbage scow" and observed that it "waddled like a duck into the channel on its four gigantic Diesel outboard motors" ("High Drama" 110). The squat, gray *CUSS I* was 260 feet long, with a derrick amidships 98 feet high. It carried 125 tons of drill pipes that could be fastened end to end in 60-foot sections to make a shaft three miles long. The shaft was lowered down a center well under the derrick and through a 38-foot funnel-shaped guide shoe to keep it from bending too much or even breaking as the ship rolled. To keep the barge in place over the hole four large outboard motors, two on each side of the barge, could counteract the pressure of wind and waves. Seawater pumped down the drill pipe cooled the drill string, which director Willard Bascom called "no more rigid than a wire one-sixteenth of an inch lowered from a twelfth-story office window to the sidewalk. With it we have to bore into rock harder than concrete" (Matthews 690). The $8,000 drill itself was a tungsten-carbide bit studded with diamond teeth that made twenty to forty rotations a minute (Matthews 693). What it extracted from the earth's core would be carried to the surface by a cable.

Life commissioned Steinbeck to write an article about the project, and though he muttered in letters to his family about "Arsenic and Old Luce," he accepted with alacrity. He wrote in the form of a log, noting that because of his comparative ignorance of submarine geology, his log would "concern itself with men and events rather than with scientific conclusions. Those will have to come later after analysis of what we find" ("High Drama" 110). Project director Bascom, with whom Steinbeck shared a compartment, was impressed with his powers of observation and his ability to judge character: "We would meet somebody and he would nail them with one shot. . . . Whatever you were, he knew what it was" (Benson 1984, 895). The scientific members of the Mohole team included "geologists, zoologists, petrologists, oceanographers, engineers of any kind you want to imagine," in addition to the hard hat workers, whom Steinbeck called "the toughest crew of oil riggers you ever saw. They look like murderers and have the delicate movements of ballet dancers, and they had better have, because to lower drill string from a heaving ship takes some doing" (*SLL* 695). Indeed it did, since the drill weighed 150,000 pounds ("Deep into the Deep," 100).

As a seagoing tug towed the clumsy craft out of San Diego harbor, Steinbeck noted the mothballed warships, "expensive reminders that the human species has not learned to make peace with itself and equally sad proof that we can always find money for violence" ("High Drama" 119). This observation turned out to be prophetic for the Mohole.

During the four-day voyage to their location 220 miles south of San Diego, the ship rolled "like a gut bucket" through heavy swells, while "the wind played on the tower like a harp so that it throbbed like plucked strings" ("High Drama" 119). Here is the Aeolian harp, a favorite image of the romantic poets, that Steinbeck had used earlier in describing the wind whistling through the guy wires of the *Western Flyer* in *Sea of Cortez,* for to him nautical research combined a sense of wonder and adventure with the scientific quest for knowledge. Steinbeck explored the ship, talked to the crew, and contemplated the nature and significance of the project, concluding that its main importance was that it was being done at all:

We spend treasures daily on fantastical sky rockets aimed feebly towards space. Our lustful eyes turn to the moon, not as the Queen of the Night, but as real estate. We spend and devise and dream toward the nearest star unreachable in a lifetime of travel. And meanwhile we know practically nothing of far the greater part of our home planet covered by the sea. The suboceanic terrain is a dark mystery to us in its nature, its components, its history and its riches. This expedition will cost less than one single glittering missile blasting from the launching pads at Canaveral, and yet this project is surely an adventure toward the discovery of a new world as were the three little lumbering ships of Columbus. And this new world is here—not a million miles away. ("High Drama" 119)

On March 26, the *CUSS I* passed Guadalupe Island, which Steinbeck called "a high waterless mountain, the top fringed with some kind of conifers," and "inhabited by goats and a herd of sea elephants and a small Mexican military radio crew" ("High Drama" 119). About midnight, in rough weather, with a twenty-five-knot wind whipping waves and swells twelve to fourteen feet, the vessel reached its drilling station, where the tug released it and the four immense outboards positioned it between anchored buoys. Almost immediately, the drilling crews began to fit together the sixty-foot sections of pipe and to lower them one a minute, along with the drill string ("High Drama" 120). With his interest in group man, Steinbeck admired their teamwork, which required them to "move with the timing and precision of a corps de ballet." They were as interdependent as Ishmael and Queequeg on each end of the *Pequod*'s monkey rope, for Steinbeck noted that "if one man makes a clumsy or ill-timed move, someone may be killed by the swinging steel. They depend on one another for their lives" ("High Drama" 120).

Despite high and bitterly cold winds and eight- to ten-foot waves, the drilling barge, aided by radar and sonar, kept its position precisely as the string whined down all day and night, when the drill rig was illuminated by powerful floodlights. Shortly after noon on the second full day of drilling, the bit touched the ocean floor and bored 110 feet below it, to bring up a sample of clay sediment full of fossils, which turned out to be twenty million years old, six times older than the general rule for the age of sediments in the deep ocean. An awestruck Steinbeck, commenting on the frantic interest of the entire team, noted that "everything is new about this, everything a discovery" ("High Drama" 120).

The next day, the cable to retrieve the corer stuck, kinked, and separated at 300 feet into the crust. The corer was lost, and the whole drill string had to be pulled up and the operation begun again. It took ten hours to pull it up and another ten hours to drop it, but despite winds as strong as forty knots that made the *CUSS I* jump "like a steeplechaser" and the tower sway dangerously, the crew persisted, bringing up samples at various depths until, on Easter Sunday, they brought up a core of volcanic basalt from 600 feet beneath the ocean floor. Later that day, the drill dug into the second layer and the core brought up more basalt and dolomite. Though the *CUSS I* broke drilling records, reaching the mantle would require digging 18,000 feet deeper, and several years of study would still be required before the actual Mohole could be dug. In the meantime, the project had to choose the best site, design new equipment, and build a larger ship to carry it. Considering the *CUSS I*'s limited success and looking at the difficulties that lay ahead, at this point, the *National Geo-*

graphic Magazine quoted Ecclesiastes 7:24, "That which is far off, and exceeding deep, who can find it out?" (Matthews 697).

Not Steinbeck, who had to leave the *CUSS I* on Easter Monday and return to New York to have surgery on a hernia he had torn while aboard the drilling barge (Benson 1984, 896). Nevertheless, he felt "a joy like a bright light" for having been a witness to "the first touching of a new world" and for having been part of the team of "a hell of a bunch of men" that made up the "motley crew of *CUSS I*" ("High Drama" 122). Steinbeck speculated that from the project's discoveries, "a whole new history of our earth may be written" ("High Drama" 122). More practically, he concluded that if it turned out that most of "the world's material wealth is under the sea, there will have to be a re-examination of international spheres of ownership and controls. Twelve miles off almost any coast now belongs to anyone who can get there. The only reason the seas have been free is because no one wanted them except for transportation and defense. Available riches may change all that" ("High Drama" 119).

CUSS I's trial run for the Mohole was a spectacular success, accomplished in a few weeks and within its budget. President Kennedy sent congratulations to everyone associated with the project "and especially to all those on board the *CUSS I* and attendant vessels who have combined their talents and energies to achieve this major success" (Greenberg 1964, 118). Saying that we must develop the ocean's abundance of food and minerals, Kennedy also asked Congress to almost double its appropriation for oceanographic research, to $97.5 million (*Newsweek*, 10 April 1961, 100). Around the world, geophysicists and engineers hailed the accomplishment of *CUSS I*.

But from the beginning there were skeptics. The 1960 Pick and Hammer Show, an annual musical spoof of the Washington Geological Society, entitled "Mo-Ho-Ho and a Barrel of Funds," had its hero, Glib Bunkum, employ a posthole digger at the bottom of the sea (Bascom 55). Soon problems arose over the amount of funding and the scope and control of the project. Should geologists simply drill through the Moho, or should they pursue a more extensive and multilevel drilling program? Should an intermediate ship be constructed to replace *CUSS I*, or should such a ship be bypassed in favor of an ultimate one?

The estimated expense escalated from an initial $15 million to as high as $150 million, and critics were calling the project a pork-barrel boondoggle. Administrative infighting became disastrous. Shortly after the success of *CUSS I*, the AMSOC Committee decided that the project was becoming too sprawling and complex and so withdrew from it. In turn the National Academy of Sciences, while continuing to recommend the project, decided that it was the wrong organization to pursue it. Both organizations advised turning the project over to a prime contractor, while urging that Willard Bascom's staff be retained, since it was chiefly responsible for the success of the operation so far. But as the National Science Foundation began to select a prime contractor, the Bascom group was gradually phased out of the picture.

Though it scored fifth in the bidding process, Brown & Root, Inc., of Houston was awarded the contract, amid charges of favoritism and conflict of interest, particularly since the firm had been a long-time supporter of Lyndon Johnson, who allegedly answered worries that if John F. Kennedy became the first Catholic president, he would dig a tunnel from the Vatican to the White House: "I'm not worried about the tunnel—as long as Brown & Root get the contract" ("Project Nohole?" 60). Critics also complained that the president of Brown & Root was a close political ally of Albert Thomas, whose congressional district was close to Houston and who was chairman of the House appropriations subcommittee, which controlled the National Science Foundation's budget.

Though the engineering aspects of the Mohole project were formidable, they became subordinated to administrative and political ones. Hostile members of Congress, mainly Republicans, attempted to hold up the National Science Foundation's budget. For five years, Project Mohole limped along, under constant fire from congressional opponents, who attempted to kill its appropriations. Meanwhile, Brown and Root considered alternative digging sites, finally rejecting one off Puerto Rico because of the hurricane belt and in 1965 approving one north of Maui. At the same time, work began on a drilling platform that was to become the world's largest oceanic laboratory. Construction and testing time for the drilling rig was estimated at over three years, pushing the actual drilling date to 1968 or 1969.

Meanwhile, with the United States now at war in Vietnam, congressional critics of the Mohole said the project was no longer affordable (thus far, federal funding had contributed $55 million to the project) and cut off funds for it in 1966, despite an attempt by President Johnson to reverse the House action. Steinbeck's observation five years earlier that we can always find money for war but are reluctant to spend it for peaceful research turned out to be painfully true. Thus the drilling rig was never built, and the Mohole was never dug. Calling the Mohole "the albatross of the scientific community," D. S. Greenberg wrote in *Science* that it had died of "multiple and needless injuries," inflicted not by scientific obstacles but by administrative and political battles (Greenberg, "Mohole: Aground on Capitol Hill," 963).

When the Mohole project was killed by the loss of federal funding, Ernest V. Heyn, editor-in-chief of *Popular Science,* invited Steinbeck to write an open letter on the issue. A longtime reader of the magazine, Steinbeck was more than happy to comply, since doing so would provide him with a forum for his frustrations and his hopes. While expressing support for the billions of dollars spent on space probes, he lamented the tunnel vision of congressional leaders unwilling to spend vastly less for a matter Steinbeck considered of both greater urgency and practicality—the exploration of the sea. Yet it was not primarily practicality that appealed to Steinbeck; rather, he wrote that human beings "are still incurable, incorrigible romantics . . . capable of a search for the Golden Fleece" and concluded that "the key to his [the human animal's] success in survival and triumph over the forces of nature, is curiosity" (Steinbeck, "Let's Go" 84–85). Certainly curiosity seemed to Steinbeck a better motivation for scientific exploration than the race to get somewhere, like the moon, before the Russians. Thus he lamented that "while the lifeless rubbled surface of the inconstant moon becomes increasingly littered with the burnt-out bones of vehicles, the bathyscaphe [*sic*] has visited the deep and unknown places of the earth only a few times" ("Let's Go" 85). In consequence, while we have changed the face of the earth, we are pitifully ignorant of the three-fifths of the earth that lie under the ocean: "We peck like sandpipers along the edges for the small treasures the restless waves wash up. We raid the procession of the migrating fishes, killing all we can" ("Let's Go" 86).

Having observed the near destruction of the sardine fisheries off Cannery Row, Steinbeck commented that "even the killer whale herds the sperm whales and kills them only when it needs food—but we have wiped out some species entirely" ("Let's Go" 86). Meanwhile, he observed that though plankton may be "the basic reservoir" for the world's future supply of protein, we have ignored completely the agricultural possibilities of the sea "except to rip out the fringes for iodine or fertilizer" ("Let's Go" 86).

Musing on the perversity of human nature that makes us require the prod of danger, war, or starvation as catalysts for our inventiveness, Steinbeck concluded that "finally we find ourselves faced with the most ghastly enemy of all—ourselves, too many of us in a world with a limited food supply. And hungry men will destroy anything, even themselves, to get food" ("Let's Go" 86). The one good that could come from this is that the depletion of supplies on land might drive us back to "our mother, the sea." Steinbeck predicted that if we could focus our inventiveness and our money on the sea, we might find four-fifths of the earth's wealth on or under the ocean floor, while with desalinization, we could make the deserts fertile.

Looking back at the Mohole project, he muttered at the howls of protest from congressional leaders against spending any more money for it, even though the preliminary drillings off Guadalupe Island caused the textbooks to be rewritten. Though he was encouraged by the work of Jacques Cousteau and of the American navy, he insisted that small, unrelated groups could never do what a coordinated effort funded by the government could accomplish. Observing that to himself "the oceans mean safety, mystery, and wonder," Steinbeck concluded, "There is something for everyone in the sea—incredible beauty for the artist, the excitement and danger of exploration for the brave and restless, an open door for the ingenuity and inventiveness of the clever, a new world for the bored, food for the hungry, and incalculable material wealth for the acquisitive—and all of these in addition to the pure clean wonder of increasing knowledge" ("Let's Go" 87). Personally, he hoped to go with the next Mohole expedition and descend "to the great black depths" ("Let's Go" 87). Tragically, he died two years and a quarter later, his hope unfulfilled.

Yet despite being aborted, Project Mohole was far from a failure.

Besides adding to our knowledge of the earth's crust and mantle, it resulted in thirty-eight deep-drilling innovations ("Drowning Mohole" 62) and new technology that developed three acoustic positioning systems, useful to the offshore oil industry for deep-sea drilling and the prevention of blowouts as well as to submarines and general underwater research. Honeywell's Ordnance Division completed 98 percent of the work on a positioning system before Congress killed funding for the Mohole, and Honeywell said that its accomplishment was "directly derived" from the Mohole phase comparison sonar (Niblock 24–25). If politicians and corporations could be less mercenary and share Steinbeck's sense of wonder, perhaps his vision could come true.

Part Five:
Overviews

SIXTEEN

How Green Was John Steinbeck?

Warren French

As early as 1933 John Steinbeck expressed concern over environmental destruction, and a note of despair is echoed forcefully in his last published work, America and Americans *(1966). But his environmental advocacy must be seen, finally, as more inspirational than practical. He offered few models for an ecologically oriented political agenda but instead optimistically relied on "moral suasion," a call to awaken the slumbering "goodness" of the American people and inspire them to live in harmony with their environment.*

At the 1989 meeting of the Western Literature Association, Cheryll Burgess pointed out that "society as a whole and our profession in particular have been faced with three crises in the last thirty years: civil rights, women's liberation, and environmental degradation. The discipline of English has addressed the concerns of civil rights, equality for minorities, and women's liberation through widespread attention . . . but has failed to respond in any significant way to the issue of the environment, the acknowledgement of our place within the natural world and our need to live beautifully with it, at the peril of our very survival" (quoted in Love 1990, 201).

The president of the association, Glen A. Love, used Burgess's indictment in a subsequent issue of the organization's journal to launch his own plea toward "Revaluing Nature" with a call for a movement toward an ecological criticism. He supported its necessity by a quotation from *Person/Planet* (1978) by Theodore Roszak, one of the best-known critics of American countercultures, about the dangers of accepting "progress" without question: "We have an economic style whose dynamism is too great, too fast, too reckless for the eco-systems that must absorb its impact. . . . The eco-damage is not mitigated in the least if it is perpetrated by a 'good society' that shares its wealth fairly and provides the finest welfare benefits for its citizens" (quoted in Love, 203).

Love winds up his comments with a reminder that the distinguished biologist Lewis Thomas "has cautioned us recently that it is time for us to grow up as a people . . . , to become the consciousness of the whole earth," but that "we have a long way to go, and are remarkably loath to begin the journey" (213).

This anthology brings together thoughtful assessments of John Steinbeck's expressions of concern with environmental degradation. A further relevant question concerns the model and inspiration that his comments may provide for those seeking to promote individual and collective actions that might improve chances of our "living beautifully" with our natural environment. What guidelines might he offer to the ecological parties that have recently enjoyed some success in England, France, and Germany? In short, how *green* was John Steinbeck? Did he simply pay lip service to environmental preservation or did he work effectively toward mitigating ecodamage?

I realize that in the following speculations I may be fighting with phantoms. I have no idea how widespread interest might be in ecological criticism, nor could I guess how useful it might prove. Could literary works make as effective contributions to environmental preservation as to feminist or ethnic minority or gay/lesbian movements? Although Nature speaks to us through rustling whispers and violent outbursts, it has no works of its own to champion action. As Lewis Thomas urges, we must recognize ourselves as Nature's articulate consciousness.

Steinbeck's writings demonstrate that one's head is not always where one's heart is. His despair about our growing up ecologically colors many of his writings, beginning as early as 1933 with a cynical vision of the suburbanization of a Californian Shangri-La in the story-cycle *The Pastures of Heaven*. The most comprehensive summary of his position appears in his last major publication, *America and Americans* (1966).

This meditation on the land he cherished began as a collection of photographs commissioned by the Viking Press, his longtime publisher, to present a colorful montage of the nation two-thirds of the way through the twentieth century. Steinbeck's participation was so-

licited to promote the reception of the project. He had recently enjoyed renewed popularity with a new generation after publishing
Travels with Charley in Search of America (1962), which had sold more
copies following its first appearance than any of his earlier works. In
the course of what he had envisioned as a few weeks' leisurely work,
he became deeply involved with the work and added to the promised
foreword nine chapters of commentary on specific subjects, containing material that he had wished to use in *Travels with Charley* but had
considered inappropriate for its format.

In one of the climactic chapters, "Americans and the Land," he
observes,

> *our rivers are poisoned by reckless dumping of sewage and toxic wastes,*
> *the air of our cities is filthy and dangerous to breathe from the belching of*
> *uncontrolled products from combustion of coal, coke, oil and gasoline.*
> *Our towns are girdled with wreckage and the debris of our toys—our*
> *automobiles and our packaged pleasures. . . . All these evils can and must*
> *be overcome if America and Americans are to survive; but many of us*
> *still conduct ourselves as our ancestors did, stealing from the future for*
> *our clear and present profit.* (127)

This dynamic rhetoric should surely stir the activist spirits of the
members of the Sierra Club and critics like Roszak, but would they
have gone along with Steinbeck's view on dealing with the malefac-
tors? Would they have agreed that "since the river-polluters and the
air-poisoners are not criminals or even bad people, *we must presume*
that they are heirs to the early conviction that sky and water are un-
owned and they are limitless"? (130; italics mine). Would they be
won over by his comforting assumption that though Americans are
"an exuberant people, careless and destructive as active children,"
"we are no longer content to destroy our beloved country. We are slow
to learn, but we learn. . . . And we no longer believe that a man by
owning a piece of America is free to outrage it" (130), or would they
regard this assertion of communal consensus as Steinbeck wishfully
speaking for himself?

For his own method of dealing with the misguided, he turned—as
often in these nostalgically patriarchal essays—to an episode from

his own distant past that illustrated a spontaneous youthful response:

Quite a few years ago when I was living in my own little town on the coast of California, a stranger came in and bought a small valley where the Sempervirens redwoods grow, some of them about three hundred feet high. . . . The emotion we felt in the grove was one of awe and humility and joy; and then one day it was gone, slaughtered. . . . And I remember that after our outrage, there was sadness, and when we passed the man who had done this, we looked away, because we were ashamed for him. (133)

The technique that Steinbeck and his youthful cohorts used was one widely endorsed by nineteenth-century militant reformers, especially during the finally successful campaign for the Eighteenth Amendment to the U.S. Constitution—moral suasion. This theory held that ostracism by an offended community awakened miscreants' repressed better natures; but suppose the culprits found that doing their own thing was better for the nurture of their egos and fortunes? Would a developer, then or now, have been embarrassed by the hangdog looks of a bunch of sentimental kids? Would such rejection reform those hacking away at the rain forests or looting savings institutions to build superfluous shopping centers or spilling oil that pollutes the seas and destroys wildlife in order to cut corners?

Lawrence Jones, a promising young critic who died just as he was beginning to share his provocative speculations, argued twenty years ago in *John Steinbeck as Fabulist* that although the novelist "was able to formulate a distinct vision of good for human life, he was unable to formulate a correspondingly distinct vision of evil; ultimately he offers a merely stipulative definition of it as a lack of unity or community," in which the student of American literature would hear "the ominously familiar ring of Emerson" (32). Although Steinbeck generally shied away from acknowledging similarities between his ideas and those of the American transcendentalists, many have been noticed since the pioneering essay by Frederick Carpenter, "The Philosophical Joads" (1941); these are not necessarily direct influences, however, but evidence of sympathetic sensibilities, permeating especially conceptions of an American Adam. Jones concludes that the trouble "seems to be that his vision of good is an obsessive one and it precludes his ability to deal squarely with evil" (32), as evidenced particularly by one of his most harshly criticized fables, the good-hearted *Burning Bright* (1950). An even more significant parallel to Steinbeck's position than the imperial Emerson's might be the homespun philosophy of a fellow twentieth-century last frontiersman, Will Rogers, who charmed his hosts of admirers when he boasted that he never met a man he didn't like. Though bitter experience disillusioned Steinbeck about communal amenities, he remained prone all his life to traumatic experiences from misplaced trust.

One example of Steinbeck's lifelong exuberance leading him into painful situations is a quarrel that once developed between him and the man whose friendship and counsel he continued to value most, marine biologist Ed Ricketts, over a matter involving their different views on tampering with the natural environment.

Steinbeck had become enthusiastic about filmmaking during the late 1930s and had studied with Pare Lorentz, whose two documentaries for the U.S. Farm Security Administration, *The Plow That Broke the Plains* and *The River,* are still honored as among the most artistically effective pleas for significant environmental preservation (through contour farming and flood control).

When Steinbeck was casting about for a new project to provide relief from the intense pressure of writing *The Grapes of Wrath* and then of surviving its unanticipated reception, he decided to try his own hand at filmmaking with documentarian Herbert Kline, who had won international praise for *Lights Out over Europe.* Kline wanted to make a film in Mexico about the peasants' struggle against landlord-dominated dictatorships, but President Roosevelt, whom Steinbeck had come to know through the contentious publicizing of his novel, wanted him to make a film with Dr. Paul de Kruif of *Microbe Hunters* fame about modern American medical advances.

Steinbeck rejected parts of both concepts and came up with his own by combining aspects of both into a plan for a film about the introduction of modern medicine into a superstitious, primitive community in the Mexican mountains. This was to become *The Forgotten Village.*

Ed Ricketts accompanied Steinbeck to Mexico for the filming, but he was upset about his friend's scenario and developed his own antiscript, "Thesis and Materials for a Script on Mexico," which protested against calling for social action to upgrade the country's obsolete medical practices. He argued that in "an inward sense, the Mexicans are more advanced than we are" and that the introduction of the United States' "mechanistic civilization" could destroy a "rich relational life." He proposed to replace Steinbeck's scenario, in which an ambitious teenage rebel brings the national health service to his village to combat an epidemic, with one in which a wise old man points out the dangers of building a high-speed road through a primitive community (Astro 1973, 59). Richard Astro, who has provided the most thorough account of the disagreement, attributes Steinbeck's dismissal of Ricketts's counterproposal to the novelist's having changed from metaphysical visionary to social propagandist (140), but this judgment oversimplifies Steinbeck's career after 1939, since the metaphysical visionary reemerged in *Cannery Row* (1945) and fitfully in later fiction. He even succeeded in combining the two in the film script for *Viva Zapata!* (1950). In fact, it may be the medium in which he was working that provides the best clue to his stubbornly insisting on sticking to his own plan for what proved to be pseudodocumentary *The Forgotten Village.*

Even staunch Greens confronted with the problem of deciding whether the demands of environmental preservation or modernization of health care takes precedence might hesitate; but it can be argued that in conceiving his film Steinbeck was concerned not with making such a choice but rather with giving a short-range problem an apparently immediate solution—even if its consequences might pose more problems than had been perceived, priority over a long-range problem that made necessary revolutionary adjustments in lifestyle through a difficult process of consciousness-raising. He may in the early 1940s have had differing conceptions of the functions of fiction and film.

He is not on record as explaining such a distinction, but he was always reluctant to discuss his writing strategies publicly. We may be able to make some assumptions, however, from two radically different versions of *The Red Pony*, the only one of his own fictional works that he himself revised for the cinema.

Without going into detailed analyses of the changes, we may observe that the basic difference is that he turned a cycle of four autonomous stories about the slow and difficult process of a boy's maturing into a continuous narrative, using material from only three of the stories with new additions to sentimentalize the short-range problem of providing the boy with a horse that will enhance his prestige among his schoolmates. Steinbeck appears to have considered fiction at this time as a vehicle for communicating to individual, contemplative readers portrayals of long-range developments in human consciousness with unpredictable outcomes, whereas he saw films as short-range presentations to mass audiences of short-range problems that could be solved if people could see how breaking through their old prejudices could produce immediate benefits.

The differences between the two approaches may be clarified by Steinbeck's changing reactions to another writer's work, Norman Douglas's 1917 novel *South Wind*, a rambling, conversational narrative about natives and visitors on a Mediterranean island resembling Capri. Steinbeck had once thought the English novelist's work "profound," but by 1962, he wrote a friend that he now "considered it full of thoughts and cleverness" but "shallow as hell" (DeMott 1984, entry 245). While Steinbeck is no more specific about his criticism of the novel, the concepts of "progress" stressed in *South Wind* may have influenced a change in his opinion.

At one point as Douglas's novel moves toward its climax, an Anglican bishop returning from Africa interjects into a conversation between an elegant, world-weary Italian count and a shrewd, hedonistic American millionaire a question about his confused notions of "progress" and "civilization." The count seizes the opportunity: "Progress is a centripetal movement, obliterating man in the mass. Civilization is centrifugal: it permits, it postulates the assertion of personality. The terms, therefore, are not synonymous; they stand for hostile and divergent movements. Progress subordinates. Civilization coordinates. The individual emerges in civilization. He is submerged in progress" (346).

The count's dexterously balanced argument could have been formulated to contrast the centripetal viewpoint of Steinbeck's "progressive" script with Ricketts's "civilized" antiscript emphasizing the preservation of traditional, individual values. The count's description of "progress" anticipates Theodore Roszak's complaint, quoted by Glen Love, that the present economic style is "too fast, too reckless for the eco-systems that must absorb its impact" (Love 203), a fear that Ricketts shares. "Progress" is viewed as an inspirational concept of incompletely understood technological advances—the kind of "modern improvements" that Thoreau described in *Walden* as "improved means to unimproved ends." Civilization requires, on the other hand, a genuine consciousness-raising that keeps people in control of changes that may produce "better natures" in both a regenerating environment and an enlightened community.

I don't think that Steinbeck would have disagreed with these generalized positions, for his feeling that "we are no longer content to destroy our beloved country" indicates the underlying agreement that preserved his friendship with Ricketts, though he may have thought change possible in an unrealistic hurry. I may, therefore, sound disingenuous if I say at this point that nothing in this essay is intended as a put-down of Steinbeck, for the question under consideration is not his powers and achievement as an artist but his potential as model and inspiration for an ecologically oriented political agenda. The question is why he could offer only shaky presumptions as established beliefs in dealing with problems of ecological degradation that he deplored.

This is not exclusively a question about Steinbeck but one that opens up the larger question of what contribution literature can make to political programs. Has agit-prop ever been successful in bringing about civilized change? Dreary perusal of the forgotten proletarian literature of the 1930s is enough to suggest an answer. Steinbeck was wise to avoid commitments; his problems began when he made them. If in this context one asks, "How 'green' was John Steinbeck?" the answer is "not very, and a good thing, too."

There is, however, an older sense of "green" that may be applicable to Steinbeck's handling of political issues. It describes those who are inexperienced, innocent, naive—as Henry James applies it to Lambert Strethers's provincial literary review in *The Ambassadors.* It can be applied to Twain's Huck Finn, to Fitzgerald's Great Gatsby, or to the central figures in Steinbeck's own earlier apocalyptic trilogy—*Tortilla Flat, In Dubious Battle,* and *Of Mice and Men*—written during his despairing years of obscurity. In his failure to deal with the sources and overcoming of evil adequately in these and later works, he was "green" in this sense of being handicapped in drawing up an activist agenda, but this may be essential to inspiring the repressed to the possibilities of a better world in which people live in harmony with their environments.

Worth pondering in considering the question of politicized novels is a letter that Frank Norris wrote to a friend while working on *The Octopus*, the most important predecessor of *The Grapes of Wrath* and also written against the background of agrarian California's socioeconomic problems. When George Sargent asked the novelist whether he had any solutions to the problems of which he had made such harrowingly dramatic use, Norris replied, "I hardly think so. The novelist by nature can hardly be a political economist; and it is to the latter rather than the former that one must look for a way out of 'present discontents' " (Crisler 157).

If Steinbeck did share Norris's reservations when writing his best early works, he did not always avoid looking for ways out of "present discontents." In one of his first "Letters to Alicia," a series of informal commentaries addressed to the dead publisher of a Long Island newspaper and published there between November 1965 and May 1967, he observes that he had been "an adviser to four Presidents— Mr. Roosevelt, Mr. Truman, Mr. Kennedy, and Mr. Johnson," even though, as he modestly disclaimed, he could find no evidence that they ever took any of his advice (*Newsday*, 11 December 1965, 3-W). After the lighthearted tone of the first letters changed in the second series beginning in December 1966 to belligerent support for the Johnson administration's conduct of the war in Vietnam, the once widely popular and revered novelist was bitterly attacked and rejected by fellow writers and liberal readers. Although he was again outspoken on short-range issues, he rarely mentioned environmental concerns, except in an enthusiastic early letter from Israel, in which he praised the new nation's reclamation of the desert for productive issues involved in the experiment "Letter to Alicia" (*Newsday*, 12 March 1966, 3W).

As one rereads Steinbeck's writings from the viewpoint of an ecological critic, however, one begins to feel that there may have been deeper reasons than a naive faith in reeducating polluters and reclaiming contested lands for Steinbeck's sidestepping "green" issues in spite of his outraged impatience with the thoughtless exploitation of irreplaceable resources.

"Impatience" is the key word here. As one ponders Steinbeck's views, one is struck with how much he resembles one of his earliest memorable creations, "The Leader of the People," Jody Tiflin's grandfather in *The Red Pony* cycle. The "people" that the old man had led were those in the vanguard of the conquest and settlement of the American West. Grandfather has scarce respect for his son-in-law, Jody's father, who is content with the sedentary life of a farmer in the farthest reaches of the land that the father-in-law had subjugated. "The Leader of the People," climax of *The Red Pony* cycle, focuses on the son-in-law's impatience with the old man's constantly retelling stories of his vanished days of glory. "That time's done," he tells his more patient and considerate wife. When the grandfather overhears one of these outbursts, he observes sadly, "Maybe you're right. The crossing is finished. Maybe it should be forgotten now it's done" (301). Later he confides to young Jody, "It wasn't the getting here that mattered. It was movement and westering. . . . That's what I should be telling instead of stories. . . . Westering has died out of the people" (303).

"Westering" is a specific manifestation of the spirited urge that drives the classical hero of Steinbeck's favorite poem, Tennyson's dramatic monologue "Ulysses," which begins,

> *It little profits that an idle king . . .*
> *. . . I mete and dole*
> *Unequal laws unto a savage race*
> *That hoard, and sleep and feed and know not me.*

> *I cannot rest from travel.*

The ancient wanderer is more philosophical about his situation than Jody's grandfather, as he is content to leave his kingship to his son Telemachus,

> *Well-loved of me, discerning to fulfill*
> *This labour, by slow prudence to make mild*
> *A rugged people, and through soft degrees*
> *Subdue them to the useful and the good.*

These contrasting figures exactly illustrate the difference that the count in *South Wind* draws between those who seek rapid "progress" and those who cultivate "civilization." Jody's grandfather does not feel, however, that he has Ulysses' option of continuing to venture restlessly into "that untraveled world, whose margin fades / For ever and for ever when I move." He has led his people down to the sea, beyond which all is now known. "Westering" is done. He can perceive no alternative outlet for his energies.

Steinbeck appears to have found himself in just such a predicament. Near the end of his commentary in *America and Americans,* he recognized that the kind of contemplative behavior that Norman Douglas's count champions is required for the establishment of civilization: "We have not had time to learn inside ourselves the things that have happened to us" (14). Rather than considering what unfinished business remains, however, such as cleaning up the mess that uncontrolled progress has left behind, Steinbeck despairs, like Jody's grandfather, that "the roads of the past have come to an end and we have not yet discovered a path to the future. I think we will find one, but its direction may be unthinkable to us now" (*AAA* 142). Lewis Thomas does not share this feeling that we are at road's end, cautioning that "it is time for us to grow up as a people," because "we have a very long way to go, and are remarkably loath to begin the journey" (quoted in Love, 213). Despite Steinbeck's generalization that "we are no longer willing to destroy our beloved country," he fails to acknowledge that the unfound path to the future requires giving up the practices that threaten it. Like the "active children," we must abandon "careless and destructive" ways and settle down to the unexciting labor of through soft degrees subduing rugged people to the useful and the good. Steinbeck expressed a tourist's admiration for the reclamation work of the Israelis, but he set off on an ill-advised trip to Vietnam that served well neither his reputation nor his health.

In *Vietnam in American Literature* (1991), Philip Melling develops the provocative thesis that American involvement in the centuries-long struggle of a culture that American leaders did not even try to understand was an anachronistic outburst of Puritan vision. The Vietnam War was part of the puritanical desire to destroy the dark devils threatening the elect's effort to establish a City on the Hill as the Kingdom of Heaven on earth. It was, in short, a last-ditch effort to keep "Westering" alive (as Frank Norris had urged Anglo-Saxons to do).

Both Steinbeck and Jody's grandfather were brave, adventurous men who took bold risks to push back frontiers; but they were too single-minded to change with the times and not tough-minded enough to face the possibility that maybe it was they rather than the times that must change. Camille Paglia, in one of her recent controversial jeremiads, makes some remarks worth pondering about the American characteristic these people share: "America is still a frontier country of wide open spaces. Our closeness to nature is one reason why our problem is not repression but regression: our notorious violence is the constant eruption of primitivism, of anarchic individualism" (216).

Our very closeness to nature makes it difficult for us to see ourselves as a part of it. We see it—as Frank Norris especially pointed out—from an adversarial viewpoint. As long as we think in terms of winning or losing rather than surviving, we remain what Norris called "motes in the sunshine." Steinbeck could not bring himself to accept such withering scorn, but he could not come up with an alternative that would confirm a positive role for the human race as an inseparable part of the natural order.

SEVENTEEN

John Steinbeck: Late-Blooming Environmentalist

Joel W. Hedgpeth

A contemporary and colleague of both John Steinbeck and Edward F. Ricketts, Joel Hedgpeth is also a native Californian, marine biologist, editor of Between Pacific Tides, *and recipient of the Browning Award for Conserving the Environment. In short, he is eminently well equipped to discuss the coevolution of Steinbeck's environmental consciousness with that of the nation at large. Hedgpeth, who defines environmentalism as the recognition that "the human race is exceeding the earth's carrying capacity at an exponential rate by overpopulation" and that "continued exploitation of the earth's resources to support our elaborate material culture is not sustainable," concludes that Steinbeck's most sophisticated thinking about the environment occurs in his later works, especially in* America and Americans *(1966), now sadly out of print.*

> Americans, even in these days of rising concern, still tend to look on nature through an eighteenth-century rose-colored window—Palladian is understood. I speak not only of the creationists, who still consider Moses the best biologist ever and vehemently reject the overwhelming testimony of scientists about evolution, but also of economists, politicians, manufacturers, and happy summer campers, for all of whom nature is forever infinitely generous, forgiving, and abundant. We cannot do any real damage to her, we still say to ourselves; she is now, as ever, a mother who never says no to her children. Eden survives for us, if only in the endlessness of our material expectations.
> —Donald Worster, *The Wealth of Nature* (1993)

John Steinbeck was a country boy, born and raised in the small town of Salinas, the principal town of an agricultural and stock-raising region, the valley and flanking hills of the Salinas River. Not far to the west there was the sea, the broad bight of Monterey Bay, with the city of Monterey and its satellite Pacific Grove on the south, its beaches teeming with the life of the sea. As a boy Steinbeck roamed this country as his own and often described it in beautiful passages, dripping with nostalgia, that added a sense of reality to his stories. That power to evoke the feeling of his natural environment remained with him all his life, and it was no surprise to see that the opening pages of *East of Eden,* the best of his later novels, were selected to accompany the 1850 painting of the Salinas Valley for that elegant collection of reproductions of paintings of California scenes, *O, California!* (Vincent 1990). This same extract was also included in a literary anthology (Michaels et al. 1989). As Wallace Stegner put it, "Steinbeck had a transcendent sense of place, (he) knew the Santa Lucia Mountains, from the stacks and skerries of the shore through the mist forests of the westward-draining canyons up through the high chamisal country to the baking ridges and waterless valleys of the rain shadow" (Stegner 1992, 149).

Fondness for scenery or remembrance of places past are not essential for environmentalists, however, and we find little in the tone of Steinbeck's early work that suggests more than a fondness for scenery, oftentimes mystical in its intensity. Most readers of Steinbeck do not think of him as an environmentalist in the modern sense of that word.

Environmentalism, as we know it today, is based on the realization that the human race is exceeding the earth's carrying capacity at an exponential rate by overpopulation and that continued exploitation of the earth's resources to support our elaborate material culture is not sustainable. Used in this sense, the term "environmentalism" did not come into common use until the observation of the first Earth Day on 21 April 1970.[1] John Steinbeck died on 20 December 1968, about fourteen months earlier. Nevertheless, our generation (I include myself as well as Steinbeck, since I am only nine years and eight months younger) began to hear about concern for protecting natural resources fairly early on. The word then was conservation, ardently espoused by Theodore Roosevelt's chief forester, Gifford Pinchot, who defined it as "wise use" of natural resources. In 1910 Pinchot published a collection of his polemics titled *The Fight for Conservation,* in which we find this statement:

The first great fact about conservation is that it stands for development. There has been a fundamental misconception that conservation means nothing but the husbanding of our resources for future generations. There could be no more serious mistake. Conservation does mean provision for the future, but it means also and first of all the recognition of the right of the present generation to the fullest necessary use of all the resources with which this country is so abundantly blessed. Conservation demands the welfare of this generation first, and afterward the welfare of the generations to follow. (Pinchot 1910, 42)

This attitude caused Pinchot much trouble with his subordinates in his own time, but it still remains a firm conviction of many conservatives in our midst who are not interested in marking the sparrow's fall as the trees are cut down but, in the current language, prefer jobs to spotted owls—or, to put it another way, believe that natural, renewable resources may be harvested on a sustained yield basis. It was obvious even in Pinchot's time, however, that our agricultural practices were endangering our most basic resource, our soil. Concern for the future of soils led to the foundation of the Soil Conservation Service in 1935.

John Steinbeck grew up in the years when the need for improving agricultural practices was in the public eye, and indeed conservation in its modern sense became a household word. John may have gained some inkling of this early on in his friendship with Ed Ricketts, as Ed stated plainly in the introduction to his first catalogue for the Pacific Biological Laboratory (1925) that he would not over-collect the organisms that were his stock in trade (I suspect this statement was intended to allay the concerns of the staff at Hopkins Marine Station): "It should be borne in mind . . . that we must, above all else, avoid depleting the region by overcollecting" (1925, n.pag.). He also declared that he would not take orders for very rare species.

Steinbeck always had a lively interest in the natural world about him, and when in 1923 his sister persuaded him to attend the summer session at Stanford's Hopkins Marine Station, John elected to take two English courses and General Zoology. Requiring no prerequisites, General Zoology was taught by C. V. Taylor, then a graduate student at Berkeley, where the received gospel was William Emerson Ritter's organismal concept of life—that parts of nature formed a whole whose existence depends on the orderly cooperation and interdependence of the parts. This sounds like the current self-regulating (homeostatic) concept of Gaia as the benign goddess ruling Mother Earth. A bit of this rubbed off on John as the phalanx idea that would become the theme of his novel *In Dubious Battle* (*SLL* 79–82). Seven years after the session at Hopkins, Steinbeck met Ed Ricketts and soon became familiar with Ricketts's somewhat similar outlook, derived from Professor W. C. Allee's theory that living organisms are interdependent or cooperate automatically. Allee's *Animal Aggregations* was one of Ricketts's most often read books, and Steinbeck probably read it also (there is a note in Ed's book list that *Animal Aggregations* had been loaned to John). The philosophical germ of our current environmental concern is present in work by both Ritter and Allee.

The friendship between Steinbeck and Ricketts blossomed rapidly. After six years of almost daily contact with Ed, Steinbeck moved to Los Gatos and began to work on the book that became *The Grapes of Wrath*. He got down to visit Ed fairly often, however, and I remember the day I drifted in unannounced, and Ed handed me the galley proofs of *The Grapes of Wrath*. He predicted that it would win the Pulitzer Prize and asked me what I thought of the ending. I was noncommittal because, having had a half hour or so to read the book, I had not finished it.

Publication of *The Grapes of Wrath* in 1939 aroused the wrath of the Associated Farmers and all sorts of conservative folk. Most of the publicity, especially in California, was hostile and unfriendly and Steinbeck's native town disowned him. He was accused of being both a Jew and a Communist. The immediate reaction to the book was generated by its socioeconomic message. Essentially a sage of people driven from their land by forces beyond their control (overlooking the fact that their own misuse of the land had set the process in motion), of confrontation in an environment where there was no new land for the taking, and no interest in the dispossessed on the part of the entrenched establishment except as seasonal field workers, *The Grapes of Wrath* was in no sense an environmental story. The Dust Bowl is a fait accompli as the novel begins, and the book is about what happens after environmental disaster.

In his excellent history of ecology, *Nature's Economy* (a phrase from

Linnaeus!), Donald Worster scolds Steinbeck for not realizing that he had selected the wrong group of farmers as typical Dust Bowl refugees for *The Grapes of Wrath*, because Salislaw, Oklahoma, whence the Joads came, "was almost on the Arkansas border and hundreds of miles east of the dust center. Steinbeck, like most other Americans, assumed too simply that people like the Joads were victims of a natural disaster that gave the banks and the landlords an excuse to put them off the land, but in truth, their somber story was only peripherally connected with the drought on the plains" (223). Actually, as Worster goes on to explain, the Joads's plight was as much the result of their bad hill country farming practices as of the drought. A later book by Worster on the problems of water and irrigation, *Rivers of Empire*, also discusses *The Grapes of Wrath* (227–30) as well as Carey McWilliams's *Factories in the Field*, published in the same year. Worster is less patronizing of Steinbeck, but goes deeper into the major problem:

Nowhere in The Grapes of Wrath *does Steinbeck draw attention to the elaborate hydraulic apparatus that has been required to create the California garden. In fact, the process of irrigation does not even appear in the text. Grapes, carrots, cotton, and the like are the products, it would seem, of spontaneous nature, not the contrivances of advanced water engineering and the social organization it has required. The Joads, unfamiliar with the new landscape, are understandably angered when they discover there is no place for the likes of them in this paradise. Nature has never been ungenerous to them before, and they cannot comprehend why this new "nature" is different. Another migrant, who has had his hopes dashed, gives them his version of what has gone wrong: "She's a nice country. But she was stole a long time ago." Steinbeck agrees too quickly with that simplified analysis. The problem in California, he indicates at many points, is that a few greedy landowners have monopolized the garden and want to keep the Joads out. If that were the only problem, then the sufficient solution would be to challenge their ownership, and, in fact, that is precisely what Steinbeck does recommend, along with setting up some clean, government-funded labor camps, pushing worker unionization, and redistributing the economic rewards of the valley. Those were all humane, useful ideas, all planks in the New Deal platform of social reform, but the reader senses that Steinbeck's heart is not really in them. To put*

*deep confidence in such distributional changes, he would have to alter
drastically his original argument. He would have to insist after all that
the land should be remade by advanced technology and that the corpora-
tized social order carrying out that redemption can everywhere, in Oklahoma as well as in California, be a good home for people like the Joads.
And he does not quite believe any of that. He is more pessimistic about
the promise of the technological dominance of nature. The inconsistency
between Steinbeck's efforts at solution and his analysis of the underlying
causes is damaging to the book, rendering it in the end unconvincing and
half-hearted. A moving indictment in its early chapters, it becomes in the
second half a straining reformist tract. The main source of his difficulty is
that Steinbeck is not prepared to admit in California what he can perceive
so clearly in Oklahoma: that it is finally the apparatus and ideology of
unrestricted environmental conquest which lies at the root of the Joads'
affliction. (Worster,* Rivers of Empire *229)*

Indeed, Steinbeck himself realized that in *The Grapes of Wrath* he
had "written a tract." It is not quite fair to fault him, however, for
overlooking the vast hydraulic apparatus of the Central Valley system; while its keystone, Shasta Dam, was under construction by
1939, the project was not completed until 1949. The unlovely word
"agribusiness," now in common use, did not appear until 1941—allegedly coined in Fresno by a renegade entomologist turned pesti-
cide salesman.

Writing *The Grapes of Wrath* in 1938, Steinbeck would not have been
aware of the 6 December 1945 California Water Conference, where
Governor Earl Warren declared in his opening address: "in my opinion we should not relax until California has adopted and put into
operation a state-wide program that will put every drop of water to
work" (Warren 1945). In California, Governor Warren's attitude has
resulted in severe damage to the state, including the loss of salmon
stock in the Sacramento River and degradation of the San Francisco
Bay delta system (Hedgpeth in Lufkin 1991, 52–60). A very similar
view, set forth by Josef Stalin, more explicitly states that the state may
destroy nature for the further development of the country.[2]

The furor about *The Grapes of Wrath* continued on into 1939, and
Steinbeck did not enjoy the notoriety. He began to visit Pacific Grove
more often, revived his interest in marine biology, and refreshed his

relationship with Ed, whose book *Between Pacific Tides* (Ricketts and Calvin 1939), was published the same month as *The Grapes of Wrath*. It was well received by the professors, in part because of the annotated bibliography and the unique natural history approach (although some of the recluses at Hopkins Marine Station did not consider ecology a serious discipline). The book is still in print and is now considered a classic in the literature of marine biology.

Shortly after its publication, Ed was asked to think about a less detailed, high school–level guide for the San Francisco Bay area. Now a published author with a book to his name (Jack Calvin, his junior author, had moved to Alaska and was no longer in the picture), Ed discussed possible joint authorship with John. He thought it would be a good thing for John to do; if John wrote most of the text, it would improve his reputation as a scientist. John did start buying books and reading up on biology and accompanied Ed on several collecting trips, including one on Christmas Day 1939 to Tomales Point, where John Steinbeck collected a specimen of *Pycnogonum rickettsi*, one of my favorite animals. The matter of a collecting trip to Baja California came up, possibly inspired in part by the 1938 publication of William Beebe's *Zaca Venture*.

Ed had been to the Estero Punta Banda just south of Ensenada a number of times and had defined the area as the southern limit of *Between Pacific Tides*. This was about as far south as the roads in Baja could be depended on to take the traveler in those days, and to reach farther south it would be necessary to drive to Guaymas, halfway down the gulf on the mainland side, and charter a collecting boat. Steinbeck volunteered to charter a boat to go all the way from Monterey and back. Not only would it be "doing something for Ed," it would enable John to escape from the uproar over *The Grapes of Wrath* (Hedgpeth 1978, pt. 2, 1).

Very little was known about the marine life of the Gulf of California in those days, except that it was a good place for big game fishing. The area had rarely been visited by scientists, although it was originally explored by General Francisco de Ulloa in 1539 under order of Hernando Cortez. The big European expeditions of the early eighteenth and nineteenth centuries had bypassed the Gulf of California. One of the earliest scientific forays in the region was the 1841–1842 collecting trip of Ilia Gavrilovich Voznesensky, collector and preparator for the Imperial Academy of Sciences in St. Petersburg. He was sent on the ship *Nasledik Alexander* from Sitka to Carmen Island in the lower gulf to gather a supply of salt for the Russian Alaskan colonies. Voznesensky collected everything he could pick or capture as well as artifacts from island and mainland Indians, but since he did not have the appropriate social rank he was not allowed to work on his material or publish anything about it (Carter 1979).[3]

Among the most successful collectors in the gulf region was the eccentric Hungarian János Xántus.[4] He was employed to install and maintain a tide gauge at Cabo San Lucas from 1859 to 1861 and at the same time was an official collector for the Smithsonian Institution. He is the naturalist "who literally did proliferate in all directions" (*LSC* 33). In a letter now in the Bancroft Library, Xántus himself confirms this matter: "I had the *muy pesaroso* duty, to take leave of the many Señoritas I had the good fortune to be acquainted with" (see Madden 1949, 148–49). I have noticed that there is a tendency in articles about the *Sea of Cortez* to shift such sexual innuendo to E. F. Ricketts.

The modern era of exploration and study of the Sea of Cortez began with the 1911 voyage of the U.S. Fisheries Commission Steamer *Albatross.* The first California Academy of Sciences expedition of the New York Zoological Society took place in the spring of 1936 (William Beebe's *Zaca Venture*). All of these expeditions were primarily concerned with biological collections and observations. The Scripps Institution of Oceanography lacked a good seagoing research vessel until the acquisition in 1937 of a 100-foot diesel schooner, promptly named the *E. W. Scripps* for her donor. In February and March 1939, the ship made its initial expedition to the Gulf of California, emphasizing hydrography, bathymetry, and plankton (just 500 years after de Ulloa's first exploration!). A second cruise, emphasizing geology, was carried out from October to December in 1940.

That was the year the *Western Flyer* sailed the same waters during the months of March and April with "a contemporary novelist, accompanied by a biologist" (as Henry Madden describes them) aboard, hunting for all sorts of marine invertebrates. Most of them were already "known to science," that is, they had been given names and described in scholarly monographs. The trip would be an attempt to bring what was already known about the invertebrates together in an ecological context as well as to collect specimens. The goal was to collect materials for a source book on the marine invertebrates of the Panamic Faunal Province. The limits of this province, as conceived by Ricketts, are narrower than suggested by later studies, and the ultimate source book for the marine invertebrates (one that would satisfy Ricketts) has since been achieved by Richard Brusca's monumental 1980 vade mecum, *Common Intertidal Invertebrates of the Gulf of California*.

Sea of Cortez: A Leisurely Journal of Travel and Research was completed and published in time to be reviewed in the Sunday papers for 7 December 1941, one of the least auspicious days for promotion of potential Christmas sales and the beginning of a four-year period of restricted civilian activity on seashores everywhere. Some years later, after Ricketts's death, Steinbeck would revise the volume. By separating the narrative-philosophical part of *Sea of Cortez* from the dual corpus of the book, adding the preface "About Ed Ricketts," and calling it *The Log from the Sea of Cortez*, Steinbeck turned the bipartite *Sea of Cortez* into a different book, for the second, technical part was the real purpose of going there in the first place.

The very first words of the *Log* are a warning of things to come: "Just about dusk one day in April 1948 Ed Ricketts stopped work in the laboratory in Cannery Row." The accident that resulted in Ricketts's death actually occurred in May, and he died a few days later on 11 May 1948, three days before his fifty-first birthday. Whether Steinbeck did not read proofs or simply did not think such details significant cannot be determined at this late date, but the error is a warning: there is fiction as well as truth in what follows, especially the gross underestimation of Ed's accomplishments and significance as a marine biologist (see Hedgpeth 1988). By this maneuver, the *Log* became a book by Steinbeck alone but does little to advance his status as an environmentalist. The most environmental part of *Log from the Sea of Cortez* is the section about the excesses of the Mexican shrimp fishery (*LSC* 294–98), and these paragraphs were written by Ed Ricketts.

Although the restricted use of private craft during World War II prevented boating to the Sea of Cortez immediately after the original publication, traffic both to the gulf and its peninsula has since increased, and there are all sorts of guidebooks and thoughtful musings on the region, the latest being *Vermilion Sea: A Naturalist's Journey in Baja California* (Janovy 1992). Nature cruises to the gulf, with informative lectures on appropriate subjects, have become a standard attraction. Yet exploitation of the Sea of Cortez has reached disastrous proportions, with gross overfishing brought about by the incredible prices paid in the Orient for fish, and consequent destruction of other marine life, such as porpoises entangled in discarded nets. Managing the fishery is evidently no concern of the Mexican government, and outside pressure by tour groups and scientists on behalf of the region that Steinbeck and Ricketts have made so attractive must be aroused.

During the late stages of work on *Sea of Cortez*, Steinbeck's life was changing. His marriage with Carol had broken up, and he had started the affair with Gwyn and was planning to leave his California homeland, a more serious change in life than he realized. As an author, he was entering a phase of writing potboilers and socializing with eminent people. In the midst of it all, Ed died. Steinbeck was no longer the local boy who depended on his environment, the clear open skies of rural California (alas, they are no longer so!). For the next ten years he could only attempt to write, producing books that did not quite come off, as if he were his own Hercules, lifting his inner Antaeus out of touch with the earth that gave him his strength.

The environmental implications of Steinbeck's writing did not become overt until the last two books written in his lifetime, *Travels with Charley* and *American and Americans*. Jackson Benson (1984, 968) suggests that the last three, including *Winter of Our Discontent*, "might be called his 'moral trilogy.' " Perhaps so, but the only passages that interest me in *Winter of Our Discontent* are vignettes of the attic with its childhood books and back issues of the *Atlantic* and of the family talisman downstairs, since such things are part of my own memory. It must be said, however, that Steinbeck's comment on page 197 is all too accurate a description of those who do not take mankind's environmental dilemma seriously: "When a condition or problem becomes too great, humans have the protection of not thinking about it" (*WOD* 197). Come to think of it, that would be a great theme for an environmental novel, and perhaps it has been used, but *Winter of Our Discontent* itself did not help its author find himself—he was still looking.

According to Kiernan (1979, 311), it was Adlai Stevenson who gave John Steinbeck the idea of making a tour around the United States and writing a book about it. Despite the protests of his wife, Elaine, he planned to travel alone (or with his dog). This way he could talk to people who did not know who he was or invite someone into his "home" for a drink. His agent, Elizabeth Otis, suggested that he make the trip by bus, but John was determined to do it in his own vehicle. In a June 1960 letter to Otis, John won her over to letting him do as he had planned, traveling incognito off the beaten track:

I am trying to say clearly that if I don't stoke my fires soon they will go out from leaving the damper closed and the air cut off—what I am posing is not a little trip or reporting, but a frantic last attempt to save my life and the integrity of my creative pulse. An image of me is being created which is a humbling, dull, stupid, lazy oaf, who must be protected, led, instructed and hospitalized. (SLL 669–70)

On 23 September 1960, John Steinbeck started off with his poodle to meet his countrymen on the expedition he had named Operation Windmill. He had not gone very far before he began to notice the waste and rubbish around the big towns and cities:

American cities are like badger holes, ringed with trash—all of them— surrounded by piles of wrecked and rusting automobiles, and almost smothered with rubbish. Everything we use comes in boxes, cartons, bins, the so-called packaging we love so much. The mountains of things we throw away are much greater than the things we use. In this, if in no other way, we can see the wild and reckless exuberance of our production, and waste seems to be the index. Driving along I thought how in France or Italy every item of these thrown-out things would have been saved and used for something. This is not said in criticism of one system or the other but I do wonder whether there will come a time when we can no longer afford our wastefulness—chemical wastes in the rivers, metal wastes everywhere, and atomic wastes buried deep in the earth or sunk in the sea. When an Indian village became too deep in its own filth, the inhabitants moved. And we have no place to which to move. (TWC 26)

In 1961, while Steinbeck was at work on *Travels with Charley*, Rachel Carson's *Silent Spring* was appearing in serial form in the *New Yorker*, but there was no indication in either *Travels with Charley* or *America and Americans* that he was aware of the installments.[5] The first general accounts of the population explosion threatening mankind in a world of limited carrying capacity appeared some years before *Silent Spring*. In 1948, two books on the subject were published: *Our Plundered Planet*, by Fairfield Osborn, and *Road to Survival*, by William Vogt. More thoroughly documented, Vogt's book was selected by the Book of the Month Club and was touted as "one of the most crucial [books] ever written," but unconvinced reviewers referred to it as another contribution from "the plundered planet school." Since books of the month often lingered on people's living room tables, John may have seen and examined Vogt's book. It may not be stretching things too far to assume that some of this did indeed get to John Steinbeck and is reflected in his allusions to too many people and chemical wastes:

The new American finds his challenge and his love in traffic-choked streets, skies nested in smog, choking with the acids of industry, the screech of rubber and houses leashed in against one another while the townlets wither a time and die. And this, I found, is as true in Texas as in Maine. Clarendon yields to Amarillo just as surely as Stacyville, Maine bleeds its substance into Millinocket, where the logs are ground up, the air smells of chemicals, the rivers are choked and poisoned, and the streets swarm with this happy, hurrying breed. This is not offered in criticism but only as observation. And I am sure that, as all pendulums reverse their swing, so eventually will the swollen cities rupture like dehiscent wombs and disperse their children back to the countryside. This prophecy is underwritten by the tendency of the rich to do this already. Where the rich lead the poor will follow, or try to. (TWC 72)

There were many other things to say, but they did not fit into his idea of what should be in the book, and many of them emerged in the essays that appeared as the text of *America and Americans*. When he arrived in Seattle, Elaine joined him for the leg to Monterey. They traveled to Monterey as fast as they could, barely pausing in the deep redwoods of Humboldt County for Charley to relieve himself on one of the biggest trees on earth, and thence on to John's home grounds in Salinas and Monterey. His adventures were not much different than if he had been driving around on Long Island, except for his sentimental farewell as he stands on Fremont's Peak overlooking the valley of his boyhood, remembering the sweet sound of hames bells[6] and the color of lupines and the town of Salinas, "where I was born now spreading like crab grass toward the foothills" (TWC 206). It was too much for him, so he turned away and took the shortest way out of California, over Pacheco Pass to Fresno, over Tehachapi Pass to the Mojave Desert, across the Colorado River and across northern Arizona and New Mexico (pausing at El Morro without looking at the great landmark of the pioneers and explorers since the fifteenth century) and on to the barbecue with Elaine's relatives in Amarillo, Texas.

John paused briefly on his way across the desert. He saw no one but a couple of coyotes, at which he aimed his rifle and then thought better of it—they belonged there and he did not—and then he pondered about man's future in this desert environment:

The desert, being an unwanted place, might well be the last stand of life against unlife. For in the rich and moist and wanted areas of the world, life pyramids against itself and in its confusion has finally allied itself with the enemy nonlife. And what the scorching, searing, freezing, poisoning weapons of non-life have failed to do may be accomplished to the end of its destruction and extinction by the tactics of survival gone sour. If the most versatile of living forms, the human, now fights for survival as it always has, it can eliminate not only itself but all other life. And if that should transpire, unwanted places like the desert might be the harsh mother of repopulation. For the inhabitants of the desert are well trained and well armed against desolation. Even our own misguided species might re-emerge from the desert. The lone man and his sun-toughened wife who cling to the shade in an unfruitful and uncoveted place might, with their brothers in arms—the coyote, the jackrabbit, the horned toad, the rattlesnake, together with a host of armored insects—these trained and tested fragments of life might well be the last hope of life against non-life. The desert has mothered magic things before this. (TWC 217–18)

This is Steinbeck at his best, aware of the world of nature around him yet concerned for man's future in an increasingly severe environment. Much more of this was building up in his head, and he needed to think more about it.

A couple of years later John did get his chance to write more about

the environment. In August 1964 his publisher asked him to undertake the simple task of writing captions for a collection of photographs of American scenes and people. John accepted, with the idea
that it would only take a couple of weeks. Then an introduction was
suggested, and finally in October 1965 John completed the text of
America and Americans: a foreword and afterword and ten essays.
These essays concern socioeconomic matters, manners and morals,
government and business, and other subjects. The eighth and tenth
essays, "Americans and Land" and "Americans and the Future,"
provide the most significant treatment of environmental concerns.

Some of the essays in *America and Americans* are written in the same
spirit as Wylie's *Generation of Vipers,* but Steinbeck is always apolo-
gizing for saying bad things and reassuring us that he still loves us
all. One wonders, however, what he would have said about our last
two presidents as role models, either the ex–movie star who thought
that it was dangerous to picnic under trees because they released carbon monoxide and that California was most lovely in spring, especially when it's all covered with horses, or the self-styled "environmental" champion who didn't do so well in Brazil and whose syntax
passed all understanding (Steinbeck felt President Eisenhower was
a poor role model for his boys because "he reads Westerns exclusively
and cannot put together a simple English sentence" [Kiernan 310]).

Let us look at some samples of what John Steinbeck did think
about our environmental problems:

*Then the trickle of immigrants became a stream, and the population be-
gan to move westward—not to grab and leave but to settle and live, they
thought. The newcomers were of peasant stock, and they had their roots
in a Europe where they had been landless, for the possession of land was
the requirement and the proof of a higher social class than they had
known. In America they found beautiful and boundless land for the taking—and they took it.*

*It is little wonder that they went land-mad, because there was so much
of it. They cut and burned the forests to make room for crops; they abandoned their knowledge of kindness to the land in order to maintain its usefulness. When they had cropped out a piece they moved on, raping the
country like invaders. The topsoil, held by roots and freshened by leaf-fall,
was left helpless to the spring freshets, stripped and eroded with the naked*

bones of clay and rock exposed. The destruction of the forest changed the rainfall, for the searching clouds could find no green and beckoning woods to draw them on and milk them. The merciless nineteenth century was like a hostile expedition for loot that seemed limitless. Uncountable buffalo were killed, stripped of their hides, and left to rot, a reservoir of permanent food supply eliminated. More than that, the Great Plains was robbed of the manure of the herds. Then the plows went in and ripped off the protection of the buffalo grass and opened the helpless soil to quick water and slow drought and the mischievous winds that roamed through the Great Central plains. There has always been more than enough desert in America; the new settlers, like overindulged children, created even more.

No longer do we Americans want to destroy wantonly, but our new-found sources of power—to take the burden of work from our shoulders, to warm us, and cool us, and give us light, to transport us quickly, and to make the things we use and wear and eat—these power sources spew pollution on our country, so that the rivers and streams are becoming poisonous and lifeless. The birds die for lack of food; a noxious cloud hangs over our cities that burns our lungs and reddens our eyes. Our ability to conserve has not grown with our power to create, but this slow and sullen poisoning is no longer ignored or justified. Almost daily, the pressure of outrage among Americans grows. We are no longer content to destroy our beloved country. We are slow to learn, but we learn. When a super-highway was proposed in California which would trample the redwood trees in its path, an outcry arose all over the land, so strident and fierce that the plan was put aside. And we no longer believe that a man, by owning a piece of America, is free to outrage it. (AAA 128–30)

Unfortunately, few people, even some who have read many of Steinbeck's books, have ever read or heard of *America and Americans*.[7]

Notes

1. A complete history of the environmental movement is yet to be written, but it should be noted that the capacity of man to change the earth he depends on was discussed in George Perkins Marsh's *Man and Nature,* one of the great classics of environmental literature, in 1864. Although the book was almost immediately translated into the major European languages (including Russian in 1866), *Man and Nature* was not widely known in this country until the 1956 Wenner-Gren Foundation Symposium "Man's Role in Changing the Face of the Earth," dedi-

cated to George Perkins Marsh (Thomas 1956). Widely used as a reference for appropriate college courses, the book probably had a significant influence in the organization of Earth Day 1970.

2. The damage caused in the Soviet Union by this approach to national resources has been colossal and may have been a major factor in the downfall of the U.S.S.R. (Weiner 1988).

3. Voznesensky is remembered in our marine fauna by the handsome intertidal isopod *Idotea wosnesenskii* (the spelling difference is attributable to German transliteration).

4. Madden devotes an entire chapter to Xántus at Cabo San Lucas (97–151).

5. The book version of *Silent Spring* appeared in 1962 at about the same time as *Travels with Charley*.

6. A note on the "hame bells" in *Travels with Charley*: I always heard (and heard of) them as hames bells, since they involved both hames, the enforcing wood or metal sides of the horse collar. They consisted of a band of tempered steel about three inches wide and twenty-one or more inches long, to which were bolted a series of five or more bells. The center bell was larger and the two pairs of flanking bells successively smaller. The diameter of the middle bell was five inches, and the flanking bells were four and three-and-a-half inches. The ends of the band were welded or bolted to iron pegs that fitted into slots on the hames. When in place the band was under tension, and movement of the heavy horses carried quickly to the bells. The purpose of the bells was to warn rigs coming downhill that a heavy wagon team was coming up, since a team pulling a heavy freight rig could not be backed downhill (even in this motorized age the vehicle coming uphill has the right of way). While hames bells do sound sweet and musical from a distance, they were intended to be heard at least a mile away and were deafening close by. I often heard them in the Sierra, coming up the Priest grade into Groveland. Hames bells are now expensive items in the antique trade.

7. Typographically *America and Americans* is an odd book. Its eight-point text on thirty-five-and-a-half-pica lines is not very easy reading. There are 52 pages of text scattered among 155 pages of photographs, some of them double-page spreads, some colored but most of them black and white. The photograph pages are unnumbered, but the text pages are numbered. It looks as if the page proofs had been assembled at random, without any effort to distribute the printed pages in even clusters between the pictures, and sixty pages of plates are dumped into the back as if the editors, having paid for them, decided to use them anyhow. An afterword is tucked away at the end of the book, where it has probably been overlooked by many browsers. Some of the clusters of text pages include parts of two topics, and some breaks between photos leave a page ending in midsentence. Obviously Viking did not take Steinbeck's text seriously, or possibly they wanted to bury the whole project. In the same year of publication, perhaps after the first press run, they released the plates to Bonanza Books, with the result that in the used book market the Viking imprint version is now priced in the $40 range and the Bonanza edition for $12 or less (I picked up the "first" edition for $6.50 at a

Good Will emporium a few years ago). Both photography and color printing have improved since 1966, so the original version does indeed look tired and out of date. The text, however, is worth saving and should be rescued from this wilderness of stale pictures and illustrated with black-and-white drawings in key with the temper of the book. The text will have to be reset, since the present line is too long for direct photographic reduction and the typeface is undistinguished at best. *America and Americans* deserves a better fate and should be reprinted in a more appealing format.

EIGHTEEN

Steinbeck's Environmental Ethic: Humanity in Harmony with the Land

John H. Timmerman

Steinbeck's ethical imperative is apparent not only in late works of his so-called "moral phase" but throughout his career. His environmental ethic in particular is trenchantly voiced in America and Americans, Travels with Charley, *and* Sweet Thursday, *where he decries America's wastefulness as a moral lapse. Informing his earliest novels is an equally compelling, if less strident, concern with human responsibility toward the environment, and throughout his oeuvre characters struggle to establish a harmonious relationship with the land.*

During his later years John Steinbeck entered a period of intense ethical reflection that inevitably influenced his literature. It occurred to such an extent, in fact, that one might be tempted to categorize the work of the last decade as the "literature of moral concern" or the period itself as a "moral phase." If one were to categorize Steinbeck's fiction in such a way, and this essay intends to demonstrate the futility of so doing, one might date the period from the publication of *East of Eden* (1952) with its gnarled philosophical speculations, its exploration of moral obligations and the effects of moral transgression, and its proliferation of biblical allusions as a sounding board for supporting echoes. The works of the next decade might seem an extension of similar speculation, one author musing upon the moral decay and ethical paralysis of a people whom he has long loved but now finds dangerously distanced from a holding center of personal and national virtues.

Such categorization and such terms, however, are decidedly insufficient, suggesting the discovery of something altogether new and unfamiliar. It is as if Steinbeck suddenly caught a moral vision the way one catches a cold—quite by accident of circumstance and condition. At the worst, such terms suggest that the literature of earlier years was somehow bereft of moral concern.

Such terminology, moreover, renders whatever moral concerns Steinbeck held during this period indefinable, simply an amorphous cloud of political opinion, petty grievances, some old-age raillery, and a dyspeptic affliction of conservatism, mixed together on the final horizon of his life. What, precisely, was this so-called moral concern about? The task, when it comes to a consideration of his ethical views as a structured pattern of both moral oughtness and also an enactment of that oughtness in human actions, is to isolate a particular instance as a case study—in this case his sense of an environmental ethic. In so doing, however, one discerns three things: first, his environmental ethic did in fact receive deliberate articulation during the final decade of his life; second, that ethic, nonetheless, had been intuitively held throughout his life; and, third, that ethic infuses his literature by providing thematic pattern and direction.

Perhaps the most overt expression of Steinbeck's moral concern appears in *America and Americans* (1966), wherein Steinbeck is invited, like an elder statesman, to reflect upon things past, the woeful present, and the uncertain future. He doesn't miss a punch. He names the enemies of the moral order as comfort, plenty, security—the very ideals that the nation sought but that, in its marvelous excess, it perverted to a poverty of spirit: cynicism, boredom, and smugness. It is Hadleyburg on a national scale. As Steinbeck lamented in a 1959 letter to Adlai Stevenson, "We can stand anything God and nature can throw at us save only plenty" (*SLL* 652).

In *America and Americans* Steinbeck traces our failure in regard to the environment to a perfidious irresponsibility with roots in the spirit of humanity. While in modern environmental ethics we are inclined to see irresponsibility in terms of criminal actions—that is, littering is a criminal act punishable by a fine, as is toxic waste dumping—Steinbeck sees this irresponsibility as a failure in understanding and sympathy. While littering may not have been, in his time, a criminal action, it was an evil action nonetheless. The distinction is important to the case here, for evil, in Steinbeck's ethics, is a positioning of the heart in regard to other living things. We either devour those things like tigers, as *Cannery Row* had it, or live with them in a respectful equilibrium.

Yet the history of Americans in regard to the land, in Steinbeck's view, is marked by a rapacious attitude that sees the land merely as something to be used or abused. Obsessed with the notion that the land was limitless, early settlers "abandoned their knowledge of kindness to the land in order to maintain its usefulness" (*AAA* 146). Implicitly whatever was not useful could be cast aside to get at what was useful.

But as Grandfather testified in "Leader of the People" in *The Red Pony,* we have learned that the land is not limitless. We have learned that the land is fragile, that the gouges of our rapacious greed forever mar its face, that taking its hidden treasures always leaves an irreparable scar. We have learned that it is susceptible to decimation and deterioration. We have learned our evil toward the land. When one acquires such knowledge, Steinbeck asserts, a pressure of outrage grows.

It must be admitted that in *America and Americans* Steinbeck does a better job of delineating problems than of offering practical solutions. So too in regard to this environmental ethic. Outrage is an important part of an ethical consideration; it constitutes, in fact, the basic premise of an ethic, for an ethic is always and ultimately incarnated in action.

An ethical person acts against a perceived evil; one who ignores it may be said to be ethically culpable for the evil itself. To do nothing is to permit; to permit is to condone. Steinbeck's ethical action is the work of revelation: to make readers mindful of our despoliation of the land. In regard to a specific program to rectify that course, however, this ethic, at least as delineated in *America and Americans,* is found wanting.

Steinbeck arrays several examples of when a people's outrage led to action, as when a California highway route was changed to avoid a stand of redwoods. But most frequently his response in *America and Americans* is formulated as a fond reminiscence for the way things once were, a profound regret for the way they are, and a tempered hope for better times ahead.

What Steinbeck specified through discursive argument in *America and Americans* was discovered more spontaneously and intuitively, however, in the earlier *Travels with Charley.* It may well be said that this work is Steinbeck's consummate ethical treatise. He undertook the journey, leaving on 23 September 1960, immediately after finishing *The Winter of Our Discontent,* not simply to investigate his country's topography but to discover his own manhood. The heart of *Travels with Charley* arises from these questions: What really matters? What endures? What beliefs do I hold about these matters? In environmental matters also these questions receive studied consideration, not first of all as a rational construct, as is the case in *America and Americans,* but out of the expediency of personal experience. In that way, *Charley* moves much closer to Steinbeck's novelistic technique—a probing of matters of the heart arising from reflection upon experience. It may also be considered the practical, historically positioned premise for the argument in *America and Americans.*

As is the case in the best travel literature, *Charley* moves deeper into the traveler with the journey itself. Here the reflections solidify, through event to a perception of the meaning of the event. In fact, the first two parts of the work seem preoccupied by person and place; the third part initiates the harder probing into uncomfortable regions of the mind and heart. Not coincidentally, that passage occurs as Rocinante heads westward across the Mississippi, noses through the flatland prairies, and nears the environment of Steinbeck's youth. Thus he begins the journey inward, for the recollection of the past and the mindfulness of the present clash with the force of runaway freight trains.

In fact, it seems to occur precisely as Steinbeck crosses the Great Divide and becomes mindful of the fact that "it is impossible to be in this high spinal country without giving thought to the first men who crossed it" (*TWC* 166). He then contrasts our rage for hurry, the fact that "we get sick if the milk delivery is late and nearly die of heart failure if there is an elevator strike" (167), to the sense of awe the first explorers held in their slow trek across a land of grandeur. While the ethical flaw noted in *America and Americans* is always the rapacious greed of a people, the flaw noted in *Travels with Charley* is similarly disturbing. It is our unmitigated hurry that leads to the thoughtless use of the land. It took the relentless throb of tires, the flickering of a speedometer, to make Steinbeck mindful of a division in our hearts, a rupture in harmony, by virtue of our hurry. It seems, at this point, that the entire travel plan of the book itself begins to slow as the traveler himself seeks a new harmony with the land.

In this matter, as in so many, the memorable Charley also tutors him. Afflicted with polyuria, Charley makes necessary stops that become more frequent and prolonged. While Steinbeck makes light of Charley's micturition, he also admits that "while waiting for him . . . I tried to reconstruct my trip as a single piece and not as a series of incidents" (168). That moment represents a transition, more important than any individual highway interchange, in *Travels with Charley,* for it redirects the way Steinbeck looks at the land. It is as if Charley cautions him to slow down, to observe, to meditate, and to draw conclusions.

He sees the hurry of the people, rushing headlong into time, as both at odds with the land and also destructive of the land. Steinbeck understands well—as his visit to Salinas would inarguably convince him—that one cannot relive the past. The point of his land ethic is not to turn the clock backward. He argues that "this sounds as though I bemoan an older time, which is the preoccupation of the old, or cultivate an opposition to change, which is the currency of the rich and stupid. It is not so" (181). Self-preoccupation, after all, serves poorly as an ethical guide. Instead, his effort is to startle recognition of what we once were, what we now are and are now doing, in order to capture a realistic ethic of living in harmony with the land. Here are the things we have forgotten; here now those we must remember. Upon such lies our future hope.

Repeatedly, then, and in a nondidactic manner, he returns in *Travels with Charley* to the theme of living in harmony with the land, capturing the theme in personal events and vignettes that lace the story to its conclusion. In effect, he takes his time—makes time—for the land's tutoring and his appropriation of its lessons. He stands in a magnificent stand of redwoods and ponders the sense of awe and respect he derives from them. These are spiritual qualities, not utilitarian ones. They are lessons of the land. And they have the capacity to change our measure of time itself, for as the great trees work their power upon his spirit, Steinbeck finds himself reflecting, "Can it be that we do not love to be reminded that we are very young and callow in a world that was old when we came into it? And can there be a strong resistance to the certainty that a living world will continue its stately way when we no longer inhabit it?" (193). In such a way the land reminds us, and in heeding the reminder humanity learns to live in harmony with the land, finding a place at one time in the timeless.

That discovery colors, in one way or another, all the following events of *Travels with Charley*. Whether arising amid the colored rocks and terrifying delicacy of the Arizona desert or in the midst of turbulent social strife in New Orleans, the essential message endures. The heart of an environmental ethic, as also in an ethical guide toward human understanding and living, resides in a deep commitment to harmonious living, respecting the life of the land itself and respecting oneself in relationship to that land.

Something of that same discovery may be seen in his fiction also. In fact, the argument here is that while his ethic of the environment received rational elucidation rather late in his career, it achieved formulation and validation much earlier in his fiction.

The evidence for that claim could be supplied from his earliest works but at considerable risk. Joseph Wayne's grappling with seasons of discontent, his druidic embrace of the dying oak tree, his frantic religion of rain, show a man deeply involved with the land but also one who loses himself for the land. No harmony arises from his madness, which seems propelled only by an insistence that all is wrong, that it should be different, but with little rational or emotional clarity of things being set right. Joseph steps from his porch, studies the dead oak, and laments, "If only it were alive . . . I would know what to do. I have no counsel anymore" (*TGU* 183). Indeed, he does not. *To a God Unknown* bitterly inscribes the circle of helplessness and disharmony, its spiral leading to the sacrifice of oneself. To claim, as deluded Joseph does, that "I am the land . . . and I am the rain" (261) seems like anything but an environmental ethic. Yes, someone might point out, but it *does* rain. And the peasants celebrate the efficacy of Wayne's sacrifice, despite the priest's scorn and threats of penance.

The real hero of the novel, as Jackson Benson points out in *The True Adventures of John Steinbeck, Writer*, "is nature, an organic whole, which has its own being apart from man's vain attempts to control, influence, or understand it deductively" (1984, 239). In effect, the novel shows humanity and nature at odds with each other and depicts a negative ethical attitude toward nature as something to be used for individual self-interest. In his discussion of the novel and

Steinbeck's thinking about nature at this stage of his life, Benson demonstrates how Steinbeck extrapolated a holistic view of nature from his study under C. V. Taylor, a disciple of William Emerson Ritter. Basically, Ritter argued a necessary harmony of parts, including humanity, in the natural whole, a view that very much defined Steinbeck's lifelong environmental ethics.

Despite the labored mysticism of the novel, then, one detects a seminal attitude of Steinbeck that grew, deepened, and matured in later years. Undeniable is the fact that Wayne's sacrifice was for the land. Even the priest recognizes this: "He thought of Joseph Wayne, and he saw the pale eyes suffering because of the land's want. 'That man must be very happy now,' Father Angelo said to himself" (264). And at the end of his life, Wayne's thinking has changed, as he sees human life as a part of a whole, natural pattern. The failure of the ethic, if it may even be called such at this stage, is that Wayne himself fails to achieve the harmonious relationship with the land—unless one points to the ironic symmetry of his corpse stretched out upon the rock. All such talk about Wayne's absorption into the cosmic flow means very little when Wayne lies dead. Ethics, finally, are the actions and attitudes of living people in a living environment. In a sense, then, *To a God Unknown* shows a negative view in regard to an environmental ethic.

To step from the demon-haunted landscape of *To a God Unknown* to the sun-washed hills of *The Pastures of Heaven* is a journey between worlds that show similarities but are finally different. This point is particularly clear in Steinbeck's attitude toward humanity and the environment. The similarity appears first, for the notorious curse of the Battle Farm seems to afflict the very earth, to live and breed in it. While different characters are content to resign the curse to demons, and to avoid the Battle land, it seems that the curse will not leave them alone. In the words of T. B. Allen, "Maybe your curse and the farm's curse has mated and gone into a gopher hole like a pair of rattlesnakes. Maybe there'll be a lot of baby curses crawling around the pastures the first thing we know" (*PH* 19).

With the increasing interest in Steinbeck's short stories during recent years, and the revelation through those stories both of Steinbeck's developing artistry and also of his thematic directions, the nature of the curse has been amply discussed. It has, in the critical views set forth, both biblical analogues to the Edenic curse and implications for Steinbeck's view of humanity in contention with the destructive forces of modern civilization. It is in relation to that thematic pattern, however, that the similarities with *To a God Unknown* end, for *The Pastures of Heaven* is ultimately a testimony to the triumph of human nature as it learns to live in harmony with the land. Paradoxically, the battle may remain, engaged upon different fronts, but the conflict may achieve amelioration, even resolution, as individuals learn their own quiet patterns of living with the land.

The pattern of person and land in a state of discord or dominion prevails throughout the stories. One can tell a great deal about the characters by how they manage the land: whether they let it grow coarse and wild, as does Junius Maltby; whether they impose a kind of tyrannical order, as do Helen Van Deventer and Raymond Banks; or whether they achieve a degree of harmony, as does John Whiteside. The pastures are full of gardens and orchards. Often they are twisted and grotesque, signifying this crooked and confusing world. At times the land responds bountifully to the human touch. In either case, the curse lies buried just out of sight. While *The Pastures of Heaven* is littered—as a place and as a novel—with the detritus of shattered dreams and broken lives, it also remains as a powerful force that reshapes those lives. Herein lies the harmony: the discovery of the land as a powerful, living thing, having intrinsic self-worth.

The epilogue of *Pastures of Heaven* serves as a kind of propaedeutics to Steinbeck's environmental ethic as he worked it out in his fiction over the course of the following two decades. Here in the epilogue, modern pilgrims arrive at the rim of the valley and feel the disconcerting tug of its allure upon their spirits. That tug is disconcerting, for it at once invites them and challenges them. Here, each one believes, things might be different. But each pilgrim comes with a sense of how he or she would use the land to make things different. It is the Edenic paradox played out all over again: does one exercise dominion over the land by thrashing it into submission to fit some concept of usefulness or by discovering its usefulness through harmonious integration with it? None of these pilgrims, at least, discovers the harmony—giving of oneself wholly in order to experience fully the beneficence and power of the land. Each tramps back aboard the tour bus slightly dismayed but packed off to a former self.

That conflict between use of the land and living at harmony with the land intensifies in later fiction. *The Grapes of Wrath,* for example, complicates the pattern dramatically, for the sun-blasted plains of Oklahoma seem unforgiving of humanity. Even here, however, the historical information given in the interchapters explains the case; the relentless scraping of the tractors so scarified the topsoil as to damage it nearly beyond repair. The unfortunate homesteaders reap the whirlwind. When these same homesteaders migrate to the land of milk and honey, they find the cycle repeated in a more treacherous way, for in the lush valleys of California rapacious use by the land-owners insists upon destroying even the plenty. Humans are set against humans in times of bounty as in time of need. In interchapter 25, Steinbeck names this greed as "a crime . . . that goes beyond denunciation. A sorrow . . . that weeping cannot symbolize" (385).

Interchapter 25 shapes one of Steinbeck's sharpest social commentaries and most carefully develops a concept of what one might call the "land-use ethic" of this period. The chapter begins with a lyrical celebration of spring in the California valleys, when the land bursts with promise. The descriptive sentence "The full green hills are round and soft as breasts" suggests connections with the life-giving act of Rose of Sharon. The lushness of the country invokes a vast promise of plenitude, until Steinbeck introduces the men "of understanding and knowledge and skill" who shape the promise to the desires of the landowners. The description of these men is carefully rendered—the images tender, the tone appreciative. "They have," he writes, "transformed the world with their knowledge" (383).

But knowledge, as in Eden, serves as a curse here when it is used to satisfy personal pride and to reap personal gain from the earth at the expense of others. Midway through the chapter, the bounty of fruit, nourished by a sea of chemicals, proliferates to the fullness of decay, which is also the decay of human responsibilities to fellow humans. The decay acquires a macabre life of its own, symbolizing a cloud of greed that covers the land: "The decay spreads over the State, and the sweet smell is a great sorrow on the land" (384). The smell of rot, Steinbeck writes, "fills the country" (385). In this case, nature's abundance is perverted to a kind of grotesque life form, manipulated by and in order to satisfy human greed. With the decay of the fruit, human values, concerns for the well-being of others, similarly rot away in disuse.

In the *Cannery Row* novels this mechanical ruin of nature's riches sharpens intensely. While *Cannery Row* takes place in the very throbbing blast of the fishing boilers, thereby creating from the start a metaphor for the "hot taste of life," *Sweet Thursday* opens with a melancholic description of the effects of that hot taste:

The canneries themselves fought the war by getting the limit taken off fish and catching them all. It was done for patriotic reasons, but that didn't bring the fish back. As with the oysters in Alice, "They'd eaten every one." It was the same noble impulse that stripped the forests of the West and right now is pumping water out of California's earth faster than it can rain back in. When the desert comes, people will be sad; just as Cannery Row was sad when all the pilchards were caught and canned and eaten. The pearl-gray canneries of corrugated iron were silent and a pacing watchman was their only life. The street that once roared with trucks was quiet and empty. (ST 3)

By this time, of course, Steinbeck had tried, tested, and finally found wanting his marine-biology analogy for human life, the notorious Group Man who is finally little more than a naturalistic particle in a random universe. However flawed the philosophical apparatus of the Group Man theory, it does pose an intriguing explanation of, and support for, Steinbeck's mandate to live in harmony with the land. As he argues in *The Log from the Sea of Cortez:*

There is tied up at the most primitive and powerful racial or collective instinct a rhythm sense or "memory" which affects everything and which in the past was probably more potent than it is now. It would at least be more plausible to attribute these profound effects to devastating and instinct-searing tidal influences active during the formative times of the early race history of organisms. The fact remains that the imprint is there. . . . The imprint lies heavily on our dreams and on the delicate threads of our nerves. . . . The harvest of symbols in our minds seems to have been planted in the soft rich soil of our prehumanity. (LSC 39)

Steinbeck's Group Man theory enforces that sense of humanity's link to the environment; its ethical implications during this period were shaped more particularly, however, by his accompanying theory of nonteleological thinking.

Nonteleological thinking also forms a sort of premise for Steinbeck's environmental ethic, since it requires that one see the thing as it is, disinterestedly, rather than through the framework of personal, or interested, use: "The truest reason for anything's being so is that it *is*. This is actually and truly a reason, more valid and clearer than all the other separate reasons, or than any group of them short of the whole. Anything less than the whole forms part of the picture only, and the infinite whole is unknowable except by *being* it, by living into it" (*LSC* 176). Such expressions of Steinbeck's attitude toward the environment testify to a persistent concern and collectively form the outlines of an ethical view guiding human responsibility toward an appreciation of the environment. Perhaps it receives some entelechy in a novel where the environmental concern is least overt, through the character of Samuel Hamilton in *East of Eden*.

Adam Trask's initial perception of Samuel Hamilton as a biblical patriarch is appropriate, for Hamilton's is the elder voice in the novel, full of tested wisdom and ancient knowledge. Especially important to Steinbeck's maturing view of the environment is the fact that this patriarchal figure knows the land from the past to the present. Hamilton holds a patriarchal view of the land itself, imbued by an acute understanding of how the land was formed and what its secret resources are. Hamilton draws a verbal map of the land for Adam Trask, explaining the forces that have so shaped it. That intensive knowledge, that suprarational intimacy, is fundamental to living with the land as opposed to merely using or abusing the land.

It is an irony in the novel that Samuel Hamilton, more pointedly than anyone, lives East of Eden, working upon the sun-baked soil of his farm quite literally by the sweat of his brow. His life's quest is for sufficient water to replenish his stony soil. But the point of the irony is not easily missed. Hamilton is the good man making the best of his way in harmony with a bad place. More so than Joseph Wayne ever dreamed, Samuel Hamilton "is the land."

When Adam Trask, now successful on his valley farm, asks Hamilton why he has stayed upon his desert hill, Hamilton professes that he never had the courage to dare greatness but instead contented himself with mediocrity. The desert farm, it seems, ensures this. But Hamilton also qualifies *mediocrity*, and by it he means precisely a harmonious living with all living things, as opposed to the aloof arrogance that is the temptation of greatness: "On one side you have warmth and companionship and sweet understanding, and on the other—cold, lonely greatness. There you make your choice" (347–48). Thus defined, mediocrity proves heroic in the novel, and Samuel Hamilton's relationship with the land—a strange mixture of contentment and contention—proves metaphorical also for his ethics of human living.

In the end, of course, Samuel is not to be apotheosized. He may be patriarchal in bearing, but he is no saint. His primary flaw, as the narrator suggests, is his denial of death as a necessary part of the fabric of living:

> Samuel may have thought and played and philosophized about death, but he did not really believe in it. His world did not have death as a member. He, and all around him, was immortal. When real death came it was an outrage, a denial of the immortality he deeply felt, and the one crack in his wall caused the whole structure to crash. I think he had always thought he could argue himself out of death. It was a personal opponent and one he could lick. (383)

In this matter, and as Abra tutors Aron, Liza is the necessary tutor or counterpart to Samuel. She is a realist, the temper to his fancy. Even heaven, in her view, is a place marked first of all by realistic comforts—clean clothes and dishes, for example. She tutors Samuel, and nowhere is the effect of her tutoring more evident than in Samuel's attitude toward that contrary horse, Doxology. Of this animal, Samuel says: "I have never in thirty-three years found one good thing about him. He even has an ugly disposition. He is selfish and quarrelsome and mean and disobedient. To this day I don't dare walk behind him because he will surely take a kick at me. When I feed him mash he tries to bite my hand. And I love him" (400). And that sums up his ethic also. Whether in contention with an ornery land, a wayward child, or a recalcitrant horse, Samuel's contention is charged with love.

Perhaps we are misled by the sometimes strident tones of Steinbeck's later nonfiction to demarcate his final years as a "moral phase." Certainly an attitude of urgency infiltrates his letters during the 1960s, and certainly the raveled moral fabric of the nation appears as a major theme in such works as *Travels with Charley* and *America and Americans*. We are misled if we see those pronouncements and that attitude as something oddly apart from all his former life. Rather, they emerge out of a developing but fairly consistent ethic located in his fiction throughout his life.

This is particularly true in Steinbeck's ethic of the environment. From his earliest years he was exploring an ethical attitude—a pattern of right living—based upon a belief in the possibility of a harmonious relationship between humanity and the environment. If one approaches the land in a self-interested way, the result will inevitably be despoliation and depletion of what it means to be human. Humanity and the environment are linked in a delicate interplay. It is inevitably so in the fiction. Respect for this linkage, seeing the land as it is in its own right, as a living and delicate thing, not only ennobles humanity and ultimately liberates humanity but also grants self-knowledge and validation through a loving and harmonious relationship between humanity and the land. While Steinbeck may have had his "moral phase," while his moral voice may even have turned shrill at times, it was only because of his deepening sense of urgency about environmental matters. But an ethic about the land, a sense of how and why one ought to live with the land, was a part of his personal nature and his public work from his earliest years. In that sense, it would be fair to say that Steinbeck engaged a moral phase from his first lines.

NINETEEN

A World to Be Cherished: Steinbeck as Conservationist and Ecological Prophet

Roy Simmonds

From The Grapes of Wrath *to* America and Americans, *John Steinbeck wrote searingly in both fiction and prose about America's despoliation of the environment. As a realist, he lashed out at wasteful farming practices; at overfishing sardines in Monterey Bay and shrimp in the Gulf of California; and, more broadly, at man's exhaustion of the earth by overpopulation. The frothy* Sweet Thursday *warns that "Man, in saving himself, has destroyed himself." As a prophet, Steinbeck preached conservation and, in his last work,* America and Americans, *tentatively advanced the hope that Americans could learn not to "destroy wantonly."*

John Steinbeck's postwar fiction has often been criticized for being intermittently overdidactic in tone. It is, indeed, a criticism at times hard to refute, but it has to be borne in mind that, in one respect, with a keen interest in and knowledge of marine biology, he must frequently have felt compelled to assume the mantle of angry prophet in warning his fellow men of the dangers, as he interpreted them, toward which the human species was thoughtlessly heading. Certainly he enjoyed the immense advantage of having a ready-made audience in the millions of readers of his best-selling books, as well as of the popular magazines in which so many of his articles and essays appeared.

While Steinbeck had long been aware that mankind's despoliation of the environment was, in his own lifetime, increasingly alarming in extent and intensity, his novels of the 1930s, such as *In Dubious Battle, Of Mice and Men,* and *The Grapes of Wrath,* tended to dwell more on the human and sociological problems besetting America's underprivileged during the depression years. In *The Grapes of Wrath,* a work that is centered on the societal consequences of one of the greatest environmental disasters of the decade, Steinbeck concentrates on the plight of migrants fleeing the Dust Bowl and seeking a new and better life in California, and he conducts a polemic against the owners and bankers who escalate the disaster by dispossessing the tenant farmers.

But in addition, he does not fail to examine for the first time in his fiction the ecological question, spelling out the root causes of that environmental disaster: the indiscriminate plowing of marginal land and the overuse of the soil, the plundering of the wells, and the depletion of the subsoil moisture:

> *The owner men went on leading to their point: You know the land's getting poorer. You know what cotton does to the land; robs it, sucks all the blood out of it.*
>
> *The squatters nodded—they knew, God knew. If they could only rotate the crops they might pump blood back into the land.*
>
> *Well, it's too late. (TGOW 33)*

Nor does Steinbeck fail to express his own cosmic perception through the mouthpiece of Jim Casy: "Maybe it's all men an' all women we love; maybe that's the Holy Sperit—the human sperit—the whole shebang. Maybe all men got one big soul ever'body's a part of" (24). Later in the book, Casy's flash of understanding is developed in chapter 17, where Steinbeck posits the "I to We" concept of human togetherness and inter-responsibility.

This philosophy of holism, encompassing as it does the essential conservation of the vulnerable environment on which the human species depends, permeated Steinbeck's work from *The Grapes of Wrath* to the end of his life, the didacticism becoming more and more insistent as the emphasis of his writing shifted increasingly from the fictive to the nonfictive mode. It is a philosophy that implies acceptance of mankind's obligation not only toward our planet earth and to every living creature or organism that exists upon it but also to the whole cosmos. It is an extension of John Donne's "No man is an Iland, intire of it selfe" and Steinbeck's own "I to We" concept. As Steinbeck and Ricketts jointly express it in *Sea of Cortez:*

> *It is a strange thing that most of the feeling we call religious, most of the mystical outcrying which is one of the most prized and used and desired*

reactions of our species, is really the understanding and the attempt to say that man is related to the whole thing, related inextricably to all reality, known and unknowable. . . . all things are one thing and that one thing is all things—plankton, a shimmering phosphorescence on the sea and the spinning planets and an expanding universe, all bound together by the elastic string of time. It is advisable to look from the tide pool to the stars and then back to the tide pool again. (SOC 216–17)

The concern expressed in *Sea of Cortez* in 1941 over the continuing rape of the environment is most powerfully manifested in chapter 27 of that book. Steinbeck and Ricketts describe how, during a visit to the Japanese dredge boats operating in the Gulf of California, they had observed the senseless waste that resulted from the bulk, indiscriminate fishing for shrimp. The warning is spelled out unequivocally:

We in the United States have done so much to destroy our own resources, our timber, our land, our fishes, that we should be taken as a horrible example and our methods avoided by any government and people enlightened enough to envision a continuing economy. With our resources we have been prodigal, and our country will not soon lose the scars of our grasping stupidity. (250)

World events, however, overshadowed the book's appearance and its message. *Sea of Cortez* was published two days before Pearl Harbor, and America had more pressing matters to engage its national mind. With the war effort demanding ever more exploitation of the country's natural resources, the concept of conservation, if it was considered at all in those days, was put on the back burner for the sometime future. For all that, Steinbeck did not entirely abandon the cause. In 1945, on the first page of his new novel, *Cannery Row,* he obliquely warned his readers of the dire consequences of the overfishing of California coastal waters:

In the morning when the sardine fleet has made a catch, the purse-seiners waddle heavily into the bay blowing their whistles. The deep-laden boats pull in against the coast where the canneries dip their tails into the bay. The figure is advisedly chosen, for if the canneries dipped their mouths into the bay the canned sardines which emerge from the other end would be metaphorically, at least, even more horrifying.

What Steinbeck was describing here, and by satirical implication deploring, was the system of floating hoppers which, in the early 1930s, had been stationed out in Monterey Bay and were connected to the canneries on shore by immense underwater pipes. The returning purse-seiners, their catches spilling from their holds, often covering the decks to the level of the gunwales, did not even have to negotiate the treacherous inshore reefs to discharge their loads. At the hoppers, the fish were sucked from the decks and out of the holds, through the underwater pipes and straight into the processing plants.

The end result of this brutal harvesting of the sea was soon to make itself evident. The records show that in the 1944–1945 season the total landing was the second largest of all time and amounted to an impressive 237,000 tons. That season came at the end of a decade or more of deliberately indiscriminate fishing and was to be the last harvest of over 200,000 tons. The following year, total landings had dropped to 145,000 tons and continued to decline year after year, until by the 1953–1954 season, when Steinbeck wrote and published his second Cannery Row novel, *Sweet Thursday*, the total landing was a mere 58 tons, and the industry was effectively dead, killed by its own greed (Hemp 110).

If Steinbeck was entitled to an "I-told-you-so" attitude in 1954, it was surely in great sorrow as well as anger that in the opening pages of *Sweet Thursday* he reflected on the mindlessness of the Monterey fishermen and cannery owners and added a further warning of additional ecological disasters on the horizon. As he observed:

The canneries themselves fought the war by getting the limit taken off fish and catching them all. It was done for patriotic reasons, but that didn't bring the fish back. . . . It was the same noble impulse that stripped the forests of the West and right now is pumping water out of California's earth faster than it can rain back in. When the desert comes, people will be sad; just as Cannery Row was sad when all the pilchards were caught and canned and eaten. (3)

Sweet Thursday was severely battered by the critics on its publication in 1954, and ever since it has been all too summarily dismissed by many Steinbeck scholars. Richard Astro, however, in his seminal study, *John Steinbeck and Edward F. Ricketts: The Shaping of a Novelist,*

has pointed to "the impact of the person and ideas of Edward F. Ricketts on the novelist's fiction" and has referred to *Sweet Thursday* as
"one of the most important works in [Steinbeck's] entire canon"
(193). That it most certainly is. As Pascal Covici, Steinbeck's editor,
sagely suggested: "Read it once to laugh and again to think."

In this book, Steinbeck endeavored, among other matters, to convey in simplified form and through a popular medium (and we
should not overlook the intended musical comedy aspect of the work)
concepts of great complexity of which he felt the world at large
should become aware. The trouble is that these concepts are all too
often diffused by the rambunctious and sentimental style and content, their essential message blurred. On the final page of the book,
for instance, Steinbeck introduces his last big joke of all. As Doc and
Suzy, in traditional musical comedy "happy ending," are about to
drive off into the sunset to begin their life together, Mack and the
boys present Doc with what they fondly believe to be the new microscope he so desperately needs for his research:

> *Doc looked at the gift—a telescope strong enough to bring the moon
> to his lap. His mouth fell open. Then he smothered the laughter that rose
> in him.*
>
> *"Like it?" said Mack.*
>
> *"It's beautiful."*
>
> *"Biggest one in the whole goddam catalogue," said Mack.*
>
> *Doc's voice was choked. "Thanks," he said. "After all, I guess it doesn't
> matter whether you look down or up—as long as you look." (272–73)*

The microscope and the telescope are surely the twin metaphors that
Steinbeck uses here to illustrate the message from *Sea of Cortez:* "to
look from the tidepool to the stars and then back to the tidepool
again" (*SOC* 217).

The wayward rape of the earth's resources, be it on a local, nationwide, or international basis, is not, however, the sole factor spelling
out ecological disaster for the human race. In *Sweet Thursday,* Steinbeck maps the terrifying progression by which the human species, through the application of accumulated scientific and medical
knowledge and practice, will inevitably create the conditions for the
ultimate catastrophe: the end of the world, certainly the world as
we know it. A passage of animated discussion between Doc and Old

Jingleballicks is ostensibly presented to the reader as yet another episode of wild banter, but beneath it all, Steinbeck speaks through his characters with a deadly serious voice. "Man, in saving himself, has destroyed himself," Old Jingleballicks argues:

Predators he has removed from the earth; heat and cold he has turned aside; communicable disease he has practically eliminated. The old live on, the young do not die. . . . The population grows and the productivity of the earth decreases. In a foreseeable future we shall be smothered by our own numbers. Only birth control could save us, and that is one thing mankind is never going to practice. . . . It is a cosmic joke. Preoccupation with survival has set the stage for extinction. (167–68)

That Old Jingleballicks's words were meant to be taken seriously by readers of the novel is evident from the fact that in one of the last articles he published, two years before his death, Steinbeck repeats almost the selfsame words, certainly the same thesis he had expounded twelve years before in the novel. In this article, "Let's Go After the Neglected Treasures Beneath the Seas," which appeared in the September 1966 issue of *Popular Science,* Steinbeck observes that "one of the definitive diagnostics of the human animal, besides being the key to his success in survival and triumph over the forces of nature, is curiosity" (85). Steinbeck charges that man has failed to show curiosity in exploring, mapping, and evaluating "the hidden places of our mother earth" and that any requests for the money to do so has "brought howls of protest from Congressional leaders and the inevitable question—is it really necessary?" (85). Steinbeck suggests that it is necessary by echoing the words he had put into Old Jingleballicks's mouth:

We have wiped out the animal predators that once decimated embattled families. We are by way of defeating the micro-enemies which secretly invaded our bodies to strike from within. And finally we find ourselves faced with the most ghastly enemy of all—ourselves, too many of us in a world with a limited food supply. And hungry men will destroy anything, even themselves, to get food. (86)

In thus recognizing three of the definitive hallmarks of the human animal—insatiable curiosity, natural tendency toward over-procreation, and an instinct for survival by whatever means necessary—

Steinbeck foresees the eventuality when man "may be driven back to our mother, the sea, because we are running out of supplies" (86). As he wryly comments: "Two [astronauts] with their pockets full of rocks will not solve the situation" (86). On the other hand, he points out that "the plankton, the basic reservoir of the world's food, live in the sea . . . , [a] boundless bank of protein food" man has "not even learned" to process for his consumption (86).

Having regard to all the informed discussion generated over the past decade or so on the horrors of global warming, and even though some sense of the worldwide urgency and the increased financial commitment by governments may at last be discernible, research into the potential wealth of the oceans and seas that constitute three-fifths of the earth's surface is still proceeding in the same haphazard (and mainly destructive) profit-seeking manner in which it was being conducted more than a quarter century ago when Steinbeck wrote his article. The national and, more important, international coordination of knowledge and skill that Steinbeck advocated has still not materialized. This, it hardly needs saying, is not in the least surprising in view of the criminal lack of international coordination in tackling those ecological problems man has created by his exploration and exploitation of the remaining two-fifths of the earth's surface.

In the article, one can observe Steinbeck the realist, Steinbeck the romantic, and Steinbeck the ecologist in contest with each other. As a realist, he accepted that it would be impossible to contain the insatiable exploitative ways of man and the inevitable accelerating growth of the world's population; and he realized, as many fail or prefer not to do, that the earth's resources are finite, that someday the minerals and materials man takes for granted will no longer be there, that someday the areas of land available for arable production will no longer be sufficient to sustain all the hungry mouths medical and scientific expertise has saved from disease and death. As he proposed:

We must explore our world and then we must farm it and harvest its plant life. We must study, control, herd, and improve the breeds of animals, because we are shortly going to need them. And we must mine the minerals, refine the chemicals to our use. Surely the rewards are beyond

anything we can now conceive, and will be increasingly needed in an
overpopulated and depleting world. (87)

Sadly, there is no reason to suppose that Steinbeck's vision of an ordered and monitored exploitation of the seas will ever come about. The same thoughtless pattern of greed and national self-interest will hold sway in the future as it had done in the past. Indeed, as Steinbeck observed, the plundering, polluting, and wasting of the sea's resources was even then well advanced:

We peck like sandpipers along the edges for the small treasures the restless
waves wash up. We raid the procession of the migrating fishes, killing all
we can. Even the killer whale herds the sperm whales and kills them only
when it needs food—but we have wiped out some species entirely. . . .
And the huge agriculture of the seas we have ignored completely, except
to rip out the fringes for iodine and fertilizer. (86)

The extent to which in the *Popular Science* article Steinbeck presents a convincing and effective forum for his ideas, rather than a display of his undoubted enthusiasms, is arguable. If today some of his ideas seem flawed, it is mainly because we have access, even at the layman's level, to knowledge he did not possess at the time and could not possibly have foreseen. He surely would not, for instance, have advocated the use of the plankton as that "boundless bank of protein food" had he been aware of the extensive damage to the ozone layer that has been revealed to us in recent years. As latest reports indicate, the enhanced levels of harmful ultraviolet radiation from the sun reaching the earth's surface are already having a seriously adverse effect on the plankton that annually absorbs half the total of carbon dioxide from the atmosphere. Any depletion of plankton, whether by radiation or by the harvesting suggested by Steinbeck, will accordingly increase the carbon dioxide levels in the atmosphere and will add to the greenhouse effect.

If as a romantic and an ecological prophet, Steinbeck can be seen as having been sometimes wrongheaded and as having confused his zest for scientific discovery with his concern for conservation, it is clear that as a species we have not heeded to any appreciable extent the warnings that he and other ecologists issued during the 1940s, 1950s, and 1960s. The squandering of the earth's bounty has been

proceeding more less unabated since Steinbeck died. The sea, despite token ges s toward conservation, is still criminally over-
fished and p d by oil spillage and the dumping of chemicals
and nuclea . The rings of trash Steinbeck so deplored in *Travels*
with Char surround the great cities of the world. Vast tracts of
land in ted States, Russia, Australia, and the Pacific remain
cont and uninhabitable as a legacy of nuclear testing. Some
a les are being hunted to extinction or are being eradi-
gh the destruction of their special environments. There
spectacular industrial accidents, such as Bhopal and Cher-
d disasters of war like the burning of Kuwait's oil fields.
ose national schemes have resulted in immense ecological ca-
es, such as the destruction of the Aral Sea in Uzbekistan. In
nesota as late as 1987, the farming practices responsible for the
st Bowl a half century before continue to be carried on.

A month after the *Popular Science* article appeared, Steinbeck's last
book, *America and Americans*, was published. In this work, written
before the article, he returned, among many other ecological matters, to the twin local themes of the proved consequences of overfishing and the inevitable consequences of the unrestricted depletion of California's natural water resources:

> The Pacific Coast pilchards were once the raw material for a great and
> continuing industry. We hunted them with aircraft far at sea until they
> were gone and the canneries had to be closed. In some of the valleys of th
> West, where the climate makes several crops a year available, which th
> water supply will not justify, wells were driven deeper and deeper fo
> gation, so that in one great valley a million acre feet more of water
> taken out than rain and melting snow could replace, and the wat
> went down and a few more years may give us a new desert. (12

On the very next page, however, Steinbeck professe
found hope for the future. "No longer do we America
stroy wantonly," he declared. "We are no longer co
our beloved country. We are slow to learn; but we
have his ideas, which he shared so eloquently
other caring ecologists of the day, really been h
pear not, or if they were, then only with a gre
The truth of all this was made evident to

we visited the West Coast in the summer of 1990.
the Golden State from a Britain that had seen no ~~had arrived in~~
weeks, and we mentioned this, for what it was wo~~fall for three~~
that our statement would at least raise some eyebro~~ticipating~~
country, of all places, such a situation should obtain. W~~in our~~
veloped the theme by revealing that drought condition~~de-~~
declared back home with the accompanying imposition o~~f~~
of water restrictions, including, for instance, the outlawin~~g~~
use of garden hoses. We received no show of sympathy, howev~~er~~
ing advised in our turn that there had been no rain in Californi~~a~~
three *years*. We were not even granted the anticipated reaction of ~~as~~
tonishment and, if nothing else, were confirmed in our long-held be~~-~~
lief that everything in America is on a far vaster scale than we are
used to at home.

To paraphrase Laurence Sterne: "They order this matter differently in the U.S.A." Indeed they do. For to our amazement, we discovered that although, after those three long years of drought, some water restrictions were in force in California, these were no more than we would regard at home as the very minimum of token gestures toward conservation. They were, moreover, as far as we could see, designed to operate only during specific hours of the day. For the rest of the time, lawn sprinklers could send forth their prolific glittering arcs, unimpeded by law or apparently even by conscience.

By the following year, so we read in our daily press and saw on television, the attitudes we had observed in California were beginning to be severely modified. Conservation was very much on the agenda. In Santa Barbara, the water reservoirs had become dangerously depleted. It was estimated that by May 1991, if the drought continued and if no solution to the problem were quickly found, there would be a frightening 80 percent shortfall in the water supply. Matters were seen to be so desperate that discussions had already been instituted to purchase cheap water from western Canada and truck it down by road, despite the huge costs involved. There were, in addition, proposals for two separate schemes for water desalination; official "drought busters" patrolled the city streets, checking reported water leaks and rooting out any wasteful use of water, and flow restrictors were being fitted to showers. House owners wishing to sell their properties and concerned that their dried-up lawns might discourage out-of-state buyers, had even been panicked into having the withered brown grass sprayed with green dye. At long last, it seemed, there was in California a universal awareness that a disaster of enormous magnitude had crept up to the front doorstep, a disaster that in many respects could make any movement of the San Andreas Fault pale into secondary significance.

This, indeed, is the potential disaster Steinbeck had been predicting for California a half century ago in the opening paragraphs of *Sweet Thursday*. Its root cause, however, lies not so much in the lack of rain as in the fact that the existing water resources are becoming more and more insufficient for an expanding California population. The circumstances that obtain in the valleys of California also obtain in other areas of the nation and in the world as a whole. If populations continue to grow unchecked in the way Old Jingleballicks predicted, then they will cancel out any doubtful advantages of the new food sources that may be gained by laying waste the rain forests or harvesting the wealth of the sea. The problem will not go away, the numbers of starving people progressively increasing in some sort of horrible version of Parkinson's Law, maintaining the gap between demand and the increased but always insufficient food supply. Even the most ideal measures of environmental conservation that can be imagined today will possibly be inadequate to ensure ultimate survival.

Significantly, Old Jingleballicks's theory of the "cosmic joke" is used as an epigraph in Dr. June Goodfield's *The Cosmic Joke*, published in conjunction with the showing on BBC Television of two documentary films bearing the same title. The book and the films detail Dr. Goodfield's "personal investigation into the likelihood of the Cosmic Joke as envisaged by John Steinbeck" (4), following her on her journeys in South East Asia, Latin America, and Africa. Her findings on the population issue seem to indicate an acceptance of the need for birth control that is by no means the universal rejection that Old Jingleballicks believed to be the case; there seems indeed to be a grassroots call for education and assistance in family planning in the Third World to which governments are responding in varying degrees. In summing up what she describes as "the unavoidable dilemma," she admits that "it is too early to say whether we will manage to stabilize the world's population at double its present numbers or whether we will surge to 15 billion, when the Cosmic Joke of John Steinbeck could engulf us in all its black humour" (44).

Steinbeck's own cosmic perception never deserted him. While he was staying in Bruton in England during 1959 and working on his never-to-be-completed *Arthur* manuscript, he was one morning "doodling" preparatory to settling down to the work of the day. This is what he wrote:

> *When I read of the expanding universe, of novas and red dwarfs, of violent activities, explosions, disappearances of suns and the birth of others, and then realize that the news of these events, carried by light waves, are records of things that happened millions of years ago, I am inclined to wonder what is happening there now. How can we know that a process and an arrangement so long past has not changed radically or revised itself? It is conceivable that what the great telescopes record presently does not exist at all, that those monstrous issues of the stars may have ceased to be before our world was formed, that the Milky Way is a memory carried in the arms of light.* (TAKA 350)

It is a vision presupposing that someday, somewhere, in the unimaginable future, someone will observe our own no longer existent planet. It will be a time that will not concern any of us today but that does not absolve us from being careful with the heritage that has been entrusted to us and from ensuring that we do not diminish the heritage we pass on to future generations. Jim Casy's flash of inspiration in his wilderness was not the imagining of a crackpot seer but, above all else, the discovery and celebration of a cosmic truth.

It is salutary to remind ourselves that a quarter century has passed since Steinbeck's death and to ask ourselves whether or not the faith he expressed in *America and Americans* that our attitude toward the environment will become more careful and more caring was entirely justified or whether it is likely that the cosmic joke will prove to be grim reality a few more generations in the future. In *Sea of Cortez*, we are told: "Ecology has a synonym which is ALL" (85). As a concept, it has irrefutable force and relevance, not only for our time, but for all the earth's conceivable time to come. It is a truth mankind ignores at its peril.

Bibliography

Principal Collections

Bancroft Library, University of California, Berkeley, California.
Bracken Library, Ball State University, Muncie, Indiana.
Columbia University, New York, New York.
Humanities Research Center, University of Texas, Austin, Texas.
John Steinbeck Library, Salinas, California.
Pierpont Morgan Library, New York, New York.
Stanford University Library, Stanford, California.
Steinbeck Research Center, San Jose State University, San Jose, California.
University of Virginia Library, Charlottesville, Virginia.

Published Works by John Steinbeck

Editors' Note: When possible, the works of John Steinbeck are cited from readily available paperback editions. Original dates of publication are included in the bibliographic entries.

America and Americans. New York: Viking Press, 1966.
Burning Bright. 1950. New York: Penguin Books, 1979.
Cup of Gold. 1929. New York: Penguin Books, 1986.
East of Eden. 1952. New York: Penguin Books, 1987.
"Fascinating Historical and Improbable Events." *Old Whalers Festival and First International Whaling Competition.* N.p.: 1966.
The Grapes of Wrath. 1939. New York: Penguin Books, 1981.
The Harvest Gypsies. 1936. Berkeley: Heyday Books, 1988.
"High Drama of Bold Thrust Through Ocean Floor." *Life* 50 (14 April 1961).
In Dubious Battle. 1936. New York: Penguin Books, 1979.
Journal of a Novel: The East of Eden *Letters.* 1969. New York: Penguin Books, 1990.
"Let's Go After the Neglected Treasures Beneath the Seas." *Popular Science* 189 (September 1966): 84–87+.
"Letter to Alicia." *Newsday* (11 December 1965): 3-W.
"Letter to Alicia." *Newsday* (12 March 1966): 3-W.
[With Edward F. Ricketts, Jr.] *The Log from the Sea of Cortez.* 1951. New York: Penguin Books, 1986.
The Long Valley. 1938. New York: Penguin Books, 1966.
The Moon Is Down. 1942. New York: Penguin Books, 1986.
Of Mice and Men [1937]/*Cannery Row* [1945]. New York: Penguin Books, 1987.

Once There Was a War. 1958. New York: Penguin Books, 1977.

The Pastures of Heaven. 1932. New York: Penguin Books, 1986.

The Pearl. 1945. New York: Penguin Books, 1992.

[With Edward F. Ricketts, Jr.] *Sea of Cortez: A Leisurely Journal of Travel and Research.* 1941. Mt. Vernon, NY: Paul P. Appel, 1989.

The Short Reign of Pippin IV. 1957. New York: Penguin Books, 1977.

Steinbeck: A Life in Letters. Edited by Elaine Steinbeck and Robert Wallsten. New York: Viking Press, 1975.

Sweet Thursday. 1954. New York: Penguin Books, 1984.

To a God Unknown. 1933. New York: Penguin Books, 1986.

Tortilla Flat. 1935. New York: Penguin Books, 1986.

Travels with Charley in Search of America. 1962. New York: Penguin Books, 1986.

Viva Zapata! 1952. New York: Viking Compass, 1975.

The Wayward Bus. 1947. New York: Penguin Books, 1988.

The Winter of Our Discontent. 1961. New York: Penguin Books, 1988.

Working Days: The Journals of the Grapes of Wrath. Edited by Robert DeMott. 1989. New York: Penguin Books, 1990.

Zapata. 1991. Edited by Robert E. Morsberger. New York: Penguin Books, 1993.

Published Works About John Steinbeck

Astro, Richard. *John Steinbeck and Edward F. Ricketts: The Shaping of a Novelist.* Minneapolis: University of Minnesota Press, 1973.

Astro, Richard, and Tetsumaro Hayashi, eds. *Steinbeck: The Man and His Work.* Corvallis: Oregon State University Press, 1971.

Astro, Richard, and Joel W. Hedgpeth, eds. *Steinbeck and the Sea: Proceedings of a Conference Held at the Marine Science Center Auditorium, Newport, Oregon, May 4, 1974.* Sea Grant College Program Publication ORESU-W-74-004. Corvallis: Oregon State University, 1975.

Bennett, Robert. *The Wrath of John Steinbeck; or, St. John Goes to Church.* Los Angeles: Albertson, 1939.

Benson, Jackson J. "Novelist as Scientist." *Novel: A Forum of Fiction* 10 (Spring 1977): 248–64.

———. "John Steinbeck's *Cannery Row.*" *Western American Literature* 12 (May 1977): 11–40.

———. *Looking for Steinbeck's Ghost.* Norman: University of Oklahoma Press, 1988.

———. *The True Adventures of John Steinbeck, Writer.* New York: Viking, 1984; Penguin, 1990.

———, ed. *The Short Novels of John Steinbeck: Critical Essays with a Checklist to Steinbeck Criticism.* Durham, NC: Duke University Press, 1990.

Bloom, Harold, ed. *Modern Critical Interpretations:* The Grapes of Wrath. New York: Chelsea House, 1988.

————. *Modern Critical Views: John Steinbeck.* New York: Chelsea House, 1987.

Buerger, Daniel. " 'History' and Fiction in *East of Eden* Criticism." *Steinbeck Quarterly* 14 (Winter–Spring 1981): 6–14.

Carpenter, Frederick. "The Philosophical Joads." *College English* 2 (January 1941): 324–25.

Carr, Duane R. "John Steinbeck, Twentieth Century Romantic: A Study of the Early Works." Ph.D. diss., University of Tulsa, 1975. *DAI* 36A (March–April 1976): 6680.

Davis, Robert Con, ed. *Twentieth Century Interpretations of* The Grapes of Wrath. Englewood Cliffs, NJ: Prentice-Hall, 1982.

Davis, Robert Murray, ed. *Steinbeck : A Collection of Critical Essays.* Englewood Cliffs, NJ: Prentice Hall, 1972.

DeMott, Robert. "*East of Eden:* A Bibliographical Checklist." *Steinbeck Quarterly* 25 (Winter–Spring 1992): 14–28.

————. *Steinbeck's Reading: Catalogue of Books Owned and Borrowed.* New York: Garland, 1984.

Ditsky, John, ed. *Critical Essays on Steinbeck's* The Grapes of Wrath. Boston: G. K. Hall, 1989.

————. *Essays on* East of Eden. Steinbeck Monograph Series. Muncie, IN: John Steinbeck Society of America/Ball State University, 1977.

————. "Steinbeck's *Travels with Charley:* The Quest That Failed." *Steinbeck Quarterly* 8 (1975): 45–50.

Donohue, Agnes McNeil, ed. *A Casebook on* The Grapes of Wrath. New York: Thomas Crowell, 1968.

Enea, Sparky. *With Steinbeck in the Sea of Cortez.* As told to Audry Lynch. Los Osos, CA: Sand River Press, 1991.

Fontenrose, Joseph. *John Steinbeck: An Introduction and Interpretation.* New York: Holt, Rinehart, and Winston, 1962.

French, Warren. *John Steinbeck.* Twayne's United States Author Series. Boston: Twayne, 1961.

————. *John Steinbeck.* Twayne's United States Author Series. Rev. ed. Boston: Twayne, 1975.

————, ed. *A Companion to* The Grapes of Wrath. New York: Viking, 1963.

Gaither, Gloria. "John Steinbeck: From the Tidal Pool to the Stars: Connectedness, Is-Thinking, and Breaking Through: A Reconsideration." *Steinbeck Quarterly* 25 (Winter–Spring 1992): 42–52.

Govoni, Mark W. " 'Symbols for Wordlessness': The Original Manuscript of *East of Eden.*" *Steinbeck Quarterly* 14 (Winter–Spring 1981): 14–23.

Hart, Richard E. "The Concept of Person in the Early Fiction of John Steinbeck." *Personalist Forum* 3.1 (Spring 1992): 67–73.

Hayashi, Tetsumaro, ed. *Steinbeck's Travel Literature: Essays in Criticism.* Steinbeck Monograph Series. Muncie, IN: John Steinbeck Society of America/Ball State University, 1980.

———, ed. *A Study Guide to Steinbeck (Part Two)*. Metuchen, NJ: Scarecrow Press, 1979.

Hayashi, Tetsumaro, and Thomas J. Moore, eds. *Steinbeck's Posthumous Work: Essays in Criticism*. Steinbeck Monograph Series. Muncie, IN: The John Steinbeck Society of America/Ball State University, 1989.

Hedgpeth, Joel W. "Ed Ricketts (1897–1948), Marine Biologist." *Proceedings of the Symposium on Managing Inflows to California's Bays and Estuaries*. Sausalito, CA: Bay Institute, 1988.

———. *The Outer Shores, Part 1: Ed Ricketts and John Steinbeck Explore the Pacific Coast*. Eureka, CA: Mad River, 1978.

———. *The Outer Shores, Part 2: Breaking Through*. Eureka, CA: Mad River, 1978.

Jones, Lawrence William. *John Steinbeck as Fabulist*. Steinbeck Monograph Series. Muncie, IN: John Steinbeck Society of America, 1973.

Kiernan, Thomas. *The Intricate Music: A Biography of John Steinbeck*. Boston: Little, Brown, 1979.

Lisca, Peter. *The Wide World of John Steinbeck*. New Brunswick, NJ: Rutgers University Press, 1958.

Marks, Lester Jay. *Thematic Design in the Novels of John Steinbeck*. The Hague: Mouton, 1971.

McCarthy, Paul. *John Steinbeck*. New York: Frederick Ungar, 1980.

Moore, Harry Thornton. *The Novels of John Steinbeck: A First Study*. Chicago: Normandie House, 1939.

Mulder, Steven. "The Reader's Story: *East of Eden* as Postmodernist Metafiction." *Steinbeck Quarterly* 25 (Summer–Fall 1992): 109–18.

Nakayama, Kiyoshi, Scott Pugh, and Shigeharu Yano, eds. *John Steinbeck: Asian Perspectives*. Osaka, Japan: Osaka Kyoiko Tosho, 1992.

Owens, Louis. *John Steinbeck's Re-Vision of America*. Athens: University of Georgia Press, 1985.

Parini, Jay. *John Steinbeck*. New York: Henry Holt, 1995.

Pratt, William. *John Steinbeck: A Critical Essay*. Contemporary Writers in Christian Perspective Series. Grand Rapids, MI: William B. Eerdmans, 1970.

Railsback, Brian. "Darwin and Steinbeck: The 'Older Method' and the *Sea of Cortez*." *Steinbeck Quarterly* 23 (Winter–Spring 1990): 27–33.

———. *Parallel Expeditions: Charles Darwin and the Art of John Steinbeck*. Moscow: University of Idaho Press, 1995.

———. "Searching for 'What Is': The Parallel Expeditions of Charles Darwin and John Steinbeck." Ph.D. diss., Ohio University, 1990.

Shamberger, Edward. "Grapes of Gladness: A Misconception of *Walden*." *American Transcendental Quarterly* 13 (Winter 1972): 15–16.

Simmonds, Roy S. " 'And Still the Box is Not Full': *East of Eden*." *San Jose Studies* 18 (Fall 1992): 56–71.

———. "The Original Manuscript." *San Jose Studies* 16 (Winter 1990): 117–32.

Steinbeck, Elaine. Interview by Robert DeMott. Nantucket, Massachusetts, 14 May 1992.

Steinbeck, Thomas. Interview by Robert DeMott. Carmel Highlands, California, 3 October 1985.

Tedlock, E. W., and C. V. Wicker, eds. *Steinbeck and His Critics.* Albuquerque: University of New Mexico Press, 1957.

Timmerman, John H. *John Steinbeck's Fiction: The Aesthetics of the Road Taken.* Norman: University of Oklahoma Press, 1986.

Wyatt, David. Introduction to *East of Eden,* by John Steinbeck. New York: Penguin Books, 1992.

Yoshizu, Shigeharu. "Emerson and Steinbeck: On the Oriental Concept of Being." *Studies in English Literature* 10 (November 1974): n.p.

Other References

Adams, Henry. *The Education of Henry Adams.* 1907. New York: Random House, 1931.

Agee, James, and Walker Evans. 1941. *Let Us Now Praise Famous Men.* Boston: Houghton Mifflin Company, 1960.

Alekseev, A. I. *The Odyssey of a Russian Scientist: I. G. Voznesenskiu in Alaska, California, and Siberia.* Translated by Wilma C. Folletee Kingston. Fairbanks: University of Alaska Press, 1987.

Allee, W. C. *Animal Aggregations.* Chicago: University of Chicago Press, 1931.

———. *Cooperation Among Animals.* New York: Henry Shuman, 1938.

Allee, W. C., et al. *Principles of Animal Ecology.* Philadelphia: W. B. Saunders, 1949.

Arvin, Newton. *Herman Melville.* American Men of Letters Series. New York: William Sloane, 1950.

Astro, Richard. *Edward F. Ricketts.* Boise, ID: Boise State University, 1976.

Bacon, Francis. *The Philosophical Works of Francis Bacon.* Edited by John M. Robertson. London: George Routledge and Sons, 1905.

Barbour, James, and Tom Quirk, eds. *Writing the American Classics.* Chapel Hill: University of North Carolina Press, 1990.

Barrow, Clyde W. *Universities and the Capitalist State.* Madison: University of Wisconsin Press, 1992.

Barrus, Clara. *The Life and Letters of John Burroughs.* 2 vols. Boston: Houghton Mifflin, 1925.

Bascom, Willard. *A Hole in the Bottom of the Sea.* Garden City, NY: Doubleday, 1961.

Beebe, William. *Galapagos: World's End.* New York: Putnam, 1924.

———. *Zaca Venture.* New York: Harcourt, Brace, 1938.

Bergson, Henri. *Creative Evolution.* Translated by Arthur Mitchell. 1911. New York: Henry Holt, 1937.

Berkman, Richard L., and W. Kip Viscusi. *Damming the West.* New York: Grossman, 1973.

Bezanson, Walter E. "*Moby-Dick:* Document, Drama, Dream." In *A Companion to Melville Studies,* edited by John Bryant. Westport, CT: Greenwood, 1986.

Blake, William. *The Complete Poetry and Prose of William Blake.* Edited by David V. Erdman. Rev. ed. New York: Doubleday, 1988.

Bockstoce, John R. *Whales, Ice, and Men: The History of Whaling in the Western Arctic.* Seattle: University of Washington Press, 1986.

Boodin, John Elof. *Cosmic Evolution.* New York: Macmillan, 1925.

———. *A Realistic Universe.* 1916. Rev. ed. New York: Macmillan, 1931.

Bowden, Charles. "At Sea with the Shepherd." *Buzzword* (March–April 1991): 39–47.

Brent, Peter. *Charles Darwin: A Man of Enlarged Curiosity.* New York: W. W. Norton, 1981.

Briffault, Robert. *The Making of Humanity.* 1919. London: G. Allen and Unwin, 1928.

———. *The Mothers.* 3 vols. New York: Macmillan, 1927.

Brodhead, Richard. *Hawthorne, Melville, and the Novel.* Chicago: University of Chicago Press, 1976.

Brower, David. *Work in Progress.* Salt Lake City, UT: Peregrine Smith, 1991.

Brown, Mark T., Stephen Tennebaum, and H. T. Odum. "Energy Analysis and Policy Perspectives for the Sea of Cortez, Mexico." *Center for Wetlands Publication 88-04.* Gainesville: University of Florida, 1991.

Brusca, Richard C. *Common Intertidal Invertebrates of the Gulf of California.* Rev. ed. Tucson: University of Arizona Press, 1980.

"Building a Platform for Project Mohole." *Business Week* (25 September 1965): 122+.

Burroughs, John. *A Sharp Lookout: Selected Nature Essays of John Burroughs.* Edited by Frank Bergon. Washington, DC: Smithsonian Institution Press, 1987.

———. *The Writings of John Burroughs.* 23 vols. Boston: Houghton Mifflin, 1904–1922.

Caldwell, Erskine, and Margaret Bourke-White. *You Have Seen Their Faces.* New York: Viking Press, 1937.

Campbell, Joseph. *The Hero's Journey: The World of Joseph Campbell.* Edited by Phil Cousineau. San Francisco: Harper and Row, 1990.

———. *The Masks of God: Primitive Mythology.* 1959. New York: Penguin, 1991.

Capra, Fritjof, and David Steindl-Rast. *Belonging to the Universe.* San Francisco: Harper and Row, 1991.

Carson, Rachel. *Silent Spring.* Boston: Houghton Mifflin, 1962.

Carter, Annetta. "I. G. Voznesenski: Early Naturalist in Baja California." *Taxon* 28 (April 1979): 27–33.

Chase, Richard. *The American Novel and Its Tradition.* 1957. Baltimore: Johns Hopkins University Press, 1980.

———. *Herman Melville: A Critical Study.* New York: Macmillan, 1949.

Clark, Ronald W. *Charles Darwin: A Biography of a Man and an Idea* [in German]. N.p.: S. Fischer, 1985.

———. *The Survival of Charles Darwin: A Biography.* New York: Random House, 1984.

Commoner, Barry. *The Closing Circle.* New York: Alfred A. Knopf, 1971.

Cook, James. *The Voyage of the* Resolution *and* Adventure. Edited by J. C. Beaglehole. Cambridge, MA: Hakluyt Society, 1961.

Crisler, Jesse S., ed. *Frank Norris: Collected Letters.* San Francisco: Book Club of California, 1986.

Curtis, James. *Mind's Eye, Mind's Truth: FSA Photography Reconsidered.* Philadelphia: Temple University Press, 1989.

Daniel, Pete, et al. *Official Images: New Deal Photography.* Washington, DC: Smithsonian Institution Press, 1987.

Darwin, Charles. *Journal of Researches . . . During the voyage of the* H.M.S. Beagle. . . . New York: Appleton, 1899.

———. *The Origin of Species.* In *Darwin,* edited by Philip Appleman. New York: Norton, 1979.

———. *The Origin of Species and The Descent of Man.* New York: Modern Library, n.d.

———. *Voyage of the Beagle.* 1839. Edited with an introduction by Janet Brown and Michael Neve. London: Penguin, 1989.

"Deep into the Deep." *Newsweek* 57 (10 April 1961): 100.

Diaz de Sandi, Jaime. *Guia Que Hacer A Donde Ir.* La Paz, Mexico: N.p., 1989.

Dietz, Robert S. "The Spreading Ocean Floor." *Saturday Evening Post* 234 (21 October 1961): 34–35+.

Douglas, Norman. *South Wind.* New York: Boni and Liveright, 1925.

"Drilling in the Ocean Floor." *Science* 143 (7 February 1964): 529.

"Drowning Mohole." *Business Week* (3 September 1966): 62.

Dryden, Edgar. *The Form of the American Romance.* Baltimore: Johns Hopkins University Press, 1988.

Dusheck, Jennie. "Female Primatologists Confer—Without Men." *Science* 249 (1990): 1494–95.

Eliade, Mircea. *Cosmos and History.* Princeton: Princeton University Press, 1971.

Ellis, William. *The Theory of the American Romance: An Ideology in American Intellectual History.* Ann Arbor, MI: UMI Research Press, 1989.

Emerson, Ralph Waldo. *Journals.* Vol. 10, 1847–1848. Edited by Merton M. Sealts, Jr. Cambridge, MA: Belknap Press, 1973.

Evans, Walker. *Walker Evans at Work.* New York: Harper and Row, 1982.

Feynman, Richard, Robert B. Leighton, and Matthew Sands. *The Feynman Lectures on Physics.* Vols. 1 and 2. Reading, MA: Addison-Wesley, 1963.

Fitzgerald, F. Scott. *The Great Gatsby.* 1925. New York: Charles Scribner's Sons, 1953.

Forbes, Edward. *The Natural History of European Seas.* 1859. New York: Arno, 1977.

Foucault, Michel. *Power/Knowledge: Selected Interviews and Other Writings, 1972–1977.* Edited by Colin Gordon. New York: Pantheon, 1980.

Fox, Stephen. *The American Conservation Movement: John Muir and His Legacy.* Madison: University of Wisconsin Press, 1981.

Frenz, Horst, ed. *Nobel Lectures: Literature, 1901–1967.* Amsterdam: Elsevier, 1969.

"From a Bizarre Barge, A Sharp Thrust into Earth's Crust." *Life* 50 (7 April 1961): 37–40.

Furgurson, E. B. "Lake Tahoe: Playing for High Stakes." *National Geographic* (March 1992): 112–32.

Ghiselin, Michael. *The Triumph of the Darwinian Method.* Berkeley: University of California Press, 1969.

Giles, Lionel, trans. *The Sayings of Lao Tzu.* London: J. Murray, 1905.

Goodfield, June. *The Cosmic Joke: A Glimpse at the Global Population Problem.* London: BBC Education and International Health and Biomedicine, 1992.

Gordon, David G., and Alan Baldridge. *Gray Whales.* Monterey: Monterey Bay Aquarium, 1991.

Gore, G. *The Art of Scientific Discovery.* London: Longmans Press, 1878.

Gould, Stephen J. "Church, Humboldt, and Darwin: The Tension and Harmony of Art and Science." In *Frederick Edwin Church,* edited by Franklin Kelly, et al. Washington, DC: National Gallery of Art, 1989.

———. *Hen's Teeth and Horses' Toes: Further Reflections in Natural History.* New York: W. W. Norton, 1983.

Graubard, Mark. *Man the Slave and Master.* New York: Covici-Friede, 1938.

Greenberg, D. S. "Mohole: Aground on Capitol Hill." *Science* 153 (26 August 1966): 963.

———. "Mohole: Drilling Site in Pacific Favored as Time Nears to Award Construction Contract for Vessel." *Science* 147 (29 January 1965): 487.

———. "Mohole: The Project That Went Awry." *Science* 143 (10–24 January 1964): 115–19, 223–27, 334–37.

———. "NSF Appropriation: Mutiny on the Mohole." *Science* 152 (13 May 1966): 895–96.

Guba, Emil F. *Nantucket Odyssey.* Lexington, MA: Lexington Press, 1965.

Gutman, Judith Mara. *Lewis Hine, 1874–1940: Two Perspectives.* London: Studio Vista, 1974.

Hair, Jay D. "Wanted—The 1990s, Decade of the Environment: Dead or

Alive?" Address presented at the Fifty-third Annual Meeting of the National Wildlife Federation, 18 March 1989, Washington, DC.

Harding, Sandra. *Whose Science? Whose Knowledge: Thinking from Women's Lives*. Ithaca: Cornell University Press, 1991.

Hare, Lloyd C. M. *Salted Tories: The Story of the Whaling Fleets of San Francisco*. Mystic, CT: Marine Historical Association, 1960.

Hayford, Harrison. " 'Loomings': Yarns and Figures in the Fabric." In *Artful Thunder: Versions of the Romantic Tradition in American Literature in Honor of Howard P. Vincent*, edited by Robert DeMott and Sanford Marovitz. Kent, OH: Kent State University Press, 1975.

Hays, Samuel P. *Beauty, Health, and Permanence: Environmental Politics in the United States, 1955–1985*. Cambridge: Cambridge University Press, 1987.

Hemp, Michael Kenneth. *Cannery Row: The History of Old Ocean View Avenue*. Monterey, CA: History Company, 1986.

Howard, Leon. *Herman Melville: A Biography*. Berkeley: University of California Press, 1951.

Humboldt, Alexander von, and Aime Bonpland. *Personal Narrative of Travels*. 1805–1823. Translated by Helen Maria Williams, 1818–1829. New York: AMS, 1966.

Hutton, James. "Theory of the Earth; or, An investigation of the laws observable in the composition, dissolution, and restoration of land upon the globe." *Transactions of the Royal Society of Edinburgh* (1788): 209–304.

Irvine, William. *Apes, Angels, and Victorians*. New York: McGraw-Hill, 1955.

Ishikawa, Tadao. "Sigaku-no Dogan tositeno Hisai Rijicho." In *Shigaku-ni Ikiru: Hisai Tadao to Kansai Daigaku*. Osaka, Japan: 21-Seiki-no Daigaku-o Kangaeru Kai, 1991.

Janovy, John, Jr. *Vermilion Sea: A Naturalist's Journey in Baja California*. New York: Houghton Mifflin, 1992.

Jay, Gregory S. *America the Scrivener: Deconstruction and the Subject of Literary History*. Ithaca: Cornell University Press, 1990.

Jeffers, Robinson. *The Selected Poetry of Robinson Jeffers*. New York: Random House, 1938.

Jehlen, Myra. *American Incarnation: The Individual, the Nation, and the Continent*. Cambridge, MA: Harvard University Press, 1986.

Jobes, Gertrude. *Dictionary of Mythology, Folklore, and Symbols*. New York: Scarecrow Press, 1992.

Joseph, Lawrence E. *GAIA: The Growth of an Idea*. New York: St. Martin's, 1990.

Kaplan, Daile. *Lewis Hine in Europe: The Lost Photographs*. New York: Abbeville Press, 1988.

Kelley, Elizabeth Burroughs. *John Burroughs: Naturalist*. New York: Exposition, 1959.

———. *John Burroughs' Slabsides*. Rhinebeck, NY: Exposition Press, 1959.

Kellner, L. *Alexander von Humboldt*. Oxford: Oxford University Press, 1963.

Kerr, Robert S. *Land, Wood, and Water*. New York: Fleet, 1960.

Kohn, David. "Darwin's Ambiguity: The Secularization of Biological Meaning." *British Journal for the History of Science* 22 (1989): 215–39.

Kolodny, Annette. *The Lay of the Land: Metaphor as Experience and History in American Life and Letters*. Chapel Hill: University of North Carolina Press, 1975.

Lange, Dorothea, and Paul Schuster Taylor. *An American Exodus: A Record of Human Erosion*. New York: Reynal and Hitchcock, 1939.

La Paz. [La Paz, Mexico]: n.p., 1989 [Not paginated]

Larsen, Stephen, and Robin Larsen. *A Fire in the Mind: The Life of Joseph Campbell*. New York: Doubleday, 1991.

Lee, A. Robert. "*Moby-Dick*: The Tale and the Telling." In *New Perspectives on Melville*, edited by Faith Pullin. Kent, OH: Kent State University Press, 1978.

Lehman, David. *Signs of the Times: Deconstruction and the Fall of Paul de Man*. New York: Poseidon Press, 1992.

Leopold, Aldo. *The River of the Mother of God and Other Essays*. Edited by Susan L. Flader and J. Baird Callicott. Madison: University of Wisconsin Press, 1991.

Lewis, R. W. B. *The American Adam: Innocence, Tragedy, and Tradition in the Nineteenth Century*. Chicago: University of Chicago Press, 1955.

Lewis, Sinclair. *Babbitt*. 1922. New York: New American Library, 1961.

Leyda, Jay. *The Melville Log: A Documentary Life of Herman Melville*. 2 vols. New York: Harcourt Brace, 1951.

Libby, Walter. *An Introduction to the History of Science*. London: George G. Harrap, 1924.

Love, Glen A. "Revaluing Nature: Toward an Ecological Criticism." *Western American Literature* 25 (November 1990): 201–13.

Lovelock, J. E. *Gaia: A New Look at Life on Earth*. Oxford and New York: Oxford University Press, 1979.

———. "Gaia as Seen Through the Atmosphere." *Atmospheric Environments* 6 (1972): 579–80.

———. "Geophysiology, the Science of Gaia." *Reviews of Geophysics* 27 (1989): 215–22.

Lufkin, Alan, ed. *California's Salmon and Steelhead: The Struggle to Restore an Imperilled Resource*. Berkeley: University of California Press, 1991.

Maclean, Norman. *A River Runs Through It and Other Stories*. 1976. New York: Pocket Books, 1992.

Macy, Obed. *The History of Nantucket*. 1835. New York: Research Reprints, 1970.

Madden, Henry Miller. *Xántus: Hungarian Naturalist in the Pioneer West*. Palo Alto, CA: Books of the West, 1949.

Marsh, George Perkins. *Man and Nature*. 1864. Edited by David Lowenthal. Cambridge, MA: Harvard University Press, 1965.

Marx, Karl. *The Economic and Philosophic Manuscripts of 1844*. Translated by Martin Milligan. Edited by Dirk J. Struik. New York: International, 1964.

Marx, Leo. *The Machine in the Garden: Technology and the Pastoral Ideal in America*. Oxford: Oxford University Press, 1976.

Mascetti, Manuela Dunn. *The Song of Eve*. New York: Simon and Schuster, 1990.

Matthews, Samuel W. "Scientists Drill at Sea to Pierce Earth's Crust." *National Geographic* 120 (November 1961): 686–97.

Mayr, Ernst. *One Long Argument: Charles Darwin and The Genesis of Modern Evolutionary Thought*. Cambridge, MA: Harvard University Press, 1991.

McCormick, John. *Reclaiming Paradise: The Global Environmental Movement*. Bloomington: Indiana University Press, 1991.

Melling, Philip. *Vietnam in American Literature*. Boston: Twayne, 1990.

Melville, Herman. *Israel Potter, His Fifty Years of Exile*. 1855. Edited by Harrison Hayford, et al. Evanston, IL: Northwestern University Press; Chicago: Newberry Library, 1982.

———. *Journal of a Visit to Europe and the Levant*. Edited by Howard C. Horsford. Princeton: Princeton University Press, 1955.

———. *The Letters of Herman Melville*. Edited by Merrell R. Davis and William H. Gilman. New Haven: Yale University Press, 1960.

———. *Moby-Dick*. 1851. Edited by Harrison Hayford, et al. Evanston, IL: Northwestern University Press; Chicago: Newberry Library, 1988.

———. *Moby-Dick*. 1851. Introduction by Leon Howard. New York: Modern Library, 1950.

———. *Moby-Dick*. 1851. Introduction by Sherman Paul. Everyman's Library. New York: E. P. Dutton, 1950.

———. *Moby-Dick*. 1851. Edited by Willard Thorp. Oxford: Oxford University Press, 1947.

———. *The Piazza Tales and Other Prose Pieces, 1839–1860*. Edited by Harrison Hayford, et al. Evanston, IL: Northwestern University Press; Chicago: Newberry Library, 1987.

Merchant, Carolyn. *Ecological Revolutions: Nature, Gender, and Science in New England*. Chapel Hill: University of North Carolina Press, 1989.

Michaels, Leonard, David Reid, and Raquel Scherr. *West of the West: Imagining California*. San Francisco: North Point Press, 1989.

"Mohole Finds a Site at Last." *Business Week* (30 January 1965): 52.

"Mohole Job Up for Grabs." *Business Week* (9 September 1961): 142–44.

"Mohole Lives." *Newsweek* 65 (25 January 1965): 89.

"Mohole May Wind Up No Hole." *Business Week* (23 November 1963): 32.

"Mohole Regress Report." *Fortune* 69 (April 1964): 106.

"Mohole Runs Gamut in Senate Committee." *Business Week* (8 September 1962): 78+.

Monod, Jacques. *Chance and Necessity.* Translated by Austryn Wainhouse. New York: Alfred Knopf, 1971.

Muir, John. *The Mountains of California.* New York: Century, 1894.

———. *The Yosemite.* New York: Century, 1912.

Nagel, Ernest. "Naturalism Reconsidered." In *Proceedings and Addresses.* Yellow Springs, OH: Antioch Press, 1954. (Presidential address to the American Philosophical Association, Eastern Division)

Nash, Roderick. *Wilderness and the American Mind.* 3d ed. New Haven: Yale University Press, 1982.

Neumann, Erich. *The Great Mother.* Princeton: Princeton University Press, 1963.

Niblock, Robert W. "Oil Companies to Use Mohole Technology." *Technology Week* 20 (17 April 1967): 24–25.

"No Mohole?" *Scientific American* 215 (July 1965): 48.

Osborn, Fairfield. *Our Plundered Planet.* Boston: Little, Brown, 1948.

Paglia, Camille. *Sex, Art, and American Culture.* New York: Vintage, 1992.

Passmore, John. *Man's Responsibility for Nature: Ecological Problems and Western Traditions.* New York: Charles Scribner's Sons, 1974.

Pinchot, Gifford. *The Fight for Conservation.* 1910. Seattle: University of Washington Press, 1967.

"A Place for the Mohole." *Scientific American* 215 (March 1965): 54.

"The Point of the Deal." *Nation* 203 (5 September 1966): 172.

Powell, John Wesley. *Down the Colorado: Diary of the First Trip Through the Grand Canyon, 1869.* New York: E. P. Dutton, 1969.

———. *Report on Lands of the Arid Region of the United States.* 2d ed. Washington, DC: Government Printing Office, 1878.

"Project Nohole?" *Newsweek* 68 (29 August 1966): 60+.

Randall, John Herman, Jr. "The Changing Impact of Darwin on Philosophy." *Journal of the History of Ideas* 22 (1961): 435–62.

Reinhold, Robert. "U.S. Says Scarce Water Supplies Won't Go to California Farmers." *New York Times* (15 February 1992): 1+.

Reisner, Marc. *Cadillac Desert: The American West and Its Disappearing Water.* New York: Penguin, 1986.

Rhodes, Richard. *The Making of the Bomb.* New York: Simon and Schuster, 1986.

Ricketts, Edward F. *Pacific Biological Laboratory Biological Specimens.* Pacific Grove, CA: Pacific Biological Laboratory, 1925.

Ricketts, Edward F., and John Calvin. *Between Pacific Tides.* 1939. Revised by Joel W. Hedgpeth and D. W. Phillips. Stanford: Stanford University Press, 1985.

Ritter, William Emerson. "The Marine Biological Station of San Diego: Its

History, Present Conditions, Achievements, and Aims." *University of California Publications in Zoology* 9.4 (1912): 137–248.

———. *The Unity of the Organism; or, The Organismal Conception of Life.* Vol. 1. Boston: Gorham, 1919.

Roach, Catherine. "Loving Your Mother: On the Woman-Nature Relation." *Hypatia* 6.2 (Spring 1991): 46–59.

Rogin, Michael. *Subversive Genealogy: The Politics and Art of Herman Melville.* New York: Alfred A. Knopf, 1983.

Rothstein, Arthur. *Photojournalism.* 4th ed. New York: Amphoto, 1979.

Santayana, George. *The Life of Reason.* 5 vols. New York: Charles Scribner's Sons, 1936.

Schoenemann, Theodore, and Helen Benedek, trans. and eds. *Travels in Southern California by John Xántus.* Detroit: Wayne State University Press, 1976.

"Science." *Time* 77 (31 March 1961): 52.

Scott, John P. *Animal Behavior.* Chicago: University of Chicago Press, 1958.

Sealts, Merton M. *Melville's Reading.* Rev. ed. Columbia: University of South Carolina Press, 1988.

Sheail, John. *Seventy-five Years in Ecology: The British Ecological Society.* Oxford: Blackwell Scientific Publications, 1987.

Sjöo, Monica, and Barbara Mor. *The Great Cosmic Mother.* San Francisco: Harper and Row, 1987.

Slotkin, Richard. *The Fatal Environment: The Myth of the Frontier in the Age of Industrialization.* New York: Atheneum, 1985.

Smith, Henry Nash. *Virgin Land: The American West as Symbol and Myth.* Cambridge, MA: Harvard University Press, 1970.

Smuts, Jan Christiaan. *Holism and Evolution.* New York: Macmillan, 1926.

Stange, Maren. *Symbols of Ideal Life: Social Documentary Photography in America, 1890–1950.* Cambridge: Cambridge University Press, 1989.

Stegner, Wallace. *Beyond the Hundredth Meridian: John Wesley Powell and the Second Opening of the West.* Boston: Houghton Mifflin, 1954.

———. *Where the Bluebird Sings to the Lemonade Springs.* New York: Random House, 1992.

Stone, Geoffrey. *Melville.* New York: Sheed and Ward, 1949.

Stoneback, H. R. "The Compleat Quest: John Burroughs and Fishing." *John Burroughs Review* 1 (1987): 17–34.

———. "John Burroughs and the American Land Conservation Ethic." *Catskill Center Newsletter* 16.1 (1987): S1–S8.

———. "John Burroughs: Regionalist." *Literature of the Mid-Hudson Valley.* Edited by Alfred H. Marks. New Paltz, NY: SUC Press, 1973.

Stott, William. *Documentary Expression and Thirties America.* Chicago: University of Chicago Press, 1986.

Stovall, Floyd. *American Idealism.* Norman: University of Oklahoma Press, 1943.

Strong, Douglas H. *Dreamers and Defenders: American Conservationalists.* Lincoln: University of Nebraska Press, 1971.

Suzuki, D. T. *Essays in Zen Buddhism: First Series.* New York: Grove, 1949.

Terrell, John U. *The Man Who Rediscovered America: A Biography of John Wesley Powell.* New York: Weybright and Talley, 1969.

Thomas, William L., Jr., ed. *Man's Role in Changing the Face of the Earth.* Chicago: University of Chicago Press, 1956.

Turner, Frederick Jackson. *The Frontier in American History.* 1892. New York: Holt, 1947.

Udall, Stewart L. *The Quiet Crisis and the Next Generation.* Salt Lake City, UT: Peregrine Smith, 1988.

Vincent, Howard. *The Trying-Out of "Moby-Dick."* 1949. Kent, OH: Kent State University Press, 1980.

Vincent, Stephen, ed. *O California! Nineteenth and Early Twentieth Century California Landscapes and Observations.* San Francisco: Bedford Arts, 1990.

Vogt, William. *Road to Survival.* New York: William Sloan Associates, 1948.

Ward, Ritchie. *Into the Ocean World: The Biology of the Sea.* New York: Alfred A. Knopf, 1974.

Warren, Earl, convener. *Proceedings of the California Water Conference.* Sacramento: State Printing Office, 1945.

Warren, Karen, and Jim Cheney. "Ecological Feminism and Ecosystem Ecology." *Hypatia* 6.1 (Spring 1991): 178–97.

Weiner, Douglas. *Models of Nature: Ecology, Conservation, and Cultural Revolution in Soviet Russia.* Bloomington: Indiana University Press, 1988.

Westbrook, Perry D. *John Burroughs.* New York: Twayne, 1974.

Wilson, Jack. "Where We Stand: Our Planet." *Look* 27 (15 January 1963): 36–38.

Worster, Donald. *Dust Bowl: The Southern Plains in the 1930s.* Oxford: Oxford University Press, 1979.

———. *Nature's Economy: A History of Ecological Ideas.* 1977. Cambridge: Cambridge University Press, 1985.

———. *Rivers of Empire: Water, Aridity, and the Growth of the American West.* New York: Pantheon, 1985.

———. *The Wealth of Nature: Environmental History and the Ecological Imagination.* Oxford: Oxford University Press, 1993.

Wotte, Herbert. *In blauer Ferne lag Amerika.* Leipzig: VEB F. A. Brockhaus Verlag, 1967.

Wylie, Philip. *Generation of Vipers.* 1942. Marietta, GA: Larlin Corporation, 1978.

Contributors

Susan F. Beegel earned her Ph.D. in 1986 from Yale University and is a visiting scholar/editor at the University of Idaho. She is editor of the *Hemingway Review,* an author society journal circulating to one thousand subscribers in twenty-seven nations. Beegel is the author of *Hemingway's Craft of Omission: Four Manuscript Examples* and the editor of *Hemingway's Neglected Short Fiction: New Perspectives.* She has published essays on Hemingway, Melville, Poe, Hardy, and Dante Gabriel Rossetti as well as composition pedagogy. Her interest in Steinbeck and the environment arose during heated discussions in the laboratory of the University of Massachusetts Nantucket Field Station, a biological research facility directed by her husband, Wes Tiffney.

The late **Stanley Brodwin** was professor of English at Hofstra University. He published extensively on nineteenth-century American authors, particularly Mark Twain, in *Journal of the History of Ideas, American Literature, Mississippi Quarterly, Criticism, Philological Quarterly, PMLA,* and other journals. He edited a collection of essays, *The Old and New World Romanticism of Washington Irving,* coedited and contributed to *William Cullen Bryant and His America,* and coedited *The Harlem Renaissance: A Reappraisal.* He was a sponsored fellow of the Jewish Theological Seminary in New York City, and a participant in a National Endowment for the Humanities Summer Seminar on Biography.

David N. Cassuto received his doctorate in American literature from Indiana University in 1993 with a subspecialty in applied ecology. His research focuses on the relationship between literature and politics regarding the evolving ecological consciousness in the nation. His book, *Cold Running River,* an ecological biography of Michigan's Père Marquette River, was published in February 1994.

Lorelei Cederstrom, professor of English at Brandon University in Brandon, Manitoba, is the author of *Fine-Tuning the Feminine Psyche: Jungian Patterns in the Novels of Doris Lessing,* as well as numerous articles and reviews on authors including William Shakespeare, Walt Whitman, Margaret Atwood, James Baldwin, and Margaret Laurence. Her archetypal analyses of *The Golden Notebook* and *Leaves of Grass* appear in two volumes of the MLA Approaches to World Literature series. Editorial work includes a second-term as women and literature editor of *Atlantis* and guest editorship of a special issue of the *Canadian Journal of Native Studies*. Funded by a three-year grant from the Social Sciences and Humanities Research Council of Canada, she is currently working on a study of archetypal patterns in women's literature.

Robert DeMott teaches American literature at Ohio University, where he has won the undergraduate and graduate teaching awards. His publications include *Artful Thunder: Versions of the Romantic Tradition in American Literature, Steinbeck's Reading, Working Days: The Journals of* The Grapes of Wrath, and *Steinbeck's Typewriter*. He is co-editor of several volumes of Steinbeck's writings in the Library of America series.

Peter A. J. Englert holds a Ph.D. in nuclear chemistry from the University of Cologne, Germany. His research is in the area of nuclear analytical chemistry. Englert's major efforts are in the analysis of extraterrestrial materials and remote analysis of planetary surfaces. He is principal investigator on NASA's Mars Observer Mission, launched in September 1992. Throughout his career, Englert has also taught and conducted research on the role of science in the arts and humanities.

Warren French is an honorary professor of American Studies at the University of Wales, Swansea. A graduate of the University of Pennsylvania, with a Ph.D. from the University of Texas—Austin, he taught at a number of southern and midwestern state universities before retiring from Indiana University, Indianapolis, in 1986. He has edited Twayne's Filmmakers Series and many titles on modern American fiction in Twayne's United States Authors series, for which he has written two books on John Steinbeck, with a third in production, as well as books on J. D. Salinger and on Jack Kerouac and the Beats.

Clifford Gladstein is vice president of PS Enterprises, a Santa Monica, California–based environmental affairs consulting group. He is PSE's chief analyst of local, state, and federal legislative matters, as well as the company's expert on ocean, energy, and transportation issues. Gladstein spent more than five years working in the California assembly on environmental, education, and urban policy issues. From 1991 to 1993, he served as president of Heal the Bay, a 12,000-member, volunteer-led environmental organization dedicated to the restoration and protection of Santa Monica Bay. He continues to serve as a board member of Heal the Bay and also serves as a director of the Coalition for Clean Air and the Southern California League of Conservation Voters. He earned a B.A. in Public Policy Studies from Duke University and master's degrees in Middle Eastern Studies, Political Science, and Urban Planning from the University of Texas at Austin and the University of California, Los Angeles.

Mimi Reisel Gladstein is a professor of English and Theater Arts at the University of Texas at El Paso where she has been chair of both the Departments of English and Philosophy. Her administrative experience includes serving her university as executive director of the Diamond Jubilee and as first director of the Women's Studies Program. Gladstein taught graduate seminars on Hemingway, Steinbeck, and Faulkner in Venezuela and Brazil during her year as a Fulbright lecturer. She has published two books and numerous articles in journals and critical anthologies. A professor in the Honors Program, she happened to be teaching the honors course in research and critical writing when Clifford Gladstein was recommended to it by his English professor.

Richard E. Hart is associate professor of philosophy at Bloomfield College in New Jersey. He edited a recently published book, *Ethics and the Environment,* and is presently coediting a collection of essays under the title *Plato's Dialogues: The Dialogical Approach.* He has published a number of essays and reviews dealing with the interface between philosophy and literature and regularly teaches Steinbeck in his introductory philosophy and aesthetics courses. He serves on the editorial boards of *Aitia,* a philosophy-humanities journal, and *Metaphilosophy* and is a national officer and board member of the American Association of Philosophy Teachers.

Joel W. Hedgpeth is emeritus professor of Oceanography at Oregon State University. A marine biologist, conservationist, and native Californian, he is a fellow of the California Academy of Sciences, a foreign member of the Linnaean Society of London, and a founder of the Society for the Prevention of Progress. Hedgpeth specializes in *Pycnogonida*, an aberrant group of marine arthropods, and is the author of numerous scientific papers, monographs, and environmental tracts, as well as *Seashore Life of the San Francisco Bay Region* and (as Jerome Tichenor) *Poems in Contempt of Progress*. Editor of *Treatise on Marine Ecology* and *The Outer Shores*, as well as several editions of *Between Pacific Tides*, Hedgpeth is a member of the advisory board of the *Quarterly Review of Biology*. In 1976 he received the Browning Award for Conserving the Environment.

James C. Kelley is an oceanographer and geologist who received his academic training at Pomona College and the University of Wyoming. For nine years he was a member of the Oceanography faculty at the University of Washington and for the past eighteen years has been dean of science and engineering at San Francisco State University. For the past nineteen years, he has taught, together with colleagues from the English department, a course titled "John Steinbeck and Ed Ricketts: Literature in the Sea," as part of San Francisco State University's NEXA Program. During this period, he has continued to conduct research on the relationship between Steinbeck and Ricketts as well as on their relationship to the Monterey Bay ecosystem about which they wrote. Dr. Kelley has traveled for forty years in Baja California and annually leads trips to the Sea of Cortez, where he introduces people to sites that figure prominently in *Sea of Cortez*. He is president of the 105-year-old California Academy of Sciences as well as chairman of the governing board of the Moss Landing Marine Laboratories, located on Monterey Bay. He has been chief scientist and expedition leader on more then fifty scientific and natural history expeditions in the oceans of the world and has published widely on the productivity of the nearshore environment.

Marilyn Chandler McEntyre is assistant professor of English at Trenton State College. Her publications include two books: *Dwelling in the House: Houses in American Fiction* and *A Healing Art: Regeneration Through Autobiography*. She teaches and writes on attitudes toward the environment in American literature and is currently at work on a book titled *Encounters with the Earth: Nature and Character in American Fiction*, which explores the ways fiction writers in America have brought their various moral and social frames of reference to bear in their representation of the natural world, and what assumptions they—and we—make about how a relationship to the natural world shapes character.

Robert E. Morsberger is professor of English and former department chair at the California State Polytechnic University, Pomona. He has published more than 160 articles, nine short stories, and ten books. He also edited John Steinbeck's screenplay *Viva Zapata!* for the Viking Press and is head of the editorial board of the *Steinbeck Quarterly*. Most recently, he published an article ("Zapata, the Man, the Myth, and the Mexican Revolution") to accompany a deluxe illustrated edition by the Yolla Bolly Press of Steinbeck's newly discovered treatment for *Viva Zapata!*. A specialist in American literature and in science fiction, he was one of five American Steinbeck specialists invited by the Society Writers Union to Moscow in 1989 for a week-long symposium commemorating the fiftieth anniversary of *The Grapes of Wrath*.

Kiyoshi Nakayama is a professor of English at Kansai University, Osaka, Japan. He was the coeditor of *Selected Essays of John Steinbeck*, one of the three translators of *Sweet Thursday*, the editor of *Uncollected Stories of John Steinbeck*, and the author of *Stainbekku Bungaku no Kenkyu: California Jidai* (*John Steinbeck's Writings: The California Years*). He is the compiler of *Steinbeck in Japan: A Bibliography* and the editor-in-chief of *John Steinbeck: Asian Perspectives*, the Asian portion of the proceedings of the Third International Steinbeck Congress, Honolulu, May 1990. Currently he is executive director of the John Steinbeck Society of Japan.

Nathaniel Philbrick is a sailing journalist and independent scholar of American literary culture. He is the author of a book, *Away Off Shore: Nantucket Island and Its People, 1602–1890*, and his scholarly articles have appeared in a variety of journals, including *New England Quarterly* and *ESQ*.

Brian Railsback, director of writing and editing at Western Carolina University, is the author of *Parallel Expeditions: Charles Darwin and the Art of John Steinbeck*. He has published articles about Steinbeck in *San Jose Studies* and the *Steinbeck Quarterly* and has presented papers about the author in the United States, Mexico, and Japan. His other interests include Native American literature and fiction writing (he is at work on a novel). He lives in Cullowhee, North Carolina, with his wife, Sandra, and children, Travis, Justin, and Cadence.

Susan Shillinglaw is director of the Steinbeck Research Center and professor of English at San Jose State University. She is editor of the *Steinbeck Newsletter,* published at SJSU, and was associate editor of the *Steinbeck Quarterly.* She wrote the introductions for *Of Mice and Men* and *Cannery Row* for the Viking Penguin New American Library. She has also given numerous papers on Steinbeck and has published several essays: " 'The Chrysanthemums': Steinbeck's Pygmalion," "California Answers *The Grapes of Wrath,*" and "Steinbeck and Ethnicity: Paisanos, Indians, and Mexicans." Presently she is coediting a book of Steinbeck reviews for Cambridge University Press and working on a biography of Steinbeck's first wife, Carol Henning Steinbeck.

Roy Simmonds lives in Billericay, Essex, England, and first began reading Steinbeck in 1940, after seeing John Ford's *The Grapes of Wrath.* He has published *The Two Worlds of William March, William March: An Annotated Checklist,* and *John Steinbeck: The War Years.* A biography of the short story anthologist Edward J. O'Brien and two books on Steinbeck are in the works. Simmonds has published essays in *Steinbeck Quarterly, San Jose Studies, London Magazine, Mississippi Quarterly, Studies in American Fiction,* the *Steinbeck Newsletter,* and the *Hemingway Review.*

H. R. Stoneback is professor of English and director of graduate studies at the State University of New York–New Paltz. He has published extensively on modern American, British, Chinese, and French literature, including scores of essays on Durrell, Faulkner, and Hemingway. He has also published fiction, poetry, and song. His publications include two books: *Selected Stories of William Faulkner* and *Cartographers of the Deus Loci,* a volume of poetry. He has been a senior Fulbright professor at Peking University, a visiting professor at the University of Paris, and director of the American Center for Students and Artists in Paris. He is presently completing several books, including a volume dealing with Hemingway's fiction.

Wesley N. Tiffney, Jr., is director of the University of Massachusetts/Boston's Nantucket Field Station. He holds a Ph.D. in botany and has taught biology at the University of Massachusetts/Boston.

Tiffney has edited two books, *Proceedings of the 1985 California Off-shore Petroleum Conference: Resources, Technology, the Environment, and Regulation* and, with R. F. Hill, *Georges Bank: Hydrocarbon Exploration and Development.* His published papers have appeared in journals including the *American Journal of Botany* and *Rhodora;* his current research involves coastal erosion on Nantucket island and the comparative development of British and North American heath vegetation relative to human land use history.

John H. Timmerman, professor of English at Calvin College, is the author of *John Steinbeck's Fiction* and the *Dramatic Landscape of Steinbeck's Short Stories.* He has contributed many articles on Steinbeck to scholarly publications.

Peter Valenti is professor of English at Fayetteville State University, where he has also served as department chair and associate dean of the College of Arts and Sciences. In 1991–1992 he was visiting professor at the United States Military Academy at West Point. He has written on British and American literature and film and is presently completing *Reading the Landscape,* an anthology of American writing about the land and human ecology.

Index